Assessment: A Sourcebook for Social Work Practice

Julia B. Rauch, Editor

Families International, Inc.
Milwaukee, Wisconsin

Library of Congress Cataloging–in–Publication Data

Assessment : a sourcebook for social work practice / Julia B. Rauch, editor.
     p.   cm.
  Includes bibliographical references.
  ISBN 0-87304-267-0
  1. Social case work—Methodology. 2. Social case work—Evaluation. 3. Family assessment. I. Rauch, Julia B. II. Families International (Milwaukee, Wis.)
HV43.A79   1993
361.3'2—dc20   93-27098

CONTENTS

PART 5: ASSESSMENT AND ETHNIC DIVERSITY

PREFACE

During 1988–1989, while serving as field liaison for the School of Social Work at the University of Maryland–Baltimore, Family and Children's Services of Central Maryland asked me to coordinate a one-year in-service training program on clinical assessment. After the topics and speakers were selected, I spoke with Ralph Burant, Director of Publications at Families International, Inc., about his interest in publishing these presentations in anthology form. In teaching introductory social work practice courses, I perceived a need for a resource that could be used both in classroom teaching and as a reference for students in their field placements. The present volume is the result of our discussion. The various chapters were drawn from two sources: (1) papers based on presentations at in-service training seminars on assessment sponsored by the Family and Children's Services of Central Maryland and subsequently published as a series of articles on assessment in *Families in Society* and (2) selected articles on assessment published in *Social Casework* and *Families in Society*.

The topics for the in-service training were selected on the basis of a survey of agency clinical staff, discussions with clinical supervisors, and consultation with two administrative staff—Michael Cenci and Cynthia Childs. The goal was to provide staff with intensive, hands-on models of assessment in specific areas. Indeed, presenters were told that their audience would include both beginning and advanced practitioners who had command of basic assessment principles. They were asked to provide structured, even "cookbook," models.

The chapters in this volume that were drawn from the in-service seminars include the following: McPhatter (family assessment), Lucco (school-aged children), Fedoroff (sexual history taking), Griffin (drug-involved clients), and Douglas (violent couples). The remaining chapters were located by reviewing articles on assessment that had been published in *Social Casework* and *Families in Society* in the past 10 years. The initial selection of articles was reviewed by Frederick DiBlasio, Geoffrey Greif, and Alfred Lucco. In addition, these reviewers were asked to recommend other important assessment topics that should be included. Following their recommendations, a second search was undertaken. Although for several of their suggestions, appropriate articles could not be located, I believe this collection does indeed provide educators, students, and practitioners with a broad array of useful information about the assessment process.

Julia B. Rauch

CONTRIBUTORS

Paula Allen-Meares
Dean and Professor
School of Social Work
University of Michigan
Ann Arbor, Michigan

Rhea Almeida
Founder/Director
Institute for Family Services
Somerset, New Jersey

Barbara Bernhardt
Genetic Counselor
Genetics and Public Policy
Johns Hopkins Medical Institute
Baltimore, Maryland

John S. Brekke
Associate Professor
School of Social Work
University of Southern California
Los Angeles, California

Robert J. Bushorn
Clinical Director
Butler County Mental
Health Center
Hamilton, Ohio

John Victor Compher*
Family Therapist and Supervisor
Philadelphia County Children and
Youth Agency
Philadelphia, Pennsylvania

W. Keith Daugherty (d. 1992)*
Executive Director
Family Service Association
Dayton, Ohio

Harriet Douglas
Instructor
School of Social Work
University of Maryland at Baltimore
Baltimore, Maryland

Donald V. Fandetti
Associate Professor
School of Social Work
University of Maryland at Baltimore
Baltimore, Maryland

O. William Farley
Associate Dean and Professor
Graduate School of Social Work
University of Utah
Salt Lake City, Utah

J. Paul Fedoroff
Forensic Division
Clarke Institute of Psychiatry
Toronto, Ontario, Canada

Cynthia Franklin
Assistant Professor
School of Social Work
University of Texas at Austin
Austin, Texas

Nydia Garcia-Preto
Clinical Director
Family Institute of New Jersey
Metuchen, New Jersey

Donald E. Gelfand
Professor
Institute of Gerontology
Wayne State University
Detroit, Michigan

Rosalind E. Griffin
Clinic Director
Substance Abuse Center
OASIS Clinic of the Institutes
for Behavior Resources, Inc.
Washington, D.C.

J. Kent Griffiths
Administrative Director
Alta View Center for Counseling
Sandy, Utah

Dean H. Hepworth
Emeritus Professor
Schools of Social Work
University of Utah
Salt Lake City, Utah
Arizona State University
Tempe, Arizona

Paulette Moore Hines
Director
Office of Prevention Services
University of Medicine and
Dentistry of New Jersey
Piscataway, New Jersey

Harriette C. Johnson
School of Social Work
University of Connecticut
West Hartford, Connecticut

Judy Kopp
Associate Professor
School of Social Work
University of Washington
Seattle, Washington

Bruce A. Lane*
School Social Worker
Lyons Township High School
District #204
Western Springs, Illinois

Alfred A. Lucco
Associate Professor
University of Maryland at Baltimore
Baltimore, Maryland

Mark A. Mattaini
Assistant Professor
School of Social Work
Columbia University
New York, New York

Monica McGoldrick
Director

Family Institute of New Jersey
Metuchen, New Jersey

Anna R. McPhatter
Associate Professor
School of Social Work
University of Pittsburgh
Pittsburgh, Pennsylvania

Ferol E. Mennen
Assistant Professor
University of Southern California
Los Angeles, California

Kathleen J. Moroz
Department of Social Work
University of Vermont
Burlington, Vermont

Nancy Morrow-Howell
Associate Professor
George Warren Brown
School of Social Work
Washington University
St. Louis, Missouri

Robert W. Nelson
Interim Executive Director
Family Service Association
Dayton, Ohio

Jack Nowicki
Clinical Director
Middle Earth Unlimited, Inc.
Austin, Texas

James D. Orten
Professor
College of Social Work
University of Tennessee
Knoxville, Tennessee

Gary W. Paquin
Assistant Professor
College of Social Work

University of Kentucky
Lexington, Kentucky

Lynn Pearlmutter
Assistant Professor
Tulane University
New Orleans, Louisiana

Jerene Petersen
Program Director
Middle Earth Unlimited, Inc.
Austin, Texas

Julia B. Rauch
Associate Professor
School of Social Work
University of Maryland at Baltimore
Baltimore, Maryland

Linda L. Rich
Director of Family Services
Salvation Army
Honolulu, Hawaii

Carla Sarno
Clinical Assistant Professor
Department of Child Psychiatry
University of Maryland at Baltimore
Baltimore, Maryland

A. James Schwab
Associate Dean and Director
Center for Social Work Research
University of Texas at Austin
Austin, Texas

Sylvia Simpson
Assistant Professor
Department of Psychiatry
School of Medicine
Johns Hopkins University
Baltimore, Maryland

Alison Solomon
Program Coordinator

WomenReach
Jewish Family and Children's
Service of Philadelphia
Philadelphia, Pennsylvania

Janet Taynor
Senior Consultant
Synthesis, Inc.
Columbus, Ohio

Elizabeth M. Tracy
Associate Professor
Mandel School of Applied
Social Sciences
Case Western Reserve University
Cleveland, Ohio

John Trapp
Systems Analyst
School of Social Work
University of Texas at Austin
Austin, Texas

Ronald R. Van Treuren*
Clinical Social Worker and
Research Associate

Dartmouth College
Hanover, New Hampshire

Florence Wexler Vigilante
Professor
Hunter College School of
Social Work
City University of New York
New York, New York

Susan Weltman
Child and Adolescent Inpatient
Services
University of Medicine and
Dentistry of New Jersey
Piscataway, New Jersey

James K. Whittaker
Professor
School of Social Work
University of Washington
Seattle, Washington

*Professional title and affiliation
at time of original publication.

INTRODUCTION

The assessment process is critical to social work practice. Practitioners' choice of service goals and methods spring from the initial data collected and their analysis of it. In fact, the effectiveness of intervention and the outcome of treatment depend in large part upon the accuracy of the initial assessment. Thus, practitioners *must* be competent assessors.

The goal of this collection is to nurture assessment skills by presenting selected assessment topics in one easy-to-use volume suitable for use in schools of social work, in-service and continuing education programs, and as a reference for beginning and seasoned practitioners who have questions about how to evaluate a particular client or problem.

What Is Assessment?

Historically, social work assessment was referred to as "diagnosis" or "psychosocial diagnosis." In recent years, however, the term diagnosis has become passé and has been supplanted by the term assessment. For some social workers, the word diagnosis connotes the "medical model" of social work (Hollis & Woods, 1981), which they regard as being negatively associated with symptoms, disease, and dysfunction (Hepworth & Larsen, 1990; Kirk, Siporin, & Kutchins, 1989).

Although the original meaning of the word "assess" has to do with setting taxes, fines, and special levies of money, its usage has grown to encompass the notion of critical evaluation and judgment. For instance, one dictionary definition of assess includes the following: "to analyze critically and judge definitively the nature, significance, status, or merit of: determine the importance, size or value of" *(Webster's,* 1964, p. 131). In this way, the concept of social work assessment is linked to the meanings of the word diagnosis, which include "a careful investigation of the facts to determine the nature of a thing" and "the decision or opinion resulting from such examination or investigation" (*Webster's,* 1983, p. 502).

Assessment and diagnosis are not interchangeable terms, however. Diagnosis focuses on symptoms and assigns individuals to nosological categories that best fit the symptom configuration, for example, manic depression or phobia. Diagnosis assumes that people with the same symptoms have the same condition and thus can be treated similarly. Moreover, the concept of diagnosis, which was borrowed from the Western medical model, assumes that symptoms are lodged within the individual. In contrast, social work assessments are holistic and transactional in nature.

Social work assessment focuses on the *person-in-situation,* that is, on the characteristics of the individual, the systems to which she or he is connected, and the transactions between them. Assessment can be defined as the process of gathering, analyzing, and synthesizing salient data into a multidimensional formulation that provides the basis for action decisions. Its purpose is to reach an individualized understanding of the problem situation and to identify and analyze the factors that maintain the problem as well as the resources that can be mobilized for change (Pincus & Minahan, 1973).

Each component of the assessment process is complex. For example, assessment of the person scrutinizes such dimensions as appearance, ego development and functioning, cognitive development, developmental stage, physical health, education, and so forth. Similarly, family assessment identifies boundaries, roles, decision-making processes, and communication patterns. Thus, social work assessments are multidimensional, drawing upon multiple sources of information and applying knowledge and constructs from human biology and the social sciences.

Assessment can be conceptualized as *stage, process,* and *product.* As a stage of treatment, assessment follows problem definition and precedes intervention planning. As process, practitioners engage in assessment from the time of initial contact with potential clients to the final contact, which may be minutes, days, weeks, months, or even years later. Assessment is also moment to moment, in that the practitioner continually decides what information does and does not merit further exploration. New information may dramatically change the practitioner's understanding of the situation, leading to a change of strategy. Thus assessment is fluid, dynamic, and continuous. As product, it is presented as a written document entered into the client's record. Formats vary from setting to setting, but they usually include definition of the problem, analysis of the factors supporting the problem situation, identification of strengths and resources, formulation of goals and objectives, and statement of the planned strategies for achieving goals and objectives.

Clinicians use generic engagement, data gathering, and analytic skills in the assessment process. Many practitioners have specialized expertise. However, particular situations may require knowledge and techniques that are new to the practitioner. For this reason, experienced clinicians, as well as students and recent graduates, may benefit from this collection.

The book is divided into five sections:

- Assessment of individuals and families
- Assessment over the life cycle
- Assessment of specific psychosocial dysfunctions
- Assessment techniques
- Assessment and ethnic diversity

The chapters cover a range of topics; however, some gaps exist. For example, out of the pool of articles from which the chapters were selected, no articles were found on the assessment of psychosocial functioning of people with HIV/AIDS, or on families with a chronically ill or disabled member. In that articles published within a ten-year period were reviewed, the specific gaps in this volume may reflect more general gaps in the professional literature.

Assessment of Individuals and Families

Ecosystems assessment. Social work has struggled to formulate a theory of knowledge and practice that takes into account the complex transactions between person and situation. The ecological-systems (ecosystems) perspective has emerged as a unifying social work paradigm. In a useful introduction to the chapters in this volume and to ecosystems assessment, Allen-Meares and Lane review key ecosystems principles and concepts. They present an assessment framework with three dimensions: critical data variables, significant ecosystems, and relevant data sources. The chapter concludes with a discussion of six ecosystems assessment principles.

Individual assessment. Mattaini presents a contextual behavior-analysis model for assessment of individuals. From the ecosystems perspective, Mattaini advocates using behavioral concepts to operationalize observations of clients' interactions with other people and institutions. He contends that this model makes available to practitioners an extensive literature on behavior change of individuals, ranging from prescriptions for specific problems to theoretical paradigms suggesting new approaches.

Family assessment. McPhatter, also writing from an ecosystems perspective, identifies five components of family assessment: problem identification, family structure, family functioning, family strengths and resources, and intervention plan and method of evaluation. She emphasizes the need to understand the family's cultural milieu; practitioners must have a working knowledge of the culture, life-style, customs, language, and history of the group with which the family is affiliated.

Paquin and Bushorn present a simple, eclectic family assessment model for novices. The nucleus of their presentation is a four-level typology of families based on family functioning and the presenting problem. Techniques appropriate for various family types are discussed. The chapter's framework allows beginning workers to draw upon prominent schools of family therapy to select appropriate assessment and therapeutic techniques.

Assessment over the Life Cycle

Infancy and toddlerhood. The infancy period is critical in that it sets the stage for future development. Thus, early intervention for high-risk infants and toddlers is recommended. Moroz and Allen-Meares present a comprehensive framework for assessment of adolescent parents and their infants in order to develop the individual family service plans (IFSPs) required by the Preschool and Early Intervention Act (P.L. 99-457) and the Education for All Handicapped Children Act (P.L. 94-142). Moroz and Allen-Meares identify specific aspects of social functioning that should be assessed as well as suggest assessment resources and techniques.

School-aged children. Lucco proposes a tripartite model for assessment of school-aged children. The first leg of this model is a developmental profile that assesses the child's progression through age-related stages in various developmental domains. The second leg is the functional profile, which examines academic, social, and family functioning. The third leg, the ecological profile, identifies neighborhood, school, and other environmental stressors that may contribute to the child's problem. Lucco recommends various qualitative and quantitative strategies for assessment of each component of the three profiles.

Adolescents. Adolescence can be a troubling period for many young people. One indication of the personal and social distress experienced by adolescents is the rising adolescent suicide rate. Hepworth, Farley, and Griffiths discuss clinical work with suicidal adolescents and their families. They identify predisposing psychosocial risk factors that should be assessed in estimating risk. These risk factors do not pertain only to suicide, however; they are associated with other problems of adolescence, such as pregnancy, truancy, and addiction. Thus, this chapter is of general and specific value to professionals who work with adolescents.

Adulthood. Emotional maturity, according to Freud, is the capacity to work and to love. These capacities are addressed in the chapters by Vigilante and Fedoroff. Vigilante provides an overview of the attributes of the work environment, the psychosocial demands of work, strategies of coping with work, and the connections between work and other domains of living. She underscores that work provides a highly complex social milieu, the understanding of which is necessary for appropriate assessment and intervention.

Sexual relations are an important expression of love. For many people, however, sex is an uncomfortable, even taboo, topic. Social workers, too, can experience discomfort dealing with sexual issues. Consequently, clients' sexual concerns are often ignored. Fedoroff discusses how to obtain a sexual history and presents some specific techniques to elicit concerns and dysfunctions in this sensitive area.

Aging. Morrow-Howell presents a multidimensional model for assessment of elderly clients. She reviews seven domains of assessment: physical health, mental health, social support, physical environments, functioning, coping styles, and formal service usage. Her discussion includes topics to be covered in each dimension, helpful assessment instruments, adaptation of interviewing skills, and use of allied professionals.

Assessment of Specific Psychosocial Dysfunctions

The disruptive child. Johnson's chapter on the disruptive child is a useful complement to Lucco's chapter on assessment of school-aged children. Using case examples, the author reviews the features of three disruptive behavioral disorders: attention-deficit hyperactivity disorder, conduct disorder, and oppositional defiant disorder. She notes the difficulty of discriminating among the three, pointing out that correct *diagnosis* is important because the appropriate interventions depend on the nature of the problem behavior. For example, depending on etiology, medication may benefit some children but not others.

Delinquency or school-related problems of children. In contrast with Johnson's diagnostic orientation, Compher approaches the problem of school behavioral problems from a systems perspective. He posits that the child's negative behavior is symptomatic of specific and current malfunctioning within the child's self–parent–school network. He identifies three interactional patterns: aggressive entanglement, passive entanglement, and adaptive response and provides strategies for changing patterns of aggressive or passive entanglement.

Alcohol and drug abuse. Because alcohol and drug abuse is epidemic in the United States, social workers likely come in contact with many clients who are involved with or affected by substance abuse. In Griffin's overview chapter, she defines salient terms, describes specific drugs and their effects, identifies indicators of drug-use problems, delineates treatment principles, and provides guidelines for assessing drug-involved clients.

Depression and affective disorders. The exorbitant personal and social costs of depression and other mood disorders include suicide, drug and alcohol abuse, and increased mortality from physical disease. Rauch, Sarno, and Simpson discuss how to screen for these conditions, which can be life threatening. They review differential diagnosis, probing for symptoms, and assessing danger signals. Because affective disorders are inherited in some families and are responsive to medication, they discuss the need for new types of clinical partnerships between social agencies and psychiatrists.

Family violence. Partner and child abuse in the United States cuts across all socioeconomic lines and appears to be increasing. However, such abuse is not always recognized even when family members are seeing a social worker. Brekke presents a strategy for detecting partner and child abuse when it is not part of the identified problem. Brekke discusses detection of abuse in various clinical contexts, presents a domestic-abuse scale, and discusses therapeutic strategies.

Brekke's approach to screening for abuse is complemented by Douglas's in-depth, dynamic assessment of couples in which partner abuse occurs. She reviews the cycle of violence and violence continuum, discussing what to look for and how to uncover it. She discusses reciprocal couple interactions, dynamics of violent relationships, the functions of violence, and violence across generations. She also offers specific criteria for estimating prognosis and identifies barriers to the detection of violence.

Incest and sexual abuse. Incest, another form of violence, occurs at the extreme end of sexual pathology. Orten and Rich argue that the sexually abused child needs to be protected from the abuser and an often dysfunctional service system. They present an assessment scale intended to evaluate objectively incestuous families' strengths and pathology. The format is designed to help practitioners evaluate the risks involved in leaving the victim and offender in the same home and the possible benefits or harm in reunifying the family during treatment. The scale can also be used to improve services by facilitating coordination of the incest response system.

Mennen and Pearlmutter's chapter on detecting childhood sexual abuse in couples therapy deals with an overlooked issue and underrecognized skill. The authors identify adult symptoms and relationship patterns associated with a history of childhood sexual abuse. Because denial and minimization are often successful in warding off the pain of abuse, the worker may need to introduce the subject of abuse. The authors present strategies for broaching the subject, for monitoring the reactions of the survivor and her partner, and for creating a trusting, supportive environment for the couple.

Assessment Techniques

Individual self-observation. The current practice literature emphasizes the importance of incorporating empowerment techniques into practice but few articles discuss how empowerment fits into the process. Kopp asserts that the technique of self-observation, or monitoring and recording one's behavior, helps empower clients by giving them control of the information used in assessment. She identifies the goals of empowerment-oriented practice and reviews self-observation techniques. Using case examples, Kopp describes how self-observation during the assessment phase may help clients obtain information about a problem or situation, gain knowledge about the environmental context of the problem, increase self-awareness and stimulate insights, and increase involvement and control.

Family assessment. Van Treuren offers a tool for family assessment that combines elements of the genogram, eco-map, and Minuchin's family diagrams. Each family member is asked to work individually to represent symbolically his or her observations of how the family has organized itself to deal with the presenting problem. A case example illustrates how the technique is used.

Family genetic histories. Bernhardt and Rauch contend that genetic family history should become part of routine social work screening and assessment. The authors present a rationale for this view and discuss basic genetic concepts, contemporary genetic services, criteria for genetic service referrals, the desired content of these histories, and various formats for recording the information.

Social networks. Social work's person-in-situation focus requires workers to understand the role of clients' social networks in problem maintenance and the potential of such networks to contribute to problem resolution. Tracy and Whittaker present a model for social network assessment that elaborates upon the widely used technique of eco-mapping, which specifies seven network domains, complemented by a grid that records information about the supportive and nonsupportive functions of network relationships. Tracy and Whittaker assert that their model enables workers to gather specific, clearly defined, and individualized social assessment information.

Effectiveness of family intervention. In the past decade, administrators, boards, and funders increasingly have demanded that family practitioners demonstrate that their interventions are effective. Taynor, Nelson, and Daugherty describe the process by which an intervention-effectiveness scale was developed for the Family Service Association of Dayton, Ohio. With this scale, the agency was able to demonstrate that families show improved functioning between the beginning and end of treatment. The authors highlight the importance of involving staff in developing such a scale.

Computerized assessment. Social agencies are moving toward computerized management information systems, although some clinicians resist computerization for various reasons. Franklin, Nowicki, Trapp, Schwab, and Petersen describe an agency's success in developing a computerized assessment system. This system was accepted by practitioners because it provided information that proved helpful in crisis intervention with youth and their families. The authors discuss steps in the process of developing a computerized management information systems, emphasizing that participatory decision making and group planning are critical to the success of such innovations.

Assessment and Ethnic Diversity

The United States population is becoming increasingly diverse, thus making it important that practitioners understand the ethnic and cultural issues of clients with whom they work. Solomon asserts that minority clients are often misdiagnosed, identifying some of the reasons why this occurs: cultural expression of symptomatology, unreliable assessment tools, clinician bias and prejudice, and institutional racism. She offers caveats and recommendations for practitioners who work with culturally diverse populations.

Gelfand and Fandetti also address ethnicity, warning social workers against reification of ethnic culture. They note that culture is emergent and that it changes over time in response to political and social pressures. Immigrants adapt in their encounters with the culture of the host nation. Referring primarily to white ethnic groups in the United States, the authors discuss factors that contribute to culture maintenance or change, presenting case examples to illustrate intraethnic group variation.

Hines, Garcia-Preto, McGoldrick, Almeida, and Weltman provide an overview of intergenerational relationships in five cultures: African American, Hispanic, Irish, Asian Indian, and Jewish. Although they do not provide an assessment model *per se*, the authors offer information that can be useful in assessing parent–child relationships in particular cultures.

A Valuable Resource

Because accurate and ongoing assessment is so critical to social work practice, educators need good tools with which they can help train students, and practitioners need resources to which they can refer in their work with clients. This volume is designed to fulfill these needs. What began as a series of in-service seminars has developed into a substantial volume of chapters on the diverse aspects of the assessment process.

Assessment affects all stages of the therapeutic process and in many ways serves as the foundation upon which the client–therapist relationship stands or crumbles. To develop accurate assessments, however, therapists need to become attuned to the underlying, often unspoken, problems and issues clients bring to the therapeutic process. This volume clarifies and speaks openly about such problems and issues. Educators, students, and practitioners should find it to be an excellent resource with which to become and remain informed about the complex as well as practical aspects of the assessment process.

REFERENCES

Hepworth, D. H., & Larsen, J. (1990). *Direct social work practice: Theory and skills.* Belmont, CA: Wadsworth Publishing Company.

Hollis, F., & Woods, M. E. (1981). *Casework: A psychosocial therapy* (3rd ed.). New York: Random House.

Kirk, S. A., Siporin, M., & Kutchins, H. (1989). The prognosis for social work diagnosis. *Social Casework, 70,* 295–304.

Pincus, A., & Minahan, A. (1973). *Social work practice: Theory and method.* Itasca, IL: F. E. Peacock.

Webster's New Universal Unabridged Dictionary. (1983). Cleveland, OH: Dorset & Baber.

Webster's Third New International Dictionary. (1964). Springfield, MA: G. & C. Merriam Co.

Part 1

Assessment of Individuals and Families

Grounding Social Work Practice In Theory: Ecosystems

*Paula Allen-Meares
and Bruce A. Lane*

1

S ound social work practice requires grounding in theory and an understanding of the profession's mission. From its beginnings, social work's mission has been to improve the interaction between persons and their natural social environment. It is imperative that different theoretical paradigms and perspectives be analyzed for their usefulness in accomplishing this mission. An abiding challenge facing the social work profession is to formulate a unified theory of knowledge and practice insofar as the historical context of practice significantly influences the relative emphasis placed on *person* and *environment*.[1]

Social work's integrative tendency, the tendency to perceive the parts of the person-in-situation complex as a whole, has set it apart from more narrowly focused professions (Bartlett, 1964). Attempts to identify this

---

1. The early settlement house workers emphasized supporting individuals through the environmental change strategies of community action and community development (illustrated as *person–ENVIRONMENT*). The introduction and acceptance of psychoanalytic and other more individually focused psychological treatment theories in the 1930s shifted the emphasis from the environment to the person (illustrated as *person–environment*). The poverty programs and social action of the 1960s brought back into focus the importance of the role of the social and physical environments in the lives of people. Today the profession is shifting toward a balanced emphasis on both the person and the environment (illustrated as *PERSON–ENVIRONMENT*). See Goroff, N. M. (1974). Social group work: An intersystemic frame of reference. In R. W. Klenk & R. M. Ryan (Eds.), *The practice of social work.* Belmont, CA: Wadsworth Publishing. See also Phillips, H. U. (1978). *Essentials of social group work skill.* Philadelphia: University of Pennsylvania, Norwood Editions.

focus and translate it into clearly defined practice principles have not produced a singular, cohesive paradigm for practice. Rather, various theories compete for recognition as the predominant guidepost for practice (Haworth, 1984).

In response to this challenge, the ecological-systems (ecosystems) theory is emerging as a macro-level theory that offers promise as a unifying paradigm for social work knowledge and practice. According to Siporin (1980):

> Ecological systems theory is such a general meta-theory, one that provides for the many, and at times contradictory, purposes and activities of social workers. It constitutes an essential element of the generic core of social work knowledge, of its common person-in-situation and dialectical perspective, and of its basic helping approach. It supports the social work assessment and interventive focus (p. 525).

This chapter reviews the historical roots of ecosystems theory and presents a conceptual framework from which practice principles are identified.

Ecosystems Principles

Although an ecological perspective is not a new phenomenon in the social sciences, only a few specialized disciplines have attempted detailed, systematic study of the complex interrelationships that exist between people and their environments. Ethology, ecological psychology, and ethnology are three such specialized disciplines that warrant the attention of social workers. Examination of these disciplines and general systems theory can assist in the identification of the critical principles of an ecosystems perspective in social work.

Formative Theories

Ethology. This scientific study of animal behavior has its origins in the European tradition of evolutionary studies (Boice, 1982; Charlesworth, 1978; Strain, Cooke, & Apolloni, 1976). It has recently been recognized to have significant conceptual and methodological potential in the study of human behavior (Charlesworth, 1978). Ethologists are concerned with obtaining a detailed knowledge of the complete behavioral repertoire of their subjects. Ethologists prefer to sample the full range of molecular behaviors and behavioral contexts to enable them to identify context-specific relationships of behaviors and the functions of the behaviors (Wohlwill, 1970). Ethological methods include longitudinal, detailed, unobtrusive, continuous naturalistic observation of the person's behavioral repertoire. The resulting data are analyzed in relation to immediate stimulus conditions and consequences, wide social ecological conditions, possible functional or survival significance, and underlying psychological mechanisms that control behavior (Barker, 1968).

Ecological psychology. This discipline recognizes that the environmental context of behavior (1) imposes major constraining, deterministic influences on individual behavior, (2) has generalized effects on broader systems of response in the individual, and (3) instigates behavior directly (Lewin, 1936). Ecological psychology has developed various conceptual models in its effort to discover "how the properties of the person and the properties of the ecological environment are related in situations" (Barker, 1968, p. 203). Lewin's (1936) assertion that "every scientific psychology must take into account whole situations, i.e., the state of both person and environment" (pp. 11–12) laid the groundwork for his law $B = f(P,E)$, which asserts that behavior is a function of the person and the environment. Barker (1968) expanded on the importance of the environmental variables of behavior settings in human interactions. He described ecological psychology as being concerned both with "the psychological environment (the world as a particular person perceives and is otherwise affected by it) and with the ecological environment (the objective, pre-perceptual context of behavior, the real-life settings within which people behave)" (p. 203). Stern's (1970, 1974) elaboration of Murray's "need-press" model describes behavior as determined by the interaction of a person's needs and the "environmental press," that is, the unique, private view each person has of life events that organizes the individual's perception, cognition, and action in specific situations. According to Skinner (1974), "Social behavior arises because one organism is important to another as part of its environment" (p. 497). His work emphasizes the analysis of the social environment, its special features, and the observable stimuli that act as determinants of behavior in social episodes. The environment is viewed as a complex set of discriminable stimuli that is real, can be measured, exists in its own right, and signals the reinforcement possibilities that influence behavior (Ittelson et al., 1974).

Ecological psychologists recognize that "person–environment" represents an interdependent, unitary field in which deviation from consistent behavioral relationships is due to the subtle dynamics of variables that often function below the general levels of awareness (Ittelson et al., 1974; Proshansky, Ittelson, & Rivlin, 1970). They are careful not to think of person and environment as separate phenomena. As Wicker (1974) points out, dichotomizing the environment of a person as "environment and nonenvironment" (p. 601) oversimplifies a complex situation. Each theorist attempts to clarify the nature of human internal functioning and its relation to the external behavioral linkage to the environment (Lewin, 1936; Barker, 1968; Gump, 1974).

Ethnology. This anthropological approach to social knowledge focuses on individuals in the course of ongoing, everyday, taken-for-granted social interactions. It examines the development of shared understanding of words, phrases, and actions and of subtle, yet complex and powerful, sets of cultural situationally specific rules or norms (Bailey, 1978; Washington, 1983). Ethnomethodology incorporates various direct, micro-level data collection methods. These methods stress the intersubjectivity or shared understandings on which social interaction is based. Ethnomethodologists argue for descriptive research oriented toward a more empirically grounded understanding of the ordinary perceptions and intentions of people in their daily lives (Bailey, 1978; Washington, 1983). Ethnologists believe that the emphasis in social research should be on the process of social interaction through which social reality is constructed and maintained, rather than on the result of such interaction (Bailey, 1978).

Systems theory. Systems theory represents a general conceptual approach to human interaction and groupings. It characterizes social systems as composed of persons or groups of persons who interact and influence one another's behaviors. Systems theory stresses the need to view the immediate system being dealt with within the context of its significant environment or the social situations within which it operates (Anderson & Carter, 1978; Siporin, 1980). It provides practitioners with some of the necessary concepts for the assessment of the "situation" or "environment." Buckley (1967) defined systems as "complexes of elements or components directly or indirectly related in a causal network, such that each component is related to at least some others in a more or less stable way within a particular period" (p. 41).

Siporin (1980) suggests that systems theory refers to a cognitive construction of reality necessary for the understanding of and operation within the intervention situation. Concepts that describe the flow of energy within the system, the differentiation and relationships of parts within the system, and the changing yet balanced steady state that exists within a system provide a broad framework from which to view social settings (Anderson & Carter, 1978). Systems should never be viewed as totally similar. Each is subtly unique, affecting individual behavior and attitudes in different ways. Intervention is both "people-helping and system-changing" (Siporin, 1980, p. 517).

Key Ecosystems Concepts

The shared similarities in theoretical assumptions, research methods, and practice principles of the approaches to human behavior discussed above provide the basis for identifying the key concepts of an ecosystems perspective. This perspective has emerged in social work and other professions through a balanced emphasis on person and environment. A number of theorists have summarized the general characteristics of an ecosystems approach to social reality (Sells, 1974; Moos & Brownstein, 1977; Schoggen, 1978). These theorists suggest that the ecosystems perspective is characterized by the following concepts:

1. The environment is a complex environment–behavior–person whole, consisting of a continuous, interlocking process of relationships, not arbitrary dualisms.

2. The mutual interdependence among person, behavior, and environment is emphasized.
3. Systems concepts are used to analyze the complex interrelationships within the ecological whole.
4. Behavior is recognized to be site specific.
5. Assessment and evaluation should be through the naturalistic, direct observation of the intact, undisturbed, natural organism–environment system.
6. The relationship of the parts within the ecosystem are considered to be orderly, structured, lawful, and deterministic.
7. Behavior results from mediated transactions between the person and the multivariate environment.
8. The central task of behavioral science is to develop taxonomies of environments, behaviors, and behavior–environment linkages and to determine their distribution in the natural world.

Siporin (1980) has emphasized the appropriateness of an ecological perspective, given the context of social work practice. He stresses the following positive contributions. An ecological model

1. Helps gain a larger, more unitary and comprehensive unit of attention, a holistic and dynamic understanding of people and the sociocultural physical milieu
2. Permits a strategy of multiple perspectives, a way of thinking about parts and wholes
3. Encourages a theoretically and technically eclectic approach
4. Is directly useful as an assessment instrument and is able to identify consistencies, conflicts, and complementarities in regard to particular systemic attributes
5. Is useful in treatment planning, helping to identify which actions to take to alter intersystemic relationships to optimize the goodness of fit
6. Because of its multifactorial nature, encourages social workers to develop and utilize a strong and varied repertoire of assessment instruments and helping interventions

The ecological perspective is important in monitoring and evaluating the larger, long-term, systems outcomes of intervention techniques (Willems, 1974). Such evaluation of ecological outcomes of social work interventions is essential for promoting practice effectiveness and accountability.

Framework for Ecological Systems Assessment

Figure 1 represents the major dimensions of a complete ecosystems assessment. The three dimensions of assessment include critical data variables, significant ecosystems, and relevant data sources. By breaking the three-dimensional block into its component cells, one can begin to identify

7

the assessment components represented by each cell. A component is a data point that represents a combination of the specific focuses of each of the major assessment dimensions. Figure 1 represents an ideal framework for assessment. In practice it may be impossible to address every component. Practice constraints (e.g., agency policy, case load, client or family resistance) may inhibit the completion of a comprehensive assessment. Implementation of this framework results in specific principles of practice.

Practice Principles

Principle one. A comprehensive ecosystems assessment requires that data be collected about multiple ecosystems (e.g., school, home, and community). What are the expectations of school personnel? How adequate are the home's resources for education? What are the educational opportunities in the community? What, if any, are the unique ethnic and cultural characteristics?

Principle two. Assessment should include data from all three data sources (person, significant others, and direct observation of the client in the environment). For example, during an interview, a child reports sadness due to separation of parents (person); parent reports child's resistance at home on behavior-rating scale (significant other); and social worker observes parent–child interaction in multiple environments (environment).

Principle three. Assessment should gather data on all of the critical data variables that describe the person (e.g., cognitive and affective characteristics, behavior, and physical attributes) and the situation (e.g., physical, psychosocial behavior, and historic normative environments). To illustrate this, consider the following example. A child's intellectual functioning on standardized tests suggests above-normal capacity (cognitive/affective), but the teacher reports inattentiveness and sleeping in the classroom (behavior), even though the child's physician does not indicate any medical problems (physical). Observation reveals an overly warm classroom (physical environment) in which students are not reinforced for constructive contributions (psychosocial–behavioral environment) and social interaction has traditionally been low (historic–normative environment).

Principle four. A comprehensive assessment should include as many components as is possible (i.e., data about as many of the critical variables and systems as are possible and relevant). Each variable and system is one piece of a total picture. A practitioner cannot achieve a clear picture of the client's situation if assessment data about each component are missing. For example, to understand the inability of a child to make friends in his or her classroom, a practitioner would also assess the child's social skill across settings, obtain information about the child's social functioning from a number of significant others, assess the specific environments in which the child functions, and draw upon objective techniques such as sociometric ratings from peers and family members. The outcome of this process is a comprehensive picture of the "child–situation."

Principle five. The assessment data must be integrated into a comprehensive picture of the client's situation. An ecosystems assessment helps

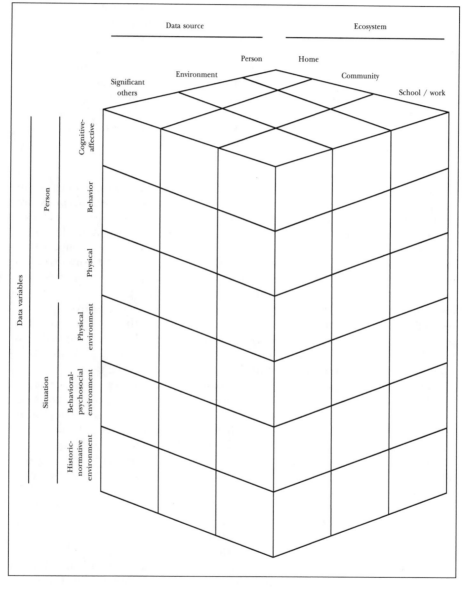

Figure 1. Ecosystems assessment framework.

the practitioner identify dysfunctional aspects of the person's interaction with his or her environments. It reminds the practitioner that the source of difficulty may be located within the person, the environment, or both.

Principle six. The ecosystems assessment must be linked to an eclectic repertoire of intervention strategies. Practitioners must have at their disposal interventions that are both person- and environment-changing. For example, a practitioner may teach a juvenile delinquent specific social skills that facilitate adjustment in society while simultaneously working with the family, school, and community agencies to develop a natural support network for the youth. Ideally, the choice of intervention should be based on strategies that have been validated (by reports from practitioners or empirically or both) for a particular situation.

The following case is presented to illustrate some of the major practice principles identified in the previous discussion. Specific details and kind and type of intervention are only briefly discussed.

Case Illustration

B, a white 13-year-old boy, was referred to the local school because his adoptive mother believed that he was a learning-disabled, hyperactive child. Data collected from the school ecosystem (teacher interviews, teacher completion of a standardized behavior-rating scale, classroom observation by means of both a process recording and a systematic observation code, and student interview) indicated no significant concerns (see principle one). B was able to meet the cognitive–affective, behavioral, and physical requirements of the school setting (see principle three). Although educational tests revealed some areas of difficulty, B's "positive attitude" toward schoolwork appeared to help compensate for these difficulties. The teachers saw no evidence of hyperactivity; rather, they saw a mildly distractible youngster who, when compared with the rest of the school's population, was very well controlled and on task (see principle two).

Data indicated that B perceived his behavior and academic performance at school as appropriate but that he lacked closeness with teachers and peers. His responses regarding peer relationships revealed significant uncertainty and discomfort. He expressed the belief that most students did not like or care about him but that his family loved him (see principles two and three).

Data gathered from the home ecosystem and about B's past living situation (interview with mother, father, and B; completion of behavior rating scale by parents; and an interview with the social worker who placed B) indicated that B was experiencing specific problems with his adoptive family (see principles one and two). B's adoptive mother believed that the school environment was negative and this resulted in her making arrangements to have B and his siblings educated at home. She indicated that while learning at home, B had experienced hyperactivity and difficulty in some skill areas but that the individualized teaching strategies and the flexibility of home instruction had lessened these problems. Moreover, she described B as having "good days" and "bad days" within their large, close-knit family and expressed concern that the number of bad days at home had increased since a custody hearing required that B return to the public school. She expressed concern that B's learning problems might eventually cause deteriorated behavior at school. B's perception of the home environment was very positive. He described the home schooling as being harder than the public schooling. He also indicated that he had a very close relationship with all of the members of his family (see principle two). The social worker who had placed B four years previously reported that he had had no such difficulty in the past; in fact, he had friends and his behavior was appropriate in all settings (see principle three).

Data regarding the community ecosystem revealed that although B's adoptive mother made special efforts to have her children involved in positive social activities with peers (e.g., YMCA groups, youth leagues, and church), the majority of B's social interaction occurred within the family group (see principles one and three). Further, since B had been in the public school, he had not continued the youth-program activities because his mother believed that he needed to put more time into his schoolwork. B appeared able to act appropriately within the community in general, but his exposure to the community was most often in the context of family activities.

The value of an ecosystems assessment is clearly demonstrated in this example. If school data alone had been collected, it is not likely that any difficulty would have been uncovered; if home data alone had been collected, the picture of B would have had a significantly negative skew. The comprehensive assessment, on the other hand, allowed one to see that B's exhibition of dysfunctional behaviors was new and occurred in the more familiar, supportive, and safe home environment (see principles four and five). Although B's school performance was acceptable, his dysfunctional behavior was seen only at home. Several alternative and working hypotheses could be relevant to this case; however, without an ecosystems approach, the important linkages between B's significant environments would not have been revealed. Also, the ecosystems assessment enabled one to explore the feasibility and appropriateness of different transenvironmental interventions. For example, B's mother, who appeared to be overly anxious, received training in parenting skills and techniques of anxiety reduction; the classroom teacher was made aware of B's educational needs and helped to develop remedial strategies to meet his learning needs; the social worker met twice a week with B to help him develop and reactivate social skills essential for establishing supportive relationships in the school (see principles five and six).

Conclusions

Although some of the concepts discussed in this chapter are found elsewhere in the social work literature, the authors' intent is to further

11

crystallize thought about ecosystems for social work assessment. The ecosystems framework provides sound principles for conducting assessment. Social workers must identify, develop, and refine the range of assessment methodologies that can be utilized to collect data for each of the components depicted in Figure 1. This challenge is complex. However, the profession demands its resolution.

REFERENCES

Anderson, R. E., & Carter, I. (1978). *Human behavior in the social environment: A social systems approach.* Chicago: Aldine Publishing.

Bailey, K. D. (1978). *Methods of social research.* New York: Free Press.

Barker, R. (1968). *Ecological psychology: Concepts and methods for studying the environment of human behavior.* Stanford, CA: Stanford University Press.

Bartlett, H. (1964). Characteristics of social work. In *Building social work knowledge: Report of a conference.* New York: National Association of Social Workers.

Boice, R. (1982). An ecological perspective on social skills research. In J. P. Curran & P. M. Monti (Eds.), *Social skills training.* New York: Guilford Press.

Buckley, W. (1967). *Sociology and modern systems theory.* Englewood Cliffs, NJ: Prentice-Hall.

Charlesworth, W. R. (1978). Ethology: Its relevance for observational studies of human adaptation. In G. P. Sackett (Ed.), *Observing behavior. Vol. 1: Theory and applications in mental retardation.* Baltimore, MD: University Park Press.

Gump, P. V. (1974). The behavior setting: A promising unit for environmental designers. In R. H. Moos & P. M. Insel (Eds.), *Issues in social ecology: Human milieus.* Palo Alto, CA: National Press Books.

Haworth, G. O. (1984). Social work research, practice, and paradigms. *Social Service Review, 58,* 343–357.

Ittelson, W. H., et al. (1974). *An introduction to environmental psychology.* New York: Holt, Rinehart, and Winston.

Lewin, K. (1936). *Principles of topological psychology.* New York: McGraw-Hill.

Moos, R., & Brownstein, R. (1977). *Environment and utopia: A synthesis.* New York: Plenum Publishing.

Proshansky, H. M., Ittelson, W. H., & Rivlin, L. G. (1970). The influence of the physical environment on behavior: Some basic assumptions. In H. M. Proshansky, W. H. Ittelson, & L. G. Rivlin (Eds.), *Environmental psychology: Man and his physical setting* (pp. 29–35). New York: Holt, Rinehart, and Winston.

Schoggen, P. (1978), Ecological psychology and mental retardation. In G. P. Sackett (Ed.), *Observing behavior: Theory and applications in mental retardation* (Vol. 1, p. 36). Baltimore, MD: University Park Press.

Sells, S. B. (1974). An interactionist looks at the environment. In R. H. Moos & P. M. Insel (Eds.), *Issues in social ecology: Human milieus.* Palo Alto, CA: National Press Books.

Siporin, M. (1980). Ecological systems theory in social work. *Journal of Sociology and Social Welfare, 7,* 507–532.

Skinner, B. F. (1974). The social environment. In R. H. Moos & P. M. Insel (Eds.), *Issues in social ecology: Human milieus.* Palo Alto, CA: National Press Books.

Stern, G. G. (1970). *People in context: Measuring person–environment in education and industry.* New York: John Wiley.

Stern, G. G. (1974). B = f(P,E). In R. H. Moos & P. M. Insel (Eds.), *Issues in social ecology: Human milieus.* Palo Alto, CA: National Press Books.

Strain, P. S., Cooke, T. P., & Apolloni, T. (1976). *Teaching exceptional children: Assessing and modifying social behavior.* New York: Academic Press.

Washington, R. O. (1983). *Ethnomethodology: An alternative framework for defining the problem in social work research.* Boston: United Community Planning Corp.

Wicker, A. W. (1974). Processes which mediate behavior–environment congruence. In R. H. Moos & P. M. Insel (Eds.), *Issues in social ecology: Human milieus.* Palo Alto, CA: National Press Books.

Willems, E. P. (1974). Behavioral technology and behavioral ecology. *Journal of Applied Behavioral Analysis, 7,* 151–165.

Wohlwill, J. F. (1970). The emerging discipline of environmental psychology. *American Psychologist, 25,* 303–312.

Contextual Behavior Analysis In the Assessment Process

Mark A. Mattaini

$$2$$

Assessment is a critical thread running through the development of social work and human services practice. Among others, Richmond (1917), Hamilton (1951), Bartlett (1970), and Meyer (1976), in their own ways and for their own times, emphasized the need for an individualized assessment as the basis for practice activities. The breadth and complexities of social problems with which practitioners struggle preclude exclusive reliance on typologies of individual pathology such as the *Diagnostic and Statistical Manual of Mental Disorders* (DSM-III-R) (American Psychiatric Association, 1987) or individual psychological functioning (Strayhorn, 1983), despite their utility in some situations. Not only have we not yet documented the most effective intervention for each type of problem, it is unlikely we will ever do so because the ecosystemic context of each client system in the real world is unique. Taking these differences into account requires a broad scan of the transactional web within which the client or client system is embedded. The ecosystems perspective (Meyer, 1976, 1983) offers a framework for doing so.

Brower (1988) suggests that this perspective must be operationalized to offer immediate practice utility. Contextual behavior analysis offers a systemic, operationalized, and prescriptive approach to assessment. This chapter sketches the contours of the ecosystems perspective and contemporary behavior analysis and presents a paradigm for the use of contextual behavior analysis using a case vignette from practice. In the process, it outlines the steps involved in implementing a broad ecobehavioral assessment as well as describes graphic instruments for organizing relevant data holistically. Finally, it considers potential advantages offered by this approach for practitioners and ultimately for clients.

The Ecosystems Perspective

Until recently, practice was generally analyzed and evaluated linearly, a situation that prevailed in the social and natural sciences as well. Such conceptualizations were anchored in views of reality—"world hypotheses" (Pepper, 1942)—that were largely unidirectional and mechanistic. In contrast, emerging conceptual frameworks are more contextual, incorporating a rigorous examination of the complex interactions and interdependencies inherent in person-in-environment configurations. Within a contextual framework, available data can be organized in multiple ways, offering alternative potential approaches to effective change.

General systems theory (GST) and ecology have made important contributions to expanding the contextual perspective in social work (Greif & Lynch, 1983). The life model of Germain and Gitterman (1980), for example, emphasizes the application of ecological principles. Concepts drawn from GST are pervasive explicitly or implicitly in the literature. For example, Reid's (1981) matrix of target of change by medium (system) of work is a systemic formulation in which the GST concept of equifinality (suggesting that an outcome, positive or negative, can be reached via multiple paths) is implicit. Meyer (1983) suggests that an ecosystemic perspective can be applied regardless of practice approach or theoretical orientation, and offers a common framework for practitioners. We can probably never step entirely outside our own world views, but a broad, integrative look at the full complexity of client situations is essential to selecting appropriate treatment modalities (Nelsen, 1975) and achieving positive client outcomes.

Although the ecosystemic perspective is conceptually appealing, the final test of its utility is its contribution to practice. Applications of systemic concepts in practice depend on the use of metaphor (as in the life model, in which principles of ecology such as "niche" are used to describe aspects of human psychosocial functioning) or operationalization, in which abstract constructs are defined by observables (Brower, 1988)—the direction taken here. Moving down the ladder of abstraction from theoretical concepts to the real world, operationalizing inevitably narrows the construct under examination. Nevertheless, it is crucial for practice implementation of more abstract models, facilitating communication between persons, and empirical testing of clinical questions. The model presented here, which is consistent with an ecosystemic perspective, is only one of many possible ways to make sense of clinical data. It serves as an effort to present a parsimonious, coherent approach with substantial practice utility.

Recent advances in chaos theory, the study of apparently random events (Gleick, 1987; Baldwin, 1988), suggest that very small changes in initial conditions can resonate within and be amplified throughout a system. This "sensitive dependence on initial conditions" may complicate prediction, but it also suggests the potential for significant change as a result of relatively small interventions, if they are well chosen. This theory offers promise for practice within a contextual perspective, while suggesting the need for ongoing monitoring of results of interventions that may not be entirely predictable.

One technique for organizing clinical data in practice suggested by the ecosystems perspective is the use of graphic tools, such as the eco-map and genogram (Hartman, 1978; Hartman & Laird, 1983). The eco-map is particularly useful in assessing client situations from a behavior analytic perspective. Complex nonlinear exchange webs can be represented and explored by practitioner and client in a holistic and integrative way. Clients often find "drawing a picture" of their life situations both enlightening and compelling. A recent study (Mattaini, 1993) offers empirical support for the potential breadth of assessment resulting from the use of an eco-map. When designed to depict exchanges of positives and aversives, the map also clarifies the behavior analytic process outlined below.

Behavior Analysis

Social workers have incorporated the principles of applied behavior analysis into practice for more than two decades (Stuart, 1970; Schwartz & Goldiamond, 1975; Thyer, 1987a; Thyer; 1987b). As was true for other models, early behavior analytic formulations were frequently linear and unidirectional (although, by definition, they were in some sense "contextual"). Recent work, however, has increasingly recognized systemic complexities and reciprocal exchanges among people (Baer, Wolf, & Risley, 1987; Kanfer & Schefft, 1988; Dumas, 1989).

Behavior analysts suggest that behavior is the most appropriate focus for attention. Their basic argument is that practitioners are interested in facilitating change. Change requires someone to act, to do something, and in that sense a focus on behavior is immediately relevant to practice. The time-honored "task" concept in social work (Studt, 1968; Bartlett, 1970; Reid & Epstein, 1972) is ultimately behavioral. The behavior of interest may be client behavior, worker behavior, or the behavior of others in the network, as determined in the assessment process. Behavior analysis is prescriptive; applying this body of theory and knowledge to practice objectives provides direction for working toward desired outcomes. I construe behavior analysis quite broadly here, including "private events" such as self-talk and imagery as covert behavior (Skinner, 1957). Contemporary debates between advocates of cognitive models and radical behaviorist models (Schnaitter, 1987; Horgan, 1987) may eventually advance our understanding of these phenomena, but their resolution is not critical for day-to-day practice.

If the clinician is dealing with a depressed client, clearly the ultimate goal is to intervene so as to improve the emotional life of the client. Nevertheless, each step from the current emotional state to the goal state requires someone—client, clinician, or significant other—to act and/or to behave differently, even if covertly. A client suffering from a nutritional deficiency may lack necessary resources (food, money) to eat properly or may not eat because of more complex interactional factors (such as with anorexia). Although the goal in each case is that the person eat, the etiological contextual factors are vastly different, calling for dissimilar interventions. Organizing practice realities conceptually in terms of these systemic relationships opens them to the robust assessment and intervention technologies of behavior analysis.

The "kernel" of behavior analysis is that behavior is "selected by consequences" over the life course, analogous to the way genes were selected in contingencies of survival (Skinner, 1981). Although some behavioral anomalies (e.g., schizophrenia) are clearly to a considerable extent biologically based, much human conduct results from the interaction of the "state of the organism" (as changed by a person's history of consequences) and the current network of consequences. (Antecedents set the stage and potentiate consequences in critical ways, as discussed below.)

History changes the person. Sometimes cultures shape and reinforce consciousness of these effects; sometimes not. In some areas humans are aware of and can describe the contingencies affecting them; in other areas they cannot. Current behavior analytic thinking has gone far beyond the classical antecedent–behavior–consequence paradigm to a reciprocal, nonlinear analysis in which a complex network of mutual contingencies affect the behavior of each individual in the network (Schwartz & Goldiamond, 1975; Lee, 1987; Kanfer & Schefft, 1988). Behavioral techniques change the probabilities of behavior in conjunction with other multiple determinants; behavioral change techniques are most accurately viewed as probabilistic rather than deterministic (Johnson & Morris, 1987; Baldwin, 1988). This recognition is compatible with previously mentioned contemporary developments in chaos theory, which suggest that even apparently random disorder may sometimes be patterned and to some extent accessible to probabilistic prediction.

Terminology

Behavioral discussions are sometimes difficult to follow due to the use of specialized, technical vocabulary. Systematic definitions are available elsewhere (Skinner, 1953, 1974; Thyer, 1987b), but it may be useful to briefly clarify crucial terms. The probability of "voluntary" behavior occurring is affected by the consequences of similar behavior in the past.

Important categories of consequences include *reinforcement* (anything that leads to an increase in behavior), *punishment* (a consequence leading to a decrease in behavior), and *extinction* (eliminating consequences that previously reinforced a behavior).

Reinforcers are generally incentives, rewards, or positive events. Affection, bonuses, or favorite foods are examples. Unpleasant events, called aversives, include punishments as well as things or situations that a person may try to escape or avoid by acting in a particular way (technically, this is called the negative reinforcement process). Although many technical aspects of positive and negative reinforcement have been intensively studied, simple rates of positives and aversives experienced have proven empirically useful in predicting and changing behavior (Bornstein & Bornstein, 1986; Goldstein, Keller, & Erné, 1985).

Antecedents are events that occur prior to a behavior and affect its probability of occurrence, often by signaling the likelihood of various consequences. For example, a child may act quite differently in a grocery store from how he or she acts at home, having learned that different consequences apply in different settings. Instructions, models, and cues related to the likelihood of consequences are called *discriminative* stimuli. Other important classes of antecedents include *potentiating* antecedents, which make consequences more powerful (e.g., deprivation), and *facilitating* antecedents, which are prerequisites of the behavior (e.g., adequate transportation is a facilitating antecedent for regular job attendance) (Stuart, 1970).

Behavior is described as "contingent" on the consequences and antecedents that have been associated with it; the relationships among behavior, consequences, and antecedents are sometimes called *contingencies*. Of course, a great deal of systematic research related to effective evaluation and modification of these factors is available, but this discussion should provide sufficient background for understanding the material that follows.

The Assessment Process

In practice, assessment and intervention are transactional and non-linear. As a general rule, however, assessment precedes intervention (Germain, 1968), and for discussion purposes it is useful to examine the process in a stepwise fashion. The following case example may be helpful in explicating the assessment process recommended here:

C, a 33-year-old native Alaskan woman, was a high school graduate who had been divorced one year. She had three children, ages ten, eight, and three. She presented complaining of lingering depression and increasing alcohol intake. She had been receiving antidepressant medication from her general physician for several months; he referred her to the mental health clinic. Her eight-year-old son had become increasingly unmanageable since the divorce, and his teacher had recently expressed serious concerns about emerging problems at school. The client continued to depend on her ex-husband for occasional sexual gratification and for extended telephone contact late at night when she was particularly depressed. Because he had been repeatedly physically abusive and had discouraged C's efforts at independent action, she did not wish to continue the relationship at its current level. The client worked in a clerical position that offered little social contact and had only minimal contacts with friends, due to fatigue and the demands of parenting. She spoke on the telephone weekly with her parents in another city. Both parents had serious drinking problems, and the client described them as generally critical and rejecting of her. Her early history reflected substantial physical and emotional neglect.

Step One: Ecosystemic Scan

The initial step in a contextual behavior analysis is taking a broad scan of the client's or client system's life-space. An eco-map can be quite valuable for this purpose. For example, Figure 1 is the map developed with C. Note that this instrument is designed to clarify exchanges of contingencies as defined above, in contrast with the less operationalized "connections" traditionally portrayed on eco-maps. This graphic depicts important persons and institutions in the client's life as well as the exchange of positives and aversives among them. The dark arrows reflect aversives exchanged among persons and systems, the light arrows, positives.

Several significant features of C's life emerge immediately from the map. The total positives currently available are few and are substantially outweighed by negatives. The most intense negatives flow between the client and her ex-husband, with whom she has contact several times a week, and between her and her eight-year-old son, who is increasingly noncompliant and demanding at home and beginning to present behavior problems in school as well. Other available positive supports are generally weak, reflected by the narrowness of the arrows connecting her with friends and extended family living in another city. Most contacts with her extended family are, in fact, aversive; this has been the situation for as long as the client can remember.

Step Two: Identification of Priority Change Targets

After exploring the broad contours of the client's life, the practitioner and client are in a position to determine priority problem areas and target goal-states collaboratively. Selection of priority areas is based on importance to the client, accessibility of the operative contingencies to intervention, and value considerations. In C's case, she identified depression as her most serious concern. The constant strains between her and her ex-husband and her and her middle child also emerged from the eco-map as clear priorities for intervention. In Figure 1, three boxes enclosing outlined numbers indicate these priority intervention foci: (1) depression, located within the client, (2) problems between her and her son, and (3) the ambivalent relationship with her ex-husband.

With these priorities determined, the worker and client can collaboratively operationalize identified problems and goal-states. In this case, scores on the Beck Depression Inventory (BDI) (Beck, 1978) as well as a

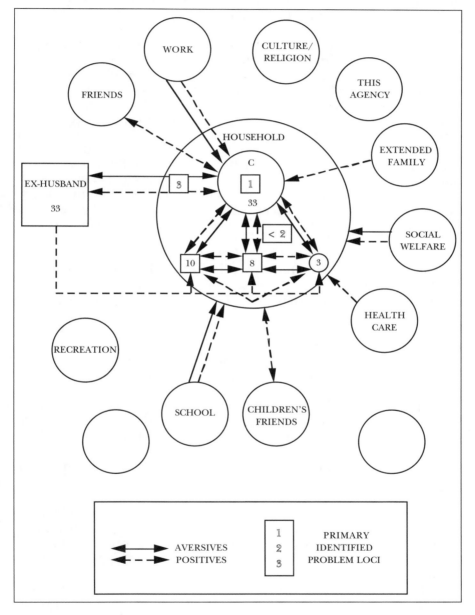

Figure 1. Eco-map depicting initial contextual scan of the C case.

self-anchored 10-point scale of mood were used to track C's level of depression. Although the other priority goal areas identified were also operationalized, for reasons of space, this chapter will focus primarily on the first identified area. C's BDI score was in the serious range at intake. On the self-anchored scale, C estimated her depressed mood as 3, not as severe as before she began taking medication, but still quite problematic.

Active, fulfilling involvement of the client in multiple activities was identified as an important goal-state. Although further specification was required, this general goal is incompatible with depression and could be addressed behaviorally. Over the course of two sessions, this goal-state was operationalized as involving more fulfilling work, engagement with a wider social network, and a possible return to school. A related instrumental goal was examination of the accuracy of the client's perception of the contingencies affecting her, and the development and testing of alternative, and perhaps more accurate, descriptions of the existing contingency web (often described as "cognitive therapy") (Skinner, 1988). These directions are in keeping with behavioral and cognitive–behavioral theories of depression (Beck, 1978; McLean, 1982) and were consistent with the picture that emerged of limited payoffs in C's life-space.

Step Three: Behavior Analysis

The steps discussed above have analogues in other practice approaches, although the focus on reinforcers and punishments in the first step and in Figure 1 offers a somewhat different emphasis. The contributions most particular to applied behavior analysis emerge in the third step, tentative identification of the contingency networks currently maintaining problems and potentially available to support new repertoires. Once again, an eco-map can be helpful in ordering the data without forcing data into an artificially linear pattern. As indicated in Figure 2, reinforcements for increased activity appeared to be potentially substantial. Although initial support might be provided largely by the practitioner, and to some extent C's physician, both C and the practitioner could see substantial, potentially available payoffs in the natural network. C's ex-husband and extended family were likely to punish efforts to open C's life-space, but the potential increase in positives from other sources seemed sufficiently powerful to outweigh these aversives, particularly if contacts with them would be few.

Nevertheless, seeing that a different life could be more fulfilling is only a preliminary step toward building and maintaining that life, particularly for a person who has overlearned that her efforts are unlikely to pay off. At this point in treatment planning, analysis of antecedents becomes critical.

Potential sources of important antecedents in Figure 2 are indicated by outlined letters. In C's network, the practitioner and physician could provide initial instructions (more technically, "rules" describing contingency relations); we could cue new efforts and describe the possible pay-offs. C herself could learn to self-instruct after such instructions had been modeled, shaped, and reinforced by the worker. Ultimately, it is essential that following these instructions lead to payoffs in the natural network; changing "thoughts" is usually insufficient to maintain behavior

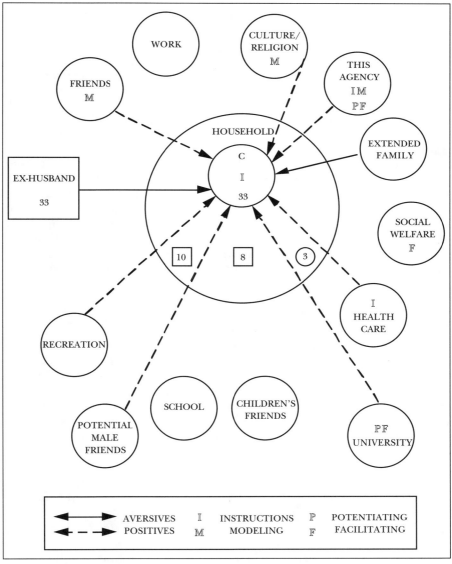

Figure 2. Eco-map portraying potential contingencies for increased client involvement in fulfilling activities.

change (Skinner, 1988). Immediate contingencies are often self-generated (e.g., self-prompts, self-talk, self-reinforcement); these are often the most accessible to intervention (note, though, that these repertoires were previously shaped by situational factors).

Other potentially positive sources of antecedents were also available in the enriched network to which the agency could connect the client. The practitioner was able to arrange to have C visit with a paraprofessional employed by the agency who was currently attending the local university. This individual later took C to the campus to sample life there and meet some students. The agency was also able to assist C with access to available financial assistance for educational and job-placement services, providing "tools" that facilitated changes in behavior. A staff member also connected C with a native Alaskan cultural group, offering models of fulfilling, active social functioning and support. Other sources of relevant antecedents and consequences in the client's network can be traced in Figure 2.

Often, a focus on the current life situation is sufficient for treatment planning. In some cases, however, particularly when it is difficult to identify contingencies supporting behavior, it is useful to take a similar scan, albeit retrospectively, of critical periods in the client's life. The history of reinforcement and punishment (whether in response to or independent of the client's behavior) experienced in some cases can offer hints for intervention, though it is essential to note that only current contingencies can be modified, and an extensive focus on the past can dissipate limited clinical time and energy.

Step Four: Identification of Tasks

A thorough behavior analysis suggests clinician, client, and collateral tasks with positive potential. Clinician tasks include providing or arranging for the necessary antecedents and consequences. Client tasks often consist of intermediate behaviors necessary to or facilitative of final, target repertoires (and providing the self-instructions necessary to cue them). Collaterals can, and often must, provide many of the critical contingencies required to shape and maintain target behaviors in the natural network. Often, a behavioral analysis of collateral behavior is also required to determine how to encourage provision of the contingencies the client requires.

Because of the difficulty and complexity of social issues, in some cases, the practitioner–client team does not have a sufficient level of influence over the most critical contingencies. A first step in such cases is to continue the behavior analysis out into the ecosystem. For example, a chronically mentally ill client can be provided with necessary cues, instructions, and models to apply for concrete assistance. In some cases, however, the powerful contingencies of an advocacy group are required to encourage public assistance agencies to provide the resources established by law, after the client has applied. Even efforts to affect legislators' behavior for the benefit of client populations can be productive if the practitioner and/or clients can affect the complex network of contingencies in which the legislator finds him- or herself (votes, interest groups, colleagues, staff, media).

Unfortunately, in practice, clinicians often are faced with client situations wherein neither the client nor the clinician has much influence or many resources and a higher-order analysis reveals no accessible intervention points. This problem is important to recognize; as Meyer (1983) indicates, the doctor who cannot cure cancer does not refuse to see it and offer to treat something else. The painful recognition of these situations remains critical for long-term advocacy.

To recapitulate, then, the four principal steps in a contextual behavior analytic assessment are (1) a broad ecobehavioral scan of the client's life situation, focusing on the contingency web in which the client is embedded; (2) the identification of priority problems and goal-states; (3) the behavior analysis of those problems and goals; and (4) the identification of tasks designed to modify the contingencies affecting the client, including reciprocal exchanges, in which the client or practitioner effects changes in the contingencies for others in the environment, who then are more likely to provide the contingencies that will positively affect the client.

Intervention incorporating the identified tasks and ongoing evaluation of effectiveness follow assessment. Because such monitoring of the effects of intervention on an ongoing basis is not specific to this approach and has been widely considered elsewhere (Auerswald, 1987; Reid, 1988; Schwartz & Goldiamond, 1975), it will not be pursued further here. Although an intensive examination of the case is not the objective here, it may be worth noting that C did begin school, form new relationships, change jobs, and learn more effective parenting skills over the course of approximately 20 sessions; her depression scores dropped into the normal range. During this time, additional goal-states were occasionally established and corresponding contextual analysis performed as changes in the network were identified or additional relationships clarified.

Contextual Behavior Analysis: Advantages for Practice

Contextual behavior analysis "enlarges the unit of attention while it sharpens the focus" (Germain, 1968), as do other approaches utilizing the ecosystemic perspective. It ensures that a broad view of the client in his or her situation is taken. To a greater extent than some other metaphoric systemic approaches, it also operationalizes the network as a web of exchanges of contingencies among persons and larger systems. This approach avoids hypothesized unobservable mental "representations" of reality suggested by cognitive formulations (Brower, 1988). Actors in the network are not viewed as exchanging abstract "information" and "feedback," but rather more tangible (and observable) contingencies.

A second advantage of the approach is that it makes an extensive litera-ture on behavior change in applied settings relevant to the practitioner, ranging from specific prescriptions for particular problems (Thyer, 1987b; Greene, Winett, Van Houten, Geller, & Iwata, 1987) to theoretical para-digms that may suggest new approaches in unique client–environment con-stellations. For example, recent work in operant matching theory suggests that increasing the general rate of free or noncontingent reinforcement in the environment may decrease existing problem behaviors without requir-ing direct action to affect the problem behavior (Mc-Dowell, 1988). This lit-erature cannot be reviewed here, but the extent of current knowledge is sub-stantial, offering the clinician a broad resource for intervention planning.

Because it is highly specified and operationalized, the approach is also quite researchable. A practitioner working with it can test hypotheses suggested by the analysis and can even contribute to the field's knowledge base by using rigorous single-case designs. For example, the practitioner and client may hypothesize that recurrent aversives from those in the social network and a lack of positives are related to parenting difficulties (Dumas, 1989). By implementing tasks that result in measurable changes in this balance and monitoring parenting tasks, this hypothesis could be tested. Alternatively, one might hypothesize that a skill deficit is responsi-ble for the problem and might then implement parent training by model-ing, instructing, and prompting (antecedents) as well as praising (rein-forcing) gradual improvements. Ultimately, success in parenting should pay off naturally in the client's life. The approach, being quantifiable, is also amenable to more traditional group designs when appropriate.

Finally, use of this approach to assessment offers direct, immediate guid-ance in treatment planning. After problem areas and goal-states are identified and analyzed, treatment options become immediately apparent. Using a broadly contextual analytic framework, the worker can identify current and potential sources of both consequences and antece-dents. Often, multiple options for intervention points exist, as is true for any truly systemic approach, and contextual behavior analysis, particularly in conjunction with diagram-matic aids such as the eco-map, simplifies identification of those points.

As can be seen in Figures 1 and 2, contemporary behavioral approach-es recognize the reciprocal influence of actors in a systemic field. These persons and systems constantly exchange incentives and aversives that affect the behavior of others in the network. Skinner (1953, 1971, 1982, 1986, 1987) has continuously argued that positive reinforcement is ulti-mately the most effective technology; clinicians also generally recognize this fact, although often using less operationalized terms.

Conclusions

The ecosystem perspective in clinical social work currently offers the best framework for conceptualizing the person-in-environment. Meyer

(1983) suggests that this perspective, which defines the range of focus for practice, can comfortably encompass multiple practice approaches. Social work is about change in the social world and therefore about human behavior in context.

Contextual behavior analysis operationalizes the perspective in a manner that is prescriptive for practice and accessible to rigorous research. Much is yet to be learned; for example, what contingencies are generally most salient for particular behaviors under what circumstances, and what contingencies practitioners can most effectively and efficiently influence in practice settings. These essential questions can be addressed and examined directly through this approach, and such explorations are urgently needed.

Many of the ethical questions that have been raised concerning control and the operant approach reflect misconceptions about and lack of familiarity with behavior analysis as well as philosophic disagreements. The interested reader is referred to Schwartz and Goldiamond (1975) for further discussion of such questions. However, ignoring such a powerful technology that may have the potential to improve radically the quality of life for clients may, in fact, be ethically questionable. The powerful have always used incentives and aversives, generally to their own advantage. Social work may now be in a position to adopt and encourage methods that can empower individuals and groups who historically have lacked access to fulfilling lives to take control of the contingencies in which their lives are embedded.

REFERENCES

American Psychiatric Association (1987). *Diagnostic and statistical manual of mental disorders* (3rd ed., rev.). Washington, DC: Author.

Auerswald, E. H. (1987). Epistemological confusion in family therapy and research. *Family Process, 26,* 317–330.

Baer, D. M., Wolf, M. M., & Risley, T. R. (1987). Some still-current dimensions of applied behavior analysis. *Journal of Applied Behavior Analysis, 20,* 315–327.

Baldwin, J. D. (1988). Mead and Skinner: Agency and determinism. *Behaviorism, 16,* 109–127.

Bartlett, H. M. (1970). *The common base of social work practice.* Silver Spring, MD: National Association of Social Workers.

Beck, A. T. (1978). *Cognitive therapy of depression.* New York: Guilford Press.

Bornstein, P. H., & Bornstein, M. T. (1986). *Marital therapy: A behavioral-communications approach.* New York: Pergamon.

Brower, A. M. (1988). Can the ecological model guide social work practice? *Social Service Review, 62,* 411–429.

Dumas, J. E. (1989). Let's not forget the context in behavioral assessment. *Behavioral Assessment, 11,* 231–247.

Germain, C. B. (1968). Social study, past and future. *Social Casework, 49,* 403–409.

Germain, C. B., & Gitterman, A. (1980). *The life model of social work practice.* New York: Columbia University Press.

Gleick, J. (1987). *Chaos: Making a new science.* New York: Penguin.

Goldstein, A. P., Keller, H., & Erné, D. (1985). *Changing the abusive parent.* Champaign, IL: Research Press.

Greene, B. F., Winett, R. A., Van Houten, R., Geller, E. S., & Iwata, B. A. (1987). *Behavior analysis in the community: 1968–1986.* Lawrence, KS: Society for the Experimental Analysis of Behavior.

Greif, G. L., & Lynch, A. A. (1983). The eco-systems perspective. In C. H. Meyer (Ed.), *Clinical social work in the eco-systems perspective.* New York: Columbia University Press.

Hamilton, G. (1951). *Theory and practice of social casework* (rev.). New York: Columbia University Press.

Hartman, A. (1978). Diagrammatic assessment of family relationships. *Social Casework, 59,* 465–476.

Hartman, A., & Laird, J. (1983). *Family-centered social work practice.* New York: Free Press.

Horgan, T. (1987). Cognition is real. *Behaviorism, 15,* 13–25.

Johnson, L. M., & Morris, E. K. (1987). When speaking of probability in behavior analysis. *Behaviorism, 15,* 107–129.

Kanfer, F. H., & Schefft, B. K. (1988). *Guiding the process of therapeutic change.* Champaign, IL: Research Press.

Lee, V. L. (1987). The structure of conduct. *Behaviorism, 15,* 141–148.

Mattaini, M. A. (1993). *More than a thousand words: Graphics for clinical practice.* Washington, DC: National Association of Social Workers Press.

McDowell, J. J. (1988). Matching theory in natural human environments. *The Behavior Analyst, 11,* 95–109

McLean, P. (1982). Behavioral therapy: Theory and research. In A. J. Rush (Ed.), *Short-term psychotherapies for depression.* New York: Guilford Press.

Meyer, C. H. (1976). *Social work practice: The changing landscape* (2nd ed.). New York: Free Press.

Meyer, C. H. (Ed.). (1983). *Clinical social work in the eco-systems perspective.* New York: Columbia University Press.

Nelsen, J. C. (1975). Social work's fields of practice, methods, and models: The choice to act. *Social Service Review, 49,* 264–270.

Pepper, S. C. (1942). *World hypotheses.* Berkeley CA: University of California Press.

Reid, W. J. (1981). Comment on "Statement on purpose of social work." *Social Work, 26,* 91–92.

Reid, W. J. (1988). The metamodel, research, and empirical practice. In E. R. Tolson (Ed.), *The metamodel and clinical social work.* New York: Columbia University Press.

Reid, W. J., & Epstein, L. (1972). *Task-centered casework.* New York: Columbia University Press.

Richmond, M. (1917). *Social diagnosis.* New York: Russell Sage Foundation.

Schnaitter, R. (1987). Behaviorism is not cognitive and cognitivism is not behavioral. *Behaviorism, 15,* 1–11.

Schwartz, A., & Goldiamond, I. (1975). *Social casework: A behavioral approach.* New York: Columbia University Press.

Skinner, B. F. (1953). *Science and human behavior.* New York: Free Press.

Skinner, B. F. (1957). *Verbal behavior.* Englewood Cliffs, NJ: Prentice-Hall.

Skinner, B. F. (1971). *Beyond freedom and dignity.* New York: Knopf.

Skinner, B. F. (1974). *About behaviorism.* New York: Knopf.

Skinner, B. F. (1981). Selection by consequences. *Science, 213,* 501–504.

Skinner, B. F. (1982). The contrived reinforcer. *The Behavior Analyst, 5,* 3–8.

Skinner, B. F. (1986). What is wrong with daily life in the Western world? In B. F. Skinner, *Upon further reflection* (pp. 15–31). Englewood Cliffs, NJ: Prentice-Hall.

Skinner, B. F. (1987). Why we are not acting to save the world. In B. F. Skinner, *Upon fur-

ther reflection (pp. 1–14). Englewood Cliffs, NJ: Prentice-Hall.

Skinner, B. F. (1988). The operant side of behavior therapy. *Recent issues in the analysis of behavior.* Columbus, OH: Merrill.

Strayhorn, J. M. (1983). A diagnostic axis relevant to psychotherapy and preventive mental health. *American Journal of Orthopsychiatry, 53,* 677–696.

Stuart, R. B. (1970). *Trick or treatment: How and when psychotherapy fails.* Champaign, IL: Research Press.

Studt, E. (1968). Social work theory and implications for the practice of methods. *Social Work Education Reporter, 16*(2), 22–24, 42–46.

Thyer, B. A. (1987a). Can behavior analysis rescue social work? (Editor's page). *Journal of Applied Behavior Analysis, 20,* 207–211.

Thyer, B. A. (1987b). Contingency analysis: Toward a unified theory for social work practice. *Social Work, 32,* 150–157.

Assessment Revisited: A Comprehensive Approach to Understanding Family Dynamics

Anna R. McPhatter

3

A ssessment is the heart and soul of the practitioner's armamentarium. It is as essential to the activities of the practitioner as breathing is to life. The assessment sets the "action agenda" for interventions with any system, from an individual to a community.

This chapter "revisits" the assessment endeavor, focusing particularly on families. Establishing a common understanding of the meaning of assessment and developing a worker philosophy are critical to assessment. A comprehensive framework for family assessment is presented.

Assessment Defined

Assessment has been conceptualized as both a product and a process (Hepworth & Larsen, 1990). As a product, the initial assessment serves as a working document designed specifically to provide a "road map" for the worker and the client system as they begin their collaborative work. As a process, the worker collects and synthesizes relevant information about the family system into a working statement of presenting and underlying problems as a basis of planning. The assessment is not cast in stone; it is an ongoing process that begins with initial client contact and continues throughout the course of work. It includes thoughtful analyses of new information and insight gained from client–worker interchanges and is incorporated into subsequent interventions. In family practice, assessment is a deliberate back-and-forth analytical process based upon a theoretical understanding of family dynamics and of common impediments to optimal family functioning. It provides working hypotheses that remain open for reframing as greater understanding of the client system unfolds.

Worker Philosophy—Prerequisite for Family Assessment

Worker philosophy can be understood as a combination of beliefs about the world and people (world view) and one's practice theory. An individual's world view, which often is not explicitly articulated, derives from one's socialization, education, and life experiences; it is one's vision of the world and how that vision relates to practice. Practice theory is essentially a working theoretical perspective regarding the nature of people's problems in living and beliefs about how change occurs, that is, what factors facilitate change and the role of the worker in the change process. Developing a practice theory begins early in the practitioner's formal education and training and continues throughout his or her professional life. Sometimes, however, workers may become locked into a practice theory early and cling to it regardless whether it is effective in specific practice situations. Beginning practitioners, in response to the ambiguity inherent in professional practice, may become wed to a particular theoretical and practice approach, using it steadfastly regardless of the presenting problems. Seasoned practitioners are more likely to have developed a solid practice theory grounded in realities of day-to-day practice, although they may rigidly adhere to particular practice approaches as well.

The worker's world view and practice theory define how he or she approaches assessment and intervention. The assumptions that undergird the worker's practice perspective guide the analytical work used to prepare the worker for initial client contact. Assumptions about the nature of people's problems and the change process dictate what questions will be asked and what areas will be explored in the assessment process. A worker who is grounded theoretically in behavioral principles, for example, will follow a line of exploration substantially different from that which a worker grounded in psychoanalytic theory will follow. Theoretical perspectives translate into practice approaches, which in turn unfold into methods and techniques of intervention.

Family Assessment Model

Theoretical Perspective

Although throughout its history the profession has vacillated in its focus on the individual or on the environment as targets of intervention, the current consensus within the profession is that a dual emphasis on individuals and the environment is optimal. The profession has expended a lot of effort in developing and building on theoretical models that are compatible with the social work practice domain. General systems theory and perspectives derived from ecology are widely used as the basis of theory and practice taught in schools of social work.

General systems theory evolved from the physical sciences as a method of analyzing complex interactions in closed systems (Von Bertalanffy, 1968). Applied to open human systems, social work systems theory is used to direct attention to "the multiplicity of systems at different levels of complexity that influence any particular situation" (Compton & Galaway, 1984). Specific principles of systems theory that are immediately applicable to families include: (1) a system is a complex of components related directly and indirectly in a causal network, with each part related to some others; (2) interrelationships of components give rise to new qualities that derive from transactions within the system; that is, change in any part of the system affects the system as a whole and its parts; (3) boundaries, which set physical and social parameters, are essential to the functioning of the system; all healthy systems have well-defined, semipermeable boundaries with ways of maintaining them; (4) open systems are goal-directed—the goal being to maintain homeostasis or a steady state; (5) tension and conflict are characteristic and necessary to adaptive systems; (6) systems have a communication network comprised of a feedback mechanism that guides information flow, responses, and modification of communication (Compton & Galaway, 1984).

The ecological perspective builds on systems theory but moves away from its mechanistic language. Ecology is concerned with relations among living entities and aspects of their environment (Germain, 1979). The ecological perspective also draws from contemporary constructs of ego psychology that highlight the importance of the individual's adaptive capacity, the link between the individual and the social environment, and a more optimistic, growth-oriented view of human functioning and potential (Goldstein, 1984). Ecological practice focuses on transactions between people and environments. It postulates that people's problems in living arise out of these complex transactions; when there are upsets in the adaptive balance or "goodness of fit" between people and environments, stress results (Germain & Gitterman, 1980). The life model (Germain & Gitterman, 1980), which was developed from the ecological perspective, suggests that stress arises in four interrelated areas of living: life transitions involving developmental changes such as entrance into puberty or a new baby entering the family, status-role changes and crisis events, the unresponsiveness of social and physical environments, and communication and relationship difficulties in families and other primary groups.

The following case vignette illustrates how the ecological approach may be used in assessing the family's situation and guiding decisions about points of intervention among several alternatives.

Mr. B was 55 years old and the primary breadwinner in a family of five. He had worked as a skilled laborer in a steel plant for 15 years when the plant suddenly shut down. Because Mr. B's training and skills had not prepared him for the high-tech and service jobs that were available, he was able to secure only minimum-wage jobs, which created extreme financial problems for the family. Unemployment/underemployment resulted in an upset in the adaptive balance that existed in the family system prior to Mr. B's layoff. Mr. B not only lost his means of providing for his family, but he lost a very important social support network as well. Family members were forced to reorient their lives from a comfortable and stable life-style to a life-style in which meeting basic needs was difficult.

The stress resulting from this "environmental" situation over which the client had no control created severe strain on the marital relationship as well as upsets in relationships among all family members. Mr. B's unexpected status-role change (as primary breadwinner) resulted in a crisis for the family and created relationship difficulties within the family. In other words, a goodness of fit no longer existed between the family and their environment. The family no longer had a positive, reciprocal interchange with the external environment (the labor force) and thus was barely able to meet intrapersonal and interpersonal needs.

In conducting an ecological assessment, the practitioner would explore in depth the impact of this imbalance between the family and the environment, perhaps focusing on helping family members see how this imbalance relates to their current situation. A primary intervention point would very likely be assisting Mr. B to restore his status as breadwinner while addressing issues of other family members who are experiencing crisis as a result of changes in their status.

The ecological approach to practice does not rule out the use of other theoretical or practice approaches. In fact, it is more inclusive than exclusive in that it broadens possible explanations for people's problems, often eliminating feelings of personal deficit and blame. Social work practitioners who are grounded in ecological systems concepts often use other intervention approaches such as behavioral therapies and structural and strategic therapy (Schwartz, 1982; Minuchin, 1974; Haley, 1976). The theoretical and practice framework that guides the family-assessment process described in the following section is grounded in ecological systems concepts.

Goals of Family Assessment

The assessment process begins with the assumption that some form of screening and determination of appropriateness of work has been made; some agreement through formal or informal contracting is presupposed. The initial assessment process typically requires several sessions to complete. For example, I see the family for a two-hour period the first session and then see members for one or two additional sessions before summarizing the results of the initial assessment. I attempt to include all members of the household initially, then decide with the family if others should be included. It is essential that the worker explain to

34

the family what the assessment process is about, what it will include, the importance of family members' participation in the process, and how the assessment will be used in getting to the root of the presenting problems in order to help them meet their goals as a family.

During the assessment process, the worker should clarify his or her approach to family work and establish time parameters for the initial assessment and further work, if that is feasible. During the second or third session, the worker, after some reflection and synthesis of information gained from the family, should share with the family his or her perceptions and ideas about the nature of the presenting problem, make clear suggestions about how the work might proceed, and begin (with the family) to develop an intervention plan to guide further work.

The primary goal of the initial assessment is to elucidate the nature of the problems presented by families at a particular point in time. The assessment serves as an appraisal of varying perceptions of the problem(s) as presented by family members (as well as people outside the family, such as the referring agency). The assessment period is often the first time all members have actually articulated for one another what they think is wrong. The process, therefore, should include a summary of these views, using explicit examples provided by family members.

A clear picture of family structure, family functioning, and inferences about underlying dynamics that contribute to and maintain the problem should emerge as a result of the assessment process. An intervention plan that reflects mutual understanding and collaboration by worker and family members flows directly from the picture of the family obtained during this process.

Guide for Family Assessment

There are five crucial areas in a comprehensive family assessment: problem identification, family structure, family functioning, family strengths and resources, and intervention plan and method of evaluation.

Problem Identification

The following areas should be included under problem identification:
- Presenting problem as described by family members
- Worker's understanding of presenting problem
- Who is involved in the problem (family members, friends)
- How members are involved in the problem
- External subsystems' involvement in the problem
- Longevity of presenting problem
- History pertinent to the presenting problem
- Intensity of presenting problem (degree to which problem is upsetting to members and the family system, crisis nature of problem, vulnerability of family members to harm)

■ Family members' motivation and commitment to engage in work to alter problem(s)

A clear statement about why the family is seeing the worker at this time should be developed. This statement should reflect each individual member's perspective on the problem as well as the worker's understanding of why the family is seeking professional assistance. It is important for the worker to state clearly what has been described as the presenting problem by a referring agency or by an intake/screening process. Problem identification should also include discussion of who family members see as being involved in the problem, how each member is involved, and the member's perception of his or her role in the presenting problem. Involvement of people outside the family should be clarified with thorough exploration of how other subsystems are involved in the problem. (This presents a good opportunity for the worker to explain the nature of systems and how each part of the system affects other parts of the system.) A determination should be made regarding the longevity of the presenting problem, including any relevant history. Particular attention should be paid to the intensity of the problem. The worker should assess the degree to which the problem upsets individual family members and the total family system, whether the presenting issues are viewed as a crisis, and whether any family member is particularly vulnerable to or at risk for physical harm, which would require immediate intervention.

Operating from the underlying assumption that the presenting problem is a systems-related problem affected by forces both internal and external to the family, the worker should thoroughly explore what factors in the physical and social environment affect the presenting problem(s). These factors include sources of stress, such as family finances and the degree to which the family is able to meet adequately food, shelter, and other instrumental needs; employment concerns; health-related issues; and neighborhood concerns, including how safe and connected the family feels in its neighborhood. Many aspects of the physical and social environment can affect families in negative and unhealthy ways. For example, families who live in poor urban areas regularly experience physical and social environments as threatening and unsafe. These families may observe violence, witness criminal activities, and be plagued with frequent and aggressive police intervention. Such environments can be debilitating for children, adolescents, and adults who struggle to keep their families safe from harm.

A firm grasp of the cultural milieu in which the family functions is critical to understanding the social context of the family's presenting problems (Green, 1982; DeVore & Schlesinger, 1987; Lum, 1986; McGoldrick, Pearce, & Giordano, 1982; Logan, Freeman, & McRoy, 1990). Race, ethnicity, gender, sexual orientation, and other sources of stress and difficulty for the family must be explored. For example, although the family may have a strong racial or ethnic identity, racism and cross-cultural conflict within our society may make it impossible for families of color to remain unscathed by the negative manifestations of these dynamics. The worker's understanding of these issues and his or her own comfort in engaging the family in discussion about such issues are essential to problem description. The practitioner needs to have a working knowledge of the culture, lifestyle, customs, language, and history of the group with which the family is affiliated. The worker must be well versed in alternative theoretical explanations to "mainstream" explanations of various cultural groups' behavior and functioning. Both observed and reported behavior by clients may appear pathological if analyzed outside the appropriate cultural context. For example, it is common for African American families to be viewed as dysfunctional by criteria based upon theoretical underpinnings foreign to their cultural environment. In fact, many characteristics believed to be dysfunctional are in actuality quite adaptive if understood within the sociocultural context in which they occur.

Norton (1978) suggests that workers adopt a "dual perspective" when working with racially, culturally, and ethnically diverse clients. The dual perspective is "the conscious and systematic process of perceiving, understanding, and comparing simultaneously the values, attitudes, and behavior of the larger societal system with those of the client's immediate family and community system" (p. 3). The goal of the dual perspective is to identify points of conflict between the nurturing system (immediate and extended family, informal helping networks, neighborhood) and the sustaining system (formal social institutions, work, schools, social welfare agencies) (Chestang, 1976). These areas of conflict produce stressors that generate or add to family dysfunction.

Chestang (1972) described the characterological response of African Americans to these conflictual and oftentimes hostile environments. The *dual response*, differentiated from dual personality, entails the development of an offensive and defensive posture of survival (the depreciated character). The *depreciated character* is often manifested in attitudes and behaviors of "getting over" at any cost, passive–aggressive behavior, and an overriding attitude of helplessness and hopelessness. The depreciated character serves as a protective function for the *transcendent character*, which Chestang describes as a force that maintains a sense of hope and optimism and a belief in the goodness of humankind. The transcendent character believes that good will come if one is patient and plays by society's rules. The depreciated character stands ready with memories of devaluing experiences to sustain the transcendent character when environmental conflicts and hostility surface. Since both characters are manifest in an individual, it is essential that the two characters unify and allow for adaptive responses of the individual. Operating alone, each character leads ultimately to dysfunction. Viewed within this context, aggressive, defensive, or unusually distrustful behavior exhibited by clients from historically oppressed groups takes on meaning contrary to typical descriptions of resistant and hostile clients.

Many tools and methods may be used to assist the worker in problem identification. The eco-map, developed by Hartman (1978), is an effective tool for gaining a visual picture of how internal and external subsystems are related to family problems and functioning. The eco-map characterizes important nurturing and adverse connections between the family and the external environment. As families participate in the development of the eco-map, they begin to understand how external stresses and intrafamilial relationships create problems within the system. It is a very effective way to involve family members and to reduce their defensiveness about providing personal information about the family (Holman, 1983). The eco-map is also a valuable tool for identifying available and absent resources as well as explicit areas where the worker and family members may begin their work (Hartman & Laird, 1983). Figure 1 shows a sample eco-map that illustrates visually the composition of a family

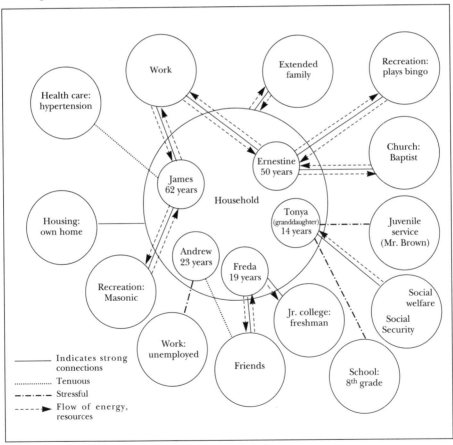

Figure 1. Sample eco-map—Clay family.

household, the various subsystems that interact with the family, the nature of members' relationship with the subsystems, and strengths and resources available to the family.

Family Structure

In order to gain more insight about the difficulties a family is experiencing, it is necessary to explore the structure of the family, which begins with an elaboration of *who* makes up the family unit. In exploring the structure of a family, the worker should not make assumptions about family composition and type based on traditional definitions of family. For example, typical American families include single mothers with children, single fathers with children, gay or lesbian couples with children, grandparent(s) with children, foster parents with children, and extended family members and nonblood relatives who are significant to the family. Moreover, African Americans may take in individuals not related by blood and include them as family members (Hill, 1972). A worker will make families feel ill at ease or defensive if he or she assumes a nuclear-family status for all families. It is useful to ask the family to describe its membership, including all people whom members see as significant to the family system. Moreover, the worker must be careful not to portray a negative valuation of a family type or composition that is unfamiliar or different from the married-couple-with-children model.

Assessment of family structure also includes specific information about family members, such as relevant historical information, current socioeconomic status of members, and the composition of the family's social network. Finally, the family's immediate physical environment should also be described, including location of family residence, description of the neighborhood, the degree to which the family feels safe and connected to its neighborhood; where children attend school; and accessibility of essential services such as health care facilities, grocery stores, shopping areas, and transportation.

The genogram is a useful method for clarifying information on family structure and functioning (Guerin & Pendagast, 1976; Holman, 1983; Hartman & Laird, 1983). It provides a "map" of the family structure spanning at least three generations, depicting factual information (such as births, illnesses, deaths, marriages, divorces, occupations, religious and ethnic affiliations) and significant physical, psychological, and social changes that have occurred within the family system (Guerin & Pendagast, 1976). As with the eco-map, the family's participation in diagramming the structure and functioning of the family helps members see themselves more clearly as a system and often reduces their reticence about sharing personal family history.

The following case vignette and sample genogram of the Clay family (Figure 2) illustrates the usefulness of this method for gaining a picture of family structure and functioning.

The Clay family was referred to the agency because their 14-year-old grand-daughter, Tonya, was ordered by the Juvenile Services Administration into a diversion program as a result of an incident of shoplifting and fighting in school. The diversion program requires family counseling. After a telephone

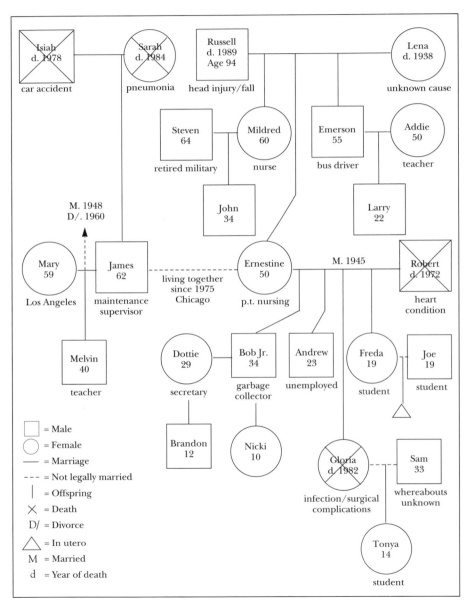

Figure 2. Sample genogram—Clay family.

intake process, the Clays—Mr. and Mrs. Clay, their granddaughter, and their daughter Freda, age 19—came in to see the social worker.

The genogram was explained to the Clays and they, at first somewhat reluctantly, agreed to participate in its construction. As indicated by the genogram, James and Ernestine, although not legally married, have formed a family unit for the past 15 years. Currently living in the home are two of Mrs. Clay's children from a previous marriage—Freda, age 19, who is unmarried and pregnant, and Andrew, age 23—and Mrs. Clay's natural granddaughter, Tonya. Prior to her father's death in 1989, Mrs. Clay also cared for her father in her home.

The Clays appear to be a close-knit family with strong ties to an extended family and the community. They live in a stable lower-middle-class neighborhood, own their home, and have fulfilling connections with the church and civic organizations. Both Mr. and Mrs. Clay are employed and feel they are managing financially. They perceived the problem as Tonya having gotten mixed up with the wrong kids since she discontinued attending church. Tonya stated that her grandparents were too strict and would not allow her to go out with her friends. She was angry that her allowance was taken away "since I get a Social Security check." Freda agreed with Tonya's view, indicating that her parents restricted her activities, while allowing her brother to do as he pleased, supporting her point by mentioning the brother's not working and involvement in illegal activities.

Family Functioning

Assessing family functioning is a broad and expansive endeavor guided by the worker's approach to therapeutic interventions. Family functioning has been conceptualized by family role assignment and performance, family boundaries, interactional processes within the family, and family life-cycle issues (Minuchin, 1974; Carter & McGoldrick, 1980; Hartman & Laird, 1983; Holman, 1983; Logan, Freeman, & McRoy, 1990.) Whatever the conceptual underpinnings that seek to clarify family functioning, the overarching goal of assessing family functioning is to learn how the family system handles day-to-day living and whether its efforts are functional and satisfactory to all members of the family. The worker must closely scrutinize specific aspects of the family's functioning in relation to presenting problems:

■ Individual members' developmental issues
■ Family developmental issues
■ How roles are identified and carried out
■ How instrumental and expressive functions are handled in the family
■ Communication styles and patterns, functionality of communication within the family
■ How the family solves problems, handles conflict
■ Family goals and degree of agreement on them

Individual developmental issues are examined to provide some understanding of the biopsychosocial status of family members (Zastrow & Kirst-Ashman, 1990). It is important to determine whether unusual stresses are occurring in relation to developmental tasks, how members are coping with stresses, and how functional these coping styles are. Fur-

41

ther, it is also necessary to explore whether family members understand their various developmental expectations; for example, are members expected to behave in ways that are beyond their capacity developmentally? Workers need to be cautious in interpreting developmental issues outside the sociocultural context in which they occur. Traditional developmental theory may offer only marginal understanding of lifespan issues of particular cultural groups.

Family life-cycle issues are also critical when viewing family functioning. Developmental transitions require change in the system and are often stressful. Family development provides the worker and the family with a broad framework for assessing functioning. Although little agreement exists as to what constitutes family *normality*, families can be viewed along a continuum from optimal functioning to dysfunction (Walsh, 1982). Exploring how the family responds to normal developmental changes, such as accepting new members or handling adolescence, can provide both the worker and family with insight into the family situation.

Role assignment in families is a function of gender and normative expectations of reference groups (Walsh, 1982). Which member will be the head of household, primary nurturer, and/or disciplinarian for children is essentially decided by cultural and societal norms. Assessing role issues is important, depending upon the degree to which roles are clearly defined, whether particular members are overloaded, and whether members feel satisfaction or dissatisfaction with assigned roles. Role transitions can generate stress. Questions of status and power are related to role issues. The family member who controls family finances or the member who is the primary nurturer often holds high status and power positions within the family. Likewise, the family member who establishes family rules or who has the "last word" in major family decisions ranks very high in the power hierarchy.

A great deal can be learned about the family's style and pattern of communication through carefully observing how family members communicate with one another during the initial assessment process. Although families often project themselves as a "well put-together" family in the early work, their customary style and patterns of communication soon surface. The worker's job is to tease out the recurring communication patterns, to assess their functionality, and to develop a sense of how to intervene in dysfunctional patterns and barriers to effective communication. Problems in communication are manifested through all aspects of the family's functioning. How the family solves problems, handles intense feelings like anger, deals with conflict, or expresses warm and caring feelings for one another are all related to issues of family communication. These areas must be attended to by the worker because they are, without fail, areas where even optimally functioning families experience difficulty.

In assessing family functioning, the worker should inquire about family goals. Although it is rare that families have established mutual goals or are in agreement about what the family goals are, exploring this area is a mechanism for getting a sense of the stability of the family unit as well as challenging the family to think about goal setting.

Family Strengths and Resources

Beset by overwhelming concerns and difficulties, families and workers alike are often hard pressed to identify assets or positive qualities in the family system. Because of the strong tendency of practitioners to focus on "what's wrong" within the system, pointing out family strengths requires a concerted effort on behalf of the worker and the family. For example, in a situation in which the mother of a pregnant adolescent consistently ventilated her frustrations about having to take off work for her daughter's clinic appointments, an inexperienced worker used this behavior to support her belief that the mother was uncaring and unsupportive of her daughter and failed to consider the fact that the mother *did* drive her daughter to her prenatal appointments. In eventually making this observation for the mother and the daughter, the worker helped them focus on the mother's caring behavior, despite its surface brusqueness. Seeking help and attending sessions consistently are indicators of strengths, even for involuntary clients. Other family resources to explore include family traditions and rituals that enhance coping strategies, supportive social institutions (the church, civic organizations, recreational outlets), and social support networks (extended family, significant friends, co-workers).

Intervention Plan

As mentioned previously, the assessment process sets the action agenda for intervention. Just as the assessment process is not a static endeavor, the intervention plan requires constant reflection and reframing in concert with the evolving assessment of family dynamics.

Several points need to be made about the intervention plan: First, although in a very real sense intervention begins with the initial contact, a concrete plan should culminate and some agreement about work be reached between the family and the practitioner. Although specific goals are not established in early sessions with families, relationship building and family members' orientation to the nature of the intervention process are occurring. Early interactions with the worker not only set the tone for later work but often serve as the deciding factor in whether the family will remain involved in the therapeutic process. It is essential that workers make explicit early in their involvement with the family why or how therapy can make a difference in the family's life. In a real sense, the worker needs to convince the family that it will benefit from therapy. Even families who are being forced into treatment by an external source need some incentive for investing in the process at more than a superficial level.

Second, the intervention plan must be clearly linked to a collaborative and mutually agreed upon definition of the issues that need to be addressed in the family work. Although the worker's broader theoretical understanding of family dynamics certainly will influence the direction of the intervention process, the family must have some understanding and agreement about issues and priorities.

Third, the goals of the intervention must be stated clearly; that is, family members and the worker should know the expected outcome of their work together. Equally important, family members need to have some understanding about how their individual participation in the intervention process can affect the outcome. A family's understanding of how systems function has the dual benefit of removing total responsibility for the family's problems from a specified member and demonstrating that the outcome of the work is every member's responsibility.

Fourth, how the work will proceed must be stated explicitly. Family members should know what is expected of them and the worker. If particular methods or techniques will be used, for example, homework assignments or behavioral modification activities, these techniques should be explained and practiced if possible. It is often helpful for the worker to explore possible repercussions of change on the family in an effort to help members anticipate obstacles or discomfort in the system.

Every intervention plan must be accompanied by a well-defined method of evaluation. Interventions without some mechanism for assessing outcome are at best a "stab in the dark." Practitioners as well as clients are at a tremendous disadvantage if they proceed without some marker indicating when they have arrived. Typically, the worker decides with the family when and how the work will be evaluated. Evaluation may consist of measuring outcome against defined goals; systematically soliciting client feedback about the intervention process in relation to methods and techniques; and soliciting evaluation of worker attributes that enhanced or stymied the helping process (Hepworth & Larsen, 1990). Although some evaluation methods are more rigorous than are others, utilizing baseline measures and formal instruments to quantify change and subjective measures of evaluation (e.g., client self-report of impact) can be advantageous in helping family members see the results of their work. Seeing positive results reinforces continued investment in future work. Moreover, systematic evaluation of one's practice creates opportunities for practitioners to share the outcome of their work with other practitioners.

Conclusion

It is presumptuous to attempt to describe everything that should be included in a family assessment. The material in this chapter is based upon recurring themes evolving out of years of practice with families in both public and private practice and with voluntary and involuntary client populations as well as upon my own professional experience and "world view" concerning what goes wrong in families and techniques that help bring about change. A belief in the validity of systems theory under-pins the approach to family assessment and intervention discussed here. Other world views and theoretical and practice approaches may be equally as valid; at best, this chapter attempts to challenge practitioners and educators to reflect upon their own assessment processes and to ana-lyze and sharpen them if necessary.

REFERENCES

Carter, E. A., & McGoldrick, M. (1980). *The family life cycle: A framework for family therapy.* New York: Gardner Press.

Chestang, L. W. (1972). *Character development in a hostile environment.* Occasional Paper No. 3. University of Chicago, Chicago.

Chestang, L. W. (1976). Environmental influences on social functioning: The black experi-ence. In P. Cafferty & L. Chestang (Eds.), *The diverse society: Implications for social policy.* New York: Association Press.

Compton, B. R., & Galaway, B. (1984). *Social work processes* (3rd ed.). Chicago: Dorsey.

DeVore, W., & Schlesinger, E. G. (1987). *Ethnic-sensitive social work practice* (2nd ed.). New York: Macmillan.

Germain, C. B. (Ed.). (1979). *Social work practice—people and environment: An ecological per-spective.* New York: Columbia University Press.

Germain, C. B., & Gitterman, A. (1980). *The life model of social work practice.* New York: Columbia University Press.

Goldstein, E. G. (1984). *Ego psychology and social work practice.* New York: Free Press.

Green, J. (1982). *Cultural awareness in the human services.* Englewood Cliffs, NJ: Prentice-Hall.

Guerin, P. J., Jr., & Pendagast, E. G. (1976). Evaluation of family system and genogram. In P. J. Guerin, Jr. (Ed.), *Family therapy: Theory and practice.* New York: Gardner Press.

Haley, J. (1976). *Problem-solving therapy.* San Francisco: Jossey-Bass.

Hartman, A. (1978). Diagrammatic assessment of family relationships. *Social Casework, 59,* 465–476.

Hartman, A., & Laird, J. (1983). *Family-centered social work practice.* New York: Free Press.

Hepworth, D. H., & Larsen, J. A. (1990). *Direct social work practice: Theory and skills* (3rd ed.). Belmont, CA: Wadsworth.

Hill, R. B. (1972). *The strengths of black families.* New York: National Urban League.

Holman, A. M. (1983). *Family assessment: Tools for understanding and intervention.* Beverly Hills, CA: Sage Publications.

Logan, S., Freeman, E. M., & McRoy, R. G. (1990). *Social work practice with black families.* New York: Longman.

Lum, D. (1986). *Social work practice and people of color: A process-stage approach.* Monterey, CA: Brooks/Cole.

McGoldrick, M., Pearce, J. K., & Giordano, J. (Eds.). (1982). *Ethnicity and family therapy.* New York: Guilford.

Minuchin, S. (1974). *Families and family therapy.* Cambridge, MA: Harvard University Press.

Norton, D. G. (1978). *The dual perspective: Inclusion of ethnic minority content in the social work curriculum.* New York: Council on Social Work Education.

Schwartz, A. (1982). *The behavior therapies: Theories and applications.* New York: Free Press.

Von Bertalanffy, L. (1968) *General systems theory.* New York: Braziller.

Walsh, F. (Ed.). (1982). *Normal family processes.* New York: Guilford.

Zastrow, C., & Kirst-Ashman, R. (1990). *Understanding human behavior and the social environ-ment* (2nd ed.). Chicago: Nelson-Hall.

Family Treatment Assessment For Novices

Gary W. Paquin
and Robert J. Bushorn

4

$\mathbf{F}$ amily treatment is now taught in virtually every social work program in the country, and has been advocated as a possible theory base for all of social work (Hartman, 1981). Most graduate programs provide an overview of the concepts and techniques used by the prominent schools of family therapy. As the beginning student soon realizes, family therapy "schools" are many and various. Initially, the variety of schools can be overwhelming. The family assessment literature is often too detailed and extensive for easy applicability in clinical practice. In addition, most "schools" have different ways of viewing and assessing families. Novices in family treatment must decide which view to take and what corresponding techniques to use. Because most family therapists identify themselves as being "eclectic" (Green & Kolevson, 1982) and little research has been done to indicate the superiority of one view of the family over another, decisions about what techniques to use in what situations are often arrived at intuitively. Novices practicing family treatment who consider themselves "eclectic" are in need of a simple, clinical diagnostic system.

Families usually present their "problems" and discuss their long-standing functioning with the worker upon intake. Most schools of family therapy see the necessity of tailoring interventions to the family's functioning as well as the presenting problem. Strategic family therapists note the difference between "first-order change" (behavioral change that keeps the system intact) and "second-order change" (changes of the rules underlying such behavior). Structural family therapists focus on the need to change the family's hierarchies and coalitions, believing that the family structure must be changed for the presenting problems to be effectively relieved. Bowenian therapists emphasize the necessity of changing the individual's "level of differentiation of self" as a way of changing the structure and functioning of the system as a whole. A preliminary family assessment should provide the worker with guidelines for when to use which theory for changing the family's functioning according to the family's presenting problem. Such a format should also be based on an eclectic model of family treatment. This article describes the current family diagnostic models in use and presents a model based on the work of Barnhill (1979) and Weltner (1986).

Barnhill's Integration of Family Treatment Theories

Efforts have been made to integrate all of the major systems of family therapy into indices of family functioning or "health." Barnhill (1979) integrated these family functioning dimensions into four themes, each of which is further divided into two subset continuums.

The first theme—*family identity*—is subdivided into individuation (independence of thought, feeling, and judgment) versus enmeshment (poorly delineated boundaries of self, identity dependent on others, symbiosis). The approaches of major theorists of these dimensions are intergenerational and structural. The other subset continuum is mutuality (sense of emotional closeness, joining, or intimacy) versus isolation (alienation or disengagement) from others. The major theorists of these dimensions are intergenerational (existential) and communications oriented.

The second theme of family functioning that Barnhill discusses is *change in the family*. This theme is subdivided into flexibility (ability to adjust in response to variation in family patterns) versus rigidity (stereotyped or repetitive responsiveness), and stability (consistency, responsibility, and security in family interactions) versus disorganization (lack of predictability and clear responsibility). The flexibility continuum is supported by strategic theorists and the stability continuum by behavioral and communications theorists.

The third theme of family functioning is *information processes within the family*. The two subset continuums within information processing are clear perception (undistorted awareness of self or others) versus unclear or distorted perception, and clear communication (clear and successful transfer of information among family members) versus unclear or distorted communication. Clear perception is discussed by intergenerational and communication theorists, whereas clear communication is discussed by strategic and communication theorists.

The fourth theme of family functioning that Barnhill discusses is *role structuring in the family*. The two subset continuums of role structuring are role reciprocity (mutually agreed-upon behavior patterns or sequences in which an individual complements the role of another family member) versus unclear roles or role conflict, and clear generational boundaries (appropriate separation between members of same-generation subsets of family members) versus diffuse (implicit alliances across generations that are not appropriate) or breached generational boundaries (alliances across subsets against a member of a same-generation subset). Role reciprocity is primarily discussed by behavioral and communications theorists, whereas clear generational boundaries are discussed by structural and strategic theorists.

The proponents of different schools of family therapy view each school as having a unique viewpoint rather than as a group of specialized techniques. Consequently, particular viewpoints are rarely viewed as contraindicated by proponents, regardless of the problem. Novice family-centered social workers have few guidelines for deciding when a particular viewpoint and its corresponding techniques are appropriate. Though assessment must direct treatment in a continuous manner (Haley, 1976), the various schools provide little validation that a sister school's viewpoint might be valuable for a particular family at a particular point. Thus a novice family worker is likely to become confused when trying to handle several theories while confronted by a deluge of family data.

Current Family Functioning Assessment Models

Family assessment schemas currently in use are either oriented toward research (Family Environment Scale by Moos) and have limited treatment practicality or are rather difficult to conduct without further training. Two of the most widely used assessment models are the McMaster Model of Family Functioning and the Olson Circumplex Model, which utilizes the "FACES" instrument.

The McMaster Model of Family Functioning (Epstein, Bishop, & Baldwin, 1982) is a sophisticated scheme of six dimensions to categorize the structure, organization, and transactional patterns of families. These dimensions are problem solving (ability to resolve problems), communications (exchange of information), roles (repetitive patterns of family behavior), affective responsiveness (ability to respond with an appropriate quantity and quality of feelings), affective involvement (interest in and value placed on the particular activities and interests of individual family members), and behavior control (ways families handle three areas: physically dangerous situations, psychobiological needs, and interpersonal socializing within and beyond the family system). This extensive diagnostic procedure is believed to be needed to allow the therapist to assess accurately the family's areas of strength rather than merely its areas of weakness as well as to discover important family problems that may influence treatment but would not become apparent if the therapist were focused only on the family problem (Epstein & Bishop, 1981).

49

These six dimensions are further broken down into a variety of subdimensions that require some specific diagnostic ability. This model has been used in treatment (Epstein & Bishop, 1981) and provides a very thorough assessment model, although unfortunately it can overwhelm the novice and still not provide guidance in utilizing those techniques in his or her repertoire. Epstein has developed a structured form of treatment—problem-centered family treatment—derived from this model of family functioning. The McMaster model may be of less value to workers who are uncommitted to this model of family treatment.

Olson, Sprenkle, and Russel (1979) developed the circumplex model of evaluating family functioning, which focuses on two dimensions: adaptability and cohesion. Adaptability is defined as "the ability of a marital/family system to change its power structure, role relationships and relationship rules in response to situational and developmental stress" (Olson et al., 1979, p. 12). Cohesion is defined as "the emotional bonding members have with one another and the degree of individual autonomy a person experiences in the family system" (p. 5). The organization of the gradations of these two dimensions produces 16 different types. A self-report measure, the Family Adaptability and Cohesion Evaluation Scale (FACES), is used as a tool in this assessment system. Olson et al. noted that formulating a diagnostic assessment of family functioning can be useful in formulating treatment goals, but the circumplex model does not specify the treatment techniques that will be useful in achieving that goal. They leave this to the discretion of the therapist, a problematic point for therapists who are developing their skills.

Family Assessment Tools

The list of research-oriented family assessment tools is quite extensive: problem lists, marital satisfaction inventories, family kinesthetic drawings, and observation of the family working on specific tasks, to name a few. Several assessment techniques have been developed from family therapy and are often used for initial assessment. These techniques include genograms, eco-maps, and family sculpting.

The genogram is a modified "family tree" diagram that allows the clinician to condense a large amount of information in such a way as to make intergenerational patterns clearer (Hartman & Laird, 1983). The eco-map diagrams the family's current connections with the environment, including the extended family, and indicates strengths and weaknesses in the family's social support system (Hartman & Laird, 1983). Family sculpting allows family members to use one another as "models" to portray the current roles and stances of various family members as perceived by each member (Duhl, Kantor, & Duhl, 1973). This visual display allows family members to break their normal roles and become "controllers" of all the other family members; this tool can be powerful therapeutically as well as useful diagnostically.

All of these techniques are valuable in helping the clinician explore different areas of difficulty with the family. Unfortunately, not all families will profit from all techniques, and assessment can become unwieldy. A broader device is needed to determine what types of specific assessment tools should be used in the most economical fashion.

Family Functioning

As Beavers (1979) notes, in functioning families spouses nurture each other, the hierarchy of power is clear, and coalitions are formed between parents so as to provide leadership. Members are involved with one another and are able to resolve differences and to accept directions or to organize in response to a task. To function well, families must devise boundaries and rules defining who does what task and how it is done (Minuchin, 1974). Boundaries allow the family to solve problems in an organized fashion. Suitable family boundaries indicate that the members have easy access to the external environment, but that movement in and out of the family is not so fluid as to cause a blurring of the family organization (Steinglass, 1987). The Beavers-Timberlawn Family Evaluation Scale (Lewis, Beavers, Gossett, & Phillips, 1976) is a clinical rating of family structure based upon the overt power structure of the family, whether the main coalitions are parent–child or parental, and the degree of closeness among family members. Weltner has developed a family classification model based upon the level of family organization and the type of problem with which the family is struggling. This model will be presented with elaboration from other models to encompass a basic family assessment model for therapists beginning family treatment.

Epstein et al. (1982) noted that families have a variety of tasks to execute in supporting and maintaining their members. They classify these tasks into three kinds: basic, developmental, and hazardous. Basic tasks involve securing fundamental resources needed for family members to survive or function: food, shelter, clothing, and so forth. Developmental tasks involve transitions the family must encounter with the normal development of its members. Members enter and leave the family, and responsibilities change as part of the life process of birth, growing up, moving away, marriage, divorce, and death. Finally, families must confront hazardous-task issues resulting from, for example, illness, loss of employment, moves, or natural disaster (the basis of crisis intervention work).

The task area reflected by the problem families present to the worker is very important with regard to how the therapist attempts to reorganize the family as opposed to simply addressing the apparent problem. A well-functioning family can be overwhelmed by a number of problems (natural disasters, illness, death), and unless the presenting problem is chronic, the therapist's primary effort should be focused on assisting members to acquire the necessary resources to resolve it before attempting to restructure the family. It should be noted that the results in these two areas may well be interrelated: a better-functioning family should be able to secure more of its own resources, and a family with sufficient resources is more likely to let its natural "infrastructure" channel these resources to its members.

Weltner (1986) developed a four-level typology of families based on family functioning and presenting problem. Each family type is discussed in light of other family assessment methods and Barnhill's (1979) work.

Weltner's Level One Families

Level one families are often considered neglectful and underorganized. They lack a leadership and control structure to meet basic nurturing and protection needs of members. According to the Beavers-Timberlawn Family Evaluation Scale (Lewis et al., 1976), these families are leaderless and have no one with enough power to structure interactions. The parental coalition is weakened or undermined by a parent–child coalition, and family closeness is amorphous and vague with indistinct boundaries among members (Weltner, 1986). These families face issues of basic resources: food, shelter, protection, education, clothing, transportation, and medical care. Faced with such deprivations, these families are rarely able to provide one another with necessary emotional nurturance (Epstein et al., 1982). Work with these families must focus on strengths. Types of problems may include an overwhelmed single mother, the strongest family member dysfunctional or incapacitated, and natural or emotional catastrophes that have depleted physical and emotional resources.

Various techniques may be used in working with such families. Ecomaps may be helpful in identifying resources that can be tapped. A structural family therapy approach, and the ecological techniques derived from it, may also be appropriate for these families (Minuchin, Montalvo, Guerney, Rosman, & Shumer, 1967). Structural treatment allows family members to develop their internal leadership ability by clarifying the hierarchical boundaries and by forming coalitions that maximize the problem-solving abilities of these families.

With level one families, therapists need to concentrate on promoting stability by strengthening or decreasing various external and generational boundaries. Adult leadership must be enhanced through therapeutic intervention and the sibling subsystem formed into a functioning coalition. Generational boundaries that govern the rights and responsibilities of family members in getting basic needs met must also be strengthened.

The worker should attempt to assist the family in evaluating and acquiring external resources from the community and/or extended family. Case management and referral to medical, income maintenance, and legal resources as well as protective services, foster home placement, and hospitalization in crises may be necessary.

The worker should provide guidance and advocacy, if they are necessary. Advocacy and guidance may occur on various levels, depending on the case. Guidance on the use of respite care and referral to substance-abuse counseling may be necessary. The worker may need to instruct the family in time and budget management as well as provide child-development information. Advocacy with school and welfare systems is often necessary.

In addition to planning for extensive change in the family's functioning, the worker must also block the family's presenting symptom in order to keep the family in treatment. Often, presenting symptoms are so extreme that families are not likely to lose sight of them. Essentially, level one families require a structural/behavioral/case-management approach to treatment.

> Mrs. R and her two children, 12 and 2 years of age, came to the clinic because Mrs. R was dependent on diazepam and her supplier had retired from medical practice. During her first session, she discussed her difficulties with welfare and how she was concerned about losing her apartment, having the utilities turned off, or being attacked by her upstairs neighbors with whom she was having a feud. She was placed on a drug-withdrawal program by the clinic psychiatrist, and the clinic worker assisted her in contacting her welfare worker to resolve misunderstandings having to do with obtaining benefits on a continued basis. As Mrs. R began assuming a measure of control over her life, welfare helped her find suitable day care so she could return to school to become a hairdresser. With education and support, her position in the family as parent with leadership responsibilities and capabilities was reinforced. She was encouraged to attend a parents' support group at the clinic.

Weltner's Level Two Families

Level two families are underorganized and out of control. They have difficulty setting limits, although the family's basic needs of minimal safety and nurturance are met. Types of problems include uncontrollable children, delinquent adolescents, and errant spouses involved in extramarital affairs, gambling, or substance abuse. Marital conflict may appear out of control and threaten dissolution of the family unit. Families in which violence is possible, although members are not in need of immediate protection, may be seen as out of control yet capable of meeting members' basic needs.

Weltner (1986) points out that the focus of treatment must be to "develop a coalition of those in charge against those needing control" (p. 53). As with level one families, this treatment approach requires structural and behavioral techniques. Family mapping of coalitions as described by Minuchin (1974) and Hartman and Laird (1983) is helpful with these families.

Often, members of these families need to be empowered. Behavioral techniques with structural considerations in mind may help empower members by allowing them to recognize their potential for modifying the behavior of other family members. In addition, behavioral techniques help clarify what the family's expectations are for the behavior of each of its members. Weltner (1986) further suggests that the worker focus on the strengths of these families. Intervention goals include blocking the key symptom that brought the family into treatment. Goals for family functioning based on Barnhill's criteria include the following: increased family stability, clearer roles and communication, and more effective executive limit-setting.

In the case discussed earlier, after Mrs. R began to assert herself with welfare authorities and to gain self-respect by attending school, she found the energy to begin assuming parental responsibilities. Therapy focused on reinforcing her generational boundary with her 12-year-old daughter, who was privy to all Mrs. R's conflicts with family, friends, and lovers. With some resistance from her daughter, including behavioral problems such as stealing, the family achieved a clearer hierarchy and the daughter's behavioral problems subsided.

Weltner's Level Three Families

According to Weltner (1986), level three families are problem focused and resistant to change. Their difficulties are related to ingrained patterns of behavior exhibited over time, yet their family structure is adequate for meeting the basic needs of their members. The Beavers-Timberlawn Family Evaluation Scale rates these families as having marked or moderate dominance (control is close to absolute, with little or no negotiation; dominance and submission are the rule) and family members are isolated and distanced from one another. Therapy with these families must challenge the existing family structure. The therapist must confront the family's tendency to remain in current patterns of behavior. With level three families, both structural and strategic family therapy techniques might be considered.

Assessment tools such as family mapping and examination of the communication and power structures around the presenting problem may be used. Intervention goals for level three families involve Barnhill's dimensions of encouraging flexibility (particularly to facilitate life-cycle transitions), clear generational boundaries, and, to a lesser extent, individuation.

The youngest child in a middle-class family of four was in the process of leaving home. The wife, who was feeling trapped and enraged, brought her husband in for marital counseling. The husband's intense compulsions, such as going to bed at exactly 9:35 P.M. for fear he would experience debilitating headaches, began to annoy his wife, and she was threatening divorce. In the husband's presence, the wife was told to turn all the clocks to a different time. The couple left the session anxious but that night were sexually intimate for the first time in months.

Weltner's Level Four Families

In level four families, basic needs are met and structural boundaries are relatively clear (Weltner, 1986). Presenting problems often focus on a desire for greater intimacy, greater sense of self, or adult independence.

Genograms extended over at least three to four generations and family sculpting may be useful in assessing patterns of behavior. Intervention goals for these families generally involve Barnhill's dimensions of individuation (to clarify personal values, meaning, awareness, and family-of-origin issues), mutuality (to increase intimacy), clear perception (to decrease distortions), and greater flexibility (to facilitate life-cycle transitions). The Bowenian family systems approach may be particularly useful with such families.

> A middle-class couple with several children entered treatment as part of the wife's rehabilitation plan after leaving an alcohol treatment facility. Other than alcoholism, no specific problems were stated on intake. The wife remained abstinent but complained of vague feelings of depression and loneliness. She began, as did her husband, to do extended family work. Contacts with family made her feel more connected and less lonely. The couple were able to weather the terminal illness of her mother in a relatively calm fashion, without the wife resorting to drinking during the grieving period.

Conclusions

Weltner's family assessment method is brief and focuses the worker with an eclectic orientation on useful assessment and therapeutic techniques. The method allows workers to fit specific assessment and intervention methods from the prominent schools of family therapy to the family at hand. Frequently, the various schools of family therapy have seen their methods more as a viewpoint than as a group of specific techniques; consequently, they do not indicate in what situations their particular viewpoint is most beneficial. The literature does not make these distinctions, although some family therapies have been shown to have a positive impact on certain problems (Gurman & Kniskern, 1981). Weltner's method allows a clearer focus on the type of technical and theoretical bases most applicable to family functioning. It is possible that the superiority of various theoretical points of view will never be validated by the research; consequently, clinicians are left with personal preference or intuition to make such judgments. Adapting Weltner's typology according to Barnhill's criteria of family functioning can provide a useful resource for narrowing applicable techniques for treating family in a structured fashion.

REFERENCES

Barnhill, L. R. (1979). Healthy family systems. *Family Coordinator, 28*(1), 94–100.
Beavers, W. R. (1979). *Psychotherapy and growth: A family systems perspective.* New York: Brunner/Mazel.
Duhl, R., Kantor, D., & Duhl, B. S. (1973). Learning, space and action in family therapy: A primer in sculpture. In D. Bloch (Ed.), *Techniques of family psychotherapy.* New York: Grune & Stratton.

Epstein, N. B., & Bishop, D. S. (1981). Problem-centered systems therapy of the family. In A. S. Gurman & D. P. Kniskern (Eds.), *Handbook of family therapy*. New York: Brunner/Mazel.

Epstein, N. B., Bishop, D. S., & Baldwin, L. M. (1982). McMaster model of family functioning: A view of the normal family. In F. Walsh (Ed.), *Normal family processes*. New York: Guilford.

Green, R., & Kolevson, M. S. (1982). Three approaches to family therapy: A study of convergence and divergence. *Journal of Marital and Family Therapy, 8*(2), 39–50.

Gurman, A. S., & Kniskern, D. P. (1981). Family therapy outcome research: Knowns and unknowns. In A. S. Gurman & D. P. Kniskern (Eds.), *Handbook of family therapy*. New York: Brunner/Mazel.

Haley, J. (1976). *Problem-solving therapy*. San Francisco: Jossey-Bass.

Hartman, A. (1981). The family: A central focus for practice. *Social Work, 26*, 7–15.

Hartman, A., & Laird, J. (1983). *Family-centered social work practice*. New York: Free Press.

Lewis, J. M., Beavers, W. R., Gossett, J. T., & Phillips, V. (1976). *No single thread: Psychological health in family systems*. New York: Brunner/Mazel.

Minuchin, S. (1974). *Families and family therapy*. Cambridge, MA: Harvard University Press.

Minuchin, S., Montalvo, B., Guerney, B. G., Rosman, B. L., & Shumer, F. (1967). *Families of the slums*. New York: Basic Books.

Olson, D. H., Sprenkle, D. H., & Russel, C. (1979). Circumplex model of marital and family systems: I. Cohesion and adaptability dimensions, family types and clinical applications. *Family Process, 18*, 3–28.

Steinglass, P. (1987). A systems view of family interaction and psychopathology. In T. Jacob (Ed.), *Family interaction and psychopathology: Theories, methods and findings*. New York: Plenum.

Weltner, J. S. (1986). A matchmaker's guide to family therapy. *Family Therapy Networker, 10*(2), 51–55.

Part 2

Assessment over the Life Cycle

Assessing Adolescent Parents and Their Infants: Individualized Family Service Planning

Kathleen J. Moroz
and Paula Allen-Meares

5

H istorically, social workers have been keenly aware of the important role environment plays in promoting dysfunctional (unhealthy) and functional (healthy) development or transactions. The passage of the Preschool and Early Intervention Act (P.L. 99-457) in 1986 as an amendment to the Education for All Handicapped Children Act of 1975 (P.L. 94-142) holds particular promise for infants born to parents who have been consistently identified as vulnerable because of their life circumstances and/or characteristics (e.g., poverty, lack of adequate prenatal and postnatal care, minority status, educational disadvantage, and/or adolescent parents).

This chapter provides a comprehensive schema for approaching the assessment of adolescent parents and their infants. Relevant theories for extrapolating directions for practice and specific scales used in assessment and intervention for the development of the individual family service plan (IFSP) are explored.

Preschool and Early Intervention Legislation—P.L. 99-457

This legislation targets children three to five years old, extending all rights and protections of P.L. 94-142 to them. All states applying for funds under P.L. 94-142 must indicate that they are providing a free and appropriate education to all children in this younger age group. However, states are not required to label children or report by disability category those whom they serve. Instead, this legislation places emphasis on family involvement and the provision of coordinated, community-based services to improve family and child functioning.

Under this same legislation, a state can also elect to extend early intervention downward to children from birth to three years of age. This program appears as a new Part H of the existing Education for All Handicapped Act and targets infants who are developmentally handicapped or at risk for developmental delays. Each state determines the specific criteria for identifying infants whose development is delayed and/or whose conditions place them at risk. Early intervention must also include comprehensive assessment and a written IFSP developed by a multidisciplinary team of professionals and the family. The IFSP must include: (1) a statement of the child's present level of development (cognitive, speech/language, psychosocial, motor, and self-help), (2) a statement of the family's needs and strengths related to enhancing the child's development, (3) a statement of major outcomes expected to be achieved for the infant and family and the criteria, procedures, and timelines for determining progress, (4) the nature of the specific early intervention services necessary to meet the needs of the infant and family (frequency and intensity of service, etc.), (5) the projected dates for initiation of services and expected duration, (6) the name of the case manager, and (7) the procedures for transferring the child from early intervention into a preschool or kindergarten program. This IFSP must be evaluated at least once a year and must be reviewed every six months or more often when appropriate. A range of services could be provided within the IFSP, for example, special education, speech and language, audiology, social work, occupational therapy, physical therapy, psychological services, medical services for diagnostic purposes, and health services. Case-management services must also be provided to every eligible infant and his or her parents at no cost to the parents (except where federal or state law provides for a system of sliding-fee payment). In addition, because the delivery of services to preschoolers and infants with special needs and their families has been characterized historically by wide variation and fragmentation, each state is now charged with developing mechanisms for coordinating services at state and local levels.

Theoretical Perspectives on Assessment

The ecological perspective of human development first elaborated by Bronfenbrenner (1979) has merit as a broad framework for assessment and intervention with children and families. From this perspective, individuals and their environments are viewed as mutually shaping systems that change over time and adapt to each other as changes occur. Thus, one examines not only the contributions of the child and the parent to the dyadic relationship but the interaction between the two. Systems that include more than two persons and the potential second and higher-order influence of one system upon another (e.g., the influence of the father's presence on the infant–mother relationship) are also analyzed.

Bronfenbrenner (1979) and others (Garbarino, 1982; Germain & Gitterman, 1980; Hobbs, 1980) have challenged us to view child development in its total context and to intervene within and across the various layers of the child's ecosystem. Both the immediate and the more distant cultural environments have an impact upon the parents and the child. Parents and children respond to the activities, beliefs, and values of their particular environmental niche. Children are at an advantage or disadvantage developmentally, depending upon their physical, emotional, and mental characteristics as well as the type of environment they inhabit and the timing of events external to them.

Similarly, a growing body of literature recognizes the crucial role that adequate social support plays in determining the level of functioning of individuals and families. Single parents, teenage parents, and geographically dislocated or isolated parents and families are vulnerable to serious maladaptation (including child neglect and abuse) when deficiencies exist in their social environments. Intervention aimed at increasing social support for teenage mothers substantiates Garbarino's (1982) contribution that an early pregnancy does not have to be an intrinsically at-risk occurrence if adequate support for the young mother is available from the family, the baby's father, friends, and others. Research by Dunst, Vance, and Cooper (1986) shows that participation by teen mothers in a comprehensive treatment program increases maternal self-esteem and internal control, decreases labor and delivery complications, and increases positive interaction between the mother and infant.

The concept of goodness-of-fit (Simeonsson, Bailey, Huntington, & Comfort, 1986; Thomas & Chess, 1977; Sprunger, Boyce, & Gaines, 1985) assumes that "the adequacy of the organism's functioning depends upon the relationship between the properties of its environment and the organism's own capacities and behavioral characteristics" (Chess, 1979, p. 105). Chess (1979) discovered that a good fit between infant and mother was characterized by maternal internal locus of control, adequate social support, a child with a relatively easy temperament, and a positive match of intrinsic mother–child characteristics such as maternal status, child birth order, child's gender, etc. Internal locus of control on the part of the mother was the strongest predictor of her positive involvement with the child, and the mother's sense of competence was the strongest predictor of overall family adjustment. Simeonsson et al. (1986) found that family and child functioning were also affected by individual characteristics and reactions to situational demands, which helps explain the fact that families with similar problems often demonstrate markedly different patterns of adjustment and adaptation in response to similar interventions.

It should be kept in mind that child development may be threatened by the absence of positive opportunities as well as by the occurrence of negative events. Optimal development for all human beings depends on the fulfillment of basic human needs for physical, emotional, and social support. The responses of each person, even in seemingly identical environments, are always unique. In cases of extreme environmental influences or severe genetic deficits, optimal conditions of the one can do much to overcome or ameliorate the risks or negative impact of the other. This factor is both the key to successful intervention and the justification for intrusion into the lives of families with young children.

Research by Garmezy (1985) and others (e.g., Werner & Smith, 1977) highlights the characteristics of individuals who successfully overcome adverse developmental conditions. These studies illuminate the strengths of young children growing up under extremely adverse conditions and point to the need for at least one source of sustained emotional support and encouragement as an important determinant that allows children to overcome the negative influences in their environments.

Finally, attachment theory (Ainsworth, 1973; Bowlby, 1982) offers an additional perspective for examining and intervening with parents and young children. Ainsworth (1973) defines attachment as an emotional or affectionate relationship developed between two specific individuals that lasts over time and across distances. Attachment thus serves to provide the infant with feelings of trust, safety, and security. For an infant, this is a major developmental task because it affects the child's ability to achieve subsequent developmental tasks (Sroufe & Waters, 1977). When infants feel basic trust and security, they are free to explore their environment and to develop physically, cognitively, and socially at an optimal rate. When fear and lack of nurturing characterize the child's early environment, motor, language, cognitive, and social development may all be undermined. Security evolves gradually and is fostered when the infant's needs are met promptly and consistently. Primary attachment will be to the person or persons who best understand and respond to the needs of the infant. Even if care is inconsistent, neglectful, or abusive, the infant will still become attached to the best available figure she or he can find, although the quality of this relationship will be less than optimal and will likely negatively affect the child's development. Interestingly, the nature of the child's attachment to his or her parents is strongly reflected in his or her capacity to form and maintain other intimate relationships throughout life.

Bowlby (1982) postulated that the nature of the young child's attachment is a reflection of the child's "inner working model" of the self as worthy or unworthy of care in response to the availability or unavailability of others when needed. A secure beginning can be undermined or damaged by later insensitive or unresponsive caregiving, just as the attachment relationship can be repaired through intervention with the mother–child pair or by helping the child develop supplementary quality relationships with significant others.

Main and Goldwyn (in press) found that not all mothers of secure infants were themselves secure as infants. Those who were not, however, seemed to have come to terms with the reality of their early lives. This "coming to terms" with the past seemed to enable them to minimize the repetition of the attachment relationships they had experienced in childhood. Ricks and Noyes (1984) obtained similar results. Mothers who had been insecurely attached as infants but who had secure attachments with their own infants had effectively reworked their childhood issues; most had begun this process during their teenage years. They currently had strong support systems, stable marriages, and positive self-esteem.

Mothers with insecurely attached children felt less accepted by their parents as adults and were still negatively affected by these feelings in such a way that their adult personalities and parenting capacities were adversely affected by a continuing sense of insecurity that had begun in childhood. For these parents, early attachment insecurity continued to dominate their adult lives and their ability to provide a secure base for their own offspring. Thus, the adolescent's capacity to nurture an infant or toddler may be undermined by his or her own developmental needs to establish adult identity and autonomy as well as by unresolved attachment issues resulting from the adolescent's own childhood experiences.

Characteristics of Adolescent Parents and Their Infants

Numerous studies have documented the immediate and long-term consequences of premature parenthood for adolescent parents and their offspring (Furstenberg, 1976; Seitz, Rosenbaum, & Apfel, 1983). Adolescent parents consistently fail to achieve their educational goals, and they and their child experience numerous pregnancy-related medical risks. These medical risks are inversely related to the mother's age and social status. Use of cigarettes, alcohol, and drugs and increased occurrence of toxemia, caesarean section, perinatal death, and low-birth-weight infants (Hardy, King, Shipp, & Welcher, 1981) characterize adolescent parenting. The long-term consequences of low birth weight for the infant include mental retardation, neurological deficits, and learning disabilities. The social and developmental risks to infants born to teen parents are related to poverty, a lack of resources, inadequate parenting skills, and sometimes family instability.

Adolescent mothers are different from older mothers, and these differences appear to be greatest for those of preterm infants. This group has been found to be significantly less verbal during interactions with the infant, less contingently responsive, less likely to engage in game playing, less likely to cradle the infant during feeding, and less likely to gaze frequently at their infants. Knowledge of child development, especially language and cognitive development, has been found to be inadequate among teen parents (Epstein, 1980).

The parenting task for adolescent parents is made more difficult by the fact that they are struggling to meet their own maturational and developmental needs while simultaneously attempting to meet the needs of a dependent infant. Thus, the normal developmental behaviors and needs of the adolescent are often in conflict with the needs of the infant. The adolescent is egocentric and tends to be present-oriented, to seek immediate gratification, to be in the process of forming an adult sexual identity, to seek independence from adults, and to experiment with various adult behaviors (e.g., alcohol, drugs, and sex). In contrast, the infant needs physical closeness and verbal and nonverbal responsiveness from at least one planful and organized person who consistently meets the infant's needs for nurturing, safety, and comfort.

Poverty, however, takes the biggest toll on teen parents and their offspring. Many adolescent parents and their infants struggle to survive in economically deprived environments. Such environments lack adequate stimulation for the infant's growth as well as needed resources to support the adolescent mother and father in their parenting roles. In addition, the economic consequences of early parenting are never fully overcome in terms of educational attainment and employment for teen mothers.

Assessment

Given our discussion of theoretical perspectives, a comprehensive assessment of the adolescent parent(s) and infant requires attention to the ability of the adolescent parent(s) to nurture, care for, and protect the infant; the resources (financial and emotional) available to support parent(s) in the parenting role; the characteristics and special needs of the infant; and the quality of the infant's relationships with mother, father, and other caregivers. There are many sources of data for the assessment process. A comprehensive assessment should include an evaluation of the adolescent's current functioning as a parent as well as his or her capacity to parent effectively, the infant's well-being and development, the quality of the infant–parent interaction, and the availability of environmental and social supports.

Parent Functioning and Capacity

To assess current parent functioning as well as parenting capacity, a variety of measures may be used, including interviews with the parents, direct observations of the parent–child interaction, self-reports by the adolescent parents, and interviews with other primary caretakers (grandparents, day-care personnel, etc.). Interviews with the adolescent mother and father should focus on how they see themselves as parents, how they feel about parenting, what they expect of and want for the child, what they enjoy about parenting, and what aspects of parenting they may find difficult. It is extremely important that practitioners actively encourage the mother and father to express their views and opinions about the infant and that their perceptions are acknowledged and valued. Other caretakers may also provide information about the day-to-day care of the baby (e.g., observations about the quality of the baby's care, interactions between baby and parents, and the parents' attention to the infant's needs). The quality of the relationship between the adolescent mother and father can play a critical role in their adjustment to parenting (Allen-Meares & Shores, 1986) and should also be assessed. Parenting capacity, including the parent's ability (or potential ability) to carry out caregiving responsibilities, to respond quickly and consistently to the child's physical needs, and to provide a safe environment, must be determined. The capacity to parent effectively also includes the ability to be aware of and respond to the infant's psychosocial and sensory needs, to cope with stress, tolerate frustration, delay one's own gratification, to avoid intense anger and resentment of the infant, and to perceive and accurately read the infant's cues and respond appropriately and consistently to them.

Infant/Toddler Development

A number of scales are available for assessing the development of infants/toddlers (Brazelton, 1973; Bayley, 1969; Frankenburg & Dodds, 1967). Data derived from these scales are useful in monitoring the infant's development and identifying delays that require attention. Efforts should be made to involve parents in the assessment process and to elicit the help of the child's caregivers in gaining the child's cooperation and best performance. Brazelton (1981) and others (e.g., Musick, Bernstein, Percansky, & Stott, 1987) discuss the benefits of this shift toward family involvement in child assessment.

Quality of Interaction

The quality of the infant–parent interaction is an important determinant of the quality of the child's attachment relationships. Parent–child interaction can be evaluated informally by observing the infant and parent(s) during play and feeding and other routine activities. Home visits, parental reports, and reports from other caretakers and professionals can offer valuable information about the child's development and the nature of the parent–child relationships. The practitioner should seek data regarding reciprocity and mutual satisfaction as well as positive affect in the parent–child relationships and the emotional availability of the adolescent parent(s). Sameroff (1982) discusses the important effect of emotional availability of parents on the emotional and cognitive development of the child. Because other studies (Epstein, 1980; Beckwith, Cohen, Kopp, Parmelee, & Marcy, 1976) have suggested that adolescent

65

mothers are less emotionally available to their infants, engage in fewer verbal interactions, and offer less cognitive stimulation to their offspring, teenage parents may need special help developing reciprocal, positive relationships with their babies. The infant's secure attachment to the mother, father, or other caregiver serves as the foundation upon which the infant can develop trust in self and others. The infant's sense of self as worthy of care and love is a reflection of the child's secure attachment to at least one capable parent. The availability of such an attachment figure enables the infant to feel safe enough to explore the environment. This sense of security is essential to the child's cognitive and motor development and to the development of internal self-regulation.

Environment and Social Support

As stated earlier, the inherent risks of early parenthood for adolescent parents and their offspring can be reduced if adequate resources and social supports are in place (Garbarino, 1982). However, insufficient attention has been focused on how practitioners should assess the environment and the quality and availability of supports within the life space of adolescent parents and their offspring. Several instruments, however, attempt to evaluate aspects of the environment and social supports.

The Home Observation for Measurement of the Environment (HOME). This instrument, developed by Caldwell (1979), uses two levels of analysis. Level one (birth to age three) assesses emotional and verbal responsivity, avoidance of restriction and punishment, organization of the physical and temporal environment, provision of appropriate play materials, maternal involvement with the child, and opportunities for variety in daily stimulation. It consists of 45 questions in a "yes" or "no" format. This instrument was normalized on the basis of use with 174 families from both welfare and nonwelfare backgrounds. It is a useful tool for screening existing and potential sources of support in the environment. Level two (for preschool children) assesses the following eight areas: stimulation through toys, games, and reading materials; language stimulation; physical environment; pride; affection and warmth; stimulation of academic behavior; modeling and encouragement of social maturity; variety of stimulation; and physical punishment. The HOME instrument has adequate predictive power to identify home environments associated with retarded development.

Resource Scale for Teenage Mothers. This scale is a modified version of the Family Resource Scale. It is designed to measure the extent to which different types of resources are deemed adequate in the adolescent mother's household (Dunst, Leet, Vance, & Cooper, 1986). The scale includes 31 items and a five-point scale that rates the adequacy of resources from "not at all" to "almost always adequate." The sum of the ratings for all 31 items provides a global measure of adequacy of resources. Individual items rated "not at all adequate" indicate that these resources are lacking and that additional support or assistance is needed.

The scale is reliable (0.92) and considered to be a valid indicator of the adequacy of resources. Items in the Resource Scale of Teenage Mothers include the following: food; money to buy necessities; dependable transportation; time for self, sleep, mate, and nurturing; a safe environment; knowledge of birth-control methods; knowledge of how to take care of child; financial assistance; and adequate living arrangements.

Assessment of the kind and level of social supports/networks is related to evaluation of the environment. Social supports can be defined as family, friends, neighbors/neighborhood, father of baby, and his family. Social networks represent the structure and functioning of social supports and include dimensions such as size, composition, density, and geographically based contacts. Unger and Wandersman (1985) reported that greater perceived support was related to greater life satisfaction and fewer concerns about parenting for adolescent mothers. Also, the importance of specific types of resources and perceived support varied over the postpartum period of parental adjustment. The adolescent mother's perception of adequate support and resources appears to have a positive effect on her child. When mothers had more social support and child-care assistance from the baby's father, infants were more responsive. Interestingly, however, the same study found that when adolescent mothers relegated too much of the parenting role to a grandparent or other caregiver, they tended to be less responsive to their baby. In other words, the availability of social networks and perceived support has potential for facilitating parental adjustment and functioning. However, too much support can retard the adolescent's transition to the role of parent and threaten the mother–infant relationship.

Family Support Scale. The Family Support Scale (FSS) (Dunst, Jenkins, & Trivette, 1984) measures qualitative aspects of support (e.g., satisfaction with support and degree of perceived helpfulness). Originally, this scale was developed as part of an investigation examining the mediating influences of social support on the personal and familial well-being and coping of parents rearing preschool handicapped children. It consists of 18 items, which the family member rates on a five-point Likert scale from "not at all helpful" (0) to "extremely helpful" (4). The sum of the ratings for all 18 items provides an overall index of the degree of helpfulness of the existing support. The sum of the items not rated (not available) provides an index of the total sources of support needed to help the respondent. The instrument was normalized on married and single parents of preschool children who were physically handicapped, mentally retarded, or developmentally at risk. Sixty percent of these parents fell into the lowest socioeconomic strata.

Individual Family Service Plan

Given the previous discussion of P.L. 99-457 and the special situation of the adolescent parent(s) and his or her offspring, developing an IFSP has important implications. The IFSP can provide the integrative framework that ties together all of the assessment data gathered from various instruments, observations, and informal sources into a comprehensive view of the child and family and a guide to strategic intervention planning. If used appropriately, it can be a powerful tool to empower not only adolescent mothers and fathers but significant others who constitute the parents' social support system. The IFSP is based upon needs and goals revealed through the assessment process as well as on those identified by the infant's caregivers. From the integration of these dimensions, an intervention plan emerges to empower the young parent(s) and to support the infant's course of development. Specific interventions are identified and roles of the adolescent parent(s) and others are defined (e.g., adolescent father, maternal and paternal grandparents, etc.). It is appropriate to go beyond the adolescent and involve significant others in the IFSP. For example, a biological grandparent may be requested to provide limited child care while the young parent completes night school. This would appear on the IFSP as a statement of support or a resource that could be mobilized to meet needs. The adolescent father and his family, social service agencies, developmental day care, and parenting classes could also be identified as resources upon which to draw. As stated earlier, a case manager works with the teenage mother and/or father and their families to identify needs, goals, and means for meeting the child's and family's needs. Case managers help the family obtain services and resources from a variety of agencies and work across agencies and disciplines to create and maintain coordination of services.

The IFSP offers practitioners the opportunity actively to involve parents in structuring and monitoring assessment, intervention, and the evaluation of outcomes. With family and professional collaboration, the social worker and other members of the early childhood intervention team can support the adolescent parents' efforts to achieve developmental milestones while fostering the healthy development of their offspring. Such concentrated and coordinated efforts offer the promise of fewer repeat pregnancies and more positive educational and economic outcomes for these parents and their children.

REFERENCES

Ainsworth, M. D. S. (1973). The development of infant–mother attachment. In B. M. Caldwell & H. N. Ricciuti (Eds.), *Review of child development research, 3* (pp. 1–94). Chicago: University of Chicago Press.

Allen-Meares, P., & Shores, D. (1986). Adolescent sexualities: Overview and principles of intervention. *Journal of Social Work and Human Sexuality, 5*(1), special issue.

Bayley, N. (1969). *The Bayley scales of infant development.* New York: The Psychological Corporation.

Beckwith, L., Cohen, S. E., Kopp, C. B., Parmelee, A. H., & Marcy, T. L. (1976). Caregiver–infant interactions and early cognitive development in pre-term infants. *Child Develop-*

ment, 47, 579–587.

Bowlby, J. (1982). Attachment and loss: Retrospect and prospect. *American Journal of Orthopsychiatry, 52,* 664–678.

Brazelton, T. B. (1973). *Neonatal behavioral assessment scale.* Philadelphia: J. B. Lippincott.

Brazelton, T. B. (1981). Assessment as a method for enhancing infant development. *Zero to Three, 2*(1), 1–7.

Bronfenbrenner, U. (1979). *The ecology of human development: Experiments by nature and design.* Cambridge, MA: Harvard University Press.

Caldwell, B. M. (1979). *Home observation for measurement of the environment.* Little Rock, AR: Center for Early Development and Education, University of Arkansas.

Chess, S. (1979). Developmental theory revisited. *Canadian Journal of Psychiatry, 24,* 101–112.

Dunst, C. J., Jenkins, V., & Trivette, C. M. (1984). The family support scale: Reliability and validity. *Journal of Individual, Family, and Community Wellness, 1*(4), 45–52.

Dunst, C. J., & Leet, H. E. (1985). *Family resource scale: Reliability and validity.* Unpublished manuscript, Family, Infant and Preschool Program, Western Carolina Center, Morganton, NC.

Dunst, C. J., Leet, H. E., Vance, S. D., & Cooper, C. S. (1986). *Resource scale for teenage mothers.* Morganton, NC: Infant and Preschool Program, Western Carolina Center.

Dunst, C. J., Vance, S. D., & Cooper, C. S. (1986). A social systems perspective of adolescent pregnancy: Determinants of parent and parent–child behavior. *Infant Mental Health Journal, 7*(1), 34–48.

Epstein, S. (1980). The self-concept: A review and the proposal of an integrated theory of personality. In E. Staub (Ed.), *Personality: Basic aspects and current research* (pp. 82–131). Englewood Cliffs, NJ: Prentice Hall.

Frankenburg, W. K., & Dodds, J. B. (1967). The Denver developmental screening test. *Journal of Pediatrics, 71,* 181–191.

Furstenberg, F. F. (1976). *Unplanned parenthood: The social consequences of teenage child-bearing.* New York: Free Press.

Garbarino, J. (1982). *Children and families in the social environment.* New York: Aldine Press.

Garmezy, N. (1985). Stress resistant children: The search for protective factors. In J. E. Stevenson (Ed.), *Recent research in developmental psychology, Journal of Child Psychology and Psychiatry, Book Supplement No. 4* (pp. 213–233). Oxford, England: Pergamon Press.

Germain, C. B., & Gitterman, A. (1980). *The life model of social work practice.* New York: Columbia University Press.

Hardy, J. B., King, T. M., Shipp, D. A., & Welcher, D. W. (1981). A comprehensive approach to adolescent pregnancy. In K. G. Scott, T. Field, & E. Robertson (Eds.), *Teenage parents and their offspring.* New York: Grune & Stratton.

Hobbs, N. (1980). An ecologically oriented, service-based system for the classification of handicapped children. In S. Salzinger, J. Antrobus, & J. Glick (Eds.), *The ecosystem of the "sick" child* (pp. 271–290). New York: Academic Press.

Main, M., & Goldwyn, R. (in press). Interview-based adult attachment classification related to infant–mother and infant–father attachment. *Developmental Psychology.*

Musick, J. S., Bernstein, V., Percansky, C., & Stott, F. M. (1987). A chain of enablement: Using community-based programs to strengthen relationships between teen parents and their infants. *Zero to Three, 8*(2), 1–6.

Ricks, M. H., & Noyes, D. (1984). *Secure babies have secure mothers.* Unpublished manuscript, Department of Psychology, University of Massachusetts.

Sameroff, A. J. (1982). Development and dialectic: The need for a systems approach. In W. A. Collins (Ed.), *Minnesota symposium on child psychology,* vol. 15 (pp. 187–244). Hillsdale, NJ: Lawrence Erlbaum.

Seitz, V., Rosenbaum, L. K., & Apfel, N. H. (1983). Effects of family support intervention: A ten-year follow-up. *Child Development, 53,* 376–391.

Simeonsson, R. J., Bailey, D. B., Huntington, G. S., & Comfort, M. (1986). Testing the concept of goodness-of-fit in early intervention. *Infant Mental Health Journal, 7*(1), 81–93.

Sprunger, L. W., Boyce, W. T., & Gaines, J. A. (1985). Family infant congruence: Routines and rhythmicity in family adaptations to a young infant. *Child Development, 56,* 564–572.

Sroufe, L. A., & Waters, E. (1977). Attachment as an organizational construct. *Child Development, 48,* 1184–1199.

Thomas, A., & Chess, S. (1977). *Temperament and development.* New York: Brunner/Mazel.

Unger, D. G., & Wandersman, L. P. (1985). Social support and adolescent mothers: Action research contributions to theory and application. *Journal of Social Issues, 41*(1), 29–45.

Werner, E. E., & Smith, R. S. (1977). *Kauai's children come of age.* Honolulu: University of Hawaii Press.

Assessment of the School-Age Child

Alfred A. Lucco

6

Sound psychosocial assessment is key to effective clinical practice. Assessment, as both product and process, is the basis for formulating treatment objectives and for selecting intervention points and strategies. Social work assessments are purposeful, focused, systematic, multidimensional, and ongoing. Generic principles of assessment, however, are implemented in specific situations. Formats and strategies are adapted to the characteristics of particular populations.

Assessment of school-age children is particularly complex, because children are in the process of developing. Their patterns of symptomatic behavior may result from any number of causes, including the stress of development itself. Although personality patterns may be evident in school-age children, personality or its pathologies are less likely to have crystallized. Thus, practitioners need to search broadly for possible sources of the surface disturbance for which the child was brought to one's attention.

Children are often less aware of what is bothering them, less focused on their distress than on their denial and survival efforts, and less able to verbalize what they are feeling. In this sense the assessment interview is best seen as a hypothesis-generating opportunity; collateral interviews with parents, teachers, and others are necessary for obtaining information and refining hypotheses. In addition, some techniques and tools are particularly helpful in obtaining information from and about a child. The following sections will discuss (1) a general framework for assessment, (2) criteria for assessment in specific areas, and (3) assessment techniques.

Framework for Assessment

Who Wants to Know?

In a general sense, the core question in assessing school-age children is "*Why* is *this child* at *this time* engaging in *this behavior?*" However, many factors shape the assessment process and the construction and content of any written report. A key question is "*Who* wants to know?"

The child seldom asks. Usually, children are involuntary clients who are referred by their parents or by institutions such as schools and the courts. The worker must be conscious simultaneously of the relationship between the referral source and the child, between the worker and the child, and between the worker and the referral source. The child may at first be distrustful and suspicious. The worker may be unable to guarantee full confidentiality, and the child may worry about what might be told to other people and how they may react. Whenever possible, begin the process with a meeting that includes the child and the relevant adult(s) (parent, guardian, teacher, principal, ward manager) concerned with the child's behavior. Begin by having everyone discuss the reasons for this assessment, including the behavior and/or emotional state of the child that is of concern, the way in which the problem affects each person, and the goals of each person with respect to the issues of concern. Within that context introduce your role (*assessment*, helping to understand why this is happening and what can be done about it; *treatment*, working to do something about this problem). After this introduction, the practitioner can begin to discuss what information will be shared with whom. In general, any information that relates to danger to the child will be disclosed and acted upon. The child's other secrets and feelings can be safely protected, and approaches to changing the environment related to such feelings can be structured in ways that protect the child's confidentiality. The child should be included in the feedback session and excused only from aspects that have to do exclusively with the adults involved.

Assessment vs. Diagnosis

Social work assessment of children involves a person-in-situation consideration of the child's functioning in biological, psychosocial, cognitive, and other domains. Assessment examines children's transactions with systems to which they belong (such as the family), taking into account the characteristics of those systems. Suppose, for example, that a child refuses to go to school. Is this behavior a symptom of fear of separation from the mother, a reaction to real dangers at school, a reaction to a demeaning teacher, or delinquency? In other words, the focus is not on the child's symptoms but on explaining these behaviors at this time with this particular child.

Assessment looks at the child's functioning compared with other children of the same age, in similar circumstances, and with the same special attributes, if any. Assessment looks for the strengths and resources of children in particular situations. It is a way of *individualizing* the child in order to develop an intervention plan for *this* child in *this* situation.

Diagnosis, on the other hand, is concerned with a child's symptoms and with assigning the child to the nosological category that best fits the symptom configuration. In this classificatory activity, the individual characteristics of the child and his or her situation are less significant than are the child's commonalities with other children. For example, a child may be categorized as having an "adjustment reaction" or "attention deficit" or "childhood schizophrenia."

Diagnosis facilitates the identification of potentially helpful approaches to intervention. Individuals with a particular disorder may well respond better to certain interventions than to others. For example, the learning-disabled child may benefit from prescriptive teaching; the child with an attention deficit is likely to benefit from medication as well as a quiet, nonstimulating environment. Diagnosis allows the reduction of symptomatic information to a category about which considerable etiological and treatment knowledge may exist. Diagnosis is one component of an assessment.

Objectivity/Subjectivity in the Assessment Process

Assessment techniques vary on a continuum from qualitative, subjective judgments based on broadly defined, descriptive criteria to quantitative, discrete measurements of narrowly defined behaviors. Assessment approaches vary, too, according to the degree to which the focus is on a particular child with particular configurations or on a child as she or he compares with established norms. The underlying theoretical assumptions vary, too, from those derived from psychoanalytic and ego developmental models to learning theory and behaviorism. More qualitative, subjective techniques rely on relatively abstract frameworks, such as dimensions of ego functioning or Piaget's stages of cognitive development, in order to focus questioning of parents, observation of the child's play, interaction with the assessor, and talk and expressive activities. The objectivity of these procedures may be increased by making use of formal developmental measures such as moral-development stories, cognitive-level tasks, and projective techniques (Copeland, 1988; Gardner, 1985). Although the latter provide some normative data, they are nonetheless *interpreted* by the assessor and are thus subject to bias according to experience, training, class, and sociocultural background. Subjective techniques have the potential to yield rich, detailed, and dynamic information about a child. However, they have been criticized by advocates of quantitative, multisource approaches (Garmezy & Rutter, 1988; Achenbach, 1988).

Quantitative approaches assume that behavior can be characterized in terms of particular behaviors (e.g., internalizer/externalizer, passive/aggressive) that can differentiate behavior patterns that occur in particular situations (states) and that manifest themselves in several situations (traits). Perhaps the best known examples of quantitative measures are intelligence (IQ) tests. Other frequently used quantitative measures include achievement tests, neuropsychological measures of cognitive functioning, and various behavior checklists that have been scientifically developed. Findings are interpreted by means of a comparison of the child's scores with those of hundreds of children of the same age and sex and, perhaps, other shared characteristics (e.g., hearing impairment). A logical extension of the quantitative approach is behavioral assessment, which focuses on specific acts (e.g., hitting sister) that occur in specific situations (e.g., at home) rather than on categories of behavior (e.g., aggression) that occur across situations.

Behavioral assessments, which provide a baseline against which changes achieved through reinforcing or extinguishing specific behaviors can be measured, will not be further discussed in this chapter. Rather, subjective and objective approaches will be outlined in an effort to provide a comprehensive framework for assessing school-age children based on a developmental/systems/ecological model.

Developmental/Systems/Ecological Model

Since the advent of the child-guidance movement, child assessment and intervention have been rooted in a developmental/systems/ecological model (Freud, 1965). Psychiatrists evaluated the child psychodynamically, psychologists administered psychometric tests, and social workers assessed the parents and the home situation. At a case conference, the diverse information was aggregated and an attempt was made to assess the child-in-situation. Within the past three decades, however, social work and the other helping professions have begun to articulate an integrative theoretical framework for this general approach. This new framework encompasses changes in foundation knowledge and theory.

Developmental psychology has changed considerably from Freud's initial emphasis on the drives and psychosexual stages. Today, ego development is emphasized to a greater extent than is id development. With the latter, the focus is upon the transformation over time from primitive drives to adaptive functioning at maturity (Greenspan, 1981). Models are now available for understanding and assessing specific spheres of ego development such as cognition (Piaget & Inhelder, 1969), moral development (Kohlberg, LaCrosse, & Ricks, 1972), and relationships between early stress and development (Rutter, 1988).

Temperament is now recognized as a factor contributing to consistency of personality over time (Thomas, Chess, & Birch, 1968; Kagan, 1984; Rutter, 1988). The child's temperament also contributes to his or her interaction with caretakers. "Goodness of fit" between the child and caregiver(s) is a factor in the life-stress experiences of children in their environments.

74

Since the 1950s, systems models of family functioning have gone through several permutations. Children's symptoms are viewed as expressions of and/or causes of family dysfunction. Assessment is concerned with psychological distance and with repetitive patterns that block or distort access of various family members to necessary resources such as nurturance, power, and value. A family-systems approach to assessing children's functioning includes exploring whether the symptom is the result of family-system dysfunction, whether it will respond to changes in the family system or is maintained through self-reinforcement, and whether it was a cause of family-system dysfunction. (Evidence that schizophrenia, affective disorders, and other mental illnesses have genetic etiology suggests that the dysfunction seen in families of psychiatric patients may be primarily reactive.) Whether a cause or a result of the child's symptomatic behavior, family functioning is a critical aspect of assessment when dealing with children.

The ecological perspective considers stresses that arise from the family system's articulation with other social groups and institutions, such as schools, mental health facilities, social agencies, and neighborhood. A "badness of fit" between the family and social groups and institutions may manifest itself in a child's behavior, for example, truancy or drug abuse. In addition, the ecological perspective emphasizes cultural variations as legitimate sources of differential developmental courses rather than assuming that divergence from Western, white, middle-class norms is the result of family or group dysfunction. Similarly, the ecological approach recognizes the relative nature of gender-oriented standards for behavior and does not view divergence from normative sex-role standards as pathological per se.

These developmental, systems, and ecological perspectives provide a sophisticated and broad-based approach to assessment of school-age children. Assessment should include the following:

- A developmental profile that includes cognitive and social development, attention span and delay of gratification, fears and anxieties, level and range of affective expression, physical and neurological development
- A temperament profile
- A functional profile, including academic performance and social relations
- Family-system functioning
- Transactions with social institutions and ecological stressors

Developmental Profile

Developmental Stages and Asynchrony

The first component of the developmental profile is the child's progression through age-related stages in various developmental domains. Considerable debate exists among developmental theorists regarding the exact nature of specific steps and the degree of certainty one can ascribe to a particular time line (Flavell, 1985). Nonetheless, general patterns of progression can be identified and transitions in the school years observed. Thus, the child's functioning can be assessed against age-graded developmental standards. This comparative evaluation provides the basis for identifying major areas of strength and vulnerability in the child's functioning.

The second component involves the assessment of discrepancies in the development of the child within and between areas. It is well known that development does not progress evenly and that some differences in the level of development in various areas are to be expected (Piaget & Inhelder, 1969). It is also well known that when environmental and/or individual factors block development within one area, other developments will continue and move ahead (a young child with a broken leg may be delayed in motor development for a period while cognitive development presses forward). Moreover, when the development block is removed, the rate of development in the affected area will accelerate (when the leg has healed, a period of rapid motor development will follow) until the general developmental pattern is reestablished.

Persistent and wide discrepancies between particular areas of development suggest the need for further study and understanding. Within an area of development (e.g., cognition) discrepancies in application (e.g., understanding mathematics vs. understanding the point of view of others in a social situation) point to problems that arise from interference in specific areas, not from general developmental delay. For example, both a retarded and an intellectually normal nine-year-old might demonstrate a high level of social egocentrism and inability to understand the perspective of another in game playing. However, the retarded child would have a general cognitive developmental level consistent with that egocentrism, whereas development of the intellectually normal child, as seen in academic tasks, would have progressed in cognitive situations, but not in social situations.

Discrepancies in level of development between different areas (e.g., motor coordination and cognitive level) may signal areas of continued blockage due to person or environmental factors. Person factors might include both natural obstacles to development (e.g., neuropsychological factors that cause specific developmental problems such as delay in language development) and overdetermined application of adaptational techniques from an earlier trauma that are self-reinforcing at the current time (e.g., the child whose affective expression is constricted as a result of living in a traumatic environment in which joy, happiness, and creative initiative were considered wrong). Obviously, such a developmental discrepancy may also be the result of current environmental factors and patterns of reinforcement (e.g., the 10-year-old child who fails to develop self-monitoring techniques because he or she lives in an environment where there is constant external monitoring and structuring).

Cognitive Development

Table 1 presents significant features of school-age children's development in the cognitive and social domains. According to Piaget and Inhelder (1969), children aged 5 to 12 develop a range of cognitive skills. These include the mental ability to perform logical operations such as computations; the ability to place themselves concretely (physically or mentally) in the place of others and to integrate others' views into their own understanding of a situation; the ability to think about thinking (meta-cognition); the ability to reflect upon and monitor behavior; skill in task planning and accomplishment; the ability to plan memory strategies to retain important information; increased understanding of social interaction and skill in determining appropriate social behaviors, including the ability to participate in social contracting and mutual decision-making activity. In contrast with the 6-year-old, the 12-year-old is able to make subtle distinctions regarding the differences between overt behavior and intent.

As the child grows older, self-definition becomes increasingly abstract and complex. Six-year-olds identify themselves concretely by name, age, physical characteristics, sex, and so forth. Twelve-year-olds can describe themselves in terms of inner thoughts, personal aspirations, and abstract

Table 1. Benchmarks of cognitive development—conceptual, social, and meta-cognition.

Age	Conceptualization	Social cognition	Meta-cognition
4–5	Egocentric thought: applies explanation based on personal experience, animistic thought, difficulty differentiating fantasy from reality, may use magical thinking to explain phenomena, fails to coordinate dimensions of objects.	Egocentric: has difficulty assuming perspective of another, can state the other perspective but unable to use it to guide behavior, views rules as being handed down by authority figure, may use rules egocentrically to promote own goals.	
6–9	Less egocentric: guides thoughts by perceptions, coordinates dimensions of objects and understands conservation of matter, time, number, etc., differentiates fantasy and reality, is able to comprehend causality if the events are perceptually available.	Can appreciate an alternative perspective but has difficulty holding own and other person's perspective simultaneously, is very concrete in self-identifications (I am what I look like and what I do), rules are absolute and must be followed rigidly.	Begins to monitor own thought processes (child can think about how he or she is doing something or about the strategy he or she is using).
10–12	Has begun to understand hypothetico-deductive reasoning, capable of hypothesis generation from a set of observations or premises, can entertain logical possibilities, is not limited to observable information.	Can take several perspectives simultaneously, appreciates the relative nature of perspective, is more abstract in self-identifications, is capable of understanding mutual roles, is concerned with social order and issues of social justice.	Develops the capacity to consider various strategies and to devise the best strategy mentally without trial and error.

qualities. For example, when a 12-year-old girl was asked who she was, she said, "I am a person who wants to be good and do good things. I'm going to be a teacher so that I can let children know that they are not alone and that someone really cares about them. I know I can do it, I love people and I know about loneliness."

The various aspects of cognitive development all share an underlying pattern of movement from egocentricity to greater attention to others and their perspectives; from concreteness to abstraction; from intuitive to rational understanding of causality; from lack of insight into one's thinking to some understanding of cognitive strategies and approaches; from manipulation of rules to suit one's purposes to mutual regulation and the ability to generate rules with another. During assessment, one needs to consider the child over time to determine whether the child's development is progressing appropriately. For example, an inability to shift from concrete thinking may be evidence of a learning disability, and difficulty in social relationships may be tied to persistent egocentrism. These cognitive developments share similar developmental trends; therefore, extensive and persistent discrepancies between areas can be very important. The 10-year-old child who remains socially egocentric while comprehending abstract concepts in class suggests overdetermined asynchrony, which points to the need for better understanding of the child's social functioning.

Information regarding a child's cognitive functioning can be obtained from various sources. During interviews, younger children often reveal aspects of cognitive functioning and level by their approach to games that involve a combination of skill, strategy, and luck. The child's ability to plan for future events and capacity to take into account the opponent's perspective and use of rules provide relevant developmental information. Similarly, and especially with older children, probing into events and interactions in their lives can reveal aspects of social cognition, perspective, conceptualization of causality, moral development, and ability to think about thought processes. Piaget's clinical method can be employed in a number of ways during an assessment (Cowan, 1978). For example, when a child is trying to explain an incident with another child, the professional can inquire as to how the other child may have seen things or how that child might have felt. Having a child explain the way a simple toy works can provide information on the child's understanding of causality. When playing a game, discussions of the rules can lead to questions about the source and modifiability of rules. More quantitative approaches to assessing cognition can be found in the work of Copeland (1988) and Gardner (1982, 1985). Benchmarks for social cognition and role taking can be found in Selman and Byrne (1977) and Strayhorn (1988).

Attention Span, Delay of Gratification, Frustration Tolerance

Difficulties in attention span, ability to delay gratification, and tolerance of frustration can potentially affect other areas of development, especially learning and social relationships. Paradoxically, however, the developmental aspect of these factors is generally overlooked. Evidence suggests that children differ in an absolute sense in their ability to persist, attend, and delay gratification (Mishel, 1984). Research also suggests that these factors change over time in both magnitude (Pick, Frankel, & Hess, 1975) and in maintenance mechanisms (Kohlberg et al., 1972).

When children enter school, they begin to improve their ability to attend selectively to stimuli, to control attention and concentrate on a specific task, to shift flexibly from one task to another, and to attend to a task when directed to do so by an authority figure. Attention span increases from a few minutes for preschoolers to 20 to 40 minutes by the fifth or sixth grade. Table 2 lists normative behaviors for these traits during the early and later school years.

Improvement in attention increases regardless of the child's starting point. However, children with attention deficits require specific training to develop these skills and more structuring of the environment to maintain them.

During assessment, one can obtain insight into the child's developmental level with respect to attention span and frustration tolerance through observations during a play session. For a more quantitative approach, the Conners Parent Rating Scale (Conners, 1980) and Conners Teacher Rating Scale (Trites, Blouin, & Laprade, 1982) measure the degree of attentional difficulty, impulse control, and hyperactivity in a child's behavior. The Child Behavior Checklist (Achenbach, 1988; Achenbach & Edelbrook, 1981) measures various aspects of the child's behavior, including maturity, school competence, and hyperactivity. These instru-

Table 2. Attention span, delay of gratification, and impulse control.

Age	Attention to task	Nature of control	Attentional behavior
5–6	A few minutes	Authority dominated.	Rapid shift of focus based on stimulus properties.
7–10	10–20 minutes	Cognitive controls involving attention to rules and expectations of the situation.	Selective attention to focal objects, decreased distractibility, increased ability to reflect.
11–12	30—40 minutes	Cognitive controls based on desire for future gain and planning a strategy.	Motivation to complete tasks and increased independence from stimulus properties of objects leading to a more flexible ability to shift between objects, increased use of logical strategies.

Note: Adapted from Mishel, W. (1984). Convergences and challenges in the search for consistency. *American Psychologist, 39,* 351–364; Pick, A.D., Frankel, D. G., & Hess, V. (1975). Children's attention: The development of selectivity. In E. M. Hetherington (Ed.), *Review of child development research,* vol. 5. Chicago: University of Chicago Press: Kohlberg, L., LaCross, J., & Ricks, D. (1972). The predictability of adult mental health from childhood behavior. In B. Wolman (Ed.), *Manual of child psychopathology.* New York: McGraw Hill; Anderson, D. R., & Levin, S. R. (1976). Young children's attention to Sesame Street. *Child Development, 47,* 806–811; Paris, S. G., & Lindauer, B. (1982). The development of cognitive skills during childhood. In B. Wolman (Ed.), *handbook of developmental psychology.* Englewood Cliffs, NJ: Prentice–Hall.

ments can be very useful when attention-deficit disorder is suspected. The assessor can also use strategies for assessing cognitive development. For example, how long can a child concentrate on a game, or how does the child behave when he or she loses?

Affective Development

The school-age child experiences various developmental transitions with respect to feelings and anxieties. In general, as the child grows older the range of expressed feelings expands and the ability to differentiate feelings and to relate appropriately to contexts increases. Fears and anxieties are age-specific; the child gradually learns to manage anxieties constructively so that they are less disruptive. Children use age-appropriate anxieties and fears to express the conflicts between change and stability that occur at critical developmental junctures. For some children, change is particularly difficult; they may linger at these junctures and express more anxiety. However, a gradual but definite developmental progression will become evident. Children who get stuck in the fears of one period and fail to progress are of greater concern. For example, the eight- or nine-year-old who has difficulty sleeping in his or her own room and sneaks into the parent's bed each night is expressing anxieties more appropriate to a four- or five-year-old. Table 3 presents age-appropriate fears and anxieties and characteristic patterns of management.

When a child manifests age-inappropriate fears and anxieties and/or management techniques to the degree that they disrupt social and/or academic functioning and serve to disorganize the child, there is cause for concern.

Eight-year-old Lisa asked to be excused to the bathroom every half hour. When questioned by the school social worker, she was too embarrassed to talk about it. After several encounters, she explained that she was worried that something was wrong with her genital area and that she had to go to look at it and check it often so that she wouldn't worry too much. Subsequently, she revealed an episode of sexual abuse by an older brother. In this instance, both the content (bodily injury) and the management technique (compulsive checking) were age-inappropriate.

Affective expression does not lend itself readily to a developmental benchmark presentation. Some developmental shifts, however, are extremely important. By school age, the child should have developed a considerable range of affective expression, including more subtle feelings such as shyness, coyness, jealousy, and envy along with more refined expressions of anger and pleasure. Feelings are more differential and relate to contextual variations to a greater extent than is true of the preschooler. However, affective intensity may be out of proportion to the stimulus event (e.g., becoming upset at the mention of bedtime even though it is a half hour away). The five- to six-year-old has little capacity

Table 3. Age-appropriate fears and anxieties and management techniques.

Age	Content	Management
5–6	Bodily injury, loss of respect, loss of significant others, fear of monsters, ghosts, etc.	Fantasy escape, change the threat, superhero for a friend, temper tantrums, and demand for reassurance.
7–8	Loss of peer group respect, loss of best friend(s), death/destruction of parents.	Anxiety signals the need for actions to avoid feared events, can take the form of changes in overt behavior (more prosocial behavior) or fantasy shifts to visions of popularity or power.
9–10	Fear of being overwhelmed by feelings, acting inappropriately, being embarrassed or disgraced.	Anxiety signals a need for action, usually in the form of sublimating feelings, daydreaming, developing a high degree of conformity and control, or reinterpretation of events to diminish their potential for negative impact.
11–12	Fear of being out of control, anxiety about acceptance by peers.	Abstract ideas and beliefs utilized to minimize problems of control, acting like everyone else increases security and acceptance.

to sustain affective expression and tends to be more superficial. By age 11 or 12, however, the child experiences greater depth of feeling and can be very intense and persistent in his or her expression of feelings. Increased ability to think abstractly leads to the development of compassion, empathy, and love based upon constructs rather than upon observations. Intensity of affective expression is more consistent with the stimulus situation. A 12-year-old is capable of expressing a wide range of feelings in appropriate ways. The practitioner should be concerned about underdeveloped areas of affective expression, inappropriate affect in relation to context, and inability to sustain feelings and expression. Each of these indicate developmental limitations and distortions.

> Jeffrey carefully ordered his pencils from the smallest to the largest. He had a very large collection of colored pencils and was an exceptional artist for a nine-year-old. He kept to himself at school and played by himself at home most of the time. He never participated in athletic activities and avoided competition. He also refused to work at developing skills that involved gross motor coordination, although he had no neurological problems. Similarly, he kept his artistic talent to himself and would not compete in activities involving this talent.

This boy's refusal to develop his aggressive drives in an age-appropriate manner suggested a developmental distortion in the expression of aggression. Subsequent work uncovered a rageful and tantrum-dominated aggressiveness held in check by a number of compulsive habits.

The affective life of the child is best assessed within the context of thematic expressions during the interview. Both the content of play and activities as well as the range and expressiveness of that content provide information about the affective level of the child and possible constrictions in expression. Techniques such as doll and puppet play, dramatization and fantasy play, storytelling, identifying and discussing feelings expressed by people in pictures and in the child's artwork are useful in determining the affective experiences of the child (Chethuk, 1988; Cooper & Wanerman, 1977; Gardner, 1985; Greenspan, 1981). The manner in which the child approaches the assessment situation and assessment techniques is also important. Although the content of the child's expressions is important, the practitioner should also pay attention to that which is not talked about or acted out and to avoidances, denials, and limitations in expressiveness. Sudden shifts in thematic content mark areas of specific anxiety that should be explored later.

Physical and Neurological Development

The school years are marked by steady progress in physical and neurological development. In kindergarten and first grade, the child is able to throw with accuracy over a five- or six-foot distance, jump rope for several minutes, kick a ball with one foot, tie shoes, and draw simple geometric shapes. More demanding tasks, such as writing and drawing intricate designs, are done clumsily. By age 12, the child's gross motor functioning is augmented by muscle development, and complex activities such as soccer and tennis can be achieved with ease. Writing becomes more fluid, and tools can be used skillfully even with small objects.

Atypical physical and neurological development may be obvious in some circumstances, for example, if a child has cerebral palsy or muscular dystrophy. Sometimes, however, medical confirmation may be needed. The practitioner should pay attention to gross and fine motor coordination in movement and play activities; visual–spatial integration during activities such as drawing, throwing, and catching; and somatic complaints and/or parental reports of illness.

Assessment of Temperament

Temperament refers to innate patterns of engagement with the environment that influence the responses of significant others. For example, one infant may engage actively with people and objects in its environment; another may assume a wait-and-see attitude. Thomas and Chess (1977) identify the following dimensions of temperament: activity level, mood, approach/withdrawal, rhythmicity, adaptability, threshold of response, intensity of reaction, distractibility, and attention span and persistence. Mussen, Conger, Kagan, and Geiwitz (1979) identified common manifestations of these traits at ages 5 and 10 (see Table 4).

Goodness-of-fit between the child's temperament and his or her environment is developmentally important. Children who manifest intense reactions, negative mood, irregular habits, and withdrawal from new situ-

Table 4. Common manifestations of temperament characteristics at ages 5 and 10.

		Age 5	Age 10
Activity level	High	Leaves table often during meals. Always runs.	Plays ball and engages in other sports. Cannot sit still long enough to do homework.
	Low	Takes a long time to dress. Sits quietly on long automobile rides.	Likes chess and reading. Eats very slowly.
Mood	Positive	Laughs loudly while watching television cartoons. Smiles.	Enjoys new accomplishments. Laughs when reading a funny passage aloud.
	Negative	Objects to putting boots on. Cries when frustrated.	Cries when he or she cannot solve a homework problem. Very "weepy" without adequate sleep.
Approach/ withdrawal	Positive	Started school unhesitatingly. Tries new food.	Goes to camp happily. Loved to ski the first time.
	Negative	Hid behind mother when starting school.	Severely homesick at camp. Does not like new activities.
Rhythmicity	Positive	Falls asleep when put to bed. Bowel movements are regular.	Eats only at mealtimes. Sleeps the same number of hours each night.
	Negative	Food intake varies, as does time of bowel movement.	Food intake varies. Falls asleep at a different time each night.
Adaptability	Adaptive	Hesitated to go to nursery school at first; now goes eagerly.	Likes camp, although homesick during first few days. Learns enthusiastically.
	Not adaptive	Has to be led into classroom each day. Bounces on bed in spite of spanking.	Does not adjust well to new school or new teacher. Comes home late for dinner even when punished.
Threshold of response	High	Always notices when mother puts new dress on for first time. Refuses milk if it is not ice-cold.	Rejects fatty foods. Adjusts shower until water is at exactly the right temperature.
	Low	Does not hear loud, sudden noises when reading. Does not object to injections.	Never complains when sick. Eats all foods.
Reactions	Intense	Rushes to greet parents. Gets hiccups when laughing hard.	Tears up an entire page of homework if one mistake is made. Slams door of room when teased by sibling.
	Mild	Drops eyes and remains silent when given a firm parental "no." Does not laugh much.	When a mistake is made, corrects it quietly. Does not comment when reprimanded.
Distractibility	Distractible	Can be coaxed out of forbidden activity by being led into something else.	Needs absolute silence for homework. Has a hard time picking out clothes in a store because they all appeal to him or her.
	Not distractible	Seems not to hear if involved in favorite activity. Cries for a long time when hurt.	Can read a book while television set is on. Does chores on schedule.
Attention span and persistence	Long	Practiced riding a two-wheel bicycle for hours until he or she mastered it. Spent more than an hour reading a book.	Reads for two hours before sleeping. Does homework carefully.
	Short	Still cannot tie shoes. Gives up when not successful. Fidgets when parents read.	Gets up frequently from homework for a snack. Never finishes a book.

ations are at risk for childhood psychopathology. Improving the good-ness-of-fit between the parents and the child can be helpful. Similarly, children who are slow to adapt may develop problems if parents push them to progress more rapidly than their natural temperament allows.

Thomas, Chess, and Birch (1968) identified a significant relationship among a child's temperament, the hospitality of the environment to the child's temperament, and the development of childhood psychopathology. Clinicians who assess school-age children need to ascertain the degree to which observed behaviors manifest temperament and the degree to which they are stimulated by environmental factors or by the combination of the two.

Ascertaining whether the observed behaviors are a manifestation of temperament or a reaction to the environment is essential. It is important to obtain information about the child's temperament during infancy and preschool years. Such information can be obtained by taking a develop-mental history that inquires about areas such as sleep, eating, and toilet-ing behaviors; reactions to new situations; regularity of pattern; sensitivity; and initial vs. eventual adaptation. Carey and Associates (1977) have developed scales that provide an objective measure of these behaviors.

Functional Profile

Academic and social functioning need to be considered when assess-ing school-age children. Difficulties in both areas may have heteroge-neous etiology. Dysfunction may reflect developmental delays and distor-tions; poorness of fit between the child and his or her environment; fam-ily pathology; or failure of the community, school, or other systems to provide needed stimulation and learning. A functional profile provides a picture of behaviors in key areas and helps identify major concerns that need to be investigated.

Academic Functioning

School performance can be evaluated with standard materials avail-able in the child's school record, report cards, and results of standard-ized achievement tests. The latter provide data about the child's academ-ic functioning compared with other children in the same grade nation-wide. However, the results must be considered in relation to the child's socioeconomic background and the quality of his or her schooling. Unfortunately, the established norms do not adequately take into account ethnic and cultural variations (Marsella & Kameoka, 1989). Thus, the social worker must make subjective allowances for these factors while not dismissing test results as biased.

Salient dimensions of academic performance include consistency over time, inconsistent performance levels across measured areas, and decreases in performance. If a child is having academic problems, refer-ral for psychological testing may be appropriate. Psychologists can provide information about cognitive ability, specific developmental disorders as measured by neuropsychological tests, and levels of achievement in various academic areas.

Social Functioning

Asking questions regarding relationships with peers can provide useful information. To determine whether a child has friends who would also choose him or her as a friend, you may ask the child, "Who are your friends?" "Whom do you like best?" and "Who likes you the best?" A child's answer to "How do you decide what to play?" suggests the degree of egocentrism as well as his or her role as leader/follower. Visiting the child's school and observing him or her interacting with peers can provide invaluable information about the child's ability to assume the perspective of others, friendship patterns, and capacity to follow and lead.

A number of good, easily administered instruments are available for assessing social skills (Marziller & Winter, 1978; Knight & Kagan, 1977; Kohn, 1977; Lambert, Essen, & Gead, 1977; Oden & Asher, 1977). Other instruments are available for use by parents and teachers. One widely used tool is the Child Behavior Checklist, which provides measures of competence and problem behaviors such as social withdrawal, popularity, maturity, aggressiveness, and impulsivity.

Assessment of social functioning should also consider the child's "citizenship" within the home. Does the child assume age-appropriate responsibilities? Is the child considerate of other members of the household? Within the limits of age, is the child aware of the family's resources and does the child limit his or her demands accordingly?

Family Functioning

Assessing family functioning is an essential part of evaluating school-age children. The family context within which a problem occurs has considerable impact on both the problem and its remediation. Consider attention deficit, one of the most common difficulties during the school years. A child who suffers from a neurologically based attention problem will most likely have a spotty academic record, poor peer relationships, low self-esteem, and problems with impulse control and conduct. If the child's family is able to communicate well and approach the child as a person with certain exceptional needs, it is possible to create a working partnership whereby the school and family cooperate in behavioral patterning and the social worker and family work to improve peer relationships, impulse control, and family citizenship. If family communication breaks down in the face of conflicts or if the family system is overloaded with demands that exceed its resources, the chances of establishing and maintaining such working alliances are minimized. In such instances, it is also likely that family interactions contribute to the impulse-control and peer-relationship components of the problem.

Family accessibility is a critical variable in determining whether the worker will (1) have access to necessary information regarding family factors that may contribute to the problem and (2) have the cooperation of the family in the intervention process. By accessibility, I mean the psychological availability of family members to participate in open discussion and to disclose significant aspects of the inner workings of the family. Many dysfunctional families have high levels of secrecy and internal rules against disclosure. Shame and guilt work together to limit access of outsiders to relevant information. These factors should not be confused with difficulties of access to the family based on issues of time, transportation, and competing demands. Rather, the question is whether significant information is shared by family members. Children from dysfunctional families are often evasive when discussing family activities or routines. They use common sex-role stereotypes, global denial ("Everything's fine"), and hostile avoidance ("It's none of your business") to avoid sharing family information. Members of inaccessible families often do not share with one another, look to a dominant family member for approval of statements, and avoid issues through disruptive behaviors or by presenting an idealistic image of their family life. In such instances, it is necessary to invest energy in the family engagement and assessment process.

Family functioning is defined here according to the capacity of the family to meet the individual needs of members for nurturance, affection, autonomy, and respect within the limits of family resources. However, the practitioner needs to distinguish between this broadly and clearly defined functionality and the particular family being observed. According to Kantor and Lehr (1975), family types may vary from traditional and closed to democratic and open to chaotic and still be functional. Thus, one must avoid simplistic assessments of family functioning based upon a comparison with a middle-class model. McPhatter (see chapter 2) elaborates on this caution, particularly as it relates to variations in class, ethnic, racial, and sexual orientation. Family assessment should be based upon the functionality of the family system, not the appearance and/or configuration of the family. The clinician may find that the various scales and measures of family functioning currently available will help to quantify this dimension (Touliatos, Perlmutter, & Straus, 1990).

Ecological Assessment

Each aspect of the child's environment can be evaluated from the viewpoint of stress-engendering factors. According to McPhatter, some, perhaps many, will relate to family stressors and hardships, the family's coping resources, and interaction patterns. The neighborhood and school are two important ecological systems that affect school-age children.

When assessing the child's neighborhood, one might ask the following questions: Are the child's family and background similar to those of peers and neighbors, or is the child an isolated minority? What recreational resources are available? Who are the child's available role models? Is the neighborhood safe? What messages does the physical environment convey regarding the value of children and families? Is the child exposed to physical agents, such as lead paint or chemical wastes, that might affect psychosocial functioning? Is the environment physically and/or psychologically destructive (Germain, 1979; Chestang, 1976)?

The school as a source of environmental stress cannot be overlooked. For the most part, schooling in the United States follows a 19th-century model. Grading based on comparison with others, rather than on one's unique capacities and learning achievements, means that failure is inevitable for many children. Similarly, games are usually competitive, generating winners and losers. Research suggests that labels attached to children influence teacher expectations and behavior and consequently children's learning. Expectations may be molded by the child's previous academic record, race, and sex and may generate self-fulfilling prophesies.

School stress may be exacerbated by poor teaching, overly large classrooms, lack of resources, and fear induced by teachers and/or peers. In addition to talking with the parents and child about the school, visiting the school and talking with the child's teacher may increase understanding of the child's daily experiences in school.

Conclusion

After the relevant information is collected and assembled, the social worker should be able to determine the following:

- The nature and area(s) of developmental delays or distortions
- The strengths and vulnerabilities of the child and whether these factors are appropriate to the child's age
- The degree to which the behavior pattern of concern reflects long-standing temperamental characteristics and/or is the result of conflict between the child's temperament and the environment, including interaction with the family, the quality of the neighborhood, and the adequacy of the school.

If the goal of the assessment is to report findings to others regarding the child's behavior, facts can be provided in detail. When the recipient of the information is part of the problem, the clinician must use tact when disseminating information so that the report will be used constructively. If the goal is intervention planning, the assessment will have established a baseline reading of the degree of impairment and will have identified the major sources of disturbance. Interventions can be directed toward several factors simultaneously or in serial order, depending upon resources and access to the family system. Multiple techniques and methods may be used, for example, advocacy with a school system, play therapy with the child, skills training for the parents.

87

The assessment model presented here can facilitate diagnosis according to *Diagnostic and Statistical Manual of Mental Disorders* (American Psychiatric Association, 1987) criteria. With children, it is important to distinguish between developmental disorders (Axis II) and other mental disorders (Axis I). A thorough developmental and functional assessment will disclose whether the behavior pattern indicates overall delay of development (mental retardation or pervasive developmental disorder), extreme delay in one or more specific areas (specific development disorders), or delays and distortions that are isolated and circumscribed in a manner consistent with other Axis I disorders.

The developmental/systems/ecological model also suggests the nature, duration, and source of stress. This information can be utilized as a basis for an Axis IV determination. The entire developmental, temperamental, and functional assessment assists in rating the current and highest level of functioning in the past year (Axis V). The diagnosis of other mental disorders requires consideration of the presenting symptoms as well as the pattern manifested in the assessment as a whole.

REFERENCES

Achenbach, T. (1988). Integrating assessment and taxonomy. In M. Rutter, A. H. Tuma, & I. Lann (Eds.), *Assessment and diagnosis in child psychopathology*. New York: Guilford Press.

Achenbach, T., & Edelbrook, C. (1981). Behavioral problems and competencies reported by parents of normal and disturbed children aged four through sixteen. *Monographs of the Society for Research in Child Development*, Vol. 46, No. 1. Chicago: University of Chicago Press.

American Psychiatric Association. (1987). *Diagnostic and statistical manual of mental disorders* (3rd ed., rev.). Washington, DC: Author.

Carey, W., & Associates. (1977). *Temperament scales.* 319 W. Front Street., Media, PA 19063.

Chestang, L. W. (1976). Environmental influences on social functioning: The black experience. In P. Cafferty & L. Chestang (Eds.), *The diverse society: Implications for social policy*. New York: Association Press.

Chethuk, M. (1988). *Techniques of child therapy.* New York: Guilford Press.

Conners, C. K. (1980). *Food additives and hyperactive children.* New York: Plenum Press.

Cooper, S., & Wanerman, L. (1977). *Children in treatment: A primer for beginning psychotherapists.* New York: Brunner/Mazel.

Copeland, R. (1988). *Piagetian activities: A diagnostic and developmental approach.* Eau Claire, WI: Thinking Publications.

Cowan, P. (1978). *Piaget with feeling.* New York: Holt, Rinehart & Winston.

Flavell, J. (1985). *Cognitive development* (2nd ed.). Englewood Cliffs, NJ: Prentice-Hall.

Freud, A. (1965). Normality and pathology in childhood: Assessments of development. *The Writings of Anna Freud, 6.* New York: International Universities Press.

Gardner, R. A. (1982). *Family evaluation in child custody litigation.* Cresskill, NJ: Creative Therapeutics.

Gardner, R. A. (1985). *Separation anxiety disorder: Psychodynamics and psychotherapy.* Cresskill, NJ: Creative Therapeutics.

Garmezy, N., & Rutter, M. (Eds.) (1988). *Stress, coping, and development in children.* Baltimore, MD: Johns Hopkins University Press.

Germain, C. B. (Ed.). (1979). *Social work practice—people and environment: An ecological perspective.* New York: Columbia University Press.

Greenspan, S. (1981). *The clinical interview of the child.* New York: McGraw Hill.

Kagan, J. (1984). *The nature of the child.* New York: Basic Books.

Kantor, D., & Lehr, W. (1975). *Inside the family.* San Francisco: Jossey-Bass.

Knight, G. P., & Kagan, S. (1977). Development of prosocial and competitive behaviors in Anglo-American and Mexican-American children. *Child Development, 48,* 1385–1394.

Kohlberg, L., LaCross, J., & Ricks, D. (1972). The predictability of adult mental health from childhood behavior. In B. Wolman (Ed.), *Manual of child psychopathology.* New York: McGraw Hill.

Kohn, M. (1977). The Kohn Social Competence Scale and Kohn Symptom Checklist for the preschool child: A follow-up report. *Journal of Abnormal Child Psychology, 5,* 249–264.

Lambert, L., Essen, J., & Gead, J. (1977). Variations in behavior ratings of children who have been in care. *Journal of Child Psychology and Psychiatry and Allied Disciplines, 18,* 335–346.

Marsella, A., & Kameoka, V. (1989). Ethnocultural issues in assessment of psychopathology. In S. Wetzler (Ed.), *Measuring mental illness: Psychometric assessment for clinicians.* Washington, DC: American Psychiatric Press.

Marziller, J. S., & Winter, K. (1978). Success and failure in social skills training: Individual differences. *Behavior Research and Therapy, 16,* 67–84.

Mishel, W. (1984). Convergences and challenges in the search for consistency. *American Psychologist, 39,* 351–364.

Mussen, P. H., Conger, J. J., Kagan, J., & Geiwitz, J. (1979). *Psychological development: A life-span approach.* New York: Harper & Row.

Oden, S., & Asher, S. R. (1977). Coaching children in social skills for friendship making. *Child Development, 48,* 495–506.

Paris, S. G., & Lindauer, B. (1982). The development of cognitive skills during childhood. In B. Wolman (Ed.), *Handbook of developmental psychology.* Englewood Cliffs, NJ: Prentice-Hall.

Piaget, J., & Inhelder, B. (1969). *The psychology of the child.* New York: Basic Books.

Pick, A. D., Frankel, D. G., & Hess, V. (1975). Children's attention: The development of selectivity. In E. M. Hetherington (Ed.), *Review of child development research,* vol. 5. Chicago: University of Chicago Press.

Rutter, M. (1988). Stress, coping and development: Some issues and some questions. In N. Garmezy & M. Rutter (Eds.), *Stress, coping and development in children.* Baltimore, MD: Johns Hopkins University Press.

Selman, R. L., & Byrne, D. F. (1977). A structural developmental analysis of levels of role taking in middle childhood. *Child Development, 45,* 803–806.

Strayhorn, J. (1988). *The competent child.* New York: Guilford Press.

Thomas, A., & Chess, S. (1977). *Temperament and development.* New York: Brunner/Mazel.

Thomas, A., Chess, S. & Birch, H. (1968). *Temperament and behavior disorders.* New York: New York University Press.

Touliatos, J., Perlmutter, B. F., & Straus, M. (Eds.). (1990). *Handbook of family measurement techniques.* Newbury Park, CA: Sage Publications.

Trites, R. L., Blouin, A. G., & Laprade, K. (1982). Factor analysis of the Conners Teacher Rating Scale based on a large normative sample. *Journal of Consulting and Clinical Psychology, 50,* 615–623.

Assessing and Treating Suicidal Adolescents and Their Families

Dean H. Hepworth, O. William Farley, and J. Kent Griffiths

7

S uicide among adolescents and young adults has tripled over the past 30 years, despite the fact that suicide rates in general have remained remarkably stable (Sudak, Ford, & Rushforth, 1984). According to recent data, half a million young people between the ages of 15 and 24 years attempt suicide each year; tragically 5,000 succeed (National Institute of Mental Health, 1986). These data tell only part of the story. Suicide often leaves untold distress for survivors and friends, who suffer acute grief and may be tormented by lifelong feelings of guilt.

Because of the prevalence and gravity of adolescent suicide, it is vital that social workers be well-informed about critical aspects of the problem. This chapter discusses psychosocial risk indicators; assessment of suicide potential, including use of an instrument recently developed for that purpose; and implications for clinical interventions with suicidal adolescents and their families. Special focus is accorded to integrating individual treatment with family therapy or group therapy.

Psychosocial Risk Indicators

Based on clinical research findings on adolescent suicide attempts, Teicher (1979) has described a three-stage process leading to a suicide attempt. The first stage, predisposing factors, consists of a long-standing history of problems from childhood to adolescence. The second stage is a period of escalation of problems related to adolescence. The final stage occurs during a period of weeks or days that immediately precede the suicide attempt. Common precipitating events of this phase include a rapid breakdown of the adolescent's social supports, including contacts and associations with peers, friends, and family.

Predisposing Factors

Traumatic losses or child abuse. Loss of parents through death or divorce predisposes children to later psychopathology, particularly to depression, which typically is associated with suicide attempts. This relationship has been studied extensively, but when all research problems are considered, little evidence documents that loss of a parent is the primary cause of a child's vulnerability to later depression. Rather, adverse psychological effects are more accurately attributed to poor parenting by the person who replaced the absent parent or to defective parenting by the earlier parent. Nevertheless, loss of a parent increases vulnerability to depression when the adolescent is faced with stress later in life (Klerman et al., 1984).

Physical abuse by parents also predisposes children to suicide in adolescence. In a study of 207 high school seniors and 901 college students, Wright (1985) found that adolescents who reported suicidal thoughts were significantly more likely than were their classmates to have been physically abused during childhood by a parent and had many conflicts with parents. Based on a comparison of his findings with previous results, Wright also concluded that adolescents who consider suicide have much in common with those who actually attempt suicide.

Family climate. Long-standing family difficulties are typically associated with suicide in adolescents. Families of adolescents who attempt suicide have been described as lacking warmth and failing to provide emotional security for family members. Research further indicates a relationship between suicide attempts and disorganized, unstable nuclear families with high levels of hostility and conflict (Williams & Lyons, 1976; McCullock & Phillip, 1967). Young persons in such families may receive subtle messages that they are unwanted and expendable (Sabbath, 1969).

Parents of adolescents who attempt suicide appear also to be troubled. One study comparing these parents with parents of adolescents who did not attempt suicide revealed that fathers of adolescents who attempt suicide were more depressed, had lower self-esteem, and consumed more alcohol than did their counterparts. Mothers of adolescents who attempted suicide were more anxious, had greater suicidal ideation, and also consumed more alcohol than did the comparison-group mothers (Tishler, McKenry, & Morgan, 1981). Thus these parents are more troubled, less stable, and less emotionally available than are other parents; they are weak models for their children.

Clearly, family climates such as those described above can have an adverse effect on the developing personalities of children. The critical ego qualities of self-esteem, impulse control, ability to cope, and interpersonal skills are particularly vulnerable to damage or to stunted development. Several researchers have documented that many adolescents who attempt suicide have long-standing personality disturbances. Friedman and co-workers (1984) found that more than 50% of adolescent patients hospitalized for affective disorders (primarily depression) manifested personality disorders. Other researchers concluded that psychiatric disorder was a necessary precondition for attempted suicide in the young people they studied (Hudgens, 1975; Crumley, 1982; Offer, 1969; Finch & Posnanski, 1971).

Behavioral indicators. The findings of one of the few prospective longitudinal studies on this population show that certain behavioral indicators observable as early as first grade are predictive of adolescent behaviors that correlate with suicide attempts (Kellam & Brown, 1986). For example, underachievement in first grade, as rated by teachers, is a strong and specific predictor of teenage depression in male children. Similarly, low ratings of psychological well-being by mothers and by clinicians of females in the first grade were predictive of teenage depression. Aggressive behavior without shyness is a strong predictor of teenage substance abuse for male first graders. Both depression and substance abuse are implicated in a high percentage of suicide attempts by adolescents.

Escalation in Adolescence

Factors cited in the preceding section predispose young persons to be ill equipped to cope with the turbulence and vicissitudes of adolescence. Moreover, low self-esteem, defective interpersonal skills, and dysfunctional behavioral patterns handicap youth in mastering the developmental tasks of adolescence, most notable of which are achieving a stable and healthy identity and developing adequate social relationships. These and other tasks are challenging even for healthy youth, but when compounded by accumulated personality deficits and by continuing lack of emotional support or escalating conflicts with family members, the consequent stresses may be insuperable. Troubled youth may thus resort to or increase dysfunctional coping behaviors that offer brief respite from pressures but intensify their problems in the long run. The following sections identify behaviors and circumstances of adolescence that are correlates of suicide attempts. As such they signal to practitioners that unless pressures are relieved, the adolescent, following a stressful precipitating event, may attempt suicide to escape what he or she perceives as an unsolvable problem situation.

School-related behavioral patterns. Dysfunctional behavioral patterns that escalate during adolescence are often manifested at school. Thus early academic underachievement can escalate into academic failure and truancy. Moreover, early problems with peers can escalate either into avoidance behavior in social situations or open peer conflicts. Impulsive behavior may also escalate in frequency and intensity. Research indicates that all of the aforementioned factors contribute to suicide potential (Jacobs, 1971).

Academic underachievement, however, is by no means the only precursor of school-related difficulties that contribute to suicide potential. A recent survey of high-achieving teenagers (listed in *Who's Who among High School Students*) found that of the sample of 5,000 students, 31% had contemplated suicide and 4% had attempted suicide. The four factors these teenagers identified as contributing most to suicide were feelings of personal worthlessness (86%), feelings of isolation and loneliness (81%), pressure to achieve (72%), and fear of failure (61%) (UPI news release, 1986). From this information, it appears that academic overachievers may struggle with troubling feelings that are similar to those of teenagers who are underachievers: doubts of personal worth, loneliness, and fear of failing. Apparently, overachievers make heroic efforts to measure up to high expectations of themselves and others; however, the consequent pressures and fears of not measuring up may become unbearable. This phenomenon may be even more prevalent in Japan, where suicides by children and teenagers soared by 44% between 1985 and 1986. Parental pressure to succeed in school is blamed for more than 25% of the deaths (UPI news release, 1987).

Substance abuse. Research findings clearly indicate that increased substance abuse over the past 25 years has been a major contributor to the increased suicide rates among the young. Based on data from several large cities, Greuling and Deblassie (1980) reported that at least 50% of the adolescents who committed suicide were involved in moderate to heavy drinking, drug abuse, or both. Data from a recent study of suicides in San Diego indicated that drug disorders were implicated in two-thirds of the suicides of young people and that 53% abused drugs or alcohol (Fowler, Rich, & Young, 1986).

Teenagers who abuse drugs and alcohol often do so to escape pressures and troubling feelings. Drugs and alcohol also create emotional highs and a counterfeit sense of well-being that temporarily supplant painful feelings of worthlessness and loneliness. Of course, other factors may also be implicated in substance abuse, including peer pressure, rebelliousness, and imitation of parents who abuse substances.

Communication deficits. Deficiencies in communication skills have also been cited as a factor in many adolescent suicides (Fish & Waldhart-Letzel, 1981). Such a deficiency may predispose a depressed adolescent who feels desperate, hopeless, and powerless to act out with self-destructive behavior. This view was supported in a study that compared delinquent adolescents in a correctional facility who had attempted suicide with adolescents in the same facility who had not attempted suicide (Miller, Chiles, & Barnes, 1982). Results indicated that those who attempted suicide had learned from their parents to use action rather than words to express troubling feelings and to cope with conflicts.

Family relationships. Cohesiveness between parents and children is typically low in families of suicidal adolescents. As adolescents strive for autonomy, however, the positive emotional connections between adolescents and their parents tend to erode even further in these families. Thus communication between suicidal adolescents and their parents is generally poor and conflict is high. In a study of adolescents who had overdosed on drugs, Hawton and co-workers (1982) found that approximately one-half of the group reported that they felt unable to discuss problems with their mothers, and 89% felt the same about communicating with their fathers. In fact, one-half of adolescents reported that their relationship with their father was constantly difficult, with severe disputes commonly occurring more than once a week. Although conflicts between adolescents and their parents or siblings frequently precipitate a suicide attempt, such conflicts generally occur in the context of long-standing strained relationships (Seiden, 1974). Moreover, adolescents' feelings of being unwanted may escalate during adolescence, and subtle messages from relatives may foster suicide attempts. Based on work with families of suicidal adolescents, Richman (1986) reported that family members may express "death wishes" for unwanted members.

Precipitating Events

Stressful events may occur that temporarily overwhelm an adolescent and produce feelings of depression and desperation. Because such events may trigger a suicide attempt, practitioners must be alert to possible suicidal ideation in these adolescents.

The major precipitant for suicidal behavior is separation or threatened separation from loved persons. The suicidal adolescent overreacts to the threatened or actual separation, its perceived finality, and subsequent association with death (Richman, 1986). Suicide attempts commonly follow quarrels with parents, siblings, or sweethearts that threaten the status of such relationships (Walker, 1980; White, 1974). Adolescents who have lost a parent of the opposite sex through death are particularly vulnerable to severe emotional reactions when a romantic relationship is terminated; the romantic relationship may have compensated for the original loss (Hepworth, Ryder, & Dreyer, 1984). Similarly, adolescents who are alienated from their parents may overinvest themselves in peer relationships or romantic involvements and may be vulnerable to suicide following losses of such relationships. Such losses may leave adolescents isolated from significant support systems, which is perilous because alienation and isolation are major correlates of adolescent suicide. Wenz (1979) studied adolescent alienation and found that the three factors that were most highly correlated with alienation (in descending order) were lack of social contact with peers in the neighborhood, conflict with parents, and broken romances. In another study of 108 adolescents who attempted suicide, Tishler and colleagues (1981) found that the reasons cited as precipitating factors for suicide attempts (in descending order) were problems with parents (52%), problems with the opposite sex (30%), school problems (30%), problems with siblings (16%), and problems with peers (15%).

A recent suicide by a relative or friend can also act as a precipitating factor. Tishler and co-workers (1981) reported that 22% of the adolescents who attempted suicide had experienced recent suicidal behavior in family members and 20% had experienced a recent death of a friend or relative preceding their attempt. More startling, however, are reports of two carefully designed studies that state that the rate of adolescent suicide increases after television news stories about suicide (Phillips & Carstensen, 1986) and television movies that depict suicide (Gould & Shaffer, 1986). Suicide attempts following exposure to suicide of others apparently involve imitative behavior by adolescents, a phenomenon of sufficient magnitude that researchers have expressed a sense of urgency about developing "a research strategy to identify the components of broadcasts that diminish suicidal behavior, if there are any, and those that encourage it" (Gould & Shaffer, 1986, p. 693).

Assessing Suicidal Risk

When the worker recognizes several risk indicators associated with suicide, especially depression, during initial contacts with an adolescent and his or her family, the practitioner should assess whether the adolescent is at risk for suicide. Information should be obtained from the following sources: (1) parents and significant others (e.g., teachers, employers, and friends), (2) interviews with the adolescent, (3) instruments devised to assess depression and suicidal risk, and (4) clinical observations.

Parents and significant others who have ongoing interaction with a young person can provide essential information about the person's behavior and possible depression. Suicidal youth often come to the attention of practitioners when parents seek help for their child for behaviors other than depression. Many distressed adolescents are not aware that they are depressed and guard against disclosing their thoughts and feelings. Moreover, parents may not realize that their child is depressed. Consequently, practitioners must be familiar with typical manifestations of adolescent depression and must alert parents to the significance of these manifestations.

- Deterioration in personal habits (personal appearance, dirty clothes, messy room)
- Decline in school achievement
- Lack of interest in activities that were previously pleasurable
- Increase in sadness, moodiness, and sudden tearful reactions
- Changes in sleep patterns (too much or too little sleep, fitful sleep, or arising too early)

■ Loss of appetite
■ Use of alcohol or drugs
■ Talk of death or dying—even in a "joking" manner
■ Sudden withdrawal from friends and family, moping about the house
  (Gold, as quoted by Ubell, 1986)

Given the mood swings and tempestuousness typical of adolescence, these warning signs should be regarded as indications of possible serious depression only when they persist for 10 days or longer.

Interviews. Although adolescents tend to guard against disclosing highly personal information, sensitive and skillful interviewing may yield sufficient information to assess suicidal risk. Skillful interviewing should explore risk factors using the following criteria: sense of self-worth, school adjustment, peer relations, family relationships (past and present), communication with parents, use of drugs or alcohol, emotional and behavioral patterns (particularly recent separations or threatened separations from parents, key peers, or sweethearts). It is also important to explore whether other family members or relatives have manifested serious depression or suicidal episodes.

Possible suicidal ideation should also be explored. When a young person acknowledges the belief that he or she would be better off dead than alive, clinicians should explore the extent of suicidal preoccupation, possible thoughts about how the young person might commit suicide, whether he or she has formulated plans (including a specific time), and whether he or she possesses means by which to commit the act. Affirmative responses to all of these inquiries indicate a high degree of risk. It is also important to assess possible deterrents to suicidal actions such as religious prohibitions that clients espouse, strong desires to accomplish certain goals, reluctance to cause anguish for significant others, and unwillingness to give up.

In addition to assessing the suicidal intent of the adolescent, it is important to evaluate the potential destructive impact of the family. This can be best accomplished in conjoint family sessions. Clinicians should be especially alert to expressions of death wishes toward the adolescent. Overt messages that place sole blame on the adolescent for family difficulties or for causing unbearable distress for the parents, such as "Our family would get along fine if it weren't for _____" or "I just don't know how much longer I can bear the pain _____ is causing," indicate that the family, either knowingly or unwittingly, is encouraging suicidal behavior. More subtle nonverbal messages include ignoring or responding with indifference to an adolescent's expression of despair or desperate plea for understanding and emotional support.

Psychological instruments. Certain diagnostic instruments can help confirm clinical judgments or assess risk when young adults reveal little information about themselves. The Clinical Measurement Package assesses depression, self-esteem, parent–child relationships, family relationships, and peer relationships (Hudson, 1982). The Scale for Suicide Ideation is an excellent tool for assessing suicidal intention (Beck, Kovacs, & Weissman, 1979). A recent instrument, the Adolescent Stress Inventory (ASI), also assesses suicidal risk (Griffiths, Farley, & Fraser, 1986). It consists of four indices: (1) problem events, (2) problem behaviors, (3) intrapersonal conflict, and (4) interpersonal conflict. Each index consists of between 14 and 25 items (72 items total) based on a careful review of the literature dealing with correlates of adolescent suicide. The instrument was tested in three groups; each group consisted of 45 adolescents between 12 and 18 years of age: (1) suicidal adolescents who were interviewed and administered the ASI two to four days after being released from emergency room treatment, (2) adolescents who had not attempted suicide but who were being treated in outpatient psychological counseling, and (3) adolescents who were hospitalized for medical problems. Analysis of the resultant scores indicated that all four indices clearly differentiated the suicidal and counseling groups from the "medical" group, which served as a "quasi normal" comparison group. Although both the suicidal and counseling groups scored relatively high on all four indices, compared with the "quasi normal" group, the suicidal group scored significantly higher than did the counseling group on the intrapersonal conflict index of the ASI. This index differentiates suicidal adolescents from other troubled adolescents. On the basis of discriminant analysis procedures, it was determined that 9 of the 25 items of this scale differentiated the suicidal group from the counseling group:

1. Feeling hopeless about the future
2. Feeling I can't be helped
3. Having thoughts about harming myself
4. Feeling others are to blame for my problems
5. Feeling unsure of my own self-worth
6. Being unable to express my feelings well
7. Having a negative attitude toward life
8. Being fearful
9. Having thoughts about sex that bother me

Adolescents who agree with all or most of these items should be regarded as high risks for suicide.

Items from the problem behaviors index of the ASI that differentiated the suicidal group from the counseling group included the following:

1. Truancy from school
2. Getting into drugs
3. Getting into alcohol

Items from the problem events index of the ASI were not sensitive to differences between the suicidal and counseling groups, but persons in the suicidal group scored significantly higher on the following two items from the ASI interpersonal conflict index:

1. Problems with amount of love or harmony in our home
2. Problems communicating with my father

Clinicians can refine their suicide assessment skills by adapting and incorporating these items into interviews.

Treatment Implications

When assessment reveals that a young person is suicidal, crisis intervention should be used during the early phase of treatment. After the situation has stabilized and the risk diminished, other interventions may be used.

Antidepressant Medication and Medical Backup

Clinicians are advised to seek psychiatric consultation for a client when suicidal risk appears high. A social worker is obligated ethically to safeguard the life of a suicidal client by seeking medical opinion and intervention, if they appear needed. Social workers who fail to take such precautionary measures are vulnerable to prosecution for negligence and malpractice should suicide occur. Moreover, antidepressant medication and hospitalization, both of which require medical management, may be indicated. Consultation also helps ease the burden of responsibility when evaluating suicidal risk. Because of the hazard of under- or over-reaction to such risk, the opinion of an emotionally uninvolved professional can greatly enhance objectivity and provide needed reassurance.

When chemical dependency is implicated in the problems of a suicidal youth, treatment for the chemical dependency should be arranged. Inpatient care in concert with family therapy is often indicated; in such instances collaboration with physicians is essential.

Individual Therapy

Because suicidal adolescents generally have long-standing mental disturbances, individual treatment, combined with family therapy or group therapy, is usually indicated. Individual treatment affords adolescents the opportunity to express troubling feelings they may be unable to verbalize in a family or group context. Moreover, the therapist can monitor clients' reactions to experiences in family or group therapy and assess suicidal risk on an ongoing basis. Because many suicidal adolescents manifest borderline personalities, practitioners should expect vicissitudes in the helping relationship.

Typical areas of therapeutic focus include assisting clients to gain awareness of and to manage painful emotions they have previously coped with by acting out, to search for more effective ways of coping with stressors, and to develop new skills in communicating and negotiating with peers and family members. Because these clients typically have difficulty expressing feelings and needs, therapists must be particularly sensitive to nonverbal cues that signal tensions and troubling emotions.

Therapists should be aware that suicidal youth may temporarily consider the therapist as their primary support system. Frequent sessions may be needed during the initial period of crisis. Flexibility is important, and shorter sessions should be used for adolescents who find it difficult to tolerate longer sessions. Therapists should give their telephone numbers to adolescents and encourage them to call if they experience suicidal impulses. It is important, of course, not to permit manipulative clients to exploit the therapist's good will by calling excessively.

Enhancing self-esteem is another major treatment focus. By discussing a client's score on the Index of Self-Esteem (Hudson, 1982), the client can begin to learn that a major part of his or her problem stems from a low sense of self-worth. The worker should help the client become aware of patterns of self-derogation and help the client negotiate a goal to monitor and curtail devaluating self-statements. Moreover, therapists should identify clients' strengths and positive attributes and provide positive feedback to clients who respond favorably to such information.

With high-achieving adolescents whose self-esteem is tenuous, it is important to explore mistaken beliefs that underlie their self-doubts. Typical beliefs include: "Excelling in school (or any other endeavor) is the only way I can be a worthwhile person" or "If I don't meet my parents' expectations, I'll be a failure and they won't love me." The worker should help the adolescent understand the unrealistic nature of these beliefs as well as their destructive impact, relinquish them in favor of more realistic beliefs, and develop satisfying activities and relationships.

Family Therapy

Whether to use family therapy or group therapy in conjunction with individual therapy depends on which mode will provide the greater emotional support to the suicidal youth. Generally, family therapy is preferred because of the potential ongoing availability of family members as a support system and the greater emotional significance of bonds with parents and siblings compared with group members. Moreover, family therapy is an effective means of engaging parents and young persons in efforts directed toward fostering constructive communication and reducing the frequency and intensity of conflicts.

Before meeting with the entire family, it is desirable to see the parents separately to assess their communication patterns. The worker should help prepare parents for later sessions by (1) clarifying the need to create a climate conducive to open communication, (2) coaching them to adopt a listening stance, and (3) emphasizing the need for them to convey willingness to focus on and to change their own dysfunctional behaviors. Although it is vital to establish rapport with parents by empathizing with their distress over the adolescent's behavior, it is equally important to construe their child's behavior as indicative of broader problems within the family. The objective, of course, is to reduce the pressure on the adolescent by countering the parents' tendency to cast him or her in the role of patient.

In sessions with the entire family, the therapist should actively confront dysfunctional interactions, especially when members attack, blame, and criticize one another. The therapist must translate negative messages into personalized statements of needs and feelings that do not elicit defensiveness and recriminations. It is also essential that the worker teach family members the importance of responding supportively and with positive feedback to one another. Positive communication strengthens family bonds, expands emotional support, and enhances self-esteem of family members.

Adolescents who experience intense parental pressure to excel should be helped to verbalize these feelings. Their parents may need help in reducing the pressures they place on their child and should be taught to provide acceptance and support not conditional upon excelling in school, music, athletics, or other activities.

Because breakdown in communication and conflict with parents are critical problems in suicidal youth, optimal benefits may be achieved by working flexibly with the parent–youth subsystem as well as with the entire family. Concentrating on dyadic interaction facilitates the dissolution of communication barriers and enhances relationships that have deteriorated because of chronic misunderstanding and conflict. Negotiating agreements between parent and youth to participate mutually in constructive activities (e.g., attending athletic or cultural events, making household or auto repairs, planning meals, shopping, or hiking) encourages positive interaction and reciprocal positive feelings. Working separately with the parents to teach them parenting skills is also effective in enhancing family interaction (a group approach can also be employed).

Activities that involve all family members foster family cohesiveness. For example, Kaslow and Friedman (1977) reported that family photos and movies help family members reexperience the past together. Laughing and reminiscing about shared events and circumstances from happier times reactivate positive connections among family members, especially if parents are coached to focus on the positive aspects of such experiences. Clinicians should also challenge parents to initiate family rituals that foster positive interaction such as planned sharing of daily experiences at the dinner table; family games; celebration of birthdays, achievements, and developmental milestones; family attendance at school, church, and athletic events; and family picnics, hikes, and camping trips.

Family therapy is sometimes contraindicated or unfeasible. One or both parents may refuse to participate or the adolescent may feel so estranged from the family that reconciliation is not realistic. In extreme instances, the family climate may be so suicidogenic and malevolent, and family patterns so deeply entrenched, that family therapy is unlikely to help.

Group Therapy and Other Support

When an adolescent's family is not a viable social support system, group therapy can be a promising alternative. Participating in a group with others provides a reference group and counters the adolescent's sense of isolation. Engaging in problem solving with others who have similar problems also counters the hopelessness and powerlessness that typify suicidal adolescents. The effectiveness of group therapy with suicidal adolescents has been documented by Ross and Motto (1984), who found no suicide attempts in their two-year follow-up study of 17 suicidal youth treated by individual and group therapy.

Contracting with group members to focus on strengths and positive qualities increases participants' self-esteem. Similarly, assisting members to adopt and to adhere to a guideline that members will personalize and "own" their feelings helps members learn to talk about feelings, which in turn decreases the adolescent's tendency to act out destructively. Goals that are particularly relevant for suicidal adolescents include mastering social skills and learning effective approaches to problem solving. Ross and Motto (1984) provide an excellent discussion of group therapy with suicidal adolescents.

Because of the importance of peer relationships, efforts to tap or to mobilize peer support systems can produce highly therapeutic benefits. Alarmed by the incidence of adolescent suicides and suicide attempts by students, some schools and youth leaders have organized hotlines and support networks for troubled adolescents. After meeting with students and faculties following suicidal incidents, Hill (1984) believes that the school is an ideal place to initiate preventive and postcrisis efforts.

For adolescents or families who participate in religious organizations, members of the pastoral staff or clergy in local churches and synagogues may be an excellent resource. These individuals may be willing to mobilize efforts to extend help to alienated adolescents. Leaders of other youth or volunteer organizations may also respond to the needs of suicidal adolescents. When such resources do not exist, clinicians may need to spearhead efforts to organize these types of social support systems.

REFERENCES

Beck, A. T., Kovacs, M., & Weissman, A. (1979). Assessment of suicidal intention: The scale for suicide ideation. *Journal of Consulting and Clinical Psychology, 47*, 343–352.

Crumley, F. E. (1982). The adolescent suicide attempt: A cardinal symptom of a serious psychiatric disorder. *American Journal of Psychotherapy, 36*, 158–165.

Finch, S. M., & Posnanski, E. O. (1971). *Adolescent suicide.* Springfield, IL: Charles C Thomas.

Fish, W. C., & Waldhart-Letzel, E. (1981). Suicide and children. *Death Education, 5*, 215–222.

Fowler, R. C., Rich, C. L., & Young, D. (1986). San Diego suicide study, II: Substance abuse in young cases. *Archives of General Psychiatry, 43*, 962–965.

Friedman, R. C., et al. (1984). The seriously suicidal adolescent: Affective and character pathology. In H. H. Sudak, A. B. Ford, & N. B. Rushforth (Eds.), *Suicide in the young.* Littleton, MA: Wright PSG.

Gould, M. S., & Shaffer, D. (1986). The impact of suicide in television movies: Evidence of imitation. *New England Journal of Medicine, 315*, 690–694.

Greuling, J. W., & Deblassie, R. R. (1980). Adolescent suicide. *Adolescence, 15*, 589–601.

Griffiths, J. K., Farley, O. W., & Fraser, M. (1986, Fall). Indices of adolescent suicide. *Journal of Independent Social Work Practice, 1*, 49–63.

Hawton, K., et al. (1982). Classification of adolescents who take overdoses. *British Journal of Psychiatry, 140*, 124–141.

Hepworth, J., Ryder, R. G., & Dreyer, A. S. (1984). The effects of parental loss on the formation of intimate relationships. *Journal of Marital and Family Therapy, 10*, 73–82.

Hill, W. H. (1984). Mobilizing schools for suicide prevention. In H. H. Sudak, A. B. Ford, & N. B. Rushforth (Eds.), *Suicide in the young.* Littleton, MA: Wright PSG.

Hudgens, R. W. (1975). Suicide communications and attempts. In *Psychiatric disorders in adolescents.* Baltimore, MD: Williams & Wilkins.

Hudson, W. W. (1982). *The clinical measurement package.* Chicago: Dorsey Press.

Jacobs, J. (1971). *Adolescent suicide.* New York: John Wiley.

Kaslow, F. W., & Friedman, J. (1977). Utilization of family photos and movies in family therapy. *Journal of Marriage and Family Counseling, 3*, 19–25.

Kellam, S. G., & Brown, C. H. (1986). Social adaptational and psychological antecedents in the first grade of adolescent psychopathology ten years later. In G. L. Klerman (Ed.), *Suicide and depression among adolescents and young adults* (pp. 149–183). Washington, DC: American Psychiatric Press.

Klerman, G. L., et al. (1984). *Interpersonal psychotherapy of depression.* New York: Basic Books.

McCullock, J. W., & Phillip, A. E. (1967). Social variables in attempted suicide. *Acta Psychiatrica Scandanavica, 43*, 341–346.

Miller, M. L., Chiles, J. A., & Barnes, V. E. (1982). Suicide attempters within a delinquent population. *Journal of Consulting and Clinical Psychology, 50*, 491–498.

National Institute of Mental Health. (1986). *Useful information on suicide.* Publication No. ADM 86-1489. Rockville, MD: U.S. Department of Health and Human Services.

Offer, D. (1969). Affects of their vicissitudes. In *The psychological world of the teenager.* New York: Basic Books.

Phillips, D. P., & Carstensen, L. L. (1986). Clustering of teenage suicides after television news stories about suicide. *New England Journal of Medicine, 315*, 685–689.

Richman. J. (1986). *Family therapy for suicidal people.* New York: Springer.

Ross, C. P., & Motto, J. A. (1984). Group counseling for suicidal adolescents. In H. H. Sudak, A. B. Ford, & N. B. Rushforth (Eds.), *Suicide in the young.* Littleton, MA: Wright PSG.

Sabbath, J. C. (1969). The suicidal adolescent—the expendable child. *Journal of the American Academy of Child Psychiatry, 8*, 272–285.

Seiden, R. H. (1974). Studies of adolescent suicidal behavior: Etiology. In R. J. Morris (Ed.), *Perspectives in abnormal behavior* (pp. 117–143). New York: Pergamon Press.

Sudak, H. S., Ford, A. B., & Rushforth, N. B. (1984). Adolescent suicide: An overview. *American Journal of Psychotherapy, 38*, 350–363.

Teicher, J. D. (1979). Suicide and suicide attempts. In J. D. Noshpitz (Ed.), *Basic handbook of child psychiatry,* vol. 2 of *Disturbances of development.* New York: Basic Books.

Tishler, C. L., McKenry, P. C., & Morgan, K. C. (1981). Adolescent suicide attempts: Some significant factors. *Suicide and Life Threatening Behavior, 11*, 86–92.

Ubell, E. (1986, November 2). Is that child bad or depressed? *Parade,* p. 10.

UPI news release. (1986, September 14). *Deseret News.* Salt Lake City, UT.

UPI news release. (1987, January 12). *Deseret News.* Salt Lake City, UT.

Walker, W. L. (1980). Intentional self-injury of school aged children. *Journal of Adolescence, 3*, 217–228.

Wenz, F. V. (1979). Sociological correlates of alienation among adolescent suicide attempts. *Adolescence, 14*, 19–30.

White, H. C. (1974). Self-poisoning in adolescence. *British Journal of Psychiatry, 124*, 24–35.

Williams, C., & Lyons, C. M. (1976). Family interaction and adolescent suicidal behavior: A preliminary investigation. *Australian and New Zealand Journal of Psychiatry, 10*, 243–252.

Wright, L. S. (1985). Suicidal thoughts and their relationships to family stress and personal problems among high school seniors and college undergraduates. *Adolescence, 20*, 575–580.

Use of Work in the Assessment And Intervention Process

Florence Wexler Vigilante

8

A principal concept affecting direct practice of social work is that work is much more than an instrument for financial support of the family. With the changing conception of the role of work and non-work, including a more accurate understanding of the demographic nature of the work force (more women, young people, and minorities; persons with different sexual orientations; greater heterogeneity), work as a social institution is being perceived in new ways (Spiegel, 1974). We increasingly understand its interface with other institutions such as the family, religion, education, and a variety of social groups, which in turn increases our understanding of interventions directed toward enhancing social functioning.

Taking into account in the assessment process a variety of psychosocial forces peculiar to work can provide more precise understanding of the working client's ability to cope. Knowledge of a client's job situation also furnishes an instrument for facilitating the use of the work experience in the treatment process. The psychosocial forces include the location and time of the work, the number of persons the worker is required to relate to, the nature of these various relationships, the dynamic relationship between how the worker experiences work and how he or she experiences his or her family, the psychological demands of required tasks, and the impact on other systems of work. This chapter will consider the interplay of these differential factors in assessment (Kurzman & Akabas, 1981).

Concept of "Fit"

Our new understanding of work is partially derived from the recent knowledge explosion in Western society. Evolving knowledge in the behavioral sciences has led us from a one-dimensional understanding of intrapsychic processes to more sophisticated perceptions of the relationships between intrapsychic processes and social functioning. We understand now that the presence of emotional problems, even fairly serious ones, does not necessarily limit the ability to work. Emotional needs do, however, influence whether we can work more comfortably in groups, in isolation, and in a variety of relationships to authority figures. We can refer to how one fits in the job. The concept of fit or complementarity of a person and his or her work suggests not only the capacity to perform the job, or the opportunity to have the job, but the more subtle psychological adaptation one must have with the work and the work space (Perlman, 1968).

Work Environment

Job requirements, performance, benefits, and opportunities may be thought of as formal attributes of work that contribute to our definition of ourselves as workers. But other attributes also influence our sense of well-being at work. Particular work environments that reflect ethnic, class, or psychological nuances and needs will contribute to a sense of well-being. The workplace that requires privacy may be experienced by some workers as isolation. On the other hand, the workplace that requires personal interaction may be experienced by a worker as an invasion. One's style in relating to authority will also influence one's sense of well-being. An authoritarian administration may make some workers feel controlled and powerless and make others secure and certain about expectations and performance. In contrast, an administration that relies on an egalitarian process of decision making may make one believe one has influence or that one is exposed to the whims of unruly peers. Social demands, such as eating lunch in groups, recreation during or after work, ages and family status of co-workers, create some of the norms and values of organizational life. Different personal needs, values, or life-styles can be labeled as deviant (Devore & Schlesinger, 1981). The need for privacy can be labeled as antisocial. Although these differences may not affect the security of a job or the ability to carry out the nature of the work, they contribute to perceptions of acceptance or rejection and, therefore, to a worker's sense of well-being (McLean, 1979).

Psychosocial Demands of Work

The nature of the work itself must also be considered in terms of individual adjustments. Tasks that have organized requirements, controlled involvement, and predictable outcomes may be perceived by one worker as soothing, as contributing to his or her ability to complete a task, and generally as work well done. To another person, the same task could be boring and tedious. Work that involves unpredictable outcomes or unpredictable involvement or constant problem definition, problem evaluation, and problem solving as part of everyday duties may be perceived as more stimulating, more creative, and, therefore, more satisfactory.

We need to understand more about work demands as these create stress or support for the individual worker and his or her family. Isolation, high expectations of socialization, or repeated work crises may be natural to the job but not to the person (McLean, 1979).

Stress needs to be understood as related to the "fit" between the worker and the job, not as the nature of the job alone or the worker alone. An example of "poor fit" is illustrated in the following situation.

G is a 26-year-old man who graduated from high school, spent several years in the army, and is currently employed as a technician with an electronics firm. He describes himself as a loner and without a winning personality. He lives in a suburban community with his mother, three siblings, and a nephew. G has never met his natural father and had a poor relationship with his stepfather, who has been separated from the family for about 10 years. He has been the family's main source of financial support since the period when he served in the army. Although he meets the financial obligations of family life, the interaction with the family is fraught with tensions and anxieties.

G is also socially avoidant and at first eased his conflict over interpersonal relationships by working at night, which meant he had little contact with his family. He also had little contact with co-workers because he was required to work with only one or two other people at night, which controlled both the psychological and social demands made on him on the job. Because of his excellent work performance he was promoted to a day shift, which required him to interact not only with many co-workers but with customers as well. Workers on the day shift had lunch together, a bowling team, and various informal family-group activities. Although the position on the day shift was clearly a promotion, this change caused G considerable anxiety, which led him to make mistakes in his work. Moreover, exposure to workers on the day shift made him appear to others as socially and psychologically deviant. In a panic, G requested a return to the night shift.

A social worker with access to the work setting helped G understand and cope with the variations of stress he experienced in the exposure to customers and co-workers on the day shift. It was possible for the worker to intervene with G's managers in order to redefine G's job so that his work space was more private. His work assignments were changed so that his lunch hour coincided with that of the fewest possible co-workers. It was possible also to remove him from constant exposure to customers.

This planning enabled G to work on the day shift, keep his promotion, and earn more money. He was able to manage the added stress of the day shift with this professional help.

Differential Means of Coping

Work itself can be relatively conflict-free and growth enhancing. Although individuals may have difficulties in intimate familial or social relationships, it is not unusual for them to find a more neutral environment at work. What may be viewed by conventional wisdom as pathological addiction to work may not be pathological. For example, the term "workaholic" connotes pathology, implying an inability to be intimate in familial and other important relationships (Machlowitz, 1980). Immersion in work, for some people, may actually indicate adaptation, not pathology. An illustration is the situation of an insurance agent whose devotion to job and customers provided a very large income as well as social interactions with other agents and customers that were altruistic, supportive, and convivial. In contrast, intimate relationships with his family resulted in anxiety, regression, feelings of powerlessness, and fear of being controlled. In response to this range of feelings, he became distant or abusive and angry with his family. His work hours precluded intimacy with the family. The more he worked, the more evenly controlled were his feelings in the presence of family members (Weiner, Akabas, & Sommer, 1973). At work, where the demands for intimacy were few compared with more superficial social demands, he functioned with minimum anxiety. In contrast, in times of illness or vacations, when the family required intimate involvement, relationships were consistently difficult and conflictual.

For some people, positive involvement with others can be maintained as long as the relationships are prescribed in content, not too frequent, and without danger of lasting commitment. These conditions are often typical of the workplace. One can feel close and engaged with work tasks without unmanageable anxiety-laden commitments. On the other hand, family life, partners, children, and in-laws may make a series of demands arousing strong and unpredictable feelings of anger, love, and even sexual feelings that can be difficult to manage emotionally. For such people, living in any situation that requires intimate arrangements may recreate earlier feelings of helplessness, of needing to submit, or of being rejected or humiliated. Family life is likely to promote these feelings. Although one may describe such a person as having serious emotional problems, the description does not actually tell us anything about the way he or she works—how successfully, how productively, or even how creatively.

The Ripple Effect

Work can help persons deal with other areas of their lives that are less conflict-free by means of a ripple effect. Positive experiences in the work setting can demonstrate to the individual that he or she has the capacity to function better in other settings. These experiences can lead to experimenting in the use of self in social or family situations outside work. The social worker may encourage the client to experiment in this manner. For example, the worker may help a client recognize that problem-solving skills successfully used in the workplace may also be applied in family life in place of the sulking, screaming, or temper tantrums that have been characteristic.

Work can be quite central to family life. Many family-life patterns are designed in reference to work. For example, the choice of where to live, when to take vacations, how much to spend for vacations, what to do for recreation and when to recreate are decisions made on the basis of work schedules and work status.

More subtle issues in understanding the meaning of work in people's lives revolve around how other systems are influenced by work demands. For example, the quality of care that can be given to family and friends may be determined not by how we feel but by our actual work time and work status.

This issue is clear in the case of a 23-year-old male with cancer who was suddenly hospitalized at a large urban research hospital 50 miles from the family's suburban community. The father, who had had a heart attack about five years previously, was a high-level manager at a suburban plant. Although he was not fired after his heart attack limited his functioning, the plant for which he worked reduced his responsibilities in conjunction with their assessment of his ability to contribute to the organization. In having his responsibilities reduced, his choices about taking time off or choosing the time he could take were also reduced because he no longer had a high-level decision-making job. The mother was a teacher at a suburban high school, where the population entering high school had decreased over the previous 10 years. This reduction in students led to a decision to reduce teaching staff. Because the mother had taken time off for her husband's illness five years earlier and, since then, to care for another child, she was in danger of losing her job should she request more time off to visit her seriously ill son. These parents regularly visited their son in the evenings but had to arrange for friends to visit their son in the daytime when they were unable to do so. They could not be with their son during the day at the time of his treatments, when the care and comfort he might receive from them could have been significant to him as well as to them. Their personal care for their son was determined not by health-care considerations, but by job-security issues.

A similar problem occurred for an 18-year-old boy from an urban community with a diagnosis of terminal cancer. He was from a single-parent family with three younger siblings. The mother was employed doing piece work and was paid an hourly minimum wage without benefits. If she were to have taken time off to visit her son, she would have lost income and likely would have been fired. Transportation to the hospital was costly, as were baby-sitters. She was seldom able to visit her child.

For the parents of both these young men, the number of visits and the quality of care they were able to provide depended not on the health needs of the children or the desires of the parents but upon the parents' work situations. Problems related to work are not usually considered in planning health-care needs. Moreover, one can only speculate about the pressures put on family members when the wage earner faces job jeopardy. Planners need to consider the possibility that illness in a family can in itself create job jeopardy, which in turn places undue pressures on the worker. The worker may then subtly pressure family members to deny, ignore, or screen needs such as illness or school problems so that the worker does not have to miss work. Single-parent families are particularly vulnerable to this set of conditions.

Social Work Intervention in the Work Setting

Social work brings special focus to the work setting. Its dual orientation to the individual and the situation sensitizes the social worker to the combination of conditions that affect behaviors at work. Social workers have developed considerable knowledge of how to function in host settings. They have developed specialized skills in helping clients negotiate systems. Enabling methods can be used alternately with advocacy to meet the differential needs of the client or clients in these settings. The social worker with access to the industrial host setting, through an employee assistance program (EAP) or otherwise, can meet with employers, union representatives, health care professionals, and supervisors. He or she is aware of the advantages and problems of various work assignments, is aware of community and company support resources, and understands how to put this knowledge to work on behalf of the worker who is a client (Ozawa, 1980).

Improved performance of clients in the work setting can be easily and directly associated with their use of social work services in an EAP or other arrangement. Social work visibility in this sense facilitates continued and more appropriate relationships among social workers, clients, and the various actors in the work setting. The more successful the social work effort, the stronger the support systems in the industrial setting. The social worker has opportunities to use supervisory personnel in a primary prevention modality. At other levels of prevention, the social worker can provide a linkage between the family and the work setting, bringing the dynamic nature of the relationship between the family and work out in the open. The worker can bring the resources of formal and informal social welfare services to bear on the needs of the work force. Referrals to community services and invitations to representatives of community agencies to speak before employers' groups and workers' groups enhance the linkages of the industrial setting to the network of community programs that can significantly enhance worker functioning (Weissman, 1975).

Work provides a highly complex social milieu, the understanding of which is necessary for appropriate assessment and intervention. The client in the workplace must cope with multiple demands that can, and usually do, affect his or her total functioning. Work has always been a central institution in the lives of people. The work experience of the client may be an important dynamic in the professional intervention process. Whether the service is offered in a community agency, in the workplace, through an EAP, or in private practice, failure to utilize the potential for growth inherent in the work experience may be considered a deficiency in practice.

REFERENCES

Devore, W., & Schlesinger, E. (1981). *Ethnic sensitive social work practice.* St. Louis, MO: C. V. Mosby.

Kurzman, P., & Akabas, S. (1981). Industrial social work as an arena for practice. *Social Work, 26,* 52–60.

Machlowitz, M. (1980). *Workaholics.* Reading, PA: Addison-Wesley.

McLean, A. A. (1979). *Work in America.* Reading, PA: Addison-Wesley.

Ozawa, M. (1980). Development of social services in industry: Why and how? *Social Work, 25,* 464–469.

Perlman, H. H. (1968). *Persona.* Chicago: University of Chicago Press.

Spiegel, H. (1974). *Not for work alone: Services at the workplace.* New York: Urban Research Center of Hunter College.

Weiner, H., Akabas, S., & Sommer, J. (1973). *Mental health care in the world of work.* New York: Association Press.

Weissman, A. (1975). A social service strategy in industry. *Social Work, 20,* 401.

Interview Techniques to Assess Sexual Disorders

J. Paul Fedoroff

9

During the past century, the clinical assessment and treatment of sexual problems have undergone a dramatic transition. One hundred years ago, the only data available to researchers were anecdotal reports of unusual sexual problems, often obtained through the criminal-justice system. Biased sampling methods and inadequate data collection contributed to the development of incorrect theories about sexuality. For example, so little was known about normal sexual behavior that Krafft-Ebing, who primarily interviewed individuals involved in forensic cases, proposed that masturbation caused mental illness (Krafft-Ebing, 1899). Since then, more careful epidemiologic surveys (e.g., Kinsey, Pomeroy, & Martin, 1948) have gradually increased our knowledge about the prevalence of normal and abnormal sexual behaviors. This growing knowledge has been accompanied by increasing awareness of the importance of sexuality in the general population (Shiavi, Schreiner-Engel, Mandeli, Schanzer, & Cohen, 1990) and in clinical populations (Swett, Surrey, & Cohen, 1990).

Evaluation and treatment of sexual problems have become more sophisticated; many sex clinics routinely use standardized psychometric tests (Derogatis & Melisaratos, 1978), sex hormone assays (Spark, White, & Connolly, 1980), nocturnal penile tumescence testing (Karacan et al., 1977), and penile plethysmography (Freund & Blanchard, 1989). Berlin's (1983) finding that a large percentage of hospitalized sex offenders have physical and mental abnormalities supports the hypothesis that, in selected cases, karyotyping, electroencephalography, and computerized tomography may be indicated as part of the assessment of sex problems. Treatments have also become more sophisticated and may now involve various forms of individual (Crown & Lucas, 1976), couple (Masters & Johnson, 1970), and group therapy (Leiblum, Rosen, & Piere, 1976) as well as pharmacotherapy (Berlin & Meinecke, 1981) and even surgery (Schmidt & Schorsch, 1981).

In addition, sex clinics themselves have tended to specialize on the basis of the types of problems they evaluate: sexual dysfunctions, paraphilias, gender-identity problems, or consequences of sexual abuse. According to current diagnostic criteria, sexual dysfunctions are defined as disorders characterized by problems of decreased sexual desire or by psychophysiologic changes that characterize the sexual response cycle (American Psychiatric Association, 1987). Gender-identity problems are characterized as involving persistent discomfort regarding one's gender. Paraphilias are sexual disorders characterized by arousal in response to stimuli that are not normally considered sexually exciting and that may interfere with a person's capacity for reciprocal, affectionate activity (American Psychiatric Association, 1987). Sex-victim clinics serve the needs of children, adolescents, and adults who have been sexually abused. Although the trend toward increasingly sophisticated and specialized sex clinics has increased awareness about the importance of sexual problems, general clinicians still tend to ignore sexual problems. This is particularly worrisome because many people first present their sex problems to their general clinician.

Given the increased sophistication of assessment procedures and the increased specialization of evaluation centers, why do general clinicians need to be able to conduct an interview about sexual behaviors and problems? There are at least four reasons.

First, sexual problems often influence nonsexual behavior. For example, a common side effect of some medications is change in sexual functioning (Barnes, Bambor, & Watson, 1979). However, because people tend to be uncomfortable talking about sexual problems, they frequently prefer to stop taking their medication rather than ask about their sexual difficulties. Thus sexual problems are one of the chief causes of noncompliance with medication. For example, a man precipitated a myocardial infarction by stopping his antihypertensive medication when he realized (correctly) that it was interfering with his ability to have sex. Had someone taken the time to discuss this common side effect, the man's heart attack might have been prevented. It is always a mistake to assume that sexual functioning is a trivial concern. Unfortunately, however, even experienced clinicians sometimes forget this, especially when treating elderly, developmentally disabled, or handicapped people.

A second reason for conducting an interview about sexual behaviors and problems is that society expects clinicians to be knowledgeable about sexual problems. Sexual behaviors, which used to be the concern of specialists, are now everyone's concern. Many legislatures now require clinicians to report to state authorities people under their care whom they suspect to be sexual abusers (Jellinek, Murphy, Bishop, Poitrost, & Quinn, 1990).

A third reason is that, in the final analysis and despite many advances in assessment procedures, the clinical interview is still the "gold standard" against which all other assessment techniques are measured. If the clinician does not consider sexual problems and is unable to conduct an interview concerning them, or the person is unwilling to discuss such issues, many problems are likely to remain undiscovered and therefore go untreated.

Finally, attending to sexual concerns and difficulties is simply part of caring for people who seek our help. Consider the following case example:

> A 65-year-old woman presented with depression. During the initial interview, I learned that she had had a colostomy for 10 years following a successful operation for cancer of the bowel. Since then she had become increasingly withdrawn and anxious that her husband would leave her. She had not responded to antidepressant medication. When asked whether she or her husband had experienced any sexual problems since her operation, she looked at me in shock—not because I had asked her about sex but because she had thought that sex was not possible with a colostomy. She had assumed that it was forbidden. Both she and her husband were unhappy with this situation but were too embarrassed to seek help or advice. As a consequence, she and her husband had moved into separate bedrooms and had not had sexual intercourse for 10 years.
>
> The remainder of the interview focused on reassuring this woman that sexual activity was possible and quite safe following a colostomy operation. The next week I learned that following our conversation she had gone home and told her husband that sex was not prohibited. That night they checked into a local motel and had sex for the first time in 10 years. On her next visit, all symptoms of depression had vanished. She also brought her husband with her. He shook my hand vigorously and said, "My wife and I have needed help for 10 years. In all that time no one ever asked us about sex. Why has it taken so long?"

Conducting an interview includes asking questions about sexual functioning, concerns, and problems. This chapter discusses ways to make this important task easier.

Types of Interviews

Not all sex interviews are the same. A common mistake is to assume that the nature of an interview is determined by its topic. However, clinical sexual and nonsexual interviews are more alike than are clinical and research interviews that both deal with sexual issues. Thus therapists who would like to conduct clinical sexual interviews should be reassured that their clinical experience is directly applicable to conducting such interviews.

Table 1 lists several types of interviews, together with the chief purpose and typical characteristics of the interview. Each type of interview could involve sexual topics, yet each would be very different. For example, late-night television talk-show hosts frequently discuss sex with their guests, but the purpose of their interview is entertainment. Talk-show hosts rarely ask questions to which they do not already know the answer. When the conversation becomes too intimate, the host or guest will frequently resort to humor in order to increase the entertainment value of the show (and decrease his or her own anxiety). Clearly, the interview style of a talk-show host is a poor example for clinicians to follow. People enter treatment to be helped, not to provide entertainment. Therefore, before the interview begins, the clinician should always let the interviewee know how the information will be recorded, who will have access to it, and what will be done with it.

Clinicians should always be honest about the purpose of the interview. Is the interview part of ongoing psychotherapy? Will it be used to generate a court report? Is it part of a research project? Because the purpose of the interview affects how the interview will be conducted, the interviewee needs to know why the interview is being conducted, especially when the interview may be used for more than one purpose. Freud's work provides an example of the sort of problems that can occur when this principle is not followed. Many of his interviews were conducted for the purpose of psychotherapeutic treatment. As part of this process, he trained his patients to speak their thoughts without censoring themselves. However, when the purpose of his interviews changed from psychotherapy to data collection in support of his developing theory of personality, Freud found it difficult to interpret what he learned. For example, during psychotherapy sessions, many of his patients reported having had sexual relations with their parents, but one could not be sure whether these reports represented fantasy or reality (Masson, 1984).

Table 1. Types of interviews.

Style	Purpose	Characteristic
Talk show	Entertainment	Superficial, leading questions
Survey	Population-based	Extensive, menu-type
Forensic	Court report	Nonspeculative, multiple informants
Therapeutic	Alleviation of problem	Feelings more important than facts
Diagnostic	Individual assessment	Problem-oriented

The Interview Process

Opening the Interview

After explaining the purpose of the interview, the clinician should be sure that the interviewee agrees to be interviewed and knows why he or she is being interviewed. Sexual problems are extremely difficult for couples to discuss. Commonly, the person with the problem remains quiet and lets the partner do the talking. It is not unusual to discover that the man who is referred for treatment because he shows too little interest in sex has never heard this complaint directly from his wife and is surprised to discover that this is the purpose of his appointment with the therapist.

Establishing Rapport

After opening the interview, some level of mutual understanding should be achieved. This process is facilitated if the interviewee feels he or she is understood and will not be judged prematurely. The clinician should clarify all terminology, especially terms such as "making love," "sexual problems," or other euphemisms. Technical terms without mutually agreed-upon definitions can also be misleading. For example, a man who says he has "premature ejaculation" may actually have inhibited sexual desire, erectile dysfunction, retarded ejaculation, retrograde ejaculation, or anorgasmia. In fact, assumptions of any type are dangerous. For example, one couple went to a sexual dysfunction clinic with the complaint that the male partner ejaculated after two minutes of sexual intercourse. The clinician interviewing the man began by explaining that he would be asking some questions about premature ejaculation. Fortunately, the man quickly interrupted to say that his wife disliked sex and complained that he took too long! Thus the clinician had made an incorrect assumption about what this couple thought their problem was based on the clinician's preconceived ideas of normal sexual behavior.

Rapport tends to increase when people feel that they are in control. In a clinical interview, it helps to tell people that they do not have to answer every question and that they can stop the interview if they feel uncomfortable. They should be encouraged to ask for clarification if they don't understand a question. People who are at ease will generally provide more information about themselves. Rapport is also facilitated if the interviewee is convinced that the *clinician* will not lose control. Clinicians frequently underestimate the degree to which clients try to protect them. A person with a shocking secret is unlikely to reveal the secret to a clinician who becomes easily flustered. Talking about sexual matters may be a new experience for some people. Some may not have achieved this level of intimacy even with their own sexual partners. The clinician should be especially alert to transference or countertransference feelings.

117

Identification of Problems

During this stage the clinician should focus on the main purpose of the interview, that is, identifying specific problems that the clinician can help resolve. People tend to be embarrassed by or ashamed of sexual problems and prefer that the clinician "discover" the problem. People tend to be unsure about what "normal" sexuality is and often attempt to find out what the interviewer thinks is normal before committing themselves. Thus the clinician should beware of answering questions about "normal" sexual behavior.

At this point in the interview, the clinician should discourage the client from offering explanations for his or her behavior. Try to "stick with facts." As in other areas of life, people who have one sexual problem often have several. Usually people will start the interview by stating the problem that they consider to be the least abnormal or least distressing. The clinician should not settle for the first sexual problem mentioned or discovered. The clinician should try to convey the impression that he or she is knowledgeable about sexuality and is unlikely to be overwhelmed by the person's current problem. Closed-ended questions, to which replies of "yes" or "no" can be made, should be avoided by the clinician. Finally, the practitioner should not jump to conclusions in diagnosing a problem. Sexual problems are extremely complex and usually involve at least two people. If only one of the parties is interviewed, the clinician knows only half the story at most.

Background Information

The first part of the interview can be used to establish what the presenting problems are, after which the therapist should obtain some background information about the person and the problem. It is helpful to ask the person his or her opinion of the problem. In my experience, these theories are usually wrong but always informative. For example, it is helpful to know early in treatment that the married man with erectile dysfunction has had an affair and believes his problem is an early symptom of syphilis.

This section of the interview can often be less structured. However, it helps to proceed in a chronological direction—either from the present backward or from the past forward. People generally provide more complete information if they are able to place it in the context of other important life events. Frequently, in the process of tracing the exact course of a problem new insights into possible causes emerge. For example, a man who presents with the complaint of premature ejaculation "all his life" may be asked whether he had this problem before he was married, before he left home, before he graduated from school, and so forth.

Completing the Interview

When is the interview over? Most interviewers agree that a single interview of more than 90 minutes is too long. Usually, it is better to have several shorter interviews. It may help to say how much time is available at the start of the interview. If people know they have only one hour, they may get to the crux of the problem faster. Other important interview topics include what the person thinks will happen if he or she doesn't get treatment. Does the person think he or she will ever get better? What type of therapy, if any, does the person think he or she needs?

At this point, the clinician should do a mental check of items to be covered. What is the primary problem? What does the person think the problem is? What does the partner think the problem is? Is the chronology clear? Does the story have any gaps? Why did the person seek help at this time? Leave the door open for further elaboration, as people are rarely able to tell their whole story in a single interview. They may hold back vital pieces of information until after they evaluate the interviewer. The clinician should double check to be sure the interview hasn't focused on the wrong issues. A comment such as the following may help: "I've asked you a lot of questions, but every person is different. What other things that we haven't discussed today have you wondered about?"

Closing the Interview

During the last few minutes of the interview, the clinician should briefly summarize what he or she has learned. The clinician should state what will happen next: schedule another appointment? an interview with the partner? referral to a specialist? A simple statement such as the following may be reassuring:

> People frequently have concerns like yours about their sexual behavior and I am glad you have trusted me enough to tell me about them. We've covered a lot of ground today and you are likely to have other thoughts about what we have talked about. If you think of anything or have any concerns, you can reach me at _____.

The point here is to reassure the person that he or she has made the right decision to seek help and to leave the door open for further dialogue. Finally, the clinician should always give the person a chance to ask questions.

Helpful Techniques

Much of the advice discussed in the foregoing sections of this article applies equally well to nonsexual clinical interviews. Several techniques, however, are especially helpful in taking sex histories. With experience, most clinicians develop their own strategies and techniques. The following techniques may be useful to clinicians with little experience in this area (Money, 1986).

Sportscaster

As mentioned earlier, it is often a mistake to invite the interviewee to spend too much time speculating on his or her behavior or problem. The "sportscaster technique" can help avoid this pitfall. Ask the person to describe an event as though he or she were a sportscaster and the event was happening right now. Typically, the person will begin talking in the past tense or start offering explanations or justifications about his or her behavior. However, after being interrupted and reminded to tell the story as if it were actually occurring, people will often begin describing important details that would have been left out otherwise. The effect can be enhanced by asking for details: for example, "What do you hear?" This technique helps the clinician learn how the event was experienced.

Topics in the Public Domain

Discussing sexual behavior with a stranger provokes anxiety in most people. However, people are often less anxious about discussing the sexual problems of others. In some cases, clinicians can encourage people to talk about sexual problems by introducing the topic through a reference to a recent news story or event. For example, attitudes toward homosexuality can be elicited by bringing up the topic of AIDS. Sexual abuse can be investigated by mentioning recent cases in the news.

Alternative Names, Hypothetical Situations

Sometimes it helps to ask the interviewee to imagine particular situations. Transsexual interests and attitudes toward the opposite sex can be assessed by asking whether the person has ever had a dream (or nightmare) about being the opposite sex. Has the person ever imagined he or she had a different name? Sometimes it's easier for people to talk about sensitive issues if they don't have to admit to their own participation. For this reason, people often find it easier to discuss sensitive topics in the subjunctive mood: What would happen if . . . ?

Sexual Fantasy Letters

As many know, some popular sex magazines regularly publish letters describing the sexual adventures of their readers. Even if clients have never read such a letter, it is often possible to convince them to compose the sort of letter they would write to such a magazine if they were to describe their "most unusual sexual experience," "best sexual experience," or the like. People who are embarrassed to talk about sex often find it easier to write about it. Asking what a person's most unusual sexual experience is elicits information about what the person *thinks* is unusual as well as about actual behavior. Asking about fantasies is especially important when evaluating paraphilic sexual disorders because responses may provide clues about the nature of the disorder. For example, a man who presents with a complaint of exhibitionism and who describes fantasies of being seen by children should be carefully evaluated for pedophilia.

Projection

It is always useful to know what the client thinks will happen in the future. By asking the person what the future will be like with and without treatment, the clinician can estimate the person's commitment to treatment. This technique also provides an index of how hopeful or hopeless the person is feeling.

Conclusion

Assessing sexual functioning requires the same kinds of skills used in assessing other aspects of people's lives. However, assessing sexual functioning is complicated by the reluctance of clinicians and clients to talk about sex due to embarrassment, shyness, or lack of knowledge. Probably the best advice on how to conduct a good sex interview can be found in Freud's papers on how to conduct psychoanalytic interviews. The principles that he advocated included avoiding clinician self-disclosure, encouraging the patient to speak freely about anything that comes to mind without censorship, and attention to dreams and fantasies (Freud, 1958).

Of the thousands of interviews that I have conducted, I have never had a patient become upset or angry because I have asked a question about sex. Some say they would rather not discuss that area of their lives and we move on to another topic. However, many more people have thanked me for giving them a chance to talk about their sexual difficulties or concerns. Sexual interviewing certainly becomes easier with practice. In the final analysis, the clinical history should be tailored to the skills of the clinician and the needs of the individual seeking help. If it is done correctly, the person is left with the impression that he or she can talk about any aspect of his or her life with an understanding, competent professional who sincerely wishes to help.

REFERENCES

American Psychiatric Association. (1987). *Diagnostic and statistical manual of mental disorders* (3rd ed., rev.). Washington, DC: Author.

Barnes, T. R. E., Bambor, R. W. K., & Watson, J. P. (1979). Psychotropic drugs and sexual behaviour. *British Journal of Hospital Medicine, 21,* 327–340.

Berlin, F., & Meinecke, C. (1981). Treatment of sex offenders with antiandrogenic medication, conceptualization review of treatment modalities and preliminary findings. *American Journal of Psychiatry, 138,* 601–607.

Berlin, F. S. (1983). Sex offenders: A biomedical perspective and a status report on biomedical treatment. In J. G. Greer & I. R. Stuart (Eds.), *The sexual aggressor: Current perspectives and treatment.* New York: Van Nostrand Reinhold.

Crown, S., & Lucas, C. J. (1976). Individual psychotherapy. In S. Crown (Ed.), *Psychosexual problems.* London: Academic Press.

Derogatis, L. R., & Melisaratos, N. (1979). The DSFI: A multidimensional measure of sexual functioning. *Journal of Sex and Marital Therapy, 5,* 244–281.

Freud, S. (1958). On beginning the treatment (Further recommendations on the technique of psychoanalysis). In J. Strachey, A. Freud, A. Strachey, & A. Tyson (Eds.), *The standard edition of the complete psychological works of Sigmund Freud.* London: Hogarth Press.

Freund, K., & Blanchard, R. (1989). Phallometric diagnosis of pedophilia. *Journal of Con-*

sulting and Clinical Psychology, 57, 100–105.

Jellinek, M. S., Murphy, J. M., Bishop, S., Poitrost, F., & Quinn, D. (1990). Protecting severely abused and neglected children—An unkept promise. *New England Journal of Medicine, 323,* 1628–1630.

Karacan, I., Scott, B., Salis, P., Attia, S., Ware, C., Altinel, A., & Williams, R. (1977). Nocturnal erections, differential diagnosis of impotence and diabetes. *Biological Psychiatry, 12,* 373–380.

Kinsey, A. G., Pomeroy, W. B., & Martin, C. E. (1948). *Sexual behavior in the human male.* Philadelphia: Saunders.

Krafft-Ebing, R. (1899). *Psychopathia sexualis with special reference to antipathic sexual instinct: A medico-forensic study.* London: Rebman Limited.

Leiblum, S. R., Rosen, R. C., & Piere, D. (1976). Group treatment format: Mixed sexual dysfunctions. *Archives of Sexual Behavior, 5,* 313–322.

Masson, J. M. (1984). *The assault on truth: Freud's suppression of the seduction theory.* New York: Straus and Giroux.

Masters, W. H., & Johnston, V. E. (1970). *Human sexual inadequacy.* Boston: Little, Brown.

Money, J. (1986). Longitudinal studies in clinical psychoendocrinology: Methodology. *Journal of Developmental and Behavioral Pediatrics, 7,* 31–34.

Schmidt, G., & Schorsch, E. (1981). Psychosurgery of sexually deviant patients: Review and analysis of new empirical finding. *Archives of Sexual Behavior, 10,* 301–323.

Shiavi, R. C., Schreiner-Engel, P., Mandeli, J., Schanzer, H., & Cohen, E. (1990). Healthy aging and male sexual function. *American Journal of Psychiatry, 147,* 766–771.

Spark, R., White, R., & Connolly, P. (1980). Impotence is not always psychogenic. *Journal of the American Medical Association, 243,* 750–755.

Swett, C., Surrey, J., & Cohen, C. (1990). Sexual and physical abuse histories and psychiatric symptoms among male psychiatric outpatients. *American Journal of Psychiatry, 147,* 632–636.

Multidimensional Assessment Of the Elderly Client

Nancy Morrow-Howell

10

O ften social workers and other social service professionals do not receive training in gerontology, yet find themselves serving older adults and their families. The demographic trends in our aging society make this situation even more likely to occur in coming years (Committee on an Aging Society, 1985). In a survey of National Association of Social Workers members, Peterson (1990) found that 26% of members currently work with older adults; 62% of members not specifically working with older adults reported that gerontological knowledge was required in their current jobs. At the same time that experienced workers are needing new training, educational programs are not preparing enough students for gerontological practice (Spaulding, 1989). The demand for personnel in the field of aging will increase well into the next century (Greene, Barusch, & Connelly, 1990), and steps must be taken to provide experienced professionals and students with the necessary knowledge and skills to work with older adults and their families.

This chapter is aimed at increasing gerontological knowledge among social service professionals. It focuses on assessment because this part of the helping process is particularly crucial with elderly clients. Due to the close interconnections of the biological, psychological, and social aspects of aging, assessment is often the most complicated part of the treatment process. Differentiating depression from dementia, discovering that paranoia stems from a hearing loss, understanding that embarrassment about incontinence is leading to social isolation—these are a few of the many challenges in accurately understanding the situation of an elderly client. Such knowledge and understanding lead to appropriate interventions; acquiring assessment knowledge and skills is imperative for any worker offering treatment to older clients and their families. Williams (1986) described how often the assessment process is overlooked, leading to the inappropriate use of long-term care, unnecessary nursing home placements, accelerated disability, and accelerated caregiver burnout.

Assessment of the elderly client often requires a medical examination, geropsychiatric workup, or evaluation of the home by an occupational therapist. In other words, the multiple impairments of the elderly cut across professional boundaries (Blazer, 1978), and social workers are not necessarily expert in all aspects of assessment. However, a social worker is often the first or only professional to see the client, assuming the role of primary clinician. Thus, social workers must have broad knowledge of aging so that important areas of need are not overlooked. Sometimes the social worker may refer the client for evaluation by other specialists, at least a physician, but often responsibility for treatment planning remains with the practitioner.

This chapter provides an overview of the process of assessing older adults by presenting seven dimensions of assessment: physical health, mental health, social support, physical environment, functioning, coping style, and formal service usage. In each dimension, basic knowledge is reviewed, helpful assessment instruments are presented, interviewing skills relevant to specific topics in the dimension are mentioned, and the use of allied professionals is addressed. One or two assessment instruments are briefly presented with ample referencing if more information is desired. Only selected interviewing skills are mentioned, not the many skills needed in the interviewing process. The few presented, which are simply basic counseling skills, are singled out because they are particularly relevant to assessing the elderly. This assessment process also relies on the practitioner's skills in rapidly building rapport. A multidimensional assessment is challenging to the older client both physically and emotionally. The establishment of a helping relationship is critical to the collection of reliable, thorough information as well as to the treatment that follows.

Physical Health

A good place to start a multidimensional assessment is with questions regarding physical health. This topic is not as threatening as others, and older clients are usually open about health problems. The practitioner must, however, remember that physical problems are not an inevitable part of old age and avoid stereotypic assumptions that prevent careful diagnosis and treatment of elderly clients. Medical conditions should be thoroughly evaluated by a competent physician, and if the client has not had a current medical evaluation, the practitioner should attain a thorough understanding of the reasons for lack of use of the health care system. Lack of resources, access problems, lack of assertiveness, fear of the findings, use of nontraditional health practices, or religious beliefs may be involved.

Given the prevalence of chronic health conditions among older adults (Allan & Brotman, 1981), practitioners should be familiar with the most common diseases affecting their clients—arthritis, osteoporosis, hypertension, congestive heart failure, and vision and hearing deficits. Sensory impairments must be ascertained early in the interview so that any possible environmental manipulations can be made to improve communication.

Assessment of medication usage is critical. Older adults often take a number of prescription medicines, and polypharmacy (the use of multiple medicines) may be at the root of problems of confusion or inability to function at maximum capacity. The practitioner must assess which medicines are being taken and when. The practitioner must also obtain a clear picture of over-the-counter drugs used. Assessment of diet should also be made, because many older clients may have been prescribed a special diet for high blood pressure or diabetes.

Use of health services includes questions about the client's current physician and satisfaction with health care services. Has the client been in regular contact with a primary physician? Does one primary physician prescribe and monitor medications? How many times and for what reasons has the client been hospitalized in recent years? How satisfied is the client with current health care?

The most useful measurement tools in the area of physical health are checklists that allow a systematic review of health conditions or medications. The Chronic Condition Checklist helps ascertain ongoing conditions and their effects on physical activity. The list includes 26 chronic health conditions, such as arthritis, emphysema, high blood pressure, and anemia. The presence of disease is ascertained as well as a rating of how the condition interferes with activities. This checklist, as well as one for medications, is found in an assessment instrument (the OARS instrument) developed by the Center for the Study of Aging and Human Development (1978) at Duke University. The OARS instrument, which is referred to several times below, is a widely used assessment instrument among clinicians and researchers. It is a multidimensional assessment tool, with questions covering five domains: physical health, functional capacity, mental health, social well-being, and economic well-being. Responses to questions in each area lead to ratings in each domain.

Skillful interviewing is critical in ascertaining the client's actual health behaviors. Ascertaining how well the client keeps medical appointments or complies with medicine or diet regimens is difficult because noncompliers may not be honest. When assessing medications, it is best to start by asking to see medicines currently being taken and recording information from the labels. Next, the practitioner can ask how the client takes medicines and if anyone assists with them. Practitioners may find it useful to normalize the difficulty of taking prescribed medicines by saying,

> Many people who take many medicines forget to take them sometimes or find it difficult to follow the prescribed schedule. Do you take medicines at the same time every day or is this difficult, given your daily schedule? In the past week, have you had any difficulties, like forgetting to take a pill (Haynes, Taylor, & Sackett, 1979)?

Similarly, compliance with diet is often approached more successfully if the practitioner attempts to normalize difficulties first and asks about barriers to compliance such as financial or preparation constraints. Information about the client's diet can be ascertained by discussing what foods the client prefers to prepare and what foods the client actually has had in the past 24 hours.

To confirm information about medicines, health conditions, or prescribed treatments, the practitioner may need to contact the client's primary physician. Clients will usually consent to having practitioners contact their physicians directly. When talking to a physician, the practitioner should indicate that client permission has been attained and the aim of the contact is to obtain information about the client's condition in order to assist the client with treatment planning. Specific, relevant questions should then be asked, rather than general queries about health status.

Geriatricians are physicians who are specifically trained to work with older adults. Practitioners must become familiar with geriatricians available in the community and be ready for referral, especially if they discover that a client has no primary physician or is dissatisfied with current care.

Mental Health

Two major components of a mental health assessment are cognitive ability and emotional health.

Cognitive Ability

Cognitive ability involves the client's orientation and memory. Practitioners must view confusion as an expression of an underlying condition or problem, not as a normal part of aging. If a thorough evaluation has not been completed on a client with cognitive impairment, the practitioner must begin an accurate assessment to arrive at a differential diagnosis. A competent physician must make the diagnosis, assisted by information gained from the practitioner's multidimensional assessment.

When an elderly client is confused, the practitioner must determine if the dementia is reversible or irreversible. Cognitive ability lost from the irreversible dementias of Alzheimer's disease (AD) and multiinfarct dementia (MID, caused by cerebrovascular accidents) cannot be regained. However, client functioning can be maximized and families helped to manage the situation as well as possible (Mace & Rabins, 1981). Reversible dementias can be alleviated. Understanding the underlying cause of a reversible dementia is challenging because so many possible causes exist: specific medications, medication interactions, certain physical illnesses, malnutrition, relocation trauma, depression, and so forth (Cohen & Eisdorfer, 1986).

In differential diagnosis, it is important to ascertain the onset and course of the confusion. For example, abrupt onset marks an MID brought on by a stroke or a reversible dementia brought on by physical illness or medication. A slow, gradual deterioration marks AD, whereas a stepwise course marks MID. Fluctuations during the day or from day to day mark an acute confusional state; although AD victims may worsen in the evening (called "sundowning"), the symptoms of AD do not change suddenly (Kane, Ouslander, & Abrass, 1984). Information from collateral sources, such as family and friends, is crucial with regard to determining onset and course and may be the only source of information about the confused patient. The practitioner must attempt to engage family members or friends in the assessment of the confused older client.

Many standardized mental exams can be used to assess disorientation and memory impairment. The Mental Status Questionnaire (MSQ) (Kahn, Goldfarb, Polack, & Peck, 1960) and the Mini-Mental State Exam (MMSE) (Folstein, Folstein, & McHugh, 1975) are among the many quick screening tools. In both exams, the older adult is asked to report information indicating orientation to place and time as well as to report historical data about self. The MSQ requires giving the name of the current and previous U.S. president, and the MMSE asks for some figure drawing.

Many older adults suffering from cognitive impairment can maintain a good social front, especially in the familiar setting of their homes. A specific mental exam is the surest way to detect problems. However, some practitioners may feel uncomfortable administering these exams. Certain skills make it easier. Mental status questions can be introduced by saying,

> These next questions may seem odd. Some are hard and some are easy, but I ask them to everyone because some people who are experiencing health problems [or the condition that is particular to the specific client at hand] have some trouble with memory.

Most clients will be cooperative and forge through the questions without resistance. The practitioner should affirm the effort associated with answering a question, whether the answer is wrong or right.

The social worker, as primary clinician, must often begin the cognitive assessment process by obtaining information in all areas of the multidimensional assessment and by performing a screening with a standardized measure. However, a diagnosis must be given by a competent physician. Physicians skilled in working with older adults can help differentiate between AD, MID, medication problems, and other acute confusional states. In urban areas, it is increasingly common to find geriatric assessment programs. These assessment teams, usually including a social worker, are gaining expertise in the diagnosis of cognitively impaired clients (Williams, 1986).

Emotional Health

Depression is the most pressing emotional health issue for older adults. In the older adult, depression must be diagnosed and treated seriously, as suicide rates are highest in the elderly population (Pollinger-Haas & Hendin, 1983). Practitioners will see clients who are in the midst of natural grieving processes, clients who are dissatisfied (or demoralized) with their current circumstances, and clients who have depressive illnesses (Blazer, 1985). Grieving and dissatisfaction have characteristics of depression, but symptoms are more severe and duration is longer with depressive illnesses.

Older adults who are grieving may be dysphoric, withdrawn, lack energy, and have cognitive disturbances for months; it may be two years before the person totally reengages in pleasurable activities. Throughout the grieving process, the person associates sadness, guilt, and thoughts about death directly with the memory of the lost loved one. Severe loss of self-esteem is not usual, and severe loss of function is not prolonged. If the grieving person has symptoms of major depression after six months or suicidal preoccupation at any time, professional intervention should be initiated (Billig, 1987).

When assessing depression, the practitioner must ascertain information about physical symptoms, emotional symptoms, and cognitive problems. The depressed older adult often presents with somatic complaints rather than with psychological symptoms. This phenomenon has been explained as a cohort effect (Blazer, 1980). It complicates the assessment of depression because older adults often have multiple physical problems and chronic pain. Thus, somatic symptoms that are suggestive of depression must be examined for physical causes before they are viewed as signs of depression. Sleeplessness is often a sign of depression, but for the older adult who may experience disturbed sleep or change in sleeping patterns for a number of reasons, this symptom must be evaluated carefully.

The practitioner must go beyond physical symptoms and investigate emotional and cognitive aspects of functioning. Emotional symptoms include sadness, hopelessness, helplessness, worthlessness, worry, and anxiety. Depressed older adults report loss of interest in activities and social connections. They report a lack of energy to take care of themselves and perform daily activities. Loss of appetite often occurs (Billig, 1987).

Cognitive impairment can be caused or exacerbated by depression. Depressed older adults report memory problems and are upset about memory loss. This impairment, sometimes called psuedodementia, must be differentiated from dementia. When taking mental status examinations, depressed older adults exhibit a lack of effort and give "don't know" answers, whereas demented clients try harder but give wrong answers. Impairment resulting from depression does not worsen at night, whereas sundowning is common with dementia. Depressed individuals have equal loss in ability to recall remote and recent events, but demented individuals lose recent memory first. Depressed adults often withdraw socially, whereas demented adults may stay socially involved (Wells, 1979).

Standard diagnostic criteria, as presented in the *Diagnostic and Statistical Manual of Mental Disorders* (American Psychiatric Association, 1987), are helpful in reviewing symptoms, onset, and duration of depression. However, the practitioner must be aware of some differences between depressed younger and older adults. Compared with younger people, depressed older adults will have more somatic complaints, less expression of sad feelings, greater loss of self-esteem, more pronounced withdrawal and apathy, and less expression of guilt (Kane, Ouslander, & Abrass, 1984). Older adults may not even use the word "depression" at all, as this word is not familiar to the current cohort (Billig, 1987). Finally, older adults are more likely to experience cognitive impairment due to depression, and it is sometimes difficult to differentiate the two conditions.

The most commonly used depression measures, like the Beck Depression Inventory (Beck, Ward, Mendelson, Mock, & Erbaugh, 1961) and the Zung Self-Rating Depression Scale (Zung, 1965), were designed and validated on younger samples, and their use with older adults is questioned by some. The Geriatric Depression Scale (GDS) was developed specifically for use with older adults and is currently being widely used (Sheikh & Yesavage, 1986; Brink, Yesavage, Owen, Heersema, Adey, & Rose, 1982). The GDS has questions regarding hopelessness, emptiness, energy level, boredom, and helplessness; scoring indicates whether depression should be suspected.

When the client is depressed, the practitioner may find it difficult to administer any depression inventory, as each question seems to further the negative state of the client. The practitioner must be sensitive to this phenomenon and should certainly avoid ending the interview with the client in a vulnerable state. The practitioner must slowly move out of this part of the assessment by turning the client's thoughts to more externally oriented, less negative content. Using some information gained about a specific problem related to the depression, such as lack of appetite or lack of energy, the practitioner may ask a question that is in context but begins the transition to a different type of discussion. For example, "You mentioned that you have trouble getting out of bed in the morning. I'm wondering if you could tell me what you do on a typical day when you are able to get up?" The practitioner can then use this information to continue the transition. "It sounds as though you watch quite a bit of television.

What programs do you prefer?" This type of interviewing should proceed until the client has regained control and assumed a more positive affect.

Inclusion of a physician in the mental health assessment is advisable when the differential diagnosis of dementia and depression is difficult and when depression is marked. Medication and health problems are often involved. Geropsychiatrists and geropsychiatric units in hospitals are growing in number; practitioners should be familiar with resources in their communities.

Social Support

Assessing social networks is clearly the domain of social work. The profession has always appreciated the need to understand the social context of clients. For the older adult, this means knowing the quantity and quality of social contacts. Quantity is easier to assess than quality; it can be done by asking questions regarding living arrangements and the identification and location of relatives. Ascertaining information about friends is equally important, given that peer relationships are closely associated with psychological well-being (Larson, Mannell, & Zuzanek, 1986). The client can be asked about membership in religious and other social organizations.

Quality of social interactions is harder to capture, but clients can be asked directly about their feelings of closeness to friends and relatives, if they have a confidant, if they would like to see people more or less often, if they find their relationships satisfactory. It is not safe to assume that a person is lonely on the basis of information about frequency of contact with others. Clients can be asked directly if they are often lonely or if they are satisfied with the way things are.

The assessment should include questions about the people available to provide care to the client. It cannot be assumed that the existence of relatives means that caregiving is available. Kulys and Tobin (1980) documented that older adults sometimes identify someone as a primary caregiver, but when that person is asked directly, he or she does not see him- or herself in that role. A relative may not have feelings of affection or obligation sufficient to motivate the provision of care. Thus, practitioners must be cautious in their assumptions about caregiving potential and pursue the topic through direct conversations with relatives. Practitioners must withhold judgment about relatives who are not enthusiastic caregivers—families have had long histories together, and providing care to needy parents out of feelings of love may not necessarily emerge from a particular family's development (Silverstone & Burack-Weiss, 1983).

The roles friends and relatives assume in caregiving should be determined. Do they meet instrumental or affectional needs? That is, do they assist the client in the physical activities of daily living or do they provide socialization and affection? Often caregivers do both. Practitioners cannot assume that caregivers are competently performing the caregiving tasks they have undertaken. Caregiver limitations must be assessed: caregivers are sometimes too frail or weak to do the job, too mentally disoriented to be depended on for medicine administration, too busy with other duties to be available to the extent required by the circumstances.

The caregiver's preferences about the caregiving situation should be ascertained, because many caregivers assume the job with reservations. Most caregivers experience problems of their own as a result of caregiving, and caregiver stress is well documented (Cantor, 1983). Practitioners should not view client care as adequate if caregivers are too burdened by their own responsibilities; this situation implies a vulnerable caregiver and a vulnerable caregiving network. Stressed caregivers need to be viewed as clients themselves, and their needs and desires should be assessed.

Issues of abuse and neglect arise with the assessment of the caregiving network. Accurate assessment of abuse and neglect is difficult, and the elderly, the caregiver, and even the human services agencies themselves may be reluctant to identify the problem (Rathbone-McCuan, 1980). Factors associated with elder abuse have been identified. The profile of an abused victim is as follows: female, older than 80, functionally dependent, and living with relatives. Risk is increased with dependency of the elder on the abuser, history of abuse in the family, life crises in the family, and environmental factors (Fulmer & O'Malley, 1987). When the practitioner encounters situations in which abuse or neglect is suspected, the older adult's mental competency, functional status, health status, and sources of assistance must be ascertained; these areas have been covered as routine parts of the multidimensional assessment. The assessment of imminent harm is most pressing. This assessment in turn determines the urgency of intervention. Fulmer and O'Malley (1987) suggest three circumstances that indicate harm is imminent: (1) the presence of life-threatening medical problems, including delirium, profuse bleeding, inability to walk or transfer, inability to eat or drink, signs of head trauma, deformity indicating possible bone fracture, indications of acute illness, such as fever, shortness of breath, and dehydration; (2) the presence of an unsafe environment, in which heat, water, or food is lacking, and situations in which a confused client is not able safely to use gas stoves or heaters; and (3) the presence of an individual with unimpeded access to the elderly person who has seriously harmed the elderly person in the past. The Elder Assessment Instrument was developed by Fulmer and O'Malley (1987) to aid in the assessment of maltreatment. This tool includes checklists to review systematically evidence of physical and emotional abuse, evidence of serious neglect, abusive actions on the part of the caregiver, financial exploitation, and physical-environment problems.

Many instruments are available to measure social resources. One of the most commonly used is the Social Resource Rating Scale, a part of the OARS instrument (Center for the Study of Aging and Human Development, 1978). A newer instrument is the Lubben Social Network Index (LSNI) (Lubben, 1988). Both instruments tap the quality and quantity of informal support through questions about amount of contact, sources of assistance, and closeness of relationships. Caregiving strain should be assessed with the caregiver directly. Several instruments are readily available, including the Burden Interview (Zarit, Reever, & Bach-Peterson, 1980) and the Caregiver Strain Index (Robinson, 1983). Both instruments query the caregiver about subjective states of discomfort, like guilt, as well as problems such as lack of sleep and loss of social activities.

Physical Environment

It is very beneficial to assess clients in their homes. Office or telephone contact is less informative than is driving through the client's neighborhood, noting access to services, proximity to neighbors, and socioeconomic status of the locale. The practitioner can note the external condition of the house and stairs. Once inside, it is important to note safety conditions, including smoke detectors, uncluttered exits, stairways and bannisters, heating/cooling deficiencies, and insect or rodent infestations. Smells of incontinence or pets may be obvious. It is possible to overhear telephone conversations or see interactions among family members. Direct observation fills out the information gained about the client.

Most clients are receptive to home visits if the practitioner expresses genuine interest and a respectful manner. Often, clients will offer a trip through the house to see photos or hobbies or to fix a cup of coffee. It is very useful to take advantage of such trips to note the client's ability to walk as well as the physical condition of the house. In the bathroom, the practitioner may see signs of plumbing problems. In the bedroom, smells of incontinence may be obvious. In the kitchen, a glimpse of the pantry or refrigerator provides information about food preparation. Of course, practitioners should take advantage of naturally occurring opportunities and not force a house tour on a reluctant client.

A list of things to observe helps ensure a thorough and systematic assessment. Items should include insect or rodent infestation, dilapidation, clutter, steps or railing in disrepair, and whether the home is in a high-traffic or high-crime area (Lubben, 1984). Most items can be observed, thus obviating the need for direct questioning.

Occupational therapists' expertise lies in assessing homes for safety and accessibility. Occupational therapists can recommend modifications to bathrooms and kitchens to make them safe and usable. They may also have knowledge about community resources to help with costs. They can recommend equipment to maximize function and train clients to use such equipment properly. Some occupational therapy programs will conduct evaluations in the home, and many home health programs provide such services.

Functional Abilities

The bottom line of the assessment described thus far is how well the client gets along on a day-to-day basis. Given the client's physical condition, mental and emotional status, and social and physical environment, how well can the client perform the activities of daily living? It is consistent with social work's professional perspective to view function as an interaction of the client's innate ability and psychosocial/physical environment; any number of causes can underlie dysfunction (Kane, Ouslander, & Abrass, 1984). The goal of the assessment is to understand the causes of dysfunction so that client function can be maximized and appropriate services put in place.

Activities of daily living include eating, bathing, grooming, toileting, walking, stair climbing, transferring, taking medications, telephoning, transportation, shopping, meal preparation, money management, housekeeping, and laundry. Ascertaining functional ability in each area is challenging. Who says what the client can do, the client, the family, or a professional? Ratings of functional ability differ by rater, with older adults overstating their abilities and relatives understating abilities relative to the judgments of nursing personnel (Rubenstein, Schairer, Weiland, & Kane, 1984). An elderly woman may claim that she can bathe herself, although a family member may say she cannot. Differences exist because of motivations (resisting service vs. wanting service). Perceptions of reality also differ—sometimes because of confusion, sometimes because of differing standards and values. Practitioners will do best to gather information both from the older adult *and* from a family member.

The role of values must be clear when assessing functional ability; that is, what constitutes acceptable bathing, grooming, and housekeeping standards? Practitioners often operate from standards different from those of the elderly client and his or her family, and differences in standards should not influence perceptions of functional ability. In other words, a practitioner cannot assess a client as unable to perform housekeeping tasks if the house is not as clean as the practitioner thinks is acceptable. This client may have always kept his or her house in this way, and the state of the house may have nothing to do with functional ability. Client preference must be a guiding principle—can the client do what he or she wants to do in his or her house, or are things not getting done because of the client's limitations? If the client cannot keep the house as he or she is accustomed to and prefers, the practitioner can assess dysfunction in housekeeping. At some point, safety and health issues challenge self-determination and intervention is required. But during the assessment process, the practitioner's job is to determine the client's functional ability and preferences so that appropriate treatment can be planned.

Besides reviewing all of the activities of daily living, it is helpful to ask clients what their typical day is like, what they do for enjoyment, and what they would like to do if they could. A central concept is one of change in activities. Has the person always been inactive or have activities been dropped in elder years due to loss of ability to drive or health limitations? Has the person given up a cherished hobby because of recent physical limitations?

Many standardized functional instruments have been developed since the pioneering work of Katz (Katz, Ford, & Moskowitz, 1963) and Lawton (Lawton & Brody, 1969). Standardized scales have been developed for the reliable measurement of functioning, and researchers use these scales verbatim to collect data (see Kane & Kane, 1981). However, practitioners often need to go beyond the exact wording of the questions for a more thorough clinical picture. For example, one could use the OARS functional assessment as a guideline, in that it offers a comprehensive list of functional areas and three levels of ability (without help, with some help, and cannot perform) within each area (Center for the Study of Aging and Human Development, 1978). The instrument is based on self-report; open-ended probing can embellish the clinical picture and lead to a more accurate understanding. Asking about the use of mechanical devices is helpful here, to ascertain whether the client has equipment such as a bathtub rail, raised commode or bedside commode, walker, and so forth.

Toileting is a particularly sensitive area of questioning in the functional domain, but its importance cannot be ignored, given the frequency of incontinence in older adults (Ouslander, 1981). Interviewing skills include normalizing the situation for people on certain medications or with particular health conditions. For example, the clinician may say, "Often people with health or mobility problems have trouble getting to the bathroom on time; does this ever happen to you?" Practitioners may need to overcome their own embarrassment to help clients feel comfortable in discussing this problem. Some types of incontinence are reversible, and some can only be managed as best as possible. The first step, however, is to assess the nature of the problem and solicit the help of a competent physician.

Coping Styles

A client's coping styles are difficult to learn about, as they are expressed subtly and can really be known only over time. Coping styles affect physical health, mental health, and social networks—all of the assessment areas discussed above. The practitioner can learn about coping styles as the assessment in each area progresses. Coping styles are revealed through statements such as "I just pray to the Lord that I'll get by" or "Thank heaven for my friends. Without them, I couldn't do this." Information about coping styles, including religiosity, can be gained through clients' comments during the interview. However, some direct questioning is called for, given the importance of coping styles and religiosity in the lives of older adults.

In asking about coping, the intent is to understand how the client handles everyday life stresses, major crises, and transitions (Kahana, Fairchild, & Kahana, 1982). Coping styles are generally consistent across adulthood and into late life, and past patterns of coping provide evidence for future patterns. A complete evaluation of coping abilities involves prior history of stressful events and the client's resources in coping with them (Gallagher, Thompson, & Levy, 1980). This assessment results in an understanding of both strengths and weaknesses—strengths that can be used and weaknesses that must be addressed in implementing treatment plans.

Religion offers a powerful coping mechanism to many clients, and the practitioner should understand the role of religion in the client's life. Questions such as the following may be helpful: Do you identify with a religion? How important is religion in your life? Do you attend church or keep in contact with other church members? How do you prefer to worship?

Several instruments are specifically designed to evaluate coping styles of older adults (see Kahana & Kahana's ECRC Coping Scale and Quayhagen & Chiriboga's Geriatric Coping Schedule, reviewed in Kahana, Fairchild, & Kahana, 1982). These instruments are used largely for research purposes, but they suggest techniques to learn about coping mechanisms (e.g., presenting a stressful scenario and asking the client what she or he might do to handle it). They also list specific coping mechanisms (e.g., talking with others, seeking information, drinking/ smoking, expecting the worst, praying) that can be reviewed with the client to ascertain frequency of use. Several open-ended questions can be used to begin to understand the client's coping style: When you are under pressure, what do you do to take care of yourself? How do you cope with a major crisis, for example, as you did when your wife (husband) passed away? How have you handled hard times in the past?

Formal Service Usage

It is important to be clear about the formal services that the client is currently receiving, both in the home and outside the home. A generic service checklist (including nursing care, personal care, home-delivered meals, and transportation) is helpful in facilitating a thorough review. Sometimes the client does not know what agency or type of professional is providing help; the client knows only that a certain person (whom she or he knows only by first name) comes two times a week and performs certain tasks. Often it is unclear who is paying for the service. Open-ended probing, using knowledge about the specific resources in the community, can help the practitioner know, for example, that a home health aide is being supported through Medicaid funds from the state.

During the assessment process, it is important to begin to understand the client's attitude toward the service system. Information about the client's satisfaction with services received and the client's experience with the service system should be ascertained. If no services are being received, the client can be asked if she or he has ever tried to get a service or thought about using one.

Financial information is critical in understanding the current or potential use of services. Asking for financial information later in the interview, after the client is more comfortable with the practitioner, may lead to more success. Sometimes it is helpful to ask general questions about finances first: "Do you have enough income to meet your needs comfortably? Do you have difficulty making ends meet?" If a problem is acknowledged, it is then easier to ask for details so that the extent of the problem can be evaluated. If a person reports no financial strain, more information may not be necessary until a specific plan calls for the expenditure of money. It is wise to ask if a patient often goes without a medicine because she or he cannot afford it or whether the person must shortchange other budget areas because of the cost of medicine.

Moving from Assessment to Treatment

The goal of the assessment process is to identify need areas for the development of a treatment plan. As a way of ending the assessment process and moving to treatment planning, the practitioner can summarize the concerns that the client has expressed throughout the interview process and ask the client to identify any others that might exist. Successful intervention usually begins with the client-expressed problems. Over time, practitioner-observed problems can skillfully be introduced to the client and accepted for intervention. Most such problems are probably long term, and it is not necessary for the professional to push for immediate intervention, which might jeopardize the willingness of the client to continue involvement with the professional (Fulmer & O'Malley, 1987). An exception to this rule would be a critical deficit in the client's situation, for example, a problem with medicine mismanagement or unsafe wandering. After client-expressed concerns are enumerated, the practitioner may express an urgent concern in a nonalienating manner.

Ethnic-sensitive knowledge and skills must be added to those presented in this article. Although the number of minorities among older adults is relatively small due to their reduced life expectancy, minority persons are a rapidly growing segment of the elderly population (Jackson, 1980). Minority elderly are more likely to have health and mental health problems stemming from inequities in the health/social care system. Further, impoverishment decreases access to needed services. The minority client may not trust a nonminority worker with the sensitive content of the assessment. Thus, the nonminority practitioner is faced with the challenge of assessing a multiproblem situation with a jeopardized relationship.

Conclusion

The assessment process described in this article is an ideal that cannot be realized in all situations. The process takes from one and a half to two hours to complete; sometimes this amount of time is not available, or clients may not have the stamina to proceed this long. The assessment may need to be broken into several sessions, but again, this is not always possible. The assessment outlined here is intended as a framework for practitioners to use during the time available to begin a thorough and systematic collection of information about an elderly client. No "one-shot" assessment will provide a complete picture of a person; the real picture will be filled out only over time.

As a final caution, having an assessment tool with comprehensive and relevant content does not assure a good assessment. A good tool goes hand-in-hand with good interviewing skills. In addition to some of the skills mentioned in this article, practitioners must have the ability to build rapport, ask effective open-ended questions, introduce difficult content, and keep the client on track while showing interest. Practitioners will find that more skill is often needed in interviewing older clients, who require more time and are more likely to have physical and mental impairments that inhibit the interviewing process.

REFERENCES

Allan, C., & Brotman, H. (1981). *Chartbook on aging in America.* The 1981 White House Conference on Aging, Washington, DC.

American Psychiatric Association. (1987). *Diagnostic and statistical manual of mental disorders* (3rd ed., rev.). Washington, DC: Author.

Beck, A. T., Ward, C. H., Mendelson, M., Mock, J. E., & Erbaugh, J. (1961). An inventory for measuring depression. *Archives of General Psychiatry. 4,* 561–571.

Billig, N. (1987). *To be old and sad.* Lexington, MA: Lexington Books.

Blazer, D. (1978). The use of the OARS multidimensional functional assessment procedure in clinical training. *Multidimensional functional assessment: The OARS methodology* (pp. 121–125). Center for the Study of Aging and Human Development, Duke University Medical Center, Durham, NC.

Blazer, D. (1980). The diagnosis of depression in the elderly. *Journal of the American Geriatric Society, 28*(2), 52–58.

Blazer, D. (1985). Depressive illness in late life. In *America's aging: Health in an older society* (Institute of Medicine and National Research Council). Washington, DC: National Press.

Brink, T., Yesavage, J., Owen, L., Heersema, P., Adey, M., & Rose, T. (1982). Screening tests for geriatric depression. *Clinical Gerontologist, 1,* 37–43.

Cantor, M. (1983). Strain among caregivers: A study of experiences in the United States. *Gerontologist, 23,* 597–604.

Center for the Study of Aging and Human Development. (1978). *Multidimensional function-*

al assessment: The OARS methodology. Duke University Medical Center, Durham, NC.

Cohen, D., & Eisdorfer, C. (1986). Dementing disorders. In E. Calkins, P. Davis, & A. Ford (Eds.), *The practice of geriatrics* (pp. 194–205). Philadelphia: W. B. Saunders.

Committee on an Aging Society. (1985). *America's aging: Health in an older society.* Washington, DC: National Academy Press.

Folstein, M. F., Folstein, S., & McHugh, P. R. (1975). Mini-mental state: A practice method for grading the cognitive status of patients for the clinician. *Journal of Psychiatric Research, 12,* 189–198.

Fulmer, T., & O'Malley, T. (1987). *Inadequate care of the elderly.* New York: Springer Publishing.

Gallagher, D., Thompson, L., & Levy, S. (1980). Clinical psychological assessment of older adults. In L. W. Poon (Ed.), *Aging in the 1980s: Psychological issues* (pp. 19–40). Washington, DC: American Psychological Associates.

Greene, R., Barusch, A., & Connelly, R. (1990). *Social work and gerontology: Status report.* Washington, DC: Association for Gerontology in Higher Education.

Haynes, R. B, Taylor, D. W., & Sackett, D. L. (1979). *Compliance in health care.* Baltimore, MD: Johns Hopkins University Press.

Jackson, J. (1980). *Minorities and aging.* Belmont, CA: Wadsworth.

Kahana, E., Fairchild, T., & Kahana, B. (1982). Adaptation. In D. Mangen & W. Peterson (Eds.), *Research instruments in social gerontology* (vol. 1) (pp. 145–193). Minneapolis: University of Minnesota Press.

Kahn, R. L., Goldfarb, A. I., Polack, M., & Peck, A. (1960). Brief objective measures for the determination of mental status in the aged. *American Journal of Psychiatry, 117,* 326–328.

Kane, R., & Kane, R. (1981). *Assessing the elderly: A practical guide to measurement.* Lexington, MA: Lexington Books.

Kane, R., Ouslander, J., & Abrass, I. (1984). *Essentials of clinical geriatrics.* New York: McGraw-Hill.

Katz, S., Ford, A. B., & Moskowitz, R. W. (1963). Studies of illness in the aged: The index of ADL. *Journal of the American Medical Association, 185,* 914–919.

Kulys, R., & Tobin, S. (1980). Older people and their responsible others. *Social Work, 25,* 138–145.

Larson, R., Mannell, R., & Zuzanek, J. (1986). Daily well-being of older adults with friends and family. *Psychological Aging, 1,* 117–126.

Lawton, M. P., & Brody, E. (1969). Assessment of older people: Self-maintaining and instrumental activities of daily living. *Gerontologist, 9,* 179–186.

Lubben, J. (1984). *Health and psychosocial assessment instruments for community-based long term care: The California Multipurpose Senior Services Project experience.* MSSP Evaluation Unit, University of California at Berkeley, Berkeley, CA.

Lubben, J. (1988). Assessing social networks among elderly populations. *Family and Community Health, 11*(3), 42–52.

Mace, N. L., & Rabins, P. (1981). *The 36-hour day.* Baltimore, MD: Johns Hopkins University Press.

Ouslander, J. G. (1981). Urinary incontinence in the elderly. *West Journal of Medicine, 135,* 482–491.

Peterson, D. (1990). Personnel to serve the aging in the field of social work. *Social Work, 35,* 412–416.

Pollinger-Haas, A., & Hendin, H. (1983). Suicide among older people: Projections for the future. *Suicide and life-threatening behavior, 13,* 147–154.

Rathbone-McCuan, E. (1980). Elderly victims of family violence and neglect. *Social Casework, 61,* 296–304.

Robinson, B. (1983). Validation of a caregiver strain index. *Journal of Gerontology, 38,* 344–348.

Rubenstein, L. Z., Schairer, C., Weiland, G. D., & Kane, R. (1984). Systematic biases in functional status assessment of elderly adults: Effects of different data sources. *Journal of Gerontology, 39,* 686–691.

Sheikh, J., & Yesavage, J. (1986). Geriatric depression scale. *Clinical Gerontologist, 5,* 165–173.

Silverstone, B., & Burack-Weiss, A. (1983). *Social work practice with the frail elderly and their families.* Springfield, IL: Charles C Thomas.

Spaulding, E. C. (1989). *Statistics on social work education in the United States: 1988.* Washington, DC: Council on Social Work Education.

Wells, C. E. (1979). Pseudodementia. *American Journal of Psychiatry, 136,* 895–900.

Williams, F. (1986). Comprehensive assessment of frail elderly in relation to needs for long-term care. In E. Calkins, P. J. Davis, & A. B. Ford (Eds.), *The practice of geriatrics* (pp. 84–92). Philadelphia: W. B. Saunders.

Zarit, S., Reever, K., & Bach-Peterson, J. (1980). Relatives of the impaired elderly: Correlates of feelings of burden. *Gerontologist, 20,* 649–655.

Zung, W. W. K. (1965). Self-rating depression scale. *Archives of General Psychiatry, 12,* 63–70.

Part 3

Assessment of Specific Problems

The Disruptive Child: Problems of Definition

Harriette C. Johnson

11

C urrently little agreement exists among professionals on how to differentiate among various kinds of disruptive behavior in children. Is a child's troublesome behavior evidence of antisocial character or attention deficit and hyperactivity, or is it simply oppositional? While awaiting definitions that can be widely agreed upon, social workers must continue to refer children for evaluation and treatment, coordinate a child's treatment plan in the capacity of case manager, treat the child, and work with the child's family. Differences of opinion about the nature of various problem behaviors, combined with the proliferation of evaluative methods and tools during the past decade, have made it extremely difficult to decide what the problem is, where to refer for evaluation, and what treatments are needed.

Accurate diagnosis is important because different interventions are helpful, depending on the nature of the problem behavior. The literature on the damage that can result from inaccurate diagnosis is extensive (Johnson, 1980, 1987a). Questions of etiology, assessment techniques, and treatment choice have also been reviewed in the literature (Johnson, 1987b, 1989). The purpose of this chapter is to clarify issues pertaining to the definition of disruptive behavior. In order to achieve this purpose, different approaches to defining behavior disorders are summarized, and the most widely used definitions, those proposed in the *Diagnostic and Statistical Manual of Mental Disorders* (DSM-III-R) (American Psychiatric Association, 1987), are outlined. Research evidence that supports or fails to support these definitions is reviewed, and implications for case evaluation are considered.

Approaches to Defining Behavior Disorders

The concept of "behavior disorder" poses some knotty questions. First, are a child's behaviors that are viewed as problematic by clinicians, parents, teachers, or acquaintances really the manifestation of a "disorder," or do they simply represent deviance from norms established and defined by the particular culture? Kagan (1984) has shown that behaviors that are normative in some cultures are considered deviant or pathological in other cultures. For example, seven-year-old boys in New Guinea are expected to perform fellatio on older boys, repeatedly, over a period of several years. In that particular culture, such behavior is considered a necessary precursor of later heterosexual competence. In American culture, however, a young boy who repeatedly engages in sexual activities with older boys is likely to be regarded by clinicians and laypersons as deviant or possibly pathological. The editors of DSM-III-R underscore the importance of exercising caution when applying DSM categories to persons from cultural backgrounds different from the clinician's: "The clinician . . . should apply DSM-III-R with open-mindedness to the presence of distinctive cultural patterns and sensitivity to the possibility of unintended bias" (American Psychiatric Association, 1987, pp. xxvi–xxvii).

Chess and Thomas (1984) circumvent the problem of absolutist definitions by viewing behavior disorders as the product of poorness of fit between the capacities of the child and environmental expectations and demands. The disorder, in this framework, lies at the point of intersection between the child and the environment, not within the child. In a similar vein, Jessor and Jessor (1977) propose an expanded view of problem behavior from the vantage point of social psychology: Problem behavior is "a nexus at which diverse sources of influence intersect" (p. 4), such as societal changes; developmental phases of youth; norms and values learned from family, peer role models, and television; and opportunities for action, to name a few of these many influences.

The DSM-III-R represents another approach to definition of problem behavior. Although the overall approach utilized in DSM-III-R is to locate problems within individuals rather than viewing them from the framework of goodness of fit with the environment, a careful reading of the work shows that the authors are cognizant of person–environment interactions. The issue of the appropriateness of DSM-III-R as a social work tool is addressed elsewhere and is beyond the scope of this article, except to note that DSM-III-R classifications are used in the discussion that follows because, by default, it is the "only game in town" (Kutchins & Kirk, 1987). Neither social work nor any other discipline, so far, has produced alternative definitions that have gained widespread acceptance.

144

According to DSM-III-R, most problem behaviors occur in so-called "normal" children some of the time. Whether the behavior is regarded as a symptom of pathology is closely related to its *intensity* (how frequently it occurs and with what degree of magnitude) and its *duration*. The classification of problem behaviors is complicated by the fact that many behaviors appear in several diagnostic categories and that most diagnostic categories include several problem behaviors. These behaviors may appear in varying configurations in any particular child and may also appear as short-term reactions, under DSM-III-R categories of "adjustment disorder with disturbance of conduct or childhood or adolescent antisocial behavior."

In most instances, DSM-III-R views problem behavior as one symptom among several for various clinical disorders. Problem behaviors are part of the presenting problem for almost every category of childhood disorders. For example, refusal to attend school or camp is a behavior that is characteristic of anxiety disorders; atypical movements are characteristic of pervasive developmental disorder, mental retardation, tic disorders, or stereotype/habit disorder; avoidance of social contact typifies avoidant disorder, schizoid disorder, and pervasive developmental disorder. Problem behavior, then, cuts across diagnostic lines.

The one exception to this view is DSM-III-R's category called disruptive behavior disorders, in which the behaviors themselves define the "disorder" rather than being symptoms of some other disorder.

Characteristics of Disruptive Behavior Disorders

According to DSM-III-R, disruptive behavior "syndromes" (constellations of characteristics) have at least one chief feature in common: their effect on the surrounding environment. The DSM-III-R category of disruptive behavior disorders includes three subclasses: *attention-deficit hyperactivity disorder* (ADHD), *conduct disorder,* and *oppositional defiant disorder* (American Psychiatric Association, 1987). These syndromes are characterized by behavior that is socially disruptive and is often more distressing to others than to the people with the disorders. (The category of attention deficit disorder [ADD] without hyperactivity, grouped with attention deficit disorder with hyperactivity in the original version of the DSM-III, has been separated from ADHD in the revised version because children with ADD without hyperactivity are not disruptive.)

Attention-Deficit Hyperactivity Disorder

This disorder is characterized by developmentally inappropriate degrees of inattention, impulsiveness, and hyperactivity (American Psychiatric Association, 1987). Persons with ADHD have difficulty sticking to tasks as well as organizing and completing work. Often they do not listen to or follow through on instructions. Work is done carelessly and impulsively, and the product is likely to be messy. Children with ADHD blurt out answers to questions before the question has been completely stated, talk out of turn, interrupt adults and other children frequently, and fail to wait for their turn in group situations. They have trouble remaining seated, run in the classroom, fidget, manipulate objects, and twist and wiggle in their seats. They are often very noisy. They frequently instigate fights and are often in the vortex of group conflict. They talk excessively, interrupt or intrude upon other family members, and may be accident-prone. They may grab objects (not maliciously) or engage in potentially dangerous actions without stopping to think about the consequences, such as running into the street without looking or riding a skateboard over rough terrain. Other characteristics of children with ADHD include low self-esteem, mood lability, low frustration tolerance, and temper tantrums.

In preschool children, overactivity and frequent shifting from one activity to another without having completed the first are common. In older children, excessive fidgeting and restlessness are more common than the gross motor overactivity seen in younger children. In adolescents, impulsivity is often displayed by initiating spur-of-the-moment activities instead of carrying out previous commitments (e.g., going for a ride with friends instead of doing homework).

Attention-deficit hyperactivity disorder typically persists throughout childhood and frequently continues into and throughout adulthood. The DSM-III-R estimates that approximately 3% of children have ADHD; other estimates of prevalence have ranged as high as 14.3% (Schachar, Rutter, & Smith, 1981).

The disorder has been studied extensively and with increasing frequency and has become the most widely researched psychiatric condition of childhood. Between 1960 and 1975, 2,000 articles were published on children with hyperactivity or minimal brain dysfunction, nomenclature that was replaced in 1980 by attention-deficit disorder with and without hyperactivity (ADD and ADD-H) and in 1987 by attention-deficit hyperactivity disorder (ADHD). Between 1977 and 1980, 7,000 articles were published (Weiss, 1985).

Conduct Disorder

The essential feature of conduct disorder is a persistent pattern of conduct in which the basic rights of others and age-appropriate societal norms or rules are violated (American Psychiatric Association, 1987). The criterion of persistence is of paramount importance because the majority of children and adolescents commit antisocial acts occasionally. Conduct disorders typically appear in several situations—at home, school, with peers, and in the community. Physical aggression is common, and children with this diagnosis may be physically cruel to people or animals. They may set fires, steal, mug, snatch purses, or engage in extortion or armed robbery. In later adolescence, they may engage in physical violence in the form of rape, assault, or, rarely, homicide. Stealing may vary from "borrowing" others' possessions to shoplifting, forgery, and breaking and entering homes or cars. Children with conduct disorder commonly lie and cheat in games and in schoolwork. They are often truant and may also run away from home. They frequently use illegal substances or tobacco on a regular basis. They show little or no concern for the feelings and well-being of others and may fail to show remorse or guilt for harm they have inflicted. They are prone to inform on their companions and to try to pin blame on others for their own infractions.

Usually, these children have low self-esteem, despite projecting an image of toughness. Characteristically, they are irritable and reckless, have temper outbursts, and are unable to tolerate much frustration. Usually, their academic achievement is below levels expected for their age and intelligence. Frequently, they meet criteria for attention-deficit hyperactivity and/or specific developmental disorders (learning disabilities), diagnoses that are carried concurrently (not preempted).

Conduct disorder refers to impaired functioning (whether in the child–environment interface or in the child) and differs from delinquency, a legal term referring either to offenses related to juvenile status (using alcohol, driving a car before the legal age limit, staying out late, truancy) or to criminal offenses (stealing, dealing drugs, committing violent acts against another person) (Kazdin, 1987). Not all conduct disorders come to the attention of the correctional system, nor do all delinquents have conduct disorder. Some delinquents may be functioning competently in relation to the conditions that exist in their particular environment (Kazdin, 1987).

Conduct disorder usually begins before puberty in males but after puberty in females. According to DSM-III-R estimates, approximately 9% of males and 2% of females younger than 18 years old are thought to have the disorder. It is more common in children whose parents have antisocial personality disorder and/or alcohol dependence than in the general population. Some differences in conduct disorders between sexes have been noted. Females with conduct disorder more frequently lie, run away from home, and abuse substances, whereas males with conduct disorder more often engage in vandalism, fighting, and stealing and frequently pose discipline problems in school (Robins, 1986). In boys, conduct disorder at an early age is predictive primarily of adult antisocial behavior. In girls, early conduct disorder predicts antisocial tendencies, but also a variety of other pathological outcomes involving "internalizing" symptoms, such as major depression, dysthymia, phobia, and obsessive–compulsive disorders (Robins, 1986).

According to DSM-III-R criteria, there are three categories of conduct disorder: the group type, in which conduct problems occur mainly as a group activity with peers; the solitary aggressive type, characterized by physical aggression toward both children and adults initiated by the child and not by a group, and the undifferentiated type, a subtype for all other children or adolescents with conduct disorder who do not fit into one of the two previous categories. As these children grow older, they are likely to become involved in repeated conflict with the law and to be adjudicated delinquents or persons (children, juveniles) in need of supervision (PINS, CHINS, or JINS, depending on the state of residence). They may be placed on probation or eventually in correctional facilities for youth. Children with conduct disorder are at high risk for antisocial personality disorder as adults.

Oppositional Defiant Disorder

This disorder is characterized by a pattern of negativistic, hostile, and defiant behavior, without more serious violation of the basic rights of others (American Psychiatric Association, 1987). Children with this diagnosis are argumentative with adults, often lose their temper, swear, are often angry and resentful, and are easily annoyed by others. They often defy rules and adult requests and deliberately annoy others. They tend to blame others for difficulties arising from their own behavior.

Usually, the child does not see him- or herself as oppositional but believes the behavior is entirely justified by the treatment he or she is receiving or by unreasonable circumstances. As in ADHD, these children show low self-esteem, emotional lability, poor frustration tolerance, and have temper outbursts. They often use alcohol, marijuana, and tobacco.

Oppositional defiant disorder (ODD) typically begins by the age of eight and usually does not start later than early adolescence. It sometimes evolves into conduct disorder or a mood disorder. Before puberty, it is more common in males than in females, but it is presumed to occur with equal frequency in both sexes in adolescence. Currently, no information exists about its prevalence. Children with ODD frequently meet criteria for ADHD.

Case Examples

Three case examples illustrate typical case situations in which a diagnosis of disruptive behavior disorder is made.

J, a six-year-old boy, was referred to a mental health clinic. He talked incessantly, was rude, did not follow directions, often got out of his seat in school, had tantrums, and was often the center of a fight in the schoolyard. J was the product of an uncomplicated pregnancy and delivery. He was a difficult baby, had colic, and could not tolerate infant vitamins. At about one year of age, he became a headbanger, which upset his mother greatly. He stopped doing this after a few months. J attended nursery school at age four, but the school asked the parents to withdraw him after six weeks because of his unruly behavior. He attended kindergarten part of the next year, then the family moved.

L was a 14-year-old girl whose father filed a PINS (person in need of supervision) petition with the family court. L was a polydrug user, was often truant, stole money from her father's wallet, consorted with a series of unsavory boyfriends (drug dealers, petty criminals), and refused to comply with any household rules (stayed out very late or all night, drank beer and smoked cigarettes and marijuana in the home, did none of the household chores assigned to her). She was negativistic and surly toward both her natural parents and her stepmother. On two instances, she disappeared for several days without telling her parents where she was, which led to their filing a missing persons alert with the police.

L lived with her father, stepmother, 18-year-old stepbrother, and 15-year-old stepsister. She had come to live with her father and stepmother after her mother, with whom she had been living up to age 13, requested that she be placed in a psychiatric hospital because of her hostile, defiant, unruly behavior. L's father brought her to live with him at that time despite her resentment toward her stepmother, whom she blamed for her father's departure from the home. L's behavior continued to worsen until her father brought action against her a year and a half after she had moved into his home.

Until her parents' separation and ensuing divorce when she was eight years old, L had posed no problem. She had been an outgoing, popular, and happy child who did well academically. Her behavior had deteriorated gradually since that time.

B, a 10-year-old boy, lived with both parents and three siblings, ages 13, 7, and 6. Since early childhood, he had been distractible, overactive, and oppositional toward adults. He had temper tantrums over small frustrations and frequently got into fights. He seemed to enjoy tormenting his younger brother and sister to the extent of inflicting physical pain (by punching, knocking them over, or twisting their arms). He was disruptive in the classroom and was frequently sent to the principal's office.

B often lied and stole money from his parents. He had been caught shoplifting and had vandalized a neighbor's car. The neighbors told his parents that they would press charges the next time an incident occurred. His parents stated that they did not believe in hitting children, but out of desperation had resorted to spanking B and even hitting him with a belt on two occasions when he hurt his younger siblings.

J's sole diagnosis was ADHD. The other two cases illustrate the overlap of diagnoses within the category of disruptive behavior disorders. Both L's and B's primary diagnosis was conduct disorder. L's behavior also met criteria for ODD (flagrant refusal to comply with household rules, negativism, and surliness). However, additional features of stealing and heavy polydrug use as well as offenses related to juvenile status (truancy, staying out late, running away) indicated a diagnosis of conduct disorder, which preempted the ODD diagnosis.

In addition to the diagnosis of conduct disorder, B also met criteria for ADHD (long history of overactivity, distractibility, fighting, temper tantrums) and oppositional defiant disorder (argumentativeness, disobedience). As in L's case, the diagnosis of ODD was preempted by the more serious diagnosis of conduct disorder. The ADHD diagnosis, however, was carried concurrently with the conduct disorder diagnosis. In contrast with B, L had no history of ADHD.

Research Evidence

Are the disruptive behavior disorders really separate entities? Extensive debate has surrounded this issue (Luk, 1985; McGee, Williams, & Silva, 1984a, 1984b; Rutter, 1983; Lahey et al., 1985; Lambert & Hartsough, 1987; Rapoport, 1983; Rapoport & Ferguson, 1981; Reeves et al., 1987; Shaffer & Greenhill, 1979; Shapiro & Garfinkel, 1986; Shekim et al., 1986; Weiss, 1985; Werry, Reeves, & Elkind, 1987). Arguing against distinct syndromes, Rutter (1983) and Shaffer and Greenhill (1979) cite variable etiologies, inability to predict outcomes from the diagnosis, and lack of clinical usefulness of the diagnoses.

Various studies support the case against specific syndromes. Stewart and associates (1981) found that two out of three hyperactive children also had a conduct disorder. Werry and co-workers (1987) reviewed studies comparing the diagnostic categories of attention-deficit, conduct, oppositional, and anxiety disorders in children and concluded that the various groups were remarkably similar, despite some differentiating characteristics. Little evidence was found to confirm the validity of the diagnoses. Shapiro and Garfinkel (1986) screened an entire elementary school population (315 children) and found that 8.9% of the children qualified for a diagnosis of attention-deficit disorder or conduct disorder (American Psychiatric Association, 1987). Although the children could be classified as having either ADD, CD, or both, no symptoms or characteristics differentiated the inattentive–overactive (ADD) from the aggressive–oppositional (CD) children; the only basis for classifying them in one or another group was the different relative importance of symptoms in the groups. Luk (1985) concluded from reviewing 25 direct observation studies that hyperactive and normal children are clearly differentiated but that evidence distinguishing conduct disorder from hyperactive syndrome is inconclusive.

Shekim and colleagues (1986) compared the categorical or syndromal approach used by DSM-III to classify children with ADHD (ADDH), in which explicit criteria must be met in order for a child to be classified with ADHD, with a dimensional or factorial approach, in which a behavioral profile of the child is obtained emphasizing dimensions of social competence. They argue for a dimensional, rather than a syndromal (categorical), approach. On the dimensional scale, characteristics not included for the ADDH diagnosis, called "internalizing factors," are included. The boys with ADDH scored as high as did boys with other psychiatric diagnoses on the "internal" factors of depression and obsessive–compulsive factors and higher on the "social withdrawal" scale than did either the other diagnosis (OD) or the normal, no diagnosis (ND) group, a surprising finding. As would be expected, boys meeting DSM-III criteria for ADDH scored higher than did either the OD or ND groups on the hyperactive and aggressive scales. Shekim and associates (1986) note that an advantage of the dimensional scale in assessment is that potentially important treatment information about the child is revealed, information that is not generated by the categorical DSM-III approach to diagnosis.

On the other hand, Weiss (1985) argued in favor of the diagnosis of attention-deficit with hyperactivity based on her observations of hyperactive persons from childhood through young adulthood, in whom she found identifiable clusters of characteristics. Numerous studies support her position.

By using various rating scales, Milich, Loney, and Landau (1982) and Trites and Laprade (1983) found that hyperactivity and aggressiveness often existed independently. Lambert and Hartsough (1987) identified four independent dimensions for inattention, hyperactivity, conduct disorder, and impulsivity. McGee and colleagues (1984a) found that in a sample of 950 children, among those with extreme behavior problems, 2.7% were hyperactive only, 3.2% were aggressive only, and 4.3% were hyperactive and aggressive. According to this study, 7.0% met criteria for hyperactivity and 7.5% for aggressivity.

In an earlier study, the same researchers found a high correlation (.61) between aggressiveness and hyperactivity based on teachers' ratings. The apparent reason for the contradiction between the high correlation in the earlier study and the independence of the dimensions in the later study was that these behavioral dimensions are more clearly independent when more extreme problem behaviors are considered (McGee et al., 1984a). Aggressive behavior appeared to be more situation-specific than did hyperactive behavior, whereas hyperactives were more likely to have long-term cognitive deficits.

Further complicating the picture, Douglas (1984) proposed a set of inclusion criteria for ADHD that differs significantly from those in DSM-III-R. She identified four primary, related predispositions in ADHD: (1) need for immediate gratification perceived as imperative by the child, (2) very weak inclination to invest energy or attention in any tasks perceived as demanding, (3) impairment in the ability to inhibit impulsive responding, and (4) impairment in the ability to modulate arousal levels in response to situational demands. Unlike other theorists, Douglas accords priority to the need for instant gratification, an emphasis that represents a departure from the focus on attention deficit.

When the third DSM-III-R "disruptive" diagnosis, oppositional defiant disorder, is considered, the waters become even muddier. The case examples presented earlier illustrate one of the major problems with the diagnosis of ODD. Many children are oppositional intermittently. Most children whose oppositional behavior is sufficiently pervasive come to the attention of a facility that uses DSM diagnoses, such as mental health clinics, also have ADHD, CD, substance abuse, or adjustment problems, in which case some diagnosis other than ODD may be more informative. For those who are pervasively oppositional, and for a period long enough to qualify for a diagnosis of ODD, one may question whether a diagnosis of ODD adds anything to another diagnosis. Could the category simply be dispensed with by describing the child's oppositional behavior as one feature of a more complex behavioral–situational problem? Rutter (1983) summarizes the issue as follows:

> The question of whether there is a nosologically distinct hyperkinetic or attentional deficit syndrome remains unresolved. [Can] overactivity, inattention, or social disinhibition . . . be validly differentiated from the broad run of behavioral and conduct disturbances of childhood (p. 8)?

The DSM-III-R classification represents an interim working hypothesis that such a distinction can be made.

In view of the wealth of evidence that supports both sides of apparently contradictory points of view, the case for dimensional diagnosis appears plausible (Shekim et al., 1986). The dimensional approach would be useful whether or not one believes that a distinct hyperactive syndrome exists and whether one prefers DSM-III-R descriptions or alternative criteria, such as those criteria that emphasize need for immediate gratification rather than attention deficit. To obtain third-party reimbursement, diagnoses are needed. However, for treatment decisions, the relevant issue is defining the child's needs. What combination of treatment approaches can meet these needs? For this purpose, dimensional diagnosis would appear to provide more relevant information than would diagnosis focused on whether a child meets criteria for a particular DSM-III-R label. Practitioners may have to wait a long time for issues of definition to be resolved. Meanwhile, they must make daily decisions about evaluation and treatment.

Implications for Case Evaluation

The case examples described earlier illustrate the principle that no matter how a child's behavior is defined or classified, treatment approaches differ according to whether the child's disruptive behavior has a significant biological component (like J's and B's), thus indicating the possible need for biological intervention; whether it is purely psychosocial in origin (like L's); whether specific educational strategies targeted on learning deficits are required or behavioral remedies are likely to suffice; and whether casework intervention should include environmental manipulation, parenting-skills training, therapeutic counseling, group treatment, or other approaches. The choice of intervention does not depend on which diagnostic label is assigned, except that children who meet criteria for ADHD usually have a biologically based condition that can be ameliorated by biological treatments in conjunction with other interventions (see Johnson, 1987b). This is so regardless of whether these children also meet criteria for other diagnoses, such as CD, ODD, or specific developmental disability (learning disability) that may require evaluation and remediation. In addition, poor fit between child and environment is likely to play a role, and the worker must evaluate the child's characteristics, the environment's characteristics, and the nature of their interaction.

Tools for assessing children who show disruptive behavior include interviews with parents; reports from schools and community agencies; medical history and physical examination; neurological examination; psychological testing; allergy evaluation; laboratory studies; interviews with and observation of the child; behavior-rating scales completed by parents, teachers, and significant others in the child's life; and self-report scales, especially by adolescents (Shekim et al., 1986; Small, 1982). The issues pertaining to referral for medical, neurological, and allergy evaluation and for psychological testing are complex. Another complicated issue is the significance of neurological "soft signs," a frequent concomitant of disruptive behavior disorders. These issues have been reviewed elsewhere (Johnson, 1989) and are only summarized briefly here. Workers who must evaluate children who present with disruptive behavior should refer to the cited work to obtain more information about these diagnostic approaches.

The most important preliminary diagnostic information is derived from the client history and description of the problem. A careful medical, behavioral, and psychosocial history is necessary in all cases of overactivity, attention deficit, or disruptive behavior. To obtain this information, behavior-rating scales filled out by parents and teachers are extremely valuable because they provide specific, measurable information about the frequency, severity, and duration of the problem behavior that can serve as a basis for developing treatment plans. The Connors scales for parents and for teachers are most widely used for hyperactivity and attention deficit (Benton & Sines, 1985). For children or adolescents in whom antisocial behavior is prominent, the Self-Report Delinquency Scale (Elliott & Ageton, 1980), the Adolescent Antisocial Behavior Checklist (Curtiss et al., 1983), and the Parent Daily Report (Patterson, Chamberlain, & Reid, 1982) may be used. Parent ratings are very useful because parents have observed the child many hours a day, in many situations, over a long period. Teachers are often excellent raters because they are able to compare the child with other children. Direct observations of the child by the worker provide only a small sample of the child's behavior in one particular situation but can be used to enrich or amplify a carefully detailed history obtained from the people who know the child best.

Medical, neurological, psychiatric, and allergy evaluations are commonly used among clinicians to "rule out" physical factors. Such an attitude harks back to the days when prevailing clinical wisdom compartmentalized problems into two categories, "organic" and "functional." Advances in diagnostic technologies and vast increments to the research base of clinical knowledge have discredited a dichotomized view of etiology (Johnson, 1984). Complex interactions among physical, psychological, and environmental factors play a role in most states of being that attract DSM labels, so it is seldom possible to rule out physical factors, nor, frequently, is it possible to rule them in decisively.

A more fruitful approach to comprehensive assessment of children with disruptive behavior disorders is to ask, "What physical factors may be operating in this particular case, and what biologically oriented treatments (medication, diet, detoxification), if any, may be indicated?" These questions are analogous to the questions that nonmedical practitioners have asked for many decades: "What intrapsychic (intrafamilial) factors may be operating, and what psychological therapies may be indicated?" A truly biopsychosocial assessment builds in parallel assessment of the "bio," "psycho," and "social" components rather than emphasizing one and neglecting one or both of the others.

The issue of *psychological testing* is complicated by at least two factors: longstanding concern about racial and ethnic bias built into test instruments and exhibited by the people who administer and interpret the tests (Williams, 1987; Kinzie & Manson, 1987) and proliferation of tests during recent decades. Controversy over *cultural and ethnic bias* in intelligence and other psychometric tests has continued for half a century. Widely used tests, such as the Wechsler Intelligence Scale for Children and the Minnesota Multiphasic Personality Inventory have been targets of criticism (Cronbach, 1975; Williams, 1987). The addition of "culture-free" or "culture-fair" tests have not solved the problem (Sattler, 1982). Positions range from wholesale repudiation of the use of psychometric instruments with ethnic and racial minorities to cautious endorsement of the use of intelligence and other psychological tests with minorities, provided that a set of safeguards are in place to minimize prejudicial interpretation (Williams, 1987). It is beyond the scope of this article to review the evidence supporting and contravening the use of various tests, but it goes without saying that social workers should familiarize themselves with literature that critically reviews the particular tests that are used with their client populations.

The array of psychometric tests now available include psychoeducational, psychodiagnostic, neuropsychological, and intelligence tests. The value of psychological tests arises from their ability to assess the specific disabilities and dysfunctions that need remediation; to identify strengths and assets to be used to develop skills and a sense of mastery and competence; and to provide baseline measures by which to evaluate progress arising from therapy, remediation, or maturation (Small, 1982; Gittelman, 1986). The kind of information that these tests can generate is often very valuable regardless of what DSM diagnosis is assigned, assuming that the test interpretation takes cultural differences into account and that treatment or educational resources are available to make use of the information. However, interpretation requires a high level of skill, faulty interpretation is a hazard, and the validity of some of the tests, especially psychodiagnostic instruments (such as the Rorschach, Thematic Apperception, and House-Figure-Drawing tests), is questionable (Small, 1982; Gittelman, 1986).

Conclusions

The jury is still out on the definition and delineation of disruptive behavior disorders. In the meantime, practitioners working with children exhibiting disruptive behaviors must be cognizant of a confusing array of definitions and assessment approaches. In order to provide meaningful input into evaluation and treatment decisions, social workers need substantive knowledge about the different diagnostic procedures that are available as well as indications and contraindications for the use of these procedures. Such information should be integrated into curricula in schools of social work and should be offered in continuing education courses for social workers who practice with children and adolescents.

REFERENCES

American Psychiatric Association. (1987). *Diagnostic and statistical manual of mental disorders* (3rd ed., rev.). Washington, DC: Author.

Benton, A. L., & Sines, J. O. (1985). Psychological testing of children. In H. I. Kaplan and B. J. Sadock (Eds.), *Comprehensive textbook of psychiatry* (pp. 1625–1634). Baltimore, MD: Williams and Wilkins.

Chess, S., & Thomas, A. (1984). *Origins and evolution of behavior disorders.* New York: Brunner/Mazel.

Cronbach, L. J. (1975). Five decades of public controversy over mental testing. *American Psychologist, 30,* 1–14.

Curtiss, G., et al. (1983). Measuring delinquent behavior in inpatient treatment settings: Revision and validation of the adolescent antisocial behavior checklist. *Journal of the American Academy of Child Psychiatry, 22,* 459–466.

Douglas, V. A. (1984). The psychological process implicated in ADD. In L. M. Bloomingdale (Ed.), *Attention deficit disorder: Diagnostic, cognitive, and therapeutic understanding.* New York: Spectrum.

Elliott, D. S., & Ageton, S. S. (1980). Reconciling race and class differences in self-reported and official estimates of delinquency. *American Sociological Review, 45,* 95–110.

Gittelman, R. (1986). Questioning the clinical usefulness of projective psychological tests for children. *Developmental and Behavioral Pediatrics, 7,* 378–382.

Jessor, R., & Jessor, S. L. (1977). *Problem behavior and psychosocial development: A longitudinal study of youth.* New York: Academic Press.

Johnson, H. C. (1980). *Behavior, psychopathology, and the brain.* New York: Curriculum Concepts.

Johnson, H. C. (1984). Biological bases of psychopathology. In F. Turner (Ed.), *Adult psychopathology* (pp. 3–72). New York: Free Press.

Johnson, H. C. (1987a). Biologically based deficit in the identified patient: Indications for psychoeducational strategies. *Journal of Marital and Family Therapy, 13,* 337–348.

Johnson, H. C. (1987b). Drugs, dialogue, or diet: Diagnosing and treating the hyperactive child. *Social Work, 33,* 349–358.

Johnson, H. C. (1989). Behavior disorders of childhood. In F. Turner (Ed.), *Child psychopathology* (pp. 73–140). New York: Free Press.

Kagan, J. (1984). *The nature of the child.* New York: Basic Books.

Kazdin, A. E. (1987). *Conduct disorders in childhood and adolescence.* Newbury Park, CA: Sage Publications.

Kinzie, J. D., & Manson, S. M. (1987). The use of self-rating scales in cross-cultural psychiatry. *Hospital and Community Psychiatry, 38,* 190–196.

Kutchins, H., & Kirk, S. A. (1987). DSM-III and social work malpractice. *Social Work, 32,* 205–211.

Lahey, B., et al. (1985). Teacher ratings of attention problems in children experimentally classified as exhibiting attention-deficit disorder with and without hyperactivity. *Journal of the American Academy of Child Psychiatry, 24,* 613–616.

Lambert, N. M., & Hartsough, C. S. (1987). The measurement of attention-deficit disorder with behavior ratings of parents. *American Journal of Orthopsychiatry, 57,* 361–370.

Luk, S. (1985). Direct observation studies of hyperactive behaviors. *Journal of the American Academy of Child Psychiatry, 24,* 338–344.

McGee, R., Williams, S., & Silva, P. A. (1984a). Behavioral and developmental characteristics of aggressive, hyperactive, and aggressive–hyperactive boys. *Journal of the American Academy of Child Psychiatry, 23,* 270–279.

McGee, R., Williams, S., & Silva, P. A. (1984b). Background characteristics of aggressive, hyperactive, and aggressive–hyperactive boys. *Journal of the American Academy of Child Psychiatry, 23,* 280–284.

Milich, R., Loney, J., & Landau, S. (1982). The independent dimensions of hyperactivity and aggression: A validation with playroom observation data. *Journal of Abnormal Psychology, 91,* 183–198.

Patterson, G. R., Chamberlain, P., & Reid, J. B. (1982). A comparative evaluation of a parent training program. *Behavior Therapy, 13,* 638–650.

Robins, L. N. (1986). The consequences of conduct disorder in girls. In D. Olweus et al. (Eds.), *Development of antisocial and prosocial behavior: Research, theories, and issues* (pp. 385–414). Orlando, FL: Academic Press.

Rapoport, J. L. The use of drugs: Trends in research. In M. Rutter (Ed.), *Developmental neuropsychiatry* (pp. 385–403). New York: Guilford.

Rapoport, J. L., & Ferguson, H. B. (1981). Biological validation of the hyperkinetic syndrome. *Developmental Medicine and Child Neurology, 23,* 667–682.

Reeves, J. C., et al. (1987). Attention deficit, conduct, oppositional, and anxiety disorders in children: II. Clinical characteristics. *Journal of the American Academy of Child and Adolescent Psychiatry, 26,* 144–155.

Rutter, M. (1983) *Developmental neuropsychiatry.* New York: Guilford.

Sattler, J. M. (1982). *Assessment of children's intelligence and special abilities* (2nd ed.). Boston: Allyn & Bacon.

Schachar, R., Rutter, M., & Smith, A. (1981). The characteristics of situationally and pervasively hyperactive children: Implications for syndrome definition. *Journal of Child Psychology and Psychiatry, 22,* 375–382.

Shaffer, D., & Greenhill, L. (1979). A critical note on the predictive validity of the hyperactive syndrome. *Journal of Child Psychology and Psychiatry, 20,* 61–72.

Shapiro, S. K., & Garfinkel, B. D. (1986). The occurrence of behavior disorders in children: The interdependence of attention deficit disorder and conduct disorder. *Journal of the American Academy of Child Psychiatry, 25,* 809–819.

Shekim, W. O., et al. (1986). Dimensional and categorical approaches to the diagnosis of attention deficit disorder in children. *Journal of the American Academy of Child Psychiatry, 25,* 653–658.

Small, L. (1982). *The minimal brain dysfunctions: Diagnosis and treatment.* New York: Free Press.

Stewart, M. A., et al. (1981). The overlap between hyperactive and undersocialized aggressive children. *Journal of Child Psychology and Psychiatry, 23,* 35–45.

Trites, R. L., & Laprade, K. (1983). Evidence for an independent syndrome of hyperactivity. *Journal of Child Psychology and Psychiatry, 24,* 573–586.

Weiss, G. (1985). Hyperactivity: Overview and new directions. *Psychiatric Clinics of North America, 8,* 737–753.

Werry, J. S., Reeves, J. C., & Elkind, G. S. (1987). Attention deficit, conduct, oppositional, and anxiety disorders in children: I. A review of research on differentiating characteristics. *Journal of the American Academy of Child and Adolescent Psychiatry, 26,* 133–143.

Williams, C. L. (1987). Issues surrounding psychological testing of minority patients. *Hospital and Community Psychiatry, 38,* 184–189.

Parent–School–Child Systems: Triadic Assessment And Intervention

John Victor Compher

12

S ince the late 1960s, several sophisticated sociologists and family therapists in their separate fields have developed a systemic perspective on delinquency and school-related problems. The previous child-centered paradigms were based on a psychoanalytic view that focused on the child's characterological deficits and the traditional sociological outlook that enumerated the general environmental variables that seemed to produce negative behaviors. The newer systems and interactionists' views maintain, however, that the child's negative conduct is symptomatic of very specific and current malfunctioning sequences of behavior within the child's human network. Therefore, it is important to look not only at the child's actions but also at the behaviors and relationships of the adult actors in the system, especially the parents and helping professionals, who relate to the child. Further, the systemic model requires a means of intervention that can then bring together the significant persons of the whole system on behalf of the child.

Although a child's personality and environmental setting indeed have relevance, the interactionist view has convincingly pointed out that specific systems of helping professionals may effectively select and at times promote youth for delinquent careers. Delinquency may not be a special kind of behavior at all, but rather a socially conferred status (Schur, 1973). For example, tracking of children in schools or teachers' lowering their expectations of children often engenders or reinforces the behavior on which such negative judgments are based. Also, the progressive notion of seeking to remediate all problems, even those that youth would naturally abandon on their own, may exacerbate and prolong difficulties (Matza, 1964). Indeed, the juvenile-justice system through its own internal inconsistencies, whether punitive or rehabilitative in intent, can further promote delinquent careers (Emerson, 1969; Platt, 1969; Schur, 1973; Wheeler et al., 1968).

Behind the inherent and complex problems within the juvenile-justice and school systems that foster negative performance and behaviors, family therapists have shown that youth who are lodged between strongly competing systems—for example, family, school, peers—may begin to manifest symptomatic conduct. Such actions may upon examination ultimately reveal strong conflicts of values and expectations among the adults of the various systems—struggles that are placed upon the child to mediate (Aponte, 1976, Tucker & Dyson, 1976).

Methodology of the Study

In order to examine more closely the nature of this intersystems problem and its potential consequences for the child, exploratory research was conducted in a public child welfare agency. The purpose of the study was to consider the quality and styles of relationships between parents and school personnel and how the interactional patterns of the adults might bear upon youths' behavior in the school setting. The research involved interviews of a small random sample of parents whose public high school children had been referred by the police for truancy. Based on these interviews, assessments were made of the parents' attitudes toward particular school personnel with whom they dealt and their reported responses to the professionals and to their children. Rather than focusing upon a child *per se*, the study examined the triadic framework in which each child operated, with special focus on the quality of the adult relationships, that is, of the parents and the school professionals.

Three Interactional Systems

Three different typologies of parent–school–child interactional systems emerged from the study: aggressive entanglement, passive entanglement, and adaptive response.

Aggressive Entanglement

The aggressive entanglement pattern (Figure 1) is characterized by overtly hostile behaviors on the part of the school and the parents, coupled with the parents' nondiscerning alliance with the child. As the school initiates behaviors toward the child or parents that the parents consider to be highly unfavorable, the parents respond in kind with active and increasingly critical behavior toward the school. The pattern escalates as the child continues behaviors at school that cannot be sanctioned by the school system.

In one sense, the child is caught in the middle of conflicting adult relationships. He or she may indeed be the communication bearer, sometimes awkwardly positioned in the crossfire of the adults, as seen in

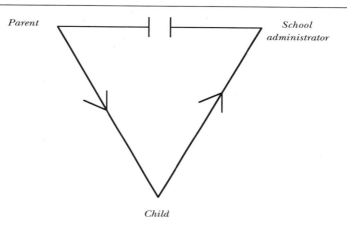

Child

Parent	Child	School administrator
■ Becomes angry with school over policy or reports of child.	■ Makes negative reports to parent, for example, that he or she is being picked on by teachers or administrators.	■ May become angry with parent for not supporting school policy.
■ Allies overtly with child against school standards.	■ With sympathy of parent, may escalate disputes with teachers, defy school rules, and appear to live up to label.	■ May engage in hostile interactions and arguments; may at times also try to avoid parent or to create bureaucratic runaround.
■ Becomes hostile and argumentative with school personnel.	■ May, although manipulative, feel caught between parent's standards and the school's; negative behaviors provide necessity or opportunity for parent and school personnel to clarify expectations.	■ Sees child as behavior problem and permits or encourages suspensions, sometimes over trivial misconduct at school.
■ May become deadlocked in this conflictual relationship, usually with a particular professional at school.	■ May cut classes and develop chronic attendance problem leading to dropout or push out.	■ May deny child access to necessary educational services and programs as well as extracurricular activities.
		■ May with time effectively push child, parent, and problem out of local school via disciplinary transfer.

Figure 1. Aggressive entanglement.

the example in which an angry principal tells the child, "Tell your Mom I want to see her at school!" Similarly, the school's acknowledged use of suspensions as a "means to get the parents into the school" puts the child in the potentially damaging situation of being the communication link between the school and the parents.

From a paradoxical perspective, the child's overt defiances at school may become a means of activating the adults of both systems to resolve a particular problem and their conflicting standards for the child. As the child acts out at school, he or she may also be riding on the shoulders of his or her parents in their disagreement with the school.

For instance, a mother in the study reported that she had argued for several years with the principal over the school's failure to provide the necessary programs that would meet her son's needs and thereby inspire him to attend school regularly and to behave acceptably. A sense of significant negative emotional involvement on the part of the mother with the principal was noted in her descriptions of the situation. This mother, with what appeared to be some legitimate school complaints, had nevertheless become locked after a period of time in an argumentative pattern with the principal. She believed that the school's rules were rigid and unfair and she argued that she could not support them. Furthermore, she would not seek behavior changes in her son, who was acting out, "until his educational needs are met." Thereby she struggled through the child against an equally "hard-nosed" principal.

Although the child had considerable manipulative power, he was also awkwardly positioned between a parent and principal who would not compromise. In some ways he was victimized in the triadic relationship; for example, the school refused to permit the child to take the school's shop course. The mother also felt that "he had been labeled as a behavior problem" and thereby was more readily tagged for disciplinary procedures. Indeed, he had been suspended several times for seemingly trivial reasons such as walking in the hallways during class time, being late to school, or not carrying his picture identification.

An escalating entanglement developed as the mother became increasingly angry and unsupportive of the school with each incident. She appeared to be in a kind of "game without end," a repetitive cycle in which her efforts to defend her son from the injustices of the school either victimized him further or gave him an implied license to maintain his rebellious conduct. Sadly, this mother reported that her son finally received a disciplinary transfer for cursing at a teacher when told to remove his hat. This type of transfer would move the problem and the parent out of the neighborhood school to a socially segregated disciplinary school where all of the children were labeled as serious discipline problems.

In sum, the aggressively entangled relationship is characterized by conflicting demands between the parent and the school. Sides are drawn and hostile interchanges occur without progress or resolution.

162

The child has the almost unconditional support of the parent and is either accused of or precipitates behaviors at school that are not sanctioned. The parent feels that the child is unfairly labeled as a behavior problem and is subsequently tagged for reprimands or exaggerated punishments by the school. Ultimately, the child suffers directly as he or she may drop out of school, be pushed out (disciplinary transfer or multiple suspensions), or may remain in school but exhibit problematic conduct.

Passive Entanglement

Similar to aggressively entangled parents, passively entangled parents are also stalemated in positions that are in conflict with school personnel. These parents, however, are less willing to enter into extended conflicts with the school; instead they tend to permit their children to miss school (Figure 2). These parents usually report that they have made some frustrated attempts to resolve the problems with the school, but now feel that the situation is hopeless. In short, they give up, and again it is the children who lose in the three-way struggle.

For instance, parents in the study often felt that they were being given bureaucratic runarounds and not being taken seriously in their early requests for help. A parent reported with strong feeling that her son was not academically inclined and should be learning a trade or practical skills at school. Her comment about conferences with the principal and later with the counselors was, "They talked and I listened." After making several trips to the school, she finally concluded, "The school doesn't have anything to offer." Tiring of the unsatisfactory situation, she then allied with her son in his desire to miss school, with the defense, "He doesn't just sit around the house, but stays active." Then, with resignation, she added, "He is just wasting time at home until he's sixteen and can go to trade school."

A complex and in many ways more disturbing extension of the passive triadic interactional pattern is characterized by parents who give the outward appearance of being allied with the school against the child because of their own ambivalence or their lack of assertive skills in an intimidating situation. In fact, the conflict between the parents and the school personnel remains submerged, undoubtedly to the confusion of the child, who may feel both supported and unsupported in a contradictory manner.

In this type of situation, the youth also may escalate negative behaviors at school, providing with each incident an opportunity or necessity for clarification by the parents and school officials as to their expectations and ultimately his or her future in the school. These parents may feel intimidated, overburdened, and hassled by a series of unsuccessful professional interventions. Although the parents take a cooperative stance, they may harbor unacknowledged resentment both toward the series of professionals involved and toward their own child.

For instance, a parent in the study reported that she was very upset to have received her first notification of her son's attendance problem only after it had become quite serious. In addition, this notification had

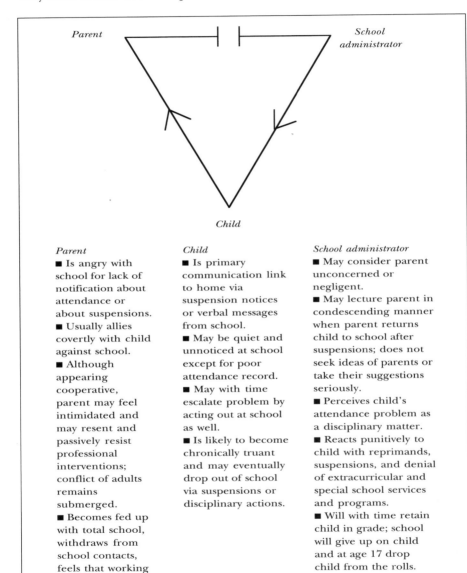

Parent	Child	School administrator
■ Is angry with school for lack of notification about attendance or about suspensions. ■ Usually allies covertly with child against school. ■ Although appearing cooperative, parent may feel intimidated and may resent and passively resist professional interventions; conflict of adults remains submerged. ■ Becomes fed up with total school, withdraws from school contacts, feels that working with the school is hopeless.	■ Is primary communication link to home via suspension notices or verbal messages from school. ■ May be quiet and unnoticed at school except for poor attendance record. ■ May with time escalate problem by acting out at school as well. ■ Is likely to become chronically truant and may eventually drop out of school via suspensions or disciplinary actions.	■ May consider parent unconcerned or negligent. ■ May lecture parent in condescending manner when parent returns child to school after suspensions; does not seek ideas of parents or take their suggestions seriously. ■ Perceives child's attendance problem as a disciplinary matter. ■ Reacts punitively to child with reprimands, suspensions, and denial of extracurricular and special school services and programs. ■ Will with time retain child in grade; school will give up on child and at age 17 drop child from the rolls.

Figure 2. Passive entanglement.

come from the district-level home-and-school visitor rather than from the local school, where it should have originated. A court case followed that the mother considered to be educationally interruptive because the youth missed additional days from school each time the hearing was postponed or continued. Although the mother was distressed, she was too intimidated to complain to the local school or to the court.

In this conflictual context, the boy's initial problem advanced from poor attendance to "bad" behavior when he was at school. The mother's first visit to the school occurred at this point as a result of a five-day suspension placed on the boy for alleged fighting. The mother believed the boy's story that he had been jumped by several other youths and was not at fault; indeed, she corroborated the story with the homeroom teacher. What appeared at first to be a supportive intervention on the part of the parent changed, however, to a negative stance as the teacher convinced her that the boy was a class clown. A meeting with the principal and the mother also took a negative direction, and the mother was not assertive enough to question the propriety of the original five-day suspension. From the mother's report it would seem that she left both meetings with the problem unresolved and with her own conflict with the school personnel submerged. Also, no attempts were made to consider the youth's social or educational needs.

Unfortunately and perhaps not surprisingly, the boy then allegedly stole a wallet at school. New court hearings for delinquency began at this point, resulting in the boy's missing more school days for continued court appearances. The probation officer became involved and tried unsuccessfully to motivate the youth. In a traditional manner, the problem continued to be seen as belonging exclusively to the boy, and there was no substantial involvement by the probation officer with the parent or with any school personnel.

In sum, this parent felt she had been informed too late of her son's absences, that the school had offered no help in resolving the problems at school, and that she and her son were essentially harassed by two court cases and by school suspensions that kept him out of school even more. The series of professionals involved focused upon the child as a "truant," "the class clown," "a behavior problem," "a delinquent," and finally as a "dropout." It is a common and perhaps classic example of a child who is caught in a context of conflicting adults and who acquires and then lives up to the labels imposed by the system. With the inability of the professionals and the parent to reach or even to seek a collaborative understanding of the youth's educational and social needs, a progression of increasingly serious behaviors were demonstrated by the youth himself.

Adaptive Response

In contrast with the two dysfunctional interactional contexts that have been described, a more adaptive response model (Figure 3) was

Initial phase: Open conflict

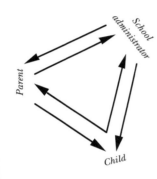

Parent
- Tries to articulate needs.
- If not "heard" or respected, may feel angry or intimidated.

Child
- Confused by school policies and treatment.
- May experiment with negative behaviors at school or continue poor attendance.

School administrator
- May not take parents' suggestions or ideas seriously.
- May seem "busy," without time to consider needs.
- Will usually treat parent in routine manner, for example, lecture or bureaucratic runaround.

Second phase: Adaptive persistence

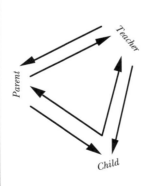

Parent
- May make a number of visits to the school until resolution is reached with administrator, for example, school to call parent rather than to suspend child.
- Sees that child's needs are recognized and that child conforms to school rules.

School administrator
- Eventually decides parent is a "concerned parent."
- Concedes to some of parent's demands.

Child
- May begin to get educational needs met and to perform better.
- Understands school and parent expectations.

Third phase: Possible circumvention

Parent
- Resolves issues with someone else in system.
- If adaptive parents are unable to resolve difficulties at second phase, they will usually seek out another school-related official (teacher, counselor) who is sympathetic and helpful.

Teacher
(or other school-related official)
- May respond to parent favorably.
- May intervene with administrator.
- Will work with parent and child toward solutions.

Child
- Is no longer communication bearer.
- Is clearer about adult expectations and performs more appropriately.

Figure 3. Adaptive model.

also suggested by the study. Although the complaints of the parents in this group were fairly similar to those of the parents in the other typologies with regard to how they were initially treated by school personnel, the adaptive parents found effective ways of coping and were able to circumvent the destructive entanglement cycles.

Moreover, the adaptive parents seemed to be able to distinguish between the school's flaws and its strengths. Although they complained strongly about similar types of school problems (inappropriate and rigid suspension and lateness policies, condescending ways in which they were treated), they were less likely to lose all hope in the school or to become stalemated in the unproductive triadic patterns. Rather than becoming embroiled in conflict or passively resigned, they persevered and seemed to demonstrate more sophisticated negotiating or maneuvering skills.

For example, a mother registered her very strong disapproval of the school's rigid lateness and class-cutting policies, which had resulted in several suspensions for her child. Although the mother was quite frustrated in her attempts to address these issues with the local school administrators, she reported favorably on her experiences with some of the teachers in the school. As she took the child's class-cutting problem around the administrators to the teacher whose class was being missed, she learned that the boy's stuttering problem was being exhibited in oral reading exercises before the class. The teacher had not been aware of the degree of the youth's embarrassment, and after consultation with the parent and the youth it was decided that he could read aloud to the teacher privately. The attendance problem was resolved in this coordinated manner as the parent circumvented the punitive attitudes of the school's administrators that had previously served to maintain the problem.

In another instance, a father had become upset with the administrator of the school for suspending his son for attendance problems, a response by the school that he felt the child himself wanted. After several visits to the school, this active father finally reached an informal agreement with the school office that he would be called directly whenever his son did not show up for school. Also, an experienced home-and-school visitor responded to the youth's interest in working afternoons and was able to find him a job and to obtain the approval of the school officials and the father. The youth began attending school regularly.

In short, the adaptive parents were able, after their initially unresolved conflicts with school administrators, to seek out or to respond to other school personnel who could be helpful. In these cases, the children's problem behavior, usually lateness or truancy, ended as the adults (the parents and school personnel) established effective communication ties. The remarkable fact is that in these cases the communication finally occurred in spite of what most parents considered to be serious initial roadblocks of policy and behaviors from within the school system itself.

Systemic Intervention

Gaining Entry into the Situation

Because the more stalemated aggressive or passive triadic systems are less likely to initiate their own referrals and will often simply encourage the youth to drop out of school eventually, the local family service or child welfare agency must look for specific means to gain entry into these seemingly deadlocked situations. Referrals from the police department provide an opportunity for intervention. These referrals indicate youth who have been picked up for truancy or for more severe acting-out behaviors such as damaging school property or attacking another pupil or a teacher. Police usually welcome voluntary social service intervention.

Another potential means of entry is created when an agency develops a collaborative relationship with a school district's home-and-school visitor's office. Frequently, such offices are understaffed and are eager to have access to the counseling and service expertise of professional social workers in the community.

Third, the social service organization concerned about the problematic interface of the family and school systems may choose to contact the local schools directly. The social worker may talk to school personnel. He or she may gain access through volunteer organizations—for example, by presenting a community education workshop to the parent–teacher's group or a similar association. Because of contacts made through such outreach efforts, interested teachers or more adaptive parents within the generally problematic setting will begin to refer the difficult cases in which they believe family service intervention can be useful.

Establishing Rapport with the Family

When contact is made between a social worker and a family whose child is having difficulty (usually through a cordial letter offering a home visit at a particular time), the social worker will, as a part of his or her general assessment process, find it helpful to determine the typical response pattern of the parents to the school system. How do the parents interpret the actions of the school personnel? How did the parents react to various school professionals (e.g., withdrawal or aggression)? Are the parents able to describe the problem from more than one perspective or are they locked into a very one-sided view? Do the parents align unconditionally with the child—either covertly or overtly? Do the parents' attitudes indicate hopelessness and helplessness? Are the parents immobilized by anger?

As the social worker gains a clearer concept of the triadic interactional style of the parent, the school personnel, and the child, the social worker will also be developing a rapport and a strategy for working with the particular type of system. With more aggressive or volatile parents, the social worker will encourage the clients to ventilate their hostile feelings about the school to the social worker rather than at the already defensive school. The social worker will help the parents acknowledge the futility of continued hostile behaviors. Can the parents recognize how the child may be further labeled or victimized by such efforts? What new behaviors would the parents be willing to consider, with the support of the social worker, that would prevent the child's further decline in the school setting? What are specific ways in which the parents can begin to take charge of the child's behavior at home? What are the objective needs of the child and how can they be articulated by the parents in ways that do not directly blame and accuse the school in a destructive manner?

In a similar way, the social worker prepares passively entangled parents for effective and collaborative communication with the school. With this type of parents, however, special attention is given to ways of motivating the parents to become more active and assertive. Are the parents aware of their parental and procedural rights—for example, reasonable notification of suspensions and unexcused absences, the right to review school records, and the right to appeal administrative decisions? Have the parents always gone to the school alone and would they want to make new efforts, in this case accompanied by the social worker, who would facilitate communication? Have the parents ever had any positive experiences with any of their children's teachers? If so, what favorable points can be drawn from these experiences to enhance self-esteem and the parents' sense of personal strength?

With both types of parents, potential adaptive capacities or experiences should be recognized and encouraged. A particularly helpful means of promoting these dynamics is role playing. Using a role play enables the parents to practice more adaptive behaviors that the social worker can model for the parents. In the role play, the parents learn to be clear about the child's needs in an assertive but nonthreatening way with school personnel. The parents are also encouraged to brainstorm solutions with the social worker that may be presented at the actual school conference.

Setting up the Family–School Conference

The school should be notified as soon as possible regarding the genuine efforts of the family in working with the social worker toward resolving troublesome issues. With this knowledge the school is generally willing to consider a meeting with the family. If the school initially resists, as may happen, for example, if the agency has not established a working relationship with the school, a premeeting between the social worker and the school counselor or vice-principal is important. At this time, the social worker can explain the casework and conference process and goals and the social worker's role in facilitating this joint meeting. The premeeting sets the stage for a new and more productive dialogue between the family and the school.

The persons invited to the school conference itself are the relevant school personnel—principal or vice-principal, school counselor, and one or two teachers who know the child well (Aponte, 1976; Tucker & Dyson, 1976). The invitation is usually through the school counselor, who acts as the social worker's liaison within the school structure. The family participants include the parents, the child, and any siblings who may attend the same school.

The general format of the family–school conference opens with an introduction by the social worker of the participants and a positive statement of purpose for the meeting. The goals of the meeting are twofold: to promote constructive interaction and dialogue between the parents and school personnel and to establish agreement on a specific mutual solution that will address the school-related problem in a new and cooperative manner. For example, the teachers may agree to advise the parents on how to tutor the child in a difficult subject area, with the parents and teachers checking in with each other for a specific number of weeks. If testing has not been done, an agreement may be reached to conduct a comprehensive academic and psychological assessment, with a follow-up meeting to discuss the child's particular educational needs.

If the youth's attendance or behavior has been a problem, the parents and teachers need to agree upon a means to inform the parents regularly of progress or setbacks at school. Parents must also indicate how they will reenforce the agreed-upon standards. The youth as well expresses his or her needs, concerns, and feelings about school expectations, peer relations, or academic or social issues; these needs must be recognized in the development of solutions. For instance, tutoring services may be needed or the youth may need an after-school job or recreational opportunity.

Above all, the beginnings of a clear and open working alliance are established in the presence of the child between the parents and school personnel—a relationship that provides appropriate guidance and nurturance to the child about school and educational issues.

A System That Works

The triadic assessment and intervention approach described here is developed out of the social worker's awareness of the powerful influences that affect children and youth within the two contexts in which they live. When a conflict, overt or covert in nature, between the values and expectations of the adults of the two systems is unresolved, a stalemate often occurs, leading to the child's eventual dismissal or dropout from the school. If the school system itself is unable to resolve the problem, the social worker's mediation effort with both systems can inspire the entangled parties to consider the possibility of new and mutual approaches that are nonblaming and specific to the needs of the child. The social worker's active intervention frees the youth from the triangulated position in the triad, making it possible for the student to relate more appropriately and productively in the educational environment.

REFERENCES

Aponte, H. J. (1976). The family–school interview: An ecostructural approach. *Family Process, 15,* 303-311.

Emerson, R. (1969). *Judging delinquents: Contexts and process in juvenile court.* Chicago: Aldine.

Matza, D. (1964). *Delinquency and drift.* New York: John Wiley.

Platt, A. M. (1969). *The child savers: The invention of delinquency.* Chicago: University of Chicago Press.

Schur, E. M. (1973). *Radical non-intervention: Rethinking the delinquency problem.* Englewood Cliffs, NJ: Prentice-Hall.

Tucker, B. Z., & Dyson, E. (1976). The family and the school: Utilizing human resources to promote learning. *Family Process, 15,* 125-143.

Wheeler, S. (1968). Agents of delinquency control: A comparative analysis. In S. Wheeler (Ed.), *Controlling delinquents* (pp. 31-60). New York: John Wiley.

Assessing the Drug-Involved Client

Rosalind E. Griffin

13

A buse of both legal (alcohol, tobacco, diazepam) and illicit (cocaine, heroin, marijuana) drugs is epidemic in the United States. Practitioners who serve children and families are likely to encounter clients who are involved with or affected by drugs, either directly or indirectly. These workers need the knowledge and skills required to assess drug involvement, to confront the abuser's denial, and to refer clients to appropriate treatment programs. Unfortunately, practitioners sometimes fail to recognize that a client or a family member is a drug abuser. This often occurs when the client does not fit the stereotype of an alcoholic or addict, for example, the elderly alcoholic or the white-collar addict. In not recognizing a drug-abuse problem, practitioners undermine their efforts to treat the identified problem.

Underrecognition of Drug Abuse and Dependence

Several factors contribute to practitioners' lack of awareness of drug involvement by individuals and families. One factor is lack of knowledge and skill. Schools of social work provide few courses in addictions. If the content is not offered in the foundation curriculum, which is required of all students regardless of specialization, students may graduate without being exposed to accurate information about psychoactive drugs and their misuse. They may not recognize signs of drug abuse and dependence. If they suspect drug abuse, they may not know how to approach the subject.

Practitioners may recognize that a drug problem is present, yet choose to avoid the topic. Drug abuse is a sensitive issue. Workers may fear that inquiries about a client's psychoactive drug use may increase that person's ambivalence and anxiety, leading the client to terminate precipitously. Theory may also contribute to the decision to delay discussion of drug use. The worker may view drug abuse and dependence as symptomatic of underlying psychopathology and believe the psychodynamic concern takes precedence over drug use. In so doing, however, the practitioner merely enables or fosters continued drug use.

Moralistic attitudes may also intrude. If the practitioner views drug use as "bad" or as a sign of moral weakness, he or she may be unable to accept and work with drug-involved people.

This chapter is intended for readers who do not have specialized expertise in drug abuse. First, basic information about psychoactive drugs is provided. The term psychoactive drugs, as employed in the *Diagnostic and Statistical Manual of Mental Disorders* (DSM-III-R) (American Psychiatric Association, 1987), is used in order to avoid the spurious distinctions frequently made between licit and illicit drugs.

The chapter also presents guidelines for conducting drug-involvement assessment interviews with adults with and without mental disorders such as schizophrenia or depression. Finally, specialized treatment options are discussed.

Use, Abuse, Dependency

Three levels of drug involvement are commonly identified: use, abuse, and dependence (addiction). *Use* refers to taking the drug for pleasure in order to achieve a sense of well-being. A drinker who has a martini after work while fulfilling his or her usual responsibilities fits this category. This type of drinker is likely to discontinue use if he or she notices undesirable consequences.

For those who *abuse* drugs, the drug and its effects interfere with the individual's ability to carry out expected responsibilities. For instance, the abuser may risk eviction by purchasing drugs instead of paying the rent or mortgage. The abuser actively pursues opportunities to use drugs and continues despite untoward results. Often the boundaries between drug abuse, dependence, and addiction are tenuous.

The *drug-dependent* individual persists in using drugs, disregarding any negative consequences and exhibiting tolerance to the drug and withdrawal symptoms when he or she cannot have the drug. Preoccupation with acquiring and using the drug results in poor judgment. For example, drug-dependent parents may leave an infant unsupervised while they seek the next "fix." In their denial, these individuals often believe that their drugged state is normal and strive to sustain it. Such psychological dependence is difficult for the drug-dependent individual to overcome. These persons are unable to control their drug use and their social functioning is inadequate.

Dependence, also known as addiction, is the preferred and most commonly used term in professional circles. The DSM-III-R states that dependence occurs when at least three of the following criteria exist (American Psychiatric Association, 1987, pp. 166–167).

■ Increased dosage
■ Loss of control of use
■ Time concentrated on acquiring and using the drug
■ Intoxication or withdrawal symptoms hinder expected duties
■ Significant social, work, recreational, or family duties are displaced with preoccupation with drug taking
■ Use persists despite undesirable consequences such as being fired or arrested
■ Withdrawal symptoms occur when drug is discontinued
■ Tolerance develops
■ Drug is taken to ameliorate or prevent withdrawal symptoms

The symptoms should have endured for at least a month or for several binge episodes.

Psychoactive Drugs

Psychoactive drugs are chemical substances that alter the functioning of brain cells (neurons). These substances may increase, decrease, or disrupt messages that are sent from neuron to neuron by neurotransmitters, the specialized biochemicals that are involved in transmission of electrical impulses in the brain (Ray & Ksir, 1987).

Psychoactive drugs mimic the body's neurochemicals. The brain does not differentiate between neurochemicals and foreign chemicals with similar structures; rather, it responds to the drug, which then interferes with normal messages and affects behaviors (Ray & Ksir, 1987). Both licit and illicit psychoactive drugs affect the brain. This fact is sometimes obscured by the media hype surrounding the "war on drugs," which battles illicit drugs primarily, despite the high personal and societal costs of legal drugs such as alcohol.

Experts are making substantial progress in knowledge about what parts of the brain are affected by specific drugs and the ways in which psychoactive drugs act upon pleasure centers in the brain. For example, it is hypothesized that cocaine operates on the dopamine receptors, which in turn contributes to cocaine dependence (Extein & Dackis, 1987).

Psychoactive drugs have two primary effects: pharmacological and psychological. Pharmacological effects manifest in physiological signs and symptoms. For example, marijuana smoking may redden eyes and dry the mouth; amphetamines and cocaine increase respiration and blood pressure (Ray & Ksir, 1987).

The most frequently misused drugs are categorized into six classes. Stimulants, including cocaine and caffeine, increase alertness and produce euphoria. In contrast, sedatives and depressants such as alcohol and barbiturates reduce anxiety and induce sleep. Narcotics such as codeine and methadone relieve pain as well as produce euphoria. Hallucinogens such as mescaline and lysergic acid diethylamide (LSD) distort perceptions and sometimes produce a psychotic-like condition. Marijuana and hashish create a euphoric state and relax inhibitions. Phencyclidine (PCP), also known as "angel dust," is a synthetic analgesic that can evoke a distorted body image, disorganized thinking, and dissociative reactions (Ray & Ksir, 1987).

Individual responses to specific drugs can vary, depending upon the dosage level, method of administration, and user's experience with the drug. For example, an experienced heroin user who injects the usual dose may feel drowsy and mildly euphoric, whereas an inexperienced user may become unconscious from the same dose.

Psychoactive drugs such as alcohol or cocaine also have detrimental effects on the unborn fetuses of pregnant women, ranging from physical deformity to mental retardation and learning disabilities (Grinspoon & Bakalar, 1990; U.S. Department of Health and Human Services, 1990).

The psychological effects of psychoactive drugs are unpredictable, ranging from short-term memory loss from marijuana use to psychosis from amphetamine use. The user's expectations and circumstances surrounding use also contribute to the psychological effects. The terms *set* and *setting* are used to describe the person's interactions with the environment. The user's set state of mind, mood, personality, and feelings influence the total response. The presence of supportive companions during drug use tends to enhance the experience. These companions, along with other physical and social conditions, constitute the setting. Set and setting reinforce use if the experience is positively rewarding. For instance, subjective reports of marijuana smokers with little experience with the drug indicate that their experience is not perceived as positively as that of experienced smokers who are aware of the desired effects and achieve them in the company of friends (Ray & Ksir, 1987).

Three biological concepts are significant in understanding individuals' responses to drugs: tolerance, cross-tolerance, and synergism. *Tolerance* refers to a user's need for increased dosages over time to obtain the same physical and psychological effects. Tolerance results from the body's adaptation to the chemical properties of the drug. Although tolerance occurs with most psychoactive drugs, the degree of tolerance depends upon the drug. In the case of barbiturates, tolerance can range from moderate to high (Ray & Ksir, 1987).

Cross-tolerance permits the user to substitute another drug with similar biochemical attributes if the desired drug is unavailable. Substitution can prevent withdrawal symptoms. Alcoholics, for example, may use diazepam to cope with the anxiety and depression associated with abstinence from alcohol. Heroin addicts may use methadone to relieve withdrawal symptoms of nausea and diarrhea.

Synergism refers to the interaction among various psychoactive drugs. With some combinations of drugs, the effects are tripled or quadrupled. The consequences can be fatal, such as when a barbiturate is used with alcohol.

Psychoactive drugs have multiple and varied effects, and the same drug may produce different effects in different individuals. Conversely, different drugs may produce similar effects in different individuals. Drug effects are multiplicatively determined, as a result of interaction among biologic susceptibility, properties of the drug, mode of administration, number of drugs used, dosage, frequency of use, degree of tolerance, and set and setting.

Principles of Drug-involvement Assessment

Abuse and dependence are often allied with behaviors that may endanger the user or other people, for example, driving while drinking, street crime, or harm to a developing fetus. Because abuse and dependence are generally accompanied by denial, practitioners need to be proactive in assessing possible drug involvement. The abuser or addict is unlikely to volunteer information.

The objectives of a psychoactive-drug-involvement assessment include the following:

■ To determine the existence, extent, and intensity of drug use
■ To determine what psychoactive drugs are being used
■ To establish the duration of the drug use
■ To learn whether a coexisting mental disorder complicates the drug use
■ To make appropriate treatment dispositions

Three principles of proactive initial assessment of psychoactive drug use are (1) self-awareness, (2) nonjudgmental acceptance, and (3) directness (see Figure 1).

Self-awareness

The practitioner needs to be aware of potential countertransference issues, such as his or her own attitude toward drugs and drug use. Attitude sets the tone for treatment and requires that the worker resist blaming the person for what appears to be self-destructive and controllable behavior. Moralism and hostility toward a drug-dependent person influence the way in which the client's problems are approached or can result in the practitioner's failure to pursue a problem.

Workers can gain insight into their attitudes by becoming aware of images associated with the labels *alcoholic* or *crack user*. For example, the worker may feel that drug-involved individuals are weak and lack willpower and self-control. To avoid countertransference, the practitioner must be able to identify and separate personal opinions and feelings that may impede pursuing drug-involvement problems.

177

Although alcohol is a socially sanctioned drug, a worker's individual attitude toward alcohol use may shape the initial assessment interviews. For some practitioners, abstinence is an unshakable value. In contrast, a worker who is a social drinker may overlook a client's drinking problem because the client's drinking habits appear to be similar to the worker's. Self-awareness helps workers systematically examine their attitudes concerning psychoactive drugs and identify ways in which their attitudes may interfere with treatment.

Nonjudgmental Acceptance

As with any client, nonjudgmental acceptance on the part of the worker is crucial. Drug-involved clients may believe that they are unworthy of respect, in part because they do not respect themselves. Demonstrating nonjudgmental acceptance, however, may be difficult. Clients commonly minimize, rationalize, project, and deny their drug problems (Zimberg, 1982). In *minimizing* the problem, clients underestimate their degree of drug use as well as the consequences of drug use. In *rationalizing* the problem, clients seek to justify their behavior by offering excuses. *Projection* deflects attention from the self to others. All of these behaviors form a *denial* mechanism that challenges the worker's ability to understand and relate to the client.

Lying, arguing, distorting, intimidating, diverting attention, or verbally attacking the worker are all manifestations of denial. For example, the client might say, "Yes, I drink, but I take care of my children. Why don't you pick on people who mess up their life? Don't I deserve to have some fun like other people? Sure, I drink, but I can handle it."

A client's asking "Do you drink?" may serve as a rebuttal to put the worker on the defensive. Workers may become angry, irritated, and frustrated at the client's exaggerated efforts to avoid dealing with his or her drug use. However, expressing hostility or impatience is unlikely to penetrate the client's denial. The practitioner should acknowledge his or her anger or irritation and firmly redirect the focus by refusing to accept the client's evasion of the problem.

The practitioner needs to express empathy and sensitivity to the client's feelings as well as understand the denial mechanism. Identifying the range of feelings that a client might have, such as embarrassment, shame, guilt, ambivalence, and anger, can help obviate problems before they occur. Simultaneously, the worker needs to gather information for the assessment and not be sidetracked by diversionary tactics.

Directness

Because drug abusers and addicts are likely to deny problems, workers need to be prepared to confront the abuser's denial. Directness and specificity of questions can facilitate data gathering and initiate confrontation. If the worker initiates discussion of a possible drug-use problem, he or she should tell the client why the line of questioning is being pursued. For example, the worker might state that he or she smells alcohol on the client's breath. Such comments should be presented as observations that have triggered concern for the person's well-being (Levinson, 1983).

Indirect questions—"How are things at home?" "How is the job going?"—are usually less productive than are focused, direct questions. More targeted questions such as "How many beers did you have last night?" or "How many times have you stayed home from work with a hangover?" are more effective.

Many drug users use multiple drugs. The practitioner should not be content with a client's admission that he or she uses only one drug. Specific questions should be asked regarding use of all licit and illicit psychoactive drugs. The quantity and circumstances of the first and most recent usages help determine the reinforcements for continuing use of the drug.

The worker should obtain the names of drugs used by using both the proper and street names of drugs. If the practitioner is unfamiliar with a name, he or she should ask the client to describe the color, size, effects, routes of administration, dosage, and frequency of use. It is crucial that the worker learn whether the individual is an intravenous drug user because of possible exposure to the human immunodeficiency virus (HIV). The worker should educate the client about AIDS and provide resources for further counseling if it is warranted.

Practitioners who normally follow their clients' leads and focus on their clients' feelings and psychodynamics may feel uncomfortable asking direct questions. However, indirect questions support denial and resistance by enabling the person to evade the issue. Workers sometimes use indirect questions to fend off their own anxiety and the client's potential wrath (Levinson, 1983).

The client is likely to become annoyed with persistent and specific probing. The worker should respectfully recognize the client's provocation and resentment but stay with his or her line of questioning. The practitioner is unlikely to identify and assess problematic drug use if he or she relies *completely* on voluntary information. However, this approach should be combined with educating the client about the consequences of continued drug use.

Introducing the Topic

The practitioner needs to learn how to introduce the subject of drug involvement. The topic can be used as a routine component of any initial assessment (Deakins, Seif, & Weinstein, 1983). The applicant might be told in a matter-of-fact manner that questions will be asked about the person's life-style. Questions or comments about drug use can be posed naturally and unequivocally, while allowing the client an opportunity to answer. A response that is direct and nondefensive usually signifies no serious problem exists. A skilled interviewer can encourage responses from a client who expresses concern about his or her drug use, even if the client is reluctant to elaborate.

It is more difficult to handle drug-abuse revelations disclosed by persons other than the client. Depending upon how the information reaches the worker, the practitioner may or may not be able to follow up on the client's drug use immediately. Regardless, the worker should help the informant deal with the drug-using client while maintaining confidentiality until a strategy can be developed to confront the client if the information is not disclosed by the client. To avoid triangulation, the practitioner must carefully examine the client's circumstances, evaluate the credibility of the informer, and review signs of drug use that may have been overlooked. Any indications of possible endangerment of children should be reported immediately to child protective authorities. Steps should also be taken to protect partners or elderly from physical abuse.

Other Indicators of Drug-use Problems

In addition to direct inquiry about drug use, the practitioner should explore the client's family life and history, social life, employment record, and legal and health problems. Drug problems are likely to affect functioning in any or all of these areas (Figure 1).

Family life and history. The worker should ask questions about family relationships, for example, whether quarrels and fights increase during drinking episodes. Specific questions should be asked regarding whether young children are expected to care for each other, prepare meals, do the laundry, and so forth.

It is critical to ascertain whether there is a family history of drug abuse. Current research points to genetic predisposition toward alcoholism (U.S. Department of Health and Human Services, 1990).

Social life. If most of the client's friends and acquaintances are alcoholics and/or drug users, a serious problem may exist. Questioning the client about his or her social life can help determine whether drugs are central to the client's social activities.

Employment history. A stable employment record may strengthen a drug user's denial because he or she can point to successful job performance as proof that a problem does not exist. A client's working at jobs below his or her educational level and personal skills may indicate job difficulties and possible drug-use problems. Several job changes may also indicate drug use.

Legal problems. A record of driving under the influence of alcohol or involvement in other illegal activities such as check forgery or theft may indicate possible drug abuse.

Physical health. Alcoholics and other drug-dependent persons develop physical complications connected with their drug use. Malnutrition is common among alcoholics. Many users of illicit drugs avoid seeking medical care to conceal their drug dependence.

Other Issues to Explore

During the assessment interview, the issue of whether the person is a drug abuser or drug dependent will inevitably arise. The client may attempt to evade this topic by entrapping the worker in terminology and stereotypes of alcoholics or addicts. To handle such evasions, the practitioner should review the details of the situation linking drug use to dysfunctional behavior, allowing the client the opportunity to make a judgment. If the worker's assessment is congruent with that of the client, their agreement should be confirmed. However, if the client does not

I. Principles
A. Attitude—Self-awareness
  1. Scrutinize own feelings to obviate moralism, hostility, or condemnation of the drug user.
  2. Do not confuse own drinking habits or other drug use with client's.
  3. Look for countertransference feelings that the drug-involved individual's responses may arouse.
B. Nonjudgmental acceptance
  1. Consider the denial system as an integral part of the defense mechanism.
  2. Control hostility toward the client by being patient yet firm and persistent.
  3. Bear in mind that the drug-involved person experiences difficulty in accepting help just as other clients do.
C. Directness
  1. Ask specific questions that elicit factual information to ascertain the behavioral consequences of the drug involvement.
  2. Pursue responses when the individual is evasive and vague.
  3. Point out inconsistencies in information and observations despite defensiveness and objections of the client.
  4. Ask for details of drug-use circumstances and behavior.

II. Areas of Inquiry
A. Types of drugs used
  1. Licit and illicit drugs used.
  2. Determine dosage, frequency of use, last use, and method of administration (e.g., how many bottles of beer, how many "snorts" of cocaine).
  3. Determine longest period of abstinence and how abstinence was managed.
B. Family life and history
  1. Quarrels and fights.
  2. Decrease in sexual relations.
  3. Have significant others expressed concern about drug use?
  4. Family violence while under influence of drugs.
  5. Determine whether mother, father, siblings, grandparents, aunts, and uncles have history of drug involvement.
C. Social life
  1. Determine whether majority of friends and acquaintances use drugs.
  2. Are social activities selected on basis of drug availability?
  3. Determine whether friendships have been terminated because of drug involvement.
D. Employment history
  1. Evidence of frequent job changes.
  2. Firings, forced resignations, or extended periods of unemployment.
  3. Frequent absences or lateness.
  4. Does employer condone drug use, specifically alcohol?
  5. Does isolated work environment conceal drug use?
E. Legal problems
  1. Driving while intoxicated.
  2. Frequent automobile accidents.
  3. History of arrests and/or convictions for disorderly conduct, prostitution, shoplifting, burglary, drug possession.
F. Health
  1. Treatment for drug overdose or drug-related illnesses such as hepatitis, cirrhosis, or AIDS.
  2. Physician has recommended that the client stop drinking.
  3. Evidence of injury from falls while drinking.
  4. Cigarette burns while intoxicated.
G. Treatment history
  1. Ascertain nature and extent of any treatment for drug involvement.
  2. Voluntary or involuntary.
  3. Length of abstinence.

Figure 1. Guidelines for assessment of drug involvement.

acknowledge drug involvement, the worker should note the divergence, pointing out reasons for concern, while recognizing that the client may find it difficult to acknowledge his or her problem.

If the worker concludes that sufficient evidence suggests that psychoactive drug use is a problem, his or her conclusion should be stated forthrightly, with an estimation of the severity of the problem, to the client. The practitioner should offer treatment options, including further interviews with the worker. The worker should emphasize that the problem can be dealt with but that the process is likely to be lengthy and perhaps painful.

Persons of color and women tend to be overlooked with regard to alcohol and drug misuse. For example, a practitioner may associate heavy drinking with African Americans and conclude that such drinking behavior among them is acceptable. Women, particularly middle-class white women, have been both protected and scorned for excessive alcohol use. The stigma and embarrassment experienced by women drug users lower their self-esteem and contribute to their unresponsiveness to intervention (Zankowski, 1987). Also, African Americans may express anger and hostility, particularly if the worker is not African American (Bell & Evans, 1983). The worker must establish rapport with these clients in order to overcome possible bias during the interview.

Some drug-involved persons have a coexisting mental disorder that complicates assessment and intervention. In such cases, intense confrontation is not recommended. Although psychoactive drugs do not cause mental disorders, they can exacerbate symptoms. Alcohol, for example, can cause organic brain syndrome. When a coexisting mental disorder is suspected, the worker should seek psychiatric consultation.

Some drug users may have attempted to decrease their use of drugs or suffered a relapse. In some cases, these individuals may be ashamed of their failure and blame treatment personnel. Review of the treatment experience may encourage these clients to recognize opportunities as well as obstacles in participating in treatment.

Treatment of drug abuse is difficult without client motivation. The worker should search out and identify any indication of motivation. Even reluctant participation in the assessment interview can be taken as a sign of motivation. Demands by family members, employers, and legal authorities may pressure the client to accept treatment. Any of these may be sufficient initially until the client is able to develop internal motivation.

The practitioner must be able to offer accessible treatment options. Programs may include residential or ambulatory detoxification services for drug-dependent clients. Live-in therapeutic communities have a drug-free treatment philosophy. Self-help groups such as Cocaine Anonymous (CA) and Alcoholics Anonymous (AA) offer peer support for the addicted person. Families of drug abusers can benefit from supportive networks such as Al-Anon and Alateen. The practitioner needs to match the client with the most appropriate services.

It may be difficult to find effective treatment facilities. Currently, the drug epidemic is dealt with primarily through law-enforcement agencies. Some population groups with drug-abuse problems are underserved: people with AIDS, women in general, pregnant women, and the homeless. The trend toward managed care through insurance programs has restricted the availability of inpatient services. Professionals need to advocate on behalf of disadvantaged populations to persuade policymakers to provide more equitable drug-abuse treatment services.

As with any assessment framework, the approach presented in this chapter may need to be modified to fit specific situations. When assessing an adolescent, for example, questions need to be congruent with the adolescent's development and inclinations toward risk taking and experimentation with drugs.

It is critical that professionals identify and assess the needs of drug-involved clients. In order to do so, workers need to acquire knowledge and skills through continuing education programs. Just as important is a commitment to advocate for comprehensive policies and treatment services that address the psychosocial causes and effects contributing to drug misuse.

REFERENCES

American Psychiatric Association. (1987). *Diagnostic and statistical manual of mental disorders* (3rd ed., rev.). Washington, DC: Author.

Bell, P., & Evans, J. (1983). Counseling the black alcoholic client. In T. Watts & R. Wright, Jr. (Eds.), *Black alcoholism* (pp. 100–121). Springfield, IL: Charles C Thomas.

Deakins, S. M., Seif, N. N., & Weinstein, D. L. (1983). In support of routine screening for alcoholism. In D. Cook et al. (Eds.), *Social work treatment of alcohol problems* (pp. 16–22). New Brunswick, NJ: Rutgers Center of Alcohol Studies.

Extein, I., & Dackis, C. A. (1987). Brain mechanism of cocaine dependency. In A. M. Washton & M. S. Gold (Eds.), *Cocaine: A clinician's handbook* (pp. 73–84). New York: Guilford Press.

Grinspoon, L., & Bakalar, J. B. (1990). Drug abuse and dependence. *The Harvard Medical School Mental Health Review. 1,* 26.

Levinson, V. R. (1983). How to conduct an alcoholism focused intake interview. In D. Cook et al. (Eds.), *Social work treatment of alcohol problems* (pp. 23–37). New Brunswick, NJ: Rutgers Center of Alcohol Studies.

Ray, O., & Ksir, C. (1987). *Drugs, society, and human behavior* (4th ed.). St. Louis: Times Mirror/Mosby.

U.S. Department of Health and Human Services. (1990). *Seventh special report to the U.S. Congress on alcohol and health.* (DHHS Publication No. ADM 90-1656). Rockville, MD: Author.

Zankowski, G. L. (1987). Responsive programming: Meeting the needs of chemically dependent women. *Alcoholism Treatment Quarterly, 4*(4), 53–66.

Zimberg, S. (1982). *The clinical management of alcoholism.* New York: Brunner/Mazel.

Screening for Affective Disorders

Julia B. Rauch, Carla Sarno, and Sylvia Simpson

14

P ractitioners in family and children's services need skills for assessing mood disorders and for referring symptomatic individuals for psychiatric evaluation. The personal and social costs of mood disorders are high and include suicide; increased mortality from physical disease; drug and alcohol abuse; and disruption of relationships, education, and careers (Akiskal & Weller, 1989; Boyd & Weissman, 1985; Brent, 1987; Goodwin & Guze, 1989; Goodwin & Jamison, 1990; Stoudemire, Frank, Hedemark, Kamlet, & Blazer, 1986; Whybrow, Akiskal, & McKinney, 1984). Unfortunately, these illnesses are underrecognized and undertreated, resulting in preventable, needless suffering for both afflicted individuals and their families (Costello, 1989). Family and children's workers are strategically positioned to screen for affective disorders and to assist affected clients and their families to secure needed psychiatric care, support services, and entitlements.

Sound assessment is a prerequisite to selection of effective intervention. Careful appraisal is particularly critical with affective disorders because they can be life threatening. Failure to diagnose a severe affective disorder may end in suicide or even homicide. Further, workers who do not recognize possible mood-disordered clients or who do not refer them for competent psychiatric evaluation are at risk for malpractice, as are their employers.

Scientific understanding of affective disorders is increasing rapidly (Keller, 1989). Etiological paradigms are changing as a result of evidence that these conditions are often inherited biological diseases and are amenable to pharmacological treatment (Akiskal, 1989; Engel, 1977; Kupfer, 1982; Group for the Advancement of Psychiatry, 1989; Marmor, 1983; Sabelli & Carlson-Sabelli, 1989). Screening for affective disorders should be a routine part of initial assessment in family and children's agencies. Additionally, workers should know how to monitor mood-disordered clients (and/or their significant others), how to assess the risks of harm to themselves or others, and when to contact the treating psychiatrist about possible changes in medication or the need for a more protective environment.

The purpose of this chapter is to update clinicians about current developments in affective disorders. It also provides guidelines for screening. The need for partnerships between family and children's services workers and psychiatrists is discussed.

Biological Aspects of Affective Disorders

Inheritance

Five decades of epidemiological research have documented that affective disorders run in families and provided evidence of biological inheritance (Blehar, Weissman, Gershon, & Hirschfeld, 1988; Gershon, 1989; Gershon, Berrettini, & Goldin, 1989; Mendlewicz, 1985; Nurnberger, Goldin, & Gershon, 1986; Tsuang & Faraone, 1990). Studies have compared (1) the incidence of mood disorders in families of unipolar or bipolar patients with control groups, (2) concordance for affective illness in identical and fraternal twins, and (3) the frequency of affective illness in biological and adoptive parents of afflicted adult adoptees and in adopted children of ill mothers.

Despite methodological difficulties, findings of these studies consistently provide evidence for genetic factors in affective disorders. Relatives of bipolar and unipolar patients have higher prevalence of mood disorders than do relatives of control groups (Mendlewicz, 1985; Gershon, 1989; Wender, Kety, Rosenthal, Schulsinger, Ortmann, & Lunde, 1986). Several studies documented higher concordance for affective disorders among identical twins than among fraternal twins (Tsuang & Faraone, 1990). Although family, twin, and adoption studies provide evidence for genetic factors in affective disorders, they also document the power of environmental factors. All families had unaffected as well as affected members.

Clinical Aspects of Affective Disorders

Characteristics

The primary symptoms of mood disorders are depression, elation, or mood swings between the two. However, disturbed mood itself is not diagnostic. Affective disorders are clinical syndromes, or clusters, of symptoms. *The Diagnostic and Statistical Manual of Mental Disorders* (DSM-

III-R) (American Psychiatric Association, 1987) identifies three categories of these conditions: major affective disorders and syndromes, other specific affective disorders, and atypical affective disorders. This chapter focuses on the first group, major affective disorders such as unipolar (depressive) and bipolar (manic depressive) syndromes. These disorders are the most common and most likely to be seen in family and children's agencies.

Affective disorders vary on several dimensions (Whybrow, Akiskal, & McKinney, 1984).

- Mood—depression, elation, or both
- Time—acute or chronic, age of onset, duration of episodes and intervals between episodes, episode frequency
- Severity—psychotic or nonpsychotic
- Etiology—symptoms primarily caused by affective disorders or by another condition (i.e., medical illness)
- Apparent response to environmental change and intervention (responsive or nonresponsive)

Thus, individual pictures vary considerably even within the same disease category. For example, one person may have a first episode of major depression in adolescence and experience it recurrently throughout life. Another person may have only a single episode in late adulthood.

Unipolar Affective Disorders

Unipolar affective disorders in which patients experience recurrent episodes of depressed mood are the most common. In depression, the "down" mood differs from ordinary sadness or "blues" and includes painful emotions and the absence of pleasure (anhedonia). The painful dimension is usually related to anxiety, guilt, anguish, and restlessness.

A diagnosis of major depressive episode is assigned when an individual has at least five of the nine symptoms listed below for at least two weeks:

- depressed mood . . . most of the day, nearly every day
- markedly diminished interest or pleasure in all, or almost all, activities
- significant weight loss or weight gain when not dieting . . . or decrease or increase in appetite
- insomnia or hypersomnia nearly every day
- psychomotor agitation or retardation
- fatigue or loss of energy nearly every day
- feelings of worthlessness, or excessive or inappropriate guilt
- diminished ability to think or concentrate, or indecisiveness
- recurrent thoughts of death . . . recurrent suicidal ideation with a specific plan, or a suicide attempt or a specific plan for committing suicide (American Psychiatric Association, 1987, pp. 222–223).

A diagnosis of melancholia (endogenous depression) requires at least five symptoms but also a history of (1) one or more major depressive episodes followed by complete, or nearly complete, recovery and (2) previous good response to specific and adequate somatic antidepressant therapy (American Psychiatric Association, 1987).

Dysthymia, according to DSM-III-R,

> is a less severe form of unipolar illness characterized by depressed mood for most of the day, more days than not, for at least two years and the presence of at least two of six other symptoms: (1) poor appetite or overeating, (2) insomnia or hypersomnia, (3) low energy or fatigue, (4) low self-esteem, (5) poor concentration or difficulty making decisions, (6) feelings of hopelessness (American Psychiatric Association, 1987, p. 230).

Bipolar Affective Disorders

Bipolar diagnoses are based on the presence of episodes of elevated mood, with or without intervening depression. In mania, a distinct period of abnormally and persistently elevated, expansive, or irritable mood is present. During the period of mood disturbance, at least three of seven symptoms must persist:

- inflated self-esteem or grandiosity
- decreased need for sleep
- more talkative than usual or pressure to keep talking
- flight of ideas or subjective experience that thoughts are racing
- distractibility
- increase in goal-directed activity (either socially, at work or school, or sexually) or psychomotor agitation
- excessive involvement in pleasurable activities which have a high potential for painful consequences, e.g., unrestrained buying sprees, sexual indiscretions or foolish business investments (American Psychiatric Association, 1987, p. 217)

The diagnostic criteria for manic episodes require sufficient symptom severity to cause marked impairment in occupational functioning or relationships, or to necessitate hospitalization to prevent harm to self or others. The person may be psychotic.

In hypomania, individuals meet all the criteria for a manic episode but without significant impairment. A diagnosis of cyclothymic disorder is assigned if numerous episodes of hypomania occur during a two-year period, along with numerous periods of depressed mood that did not meet criteria for major depression (American Psychiatric Association, 1987).

Differential Diagnosis

One complexity of differential diagnosis is distinguishing mood disorders from the normal emotional ups and downs that everyone goes through and from expected responses to loss and other psychosocial stressors. The line between normality and psychopathology is blurred. Some experts contend that affective disorders vary along a continuum;

others assert that affective disorders are qualitatively different from other variations in mood (Whybrow, Akiskal, & McKinney, 1984). In addition, normal reactions to catastrophic losses may include severe, disturbing symptoms similar to those found in affective disorders. For example, bereaved people may report seeing and hearing the lost loved one and express fears that they are going crazy.

The concept of *autonomy* helps to define the boundaries between normality and psychopathology (Whybrow, Akiskal, & McKinney, 1984). Autonomy means that the illness develops according to its own characteristics; it may emerge suddenly without any discernible reason for onset and may manifest mood and symptoms that are inappropriate to the person's situation.

Differential diagnosis is also complicated because symptoms of different mental illnesses can overlap. For example, symptoms of hallucinations and delusions can occur in both bipolar illness and schizophrenia. In those instances, it is useful to look at the course of the person's illness and the family history. Making the correct diagnosis has important treatment ramifications. Increasing knowledge of the biology of affective disorders may make it possible in the future to diagnose on the basis of biochemical laboratory tests (DePaulo, Simpson, Folstein, & Folstein, 1989).

Masking of depressive symptoms may also hinder differential diagnosis. Depression may manifest as stomach pains, headaches, backaches, palpitations, and a host of other physical complaints. People with masked depression may claim to have no sad feelings, although they may admit to being upset about their health. According to one study, one-third to two-thirds of all hospitalized medical and surgical patients older than 40 are suffering from masked depression and not the disease for which they are receiving treatment (Hamilton, 1989). Drug and alcohol abuse, eating disorders, and antisocial behavior may also conceal underlying depression.

Differential diagnosis in children and adolescents is also complex. Early symptoms of bipolar illness in children may appear as attention-deficit hyperactivity disorder (Schmidt & Friedson, 1990). Adolescents who appear to be angry and conduct disordered may have a mixed state, that is, simultaneous presentation of significant symptoms of depression and mania (Puig-Antich, Ryan, & Rabinovich, 1985).

Medical disorders accompanied apparently by psychiatric symptoms also complicate differential diagnosis. Depressed mood and allied symptoms appear with numerous medical "mimickers." These include hypothyroidism, diabetes, and other endocrine diseases; neurological problems such as multiple sclerosis, stroke, and Parkinson's disease; some cancers; heart disease; infectious diseases such as mononucleosis and infectious hepatitis; and autoimmune disorders (lupus).

Drugs and alcohol are powerful mood-altering substances; licit drugs (such as birth control pills) and illicit drugs (such as cocaine) can cause symptoms that mimic depression and mania and can also trigger episodes of these illnesses. A relatively common but underrecognized cause of depressed feelings is undernutrition, particularly in poor people and others with poor diets (Belle, 1982; Cassel, 1987; Wortis, 1985).

Guidelines for Screening Affective Disorders

Probing for Symptoms

Although psychiatric expertise is required for full diagnosis of complex conditions involving affective disorders, nonpsychiatric clinicians can provide a valuable service to their clients by screening for these disorders. Clients' presenting problems may include disturbed mood, for example, persistent depressed feelings or unusual irritability. Much information may be obtained by probing clients' statements while using diagnostic criteria as a guide (Tables 1 and 2). For example,

> You say that you are feeling pretty low. Could you tell me more about that? When did you start feeling this way?

If a client's narrative omits important symptom clusters, the worker should ask directly about specific symptoms to make sure that the possibility of an affective disorder is not overlooked.

> I would like to ask you about something that we haven't talked about yet—your appetite. Have your eating habits changed since you began to feel blue? That is,

Table 1. Screening questions for depression.

Over the past two weeks:

Has your mood been sad or irritable most of the time?

Do you have less interest or pleasure in doing things most of the time?

Have you lost or gained weight? If so, how much?

Are you sleeping too much or too little?

Do you feel restless or tired?

Do you feel tired or run down nearly every day?

Are you having feelings of worthlessness or severe guilt?

Are you having trouble concentrating or having a hard time making up your mind?

Have you been thinking about death or suicide?

Have you lost a close relative or loved one within the past year?

Are you taking any medicines? If so, what are they?

Do you use alcohol or drugs? If so, what do you use and how often do you use it (them)?

Have you ever been treated for depression or had a psychiatric hospitalization? If so, how often and when?

Table 2. Screening questions for mania.

Have you ever felt unusually excited, energetic, or irritable?

If the person answers "yes" to this question, proceed with the questions below. Even if the person clearly answers "no," proceed with the additional screening questions if you suspect that the person may have been manic. If you are confident that the person has never been manic, you may stop here.

During the time your mood changed, did you ever feel that you had special powers or gifts?

Did you ever feel that you needed less sleep? For example, have you ever felt rested after three hours of sleep?

During the time you felt unusually excited or energetic, did people tell you that you talked too much or too fast?

Did you feel your thoughts were racing or going too fast?

During the time when your mood changed, did you feel easily distracted or drawn to unimportant details?

Did you ever feel that you had so much energy that you needed to keep moving?

Did you ever do things that could have hurt or injured you?

Did you lose a job or friend during the time you felt unusually energetic?

---

do you eat more than you used to, are you eating less, or are you eating about the same?

When obtaining data for assessment, workers should ask about mood, even if the client has not mentioned disturbed feelings.

Many people who are having trouble with their children feel pretty down, pretty hard on themselves. What about you? Have you been feeling more depressed than you usually do?

As mentioned above, disturbed mood itself is not diagnostic; in some cases, a person with an affective disorder may not report disturbed mood. For this reason, workers should systematically explore whether symptoms are present.

Assessment of Danger

Dealing with risk of suicide is difficult but essential. Practitioners should ask directly whether the depressed client is thinking about killing him- or herself. Such questions can be asked tactfully in response to the client's description of low mood:

You say that you've been feeling pretty low recently. Have you been feeling so badly that you think about killing yourself?

Some workers may worry that asking a client about suicide will "plant" the idea. However, clients are usually relieved that someone takes them seriously and appreciates how badly they feel (Puryear, 1984; McAlpine, 1987).

The client's response should be probed in some detail. If the client has a specific plan, the means for carrying it out (gun, pills, rope), and the intention of implementing the plan, suicide risk is high. Workers should also determine whether clients have previously attempted to kill themselves and if they have known anyone who committed suicide. Famous people (e.g., Janis Joplin or Jimi Hendrix) may be role models for the potentially suicidal person. Social contagion may occur, as has happened in some high schools and communities in which suicide "epidemics" have occurred (Brent, Kerr, Goldstein, Bozigar, Martella, & Allan, 1989).

If the person has a plan and the means to commit suicide, the practitioner must act quickly. The worker should not attempt to resolve the situation alone but should consult with colleagues. If the client will not agree to see a psychiatrist or go to a hospital, the worker should notify relatives (or other legally responsible persons) of the danger. Significant others should be advised of (1) the client's need for evaluation and hospitalization and (2) the process for obtaining an emergency petition, if the person is unwilling to seek help voluntarily. They should be told to remove instruments of suicide from the home and to not leave the person alone. The worker should stay closely in touch with the family until hospitalization is achieved.

If the client has no relatives or if the family is unwilling to cooperate, the practitioner may need to file for an emergency petition and call the police to transport the client to a psychiatric emergency service. Because the person should not be left alone, the practitioner may need to cancel other appointments and stay with the person until other arrangements are made.

Practitioners should continue to monitor risk for suicide, even if the client protests that she or he is OK. Paradoxically, some people commit suicide when they are recovering from a depressive episode. Severely depressed people may not have enough energy to act. However, when the antidepressants kick in, the person is energized and thus may take the steps necessary, such as buying a gun, to implement the plan.

Clients may insist that they will never kill themselves. However, commission of suicide is "state dependent." Although the client may not be planning death *now*, he or she may become more deeply depressed and suicidal in the future. It is better to err on the side of overestimating risk than minimizing it. For example, some clients use talk about suicide as a histrionic, emotional, and frequently manipulative tactic. It may be tempting to believe that the client does not "really mean it." Such clients, however, may kill themselves impulsively, their gesture inadvertently proving lethal. A common method is overdose with antidepressants.

Several variables are associated with increased risk of suicide (Mollica, 1989; Hirschfeld & Cross, 1982; Roy, 1989):

■ Age 45 years or older
■ Male

- Divorced or widowed
- Unemployed or retired
- Conflictual interpersonal relationships
- Chronic illness and/or hypochondriasis
- Family history of suicide
- Substance abuse
- Severe personality disorder
- Frequent, intense, and prolonged suicidal ideation
- Previous suicide attempts
- Suicide plan, especially one that makes rescue before death unlikely
- Unambiguous wish to die
- Method lethal and available
- Feeling of guilt and self-blame
- Poor achievement, lack of success
- Poor insight
- Social isolation
- Unresponsive family

Each suicide is idiosyncratic, of course. Nonetheless, if a client reports, for example, that she is worried about her 67-year-old retired, recently widowed father who is losing weight and not sleeping well, the worker should be instantly attuned to the possibility of the father's suicide.

Risks with Mania

People who are in manic states are unlikely to cooperate with mental health professionals and may be dangerous. At first, changes in mood are not seen as problematic and may be welcomed if the person has been depressed. The manic individual becomes cheerful, enthusiastic, and appears to relish life. This zest may be infectious, and other people may enjoy being with the manic person. Thus, the manic individual (and significant others) may see no need for intervention. Only if there is family history of mania are members likely to view apparent well-being as a warning.

The euphoric mood, however, is volatile and can quickly change at the slightest frustration into anger, resentment, hostility, and unpredictable behavior. Manic people may be delusional or hear voices telling them to harm or kill themselves or others.

Family members and clinicians involved directly with manic individuals should follow safety precautions (Hirsh, 1988). First the potential for violence should be assessed. Predictors include a recent history of violence, recent acquisition of a weapon, presence of command hallucinations, preoccupation with thoughts of death, and a culture of violence in the individual's family or neighborhood. It is important that the manic individual, family members, and/or clinician all have the ability to escape a dangerous situation. The ability to secure help, for example, the police, is critical when dealing with unpredictable and potentially violent people.

Developing Partnerships

Contemporary Treatment

Treatment of affective disorders has progressed since the days of leeching by the ancient Greeks (Goodwin & Jamison, 1990). More new treatments have been developed in the 20th century than in all preceding epochs. An important change is the way in which psychiatric symptoms are classfied (Levy, 1982). In the past, categorization was based on inferences about unconscious processes. Reliance on inferences rather than observable, measurable characteristics created much disagreement among researchers and hindered research. Today, agreement about diagnoses is easier to achieve because clusters of symptoms are used as the basis for classification. Because diagnostic categories are based on measurable observation, they can be tested for usefulness in communication, etiological research, and prediction of clinical course (Hirschfeld & Shea, 1989).

Contemporary psychiatric classification is particularly useful in assessing the effectiveness of particular medications and psychotherapies for specific conditions because before and after measurements can be obtained. Psychotherapies have been developed and evaluated for their effectiveness (Hirschfeld & Shea, 1989). Most therapies are short-term and aim to correct specific aspects of depression, including cognition, behavior, and affect. Psychoanalytic, interpersonal, behavioral, and cognitive models have been formulated and used (Hirschfeld & Shea, 1989). Most people with mood disorders respond to the first antidepressant with which they are treated. New antidepressants and mood stabilizers are now available for treating persons with more presistent forms of mood disorders.

Moving from Consultantship to Partnership

Nonpsychiatric clinicians have and will continue to have an important psychotherapeutic role, especially with clients who do not require hospitalization and can be seen in community settings. They will also continue to play other roles, such as case manager, needs assessor, program developer, and program administrator. However, a clinician/psychiatric *partnership* must be nurtured.

A thorough psychiatric and medical history and examination of individuals with symptoms of affective disorders are necessary to detect any potential medical causes of symptoms before psychosocial interventions can be selected. In some instances, no services may be required; in other instances, multiple services may be needed.

Family and children's agencies historically have utilized psychiatric consultation. In the past, consultants tended to be psychoanalytically oriented. The psychiatrist provided insight into psychodynamic factors and suggested appropriate psychotherapeutic methods. Advice was usually given in response to case presentations, and the psychiatrist did not interview the client. Current knowledge of biological determinants of affective disorders requires that the role of the agency-affiliated psychiatric consultant be redefined. The agency must assure that symptomatic clients obtain a competent medical and psychiatric evaluation.

In some cases, clients may have a regular source of medical care and may have recently had a diagnostic workup. However, relying on clients' health care providers can be risky. Some clients do not have adequate health care coverage and may not have access to quality health care. Busy physicians may not keep up to date on new developments and may have little time to spend with patients. Thus, the examination may be superficial, the right questions may not be asked, and potentially helpful tests may not be administered. It may be advisable to suggest that the client obtain a second opinion.

In selecting psychiatric consultation, the agency and/or clinician should inquire about psychiatrists' training, type of practice, hospital affiliations, illness model, approach to treatment, and, of course, attitudes toward nonpsychiatric mental health practice. The goal should be to obtain competent consultants who have a *biopsychosocial* perspective.

Once a diagnosis is established and a treatment plan is designed, agencies can offer the specific counseling and support services to enable mood-disordered individuals and their families to cope with the disease. Achieving this goal, however, depends upon schools of social work and agencies providing the needed foundation knowledge, in-service training, and continuing education to prepare practitioners for their role in this emerging partnership.

REFERENCES

Akiskal, H. S. (1989). New insights into the nature and heterogeneity of mood disorders. *Journal of Clinical Psychiatry, 50* (Suppl.), 6–10.

Akiskal, H. S., & Weller, E. (1989). Mood disorders and suicide in children and adolescents. In H. I. Kaplan & B. J. Sadock (Eds.), *Comprehensive textbook of psychiatry* (vol. 2, 5th ed.) (pp. 1710–1715). Baltimore: Williams & Wilkins.

American Psychiatric Association. (1987). *Diagnostic and statistical manual of mental disorders* (3rd ed., rev.). Washington, DC: Author.

Belle, D. (1982). *Lives in stress: Women and depression.* Beverly Hills, CA: Sage Publications.

Blehar, M. C., Weissman, M. M., Gershon, E. S., & Hirschfeld, M. A. (1988). Family and genetic studies of affective disorders. *Archives of General Psychiatry, 45,* 289–292.

Boyd, J. H., & Weissman, M. M. (1985). Epidemiology of affective disorders. In R. Michaels, J. O. Cavernar, H. K. H. Brodie, A. M. Cooper, S. B. Guze, L. L. Judd, G. L. Klerman, & A. S. Solnit (Eds.), *Psychiatry* (vol. 3, rev.) (pp. 1–16). Philadelphia: J. B. Lippincott.

Brent, D. A. (1987). Correlates of the medical lethality of suicide. *Journal of the American Academy of Child and Adolescent Psychiatry, 26,* 87–91.

Brent, D. A., Kerr, M. M., Goldstein, C., Bozigar, J., Martella, M., & Allan, J. (1989). An outbreak of suicide and suicidal behavior in a high school. *Journal of the American Academy of Child and Adolescent Psychiatry, 28,* 918–924.

Cassel, R. N. (1987). Use of select nutrients to foster wellness. *Psychology: A Quarterly Journal of Human Behavior, 24,* 24–29.

Costello, E. J. (1989). Developments in child psychiatric epidemiology: Introduction. *Journal of the American Academy of Child and Adolescent Psychiatry, 28,* 836–841.

DePaulo, J. R., Jr., Simpson, W., Folstein, S. F., & Folstein, M. F. (1989). The new genetics of bipolar affective disorder: Clinical implications. *Clinical Chemistry, 35,* B28–B32.

Engel, G. L. (1977). The need for a new medical model: A challenge for biomedicine. *Science, 196,* 129–135.

Gershon, E. S. (1989). Recent developments in genetics of manic depressive illness. *Journal of Clinical Psychiatry, 50* (Suppl.), 4–7.

Gershon, E. S., Berrettini, W. H., & Goldin, L. R. (1989). Mood disorders. In H. I. Kaplan & B. J. Sadock (Eds.), *Comprehensive textbook of psychiatry* (vol. 1, 5th ed.). Baltimore: Williams & Wilkins.

Goodwin, D. W., & Guze, S. B. (1989). *Psychiatric diagnosis* (4th ed.). New York: Oxford University Press.

Goodwin, F. K., & Jamison, K. R. (1990). *Manic depressive illness.* New York: Oxford University Press.

Group for the Advancement of Psychiatry. Committee on the Family (1989). The challenge of relational diagnoses: Applying the biopsychosocial model in DSM-IV. *American Journal of Psychiatry, 140,* 1492–1494.

Hamilton, M. (1989). Mood disorders: Clinical features. In H. I. Kaplan & B. J. Sadock (Eds.), *Comprehensive textbook of psychiatry* (vol. 1, 5th ed.). Baltimore: Williams & Wilkins.

Hirsh, P. R. (1988). Psychiatric emergencies for nonpsychiatrists. *Treatment trends. A newsletter of Taylor Manor Hospital, 3*(2), 1–7.

Hirschfeld, R. M. A., & Cross, C. K. (1982). Epidemiology of affective disorders: Psychosocial risk factors. *Archives of General Psychiatry, 39,* 35–46

Hirschfeld, R. M. A., & Shea, M. T. (1989). Mood disorders: Psychosocial treatments. In. H. I. Kaplan & B. J. Sadock (Eds.), *Comprehensive textbook of psychiatry* (vol. 1, 5th ed.) (pp. 933–944). Baltimore: Williams & Wilkins.

Keller, M. B. (1989). Current concepts in affective disorders. *Journal of Clinical Psychiatry, 50,* 153–162.

Kupfer, D. J. (1982). Toward a unified view of affective disorders. In N. I. Zale (Ed.), *Affective and schizophrenic disorders* (pp. 225–262). New York: Brunner/Mazel.

Levy, R. (1982). *The new language of psychiatry.* Boston: Little, Brown.

Lipton, M. A. (1982). The evolution of the biological understanding of affective disorders. In M. R. Zales (Ed.), *Affective and schizophrenic disorders* (pp. 5–28). New York: Brunner/Mazel.

Marmor, J. (1983). Systems thinking in psychiatry. *American Journal of Psychiatry, 140,* 833–838.

McAlpine, D. E. (1987). Suicide: Recognition and management. *Mayo Clinic Proceedings, 62,* 778–781.

Mendlewicz, J. (1985). Genetic research in depressive disorders. In E. E. Peckham & W. R. Leber (Eds.), *Handbook of depression: Treatment, assessment, and research.* Homewood, IL: Dorsey Press.

Mollica, R. F. (1989). Mood (affective) disorders. In H. I. Kaplan & B. J. Sadock (Eds.), *Comprehensive textbook of psychiatry* (vol. 1, 5th ed.) (pp. 859–867). Baltimore: Williams & Wilkins.

Nurnberger, J. I., Goldin, L. R., & Gershon, E. S. (1986). Genetics of psychiatric disorders. In G. Winokur & P. Clayton (Eds.), *The medical basis of psychiatry* (pp. 486–522). Philadelphia: W. B. Saunders.

Puig-Antich, J., Ryan, N. D., & Rabinovich, H. (1985). Affective disorders in childhood and adolescence. In J. M. Wiener (Ed.), *Diagnosis and psychopharmacology of childhood and adolescent disorders* (pp. 152–173) New York: John Wiley.

Puryear, D. A. (1984). *Helping people in crisis.* San Francisco: Jossey-Bass.

Roy, A. (1989). Suicide. In H. I. Kaplan & B. J. Sadock (Eds.), *Comprehensive textbook of psychiatry* (vol. 2, 5th ed.) (pp. 1414–1426). Baltimore: Williams & Wilkins.

Sabelli, H. C., & Carlson-Sabelli (1989). Biological priority and psychological supremacy: A new integrative paradigm derived from process theory. *American Journal of Psychiatry, 146,* 1541–1551.

Schmidt, K., & Friedson, S. (1990). Atypical outcome in attention deficit hyperactivity disorder. *Journal of the American Academy of Child and Adolescent Psychiatry, 29,* 566–569.

Stoudemire, A., Frank, R., Hedemark, N., Kamlet, M., & Blazer, D. (1986). The economic burden of depression. *General Hospital Psychiatry, 8,* 387–394.

Tsuang, M. T., & Faraone, S. V. (1990). *The genetics of mood disorder.* Baltimore: Johns Hopkins University Press.

Wender, P. H., Kety, S. S., Rosenthal, D., Schulsinger, F., Ortmann, J., & Lunde, I. (1986). Psychiatric disorders in the biological and adoptive families of adopted individuals with affective disorders. *Archives of General Psychiatry, 43,* 923–929.

Whybrow, P. C., Akiskal, H. S., & McKinney, W. T., Jr. (1984). *Mood disorders: Toward a new psychobiology.* New York: Plenum Press.

Wortis, J. (1985). Irreversible starvation. *Biological Starvation, 20,* 465–466.

Detecting Wife and Child Abuse In Clinical Settings

John S. Brekke

15

T he incidence of wife and child abuse in the United States is staggering and cuts across all socioeconomic lines (Straus, Gelles, & Steinmetz, 1980; Schulman, 1979).[1] Recent research has uncovered similar rates of violence among unmarried couples (Makepeace, 1981; Carlson, 1987; Cate, Henton, Koval, Christopher, & Lloyd, 1982). Even though the effects of this abuse on the victims are profound, less than 10% of abused children and their parents are accurately identified and treated by legal, medical, or social service professionals (Meier, 1985); the percentage is much lower for victims and perpetrators of wife abuse (Roy, 1982; Borkowski et al., 1983).

Not only has the social and institutional response to these forms of abuse been ponderous and contradictory, especially in the case of wife abuse, but both the perpetrators and victims have engaged in a conspiracy of silence (Finkelhor, 1983; Martin, 1977; Walker, 1979; Bowker, 1983; Bass & Rice, 1979; Meier, 1985). The perpetrators struggle to avoid detection, and the victims fear reprisals or even develop a brainwashed loyalty to the abuser. Nevertheless, the symptoms that have been noted in victims of child and wife abuse range from severe depression to agitated hostility, from enuresis to marked somatization (Hilberman & Munson, 1977–1978; Hilberman, 1980).

---

1. The term "wife," as used here, refers to the female partner in a committed, intimate relationship, whether the couple is married and living together or not.

Hence, the effects on the victims are far greater than the bruises or lacerations that may or may not be visible. In fact, some victims have reported that the psychological and emotional abuse, as opposed to the physical abuse, has a more debilitating impact on them (Walker, 1979; Pagelow, 1984).

Several factors impede the identification and treatment of victims and perpetrators of violence in families: the abuser's denial; the victim's shame and fear; the practitioner's denial; and a lack of awareness and coordination among legislative, judicial, police, and social service efforts (Carlson, 1984). Battered women are underidentified by 800% in emergency room settings, and it is argued that mental health practitioners have a much larger number of victims and abusers among their clients than they realize (Stark et al., 1979; Saunders, 1982).

This chapter provides clinicians with a nonthreatening and effective strategy for detecting wife and child abuse when it is not part of the presenting or identified problem. The contexts in which detection occurs and the clinical indicators that suggest abuse are discussed.

Overarching Principles

The present analysis is based on the following principles. First, the terms child and wife abuse are used in place of family or domestic violence, because the most pernicious abuse in families tends to occur between individuals with the greatest differential in power—husband to wife, parent to child, older to younger, male to female (Finkelhor, 1983; Straus et al., 1980). Second, the abuse is not considered to be the result of family pathology; rather it is viewed as a function of a perpetrator who uses violence to dominate others or to resolve conflict (instrumental aggression) or who "takes out" his or her frustrations on others (expressive aggression). Hence, clinical services for ending the abuse must focus on the abused and the abuser separately, rather than on manipulating the marital or family system (Walker, 1979; Saunders, 1984; Brekke, 1990; Bograd, 1982). Moreover, the familial or marital dysfunction that exists is considered an effect, not a cause, of the abuse (Walker, 1984). Clearly, systems-oriented interventions are useful at later stages of treatment. Initially, however, treatment should focus on helping the abuser gain control of his behavior and on securing the safety and recovery of the victim, which suggests the need for specialized and violence-focused intervention.

Finally, if abuse occurs during the treatment period but is not detected, two consequences are likely to result. First, the treatment may become perplexingly unproductive, and second, the clinician becomes an unwitting accomplice to the continuing abuse by reinforcing the denial of the victim or perpetrator. Hence, detection is an important part of the effort to end abuse in families.

Table 1. Clinical contexts for detecting abuse.

	Direct detection	Indirect detection
Wife abuse	Husband, wife, marital unit, family	Children
Child abuse	Perpetrator (mother or father), abused child, marital unit, family	Nonabusive parent, nonabused sibling

Definitions and Contexts

Wife and child abuse is defined as the use of physical force by a perpetrator with the intent or perceived intent to hurt or attempt to hurt the victim. Abuse ranges from threats, pushes, slaps, and punches to attacks with a knife or gun and rape. Forms of psychological aggression (screaming, swearing, belittling, extreme jealousy, and domination) are also included in this definition because this kind of abuse has pernicious effects and tends to escalate into physical aggression (Walker, 1979; Pagelow, 1984; Straus et al., 1980).

The worker must be not only a detector of wife and child abuse, but also an advocate for treatment and a protector. When the secret of abuse is uncovered, severe consequences may result for the woman or child. Therefore, the strategies for detection feature techniques that maximize the safety of the victim. Naturally, undetected abuse is confounding; careless detection, however, can create severe problems for the abused as well as minimize the chances for effective intervention.

Detection occurs in many clinical contexts. The following paradigm helps to distinguish these contexts and provides a means of organizing the various indicators (see Table 1). The first context is direct detection, which occurs when the perpetrator or victim is present. In the case of wife abuse, it occurs when the husband or wife is being seen alone or when either is present in family or marital treatment. In the case of child abuse, it occurs when the perpetrator or abused child is being seen alone or with a parent.

The indirect context involves any family member other than the perpetrator or direct victim. In the case of wife abuse, detection may occur when a child is in treatment, and in the case of child abuse, detection may occur when only the nonabusive parent or nonabused children are being treated. The point is that detection can occur in any of these contexts and that differing clinical signals of abuse may exist, depending on the context.

Wife Abuse

Indirect Context

A child who is in treatment because of child abuse or who shows signs of abuse is an indicator that the mother is being assaulted, regardless whether the child's abuser is the mother, father, or both. Various studies indicate that between 30% to 40% of wife abusers also abuse their children. According to Straus et al. (1980), child abuse is thirty times more likely to occur in homes in which the mother is being assaulted than it is in homes in which she is not. A recent study reported that in 50% of reported child sexual-molestation cases, the mother was also being abused by her husband (Herman & Hirschman, 1981).

If these overt indicators do not exist, the children of mothers who are being abused show evidence of problems ranging from depression to enuresis. Generally, however, a child who shows any of the following symptoms might be suffering the effects of living in a home in which his or her mother is being abused:

1. Pronounced hostility or aggression directed toward him- or herself or others
2. Depression
3. Extreme passivity or withdrawal
4. Fearfulness and lack of trust in the presence of adults
5. Overprotectiveness or hostility toward his or her mother
6. Unexplainable or recurrent illnesses or psychosomatic problems

Direct Context

The husband. When treating a man individually, several signals suggest that he is a perpetrator of abuse:

1. General hostility or passivity with the worker, family members, or others outside the family
2. Rigid sex-role perceptions
3. Patriarchal attitudes
4. History of abuse in his family of origin either as a witness of wife abuse or a victim
5. Feelings of being victimized by women
6. Isolation from significant relationships outside the family
7. Extreme jealousy
8. Inability to discriminate emotional states other than anger or frustration
9. Extreme dependency on the partner to satisfy his emotional needs

The wife. When treating a woman individually, several signals indicate that she may be a victim of abuse:

1. Evidence of physical injuries and an unwillingness to discuss them
2. Depression
3. Fear of emotional expression
4. Depersonalization
5. Passivity
6. Violence in her nuclear family of origin
7. Fear of sexual intimacy
8. Hostility toward her partner or others in the family

9. Self-deprecation

10. Overconcern for the safety of the children

11. Suicide attempts

Taken alone, none of these indices should be viewed as indicative of abuse. The clinician should look for patterns of behavior. In a family or marital session, the following behaviors may indicate wife abuse: any interaction of the above-listed indicators for the abusive man or battered woman, for example, hostile man and passive woman or passive man and hostile woman; rigid patterns of interaction; male dominance of the emotional or psychological atmosphere of the marriage or marital sessions; or evidence of extreme conflict or little or no conflict. Any combination of these indicators suggests the possibility of abuse.

Child Abuse

Direct Context[2]

The perpetrator. Any combination of the following indicators in either parent suggests the possibility of child abuse:

1. Mother abused by father

2. Isolation and a lack of trust

3. History of assault as children or violence in the family of origin

4. Excessive criticism of child, unrealistic expectations of child

5. Lack of concern about physical injuries, contradictory reports about the occurrence of injuries

6. Belief in or the use of harsh punishment

7. Lack of affection for child

8. Much conflict in marital relationship

9. Verbal aggression directed toward child

10. Lack of understanding regarding child's emotional and physical needs

The child. Indicators of abuse in children include the following:

1. Aggression or destructiveness toward self or others

2. Extreme passivity or withdrawal

3. Fear of adults and of physical contact or affection

4. Learning problems that cannot be satisfactorily explained

5. Inability to concentrate and self-absorption

6. Reluctance to return home after school

7. Extreme attachment toward parent(s)

8. Extreme attentiveness to the needs of the parent(s)

9. Sudden changes in behavior

10. Lethargy and tiredness at school

11. Repeated truancy from school

12. Inappropriate sexual acting out (any age)

2. Indicators for the direct context compiled from Meier (1985) and Straus et al. (1980).

13. Evidence of not being properly cared for

As in the case of wife abuse, indicators of child abuse in the family and marital contexts include any combination of the indicators listed above as well as rigid patterns of familial or marital interaction.

Indirect Context

The nonabusing parent. Indicators of child abuse in a nonabusing parent include the following:

1. Emotional lability
2. Reticence regarding conflict in the family
3. Nonspecific anger toward marital partner
4. Fear of partner's emotional expression
5. Concern about how the other parent disciplines the children
6. Unwillingness to leave other parent alone with the children
7. Labeling child a "problem child"

The nonabused sibling(s). Indicators of child abuse in a nonabused sibling include the following:

1. Reluctance to talk about the victimized child or forgetting to mention the victim in discussion of family interactions
2. Evidence of the nonphysical symptoms listed for the abused sibling
3. Overconcern for the abused sibling
4. Reluctance to discuss the behavior of the parents

Clearly, the characteristics of the wife or child abuser, the effects of the abuse on the victims, and the actual occurrence of the abuse can be similar in wife- and child-abuse cases. Nevertheless, it is extremely important to detect the kind of abuse that is occurring. It is easier to obtain accurate information when a particular family relationship is targeted and the client is less likely to be overwhelmed.

Strategy for Detection: Funneling

The best way to detect wife or child abuse is to ask about it; however, the most fruitful way to ask is to use a technique called funneling. An abrupt or poorly managed attempt to broach the subject of abuse can create defensiveness in the client and keep the secret from being exposed. Funneling is the same regardless of the treatment context, although the referents will change somewhat depending on whether the detection is for child or wife abuse and the context. The following example illustrates the detection by funneling of wife abuse in a perpetrator who was being individually treated. Changes in the referents to reflect child abuse are provided in parentheses.

Step one: Direct the interview to conflict. "Mr. Jones, up to now we have been talking about your problems at work and the lack of support you feel that you receive from your wife. I'd like to switch topics and talk about how conflict is handled at home."

Step two: Define conflict. "Conflict is whenever two or more people disagree about something."

Step three: Normalize and generalize conflict. "As you can see from the definition, all families or marriages have conflict. In fact, it is impossible not to have conflict in relationships. Conflict can occur over which movie to see, when to change the kitty litter, or how to raise the kids."

Step four: Personalize areas of conflict. "Mr. Jones, would you describe some of the conflicts between you and your wife (child)?"

Step five: Address solutions to conflict. "Usually, it is how we handle conflict that is the problem, rather than the conflict itself. For example, some couples (parents) sit and talk it out, others scream or yell, and still others feel it is better not to discuss the conflict and hope it will go away."

Step six: Personalize solutions to conflict. "Mr. Jones, would you tell me some of the ways you and your wife (child) have handled conflict?"

Step seven: Recent example. "Would you give me a recent example of a conflict (upset), what the conflict was about, and who did or said what to whom?"

Step eight: Example of serious conflict. "Would you tell me about the most serious conflict (upset) between you and your spouse (child)—the one that sticks out in you mind—what it was about and what happened?"

Step nine: Probe for threats or use of violence. "Mr. Jones, have you or your wife (child) ever been so angry that you said or did something that you later wish you had not?"

Step ten: Administer the domestic abuse scale.

The domestic abuse scale (Figure 1), which is a modification of Straus's (1979) Conflict Tactics Scale, allows the clinician to get an accurate picture of the specific kinds of abuse that have occurred. Although it does not measure frequency of the acts, it can be assumed that one occurrence implies others. It is given orally to the client, after which it and the client's responses are reviewed with him or her. Finally, the client is asked to reflect on the abuse that has occurred and how it might relate to the problems that they have been experiencing.

The funneling technique brings up the subject of abuse gradually; in this way the clinician is likely to obtain more complete and accurate information. However, the following should be taken into consideration.

First, in work with small children, puppet interviews can be very useful (Irwin, 1983).

Second, the topic of abuse can be very painful, so the clinician must remain sensitive to the client's emotional state and pace the interview accordingly. The client should be allowed to explain, perhaps at great length, the situation that led up to the abusive incident. In general, the more comfortable the client feels, the more he or she is likely to reveal accurate information.

Third, the two most salient criteria for detecting abuse are the actual incidents reported and the client's reaction to them. Clearly, however, the more serious the abuse, the more likely abuse is a primary problem that deserves special attention. It is also important to remember that the

I will read you a list of things that you may or may not have done to your partner during an argument or at any other time. Please tell me whether or not you behaved in each of these ways at any time in your relationship with your partner. Some of these items may be painful to consider, so take as much time as you need.

Psychological abuse — Yes / No

1. Did or said something to spite her
2. Sulked or refused to talk about an issue
3. Stomped out of the room, house, or yard
4. Insulted her or swore at her
5. Interrupted her eating or sleeping
6. Said she could not leave or see certain people
7. Verbally pressured her to have sex
8. Threatened to leave the relationship
9. Threatened to withhold money, take away children, have an affair, and so forth
10. Withheld sex from her
11. Screamed or yelled
12. Smashed, kicked, or hit an object

Physical aggression

13. Threatened to hit her or throw something at her
14. Pushed, carried, restrained, grabbed, or shoved her
15. Slapped or spanked her
16. Drove recklessly to frighten her
17. Burned her
18. Threw an object at her
19. Kicked her or hit her with a fist
20. Threw her bodily
21. Physically forced sex on her
22. Hit her or tried to hit her with something

Life-threatening violence

23. Beat her up (multiple blows)
24. Choked or strangled her
25. Threatened her with a knife or gun
26. Used a knife or gun

This scale should be administered to both the perpetrator and the female victim. For use with victims, change all personal pronouns from "her" and "she" to "you." For detecting child abuse some items might not apply and can be eliminated. Pronouns may also be changed when detecting in the indirect contexts. (Based on Straus [1979].)

Figure 1. Domestic abuse scale.

purpose of the detection is not to diagnose someone as a victim or perpetrator, but to alert those involved to the potential need for further treatment in this area.

Fourth, when working in treatment contexts in which both the victim and perpetrator are present, it is very important not to put the victim in the position of revealing information that will lead to later retaliation by the abuser. If the atmosphere of the interview becomes too tense, the detection may have to be postponed. For example, in family or marital sessions, the clinician may notice uncharacteristic verbal or nonverbal tension when reaching step five or step six—address solutions to conflict, personalize solutions to conflict—of the detection. If this occurs, it may indicate that abuse is indeed occurring. At this point, the therapist should postpone the detection procedure in the following manner: "Well, it appears that the subject of conflict is a delicate one here—perhaps we can return to it later. For now I would like to turn to . . . " This may not prevent the revelations from emerging, but it does give the victim a way out.

Should it become necessary to terminate the detection process for reasons of victim safety, it is important to suggest separate interviews with the partners or children in order to complete the detection process individually. Victims will usually comply with the abuser's minimization and denial of the problem until they feel safe in individual treatment sessions. The abuser may also feel less pressure to conceal his or her behavior in individual treatment. However, the clinician should always avoid raising the abuser's suspicions by telling him or her that separate interviews are a routine and periodic part of the treatment process. No reference should be made to the detection of abuse.

In some cases, however, it is almost impossible to prevent the revelation of abuse once the detection process begins. The victim may insist on breaking the silence once given the chance and can sometimes appear quite hostile and fearless. If this occurs, the therapist must spend a few minutes with the victim(s) alone at the end of the session in order to avail them of crisis, shelter, and police services in their community. They will need options should the abuser retaliate.

Most clinicians, it is assumed, inform their clients of mandatory child-abuse reporting at the beginning of treatment. Clearly, if child abuse is detected it must be reported. It is also important to search for evidence of wife abuse if the children are being assaulted. Adequate treatment must target all extant forms of abuse. The trauma that clinicians sometimes feel in reporting child abuse can be offset by a consideration of the possible motivation for treatment that may result after the client's anger has been explored.

Finally, if abuse is detected, what then? With wife abuse, the ideal solution is to refer the family to an agency that specializes in the assessment and treatment of battered women and abusing men. Further treatment decisions can then be coordinated with the referring agency or practitioner. Descriptions of programs for aiding abused women are available in the social work literature (Star, 1983; Saunders, 1984), and local mental health agencies or feminist organizations sometimes have lists of appropriate centers or practitioners. In addition, many urban areas have shelters for abused women and programs for men who batter.

It must be remembered, however, that victims and perpetrators of wife and child abuse are likely to deny the severity of the problem even when the abuse is extreme, which puts the practitioner in the position of having to identify a problem for which none of the parties may want treatment. In the case of child abuse, this problem can be handled with legally coercive means. With wife abuse, further treatment can be made contingent upon those involved or affected seeking specialized help, or the worker can continue seeing the clients while working slowly toward such an agreement. (Clinical strategies for working with perpetrators and victims of wife abuse can be found in Brekke [1990] and Saunders [1982].) Whatever treatment strategies are chosen, the growing sensitivity generally to family violence and the worker's sense of professional responsibility will keep him or her from ignoring the problem.

REFERENCES

Bass, D., & Rice, J. (1979). Agency responses to the abused wife. *Social Casework, 60,* 338–342.

Bograd, M. (1982). Battered women, cultural myths and clinical interventions: A feminist analysis. In New England Association for Women in Psychology (Ed.), *Current feminist issues in psychotherapy.* New York: Haworth Press.

Borkowski, M., et al. (1983). *Marital violence: The community response.* New York: Tavistock Publications.

Bowker, L. (1983). *Beating wife-beating.* Lexington, MA: Lexington Press.

Brekke, J. (1990). Crisis intervention with victims and perpetrators of spouse abuse. In H. Parad & L. Parad (Eds.), *Crisis intervention, book 2.* Milwaukee, WI: Family Service America.

Carlson, B. (1987). Dating violence: A research review and comparison with spouse abuse. *Social Casework, 68,* 16–23.

Carlson, B. E. (1984). Causes and maintenance of domestic violence: An ecological analysis. *Social Service Review, 58,* 569–587.

Cate, R. M., Henton, J. M., Koval, J., Christopher, F. S., & Lloyd, S. (1982). Premarital abuse: A social psychological perspective. *Journal of Family Issues, 3,* 79–90.

Finkelhor, D. (1983). Common features of family abuse. In D. Finkelhor, et al. (Eds.), *The dark side of families.* Beverly Hills, CA: Sage Publications.

Herman, J., & Hirschman, L. (1981). Families at risk for father–daughter incest. *American Journal of Psychiatry, 138,* 967–970.

Hilberman, E. (1980). Overview: The "wife-beater's wife" reconsidered. *American Journal of Psychiatry, 137,* 1336–1348.

Hilberman, E., & Munson, K. (1977–78). Sixty battered women. *Victimology, 2*(3–4), 460–470.

Irwin, E. C. (1983). The diagnostic and therapeutic use of pretend play. In C. Schaefer & K. O'Connor (Eds.), *Handbook of play therapy.* New York: John Wiley.

Makepeace, J. (1981). Courtship violence among college students. *Family Relations, 30,* 97–102.

Martin, D. (1977). *Battered wives.* New York: Pocket Books.

Meier, J. H. (1985). Definition, dynamics and prevalence of assault against children: A multifactorial model. In J. H. Meier (Ed.), *Assault against children.* San Diego, CA: College Hill Press.

Pagelow, M. (1984). *Family violence.* New York: Praeger.

Roy, M. (1982). *The abusive partner: An analysis of domestic battering.* New York: Van Nostrand Reinhold.

Saunders, D. (1982). Counseling the violent husband. In P. Keller & L. G. Ritt (Eds.), *Innovations in clinical practice,* vol. 1. Sarasota, FL: Professional Resources Exchange.

Saunders, D. (1984). Helping husbands who batter. *Social Casework, 65,* 347–353.

Schulman, M. (1979). *A survey of spousal violence against women in Kentucky.* New York: Louis Harris Association.

Star, B. (1983). *Helping the abuser: Intervening effectively in family violence.* New York: Family Service Association of America.

Stark, E., et al. (1979). Medicine and patriarchal violence: The social construction of a private event. *International Journal of Health Services, 9,* 461–493.

Straus, M. (1979). Measuring intrafamily conflict and violence: The conflict tactics (CT) scales. *Journal of Marriage and the Family, 41,* 75–89.

Straus, M. A., Gelles, R. J., & Steinmetz, S. (1980). *Behind closed doors, violence in the American family.* New York: Doubleday/Anchor.

Walker, L. (1979). *The battered woman.* New York: Harper and Row.

Walker, L. (1984). *The battered woman syndrome.* New York: Springer.

Assessing Violent Couples

Harriet Douglas

16

Couple violence is a major social problem. The U.S. Department of Justice estimates that 95% of assaults on spouses or ex-spouses are committed by men against women (Bureau of Justice Statistics, 1983). It is estimated that more than two million women are beaten each year, 75% of whom never seek emergency shelter (Herman, 1989). The problem is underreported and often undetected by mental health professionals, especially in the early stages. As a result, professional awareness of the problem has tended to focus on the crisis state, not on the violence that may occur well before crisis erupts.

Practitioners need to be aware that couple violence is a hidden problem. They need skills to identify the violence and to assess how and why it is occurring with a particular couple. However, clinical assessment is sometimes confounded by language and concepts necessary for the political processes of advocacy, lawmaking, funding, and provision of crisis services. Conceptualizing a criminal act of assault and battery that involves an assailant who must be punished and a victim who must be protected and sheltered simplifies the process and makes clear to social agencies the protective laws and services that are needed. However, both the conceptual polarization of assailant/victim and giving attention exclusively to the violent act preclude exploration of the ongoing, complex, intimate relationship between partners. This is not assault and battery between strangers on the street. Clinicians need to be aware that conceiving of the battered woman solely as a victim may have unintended, countertherapeutic effects. This chapter provides a model for assessing couple violence within an empowerment-based practice approach.

It is important not to carry political language and concepts of domestic violence into the clinical arena. The concept of women as victims of domestic assault is biased in that a victim requires a rescuer, which offers possible gratification to the rescuer but weakens the woman by subtly stripping her of confidence and self-determination. Therefore, an effective clinical relationship avoids parallels to the power imbalance between the abuser and abused. Assessment should seek the strengths of both partners and the relationship as well as identify the problems to be solved. Empowering clients to make their own decisions and changes in their lives operationalizes client self-determination.

When clinicians broaden their focus to include the precrisis relationship, preventive intervention becomes possible. Couple violence involves an intricate process between intimate partners. Clinical preventive intervention explores the complex interactions and meanings surrounding the violence in the relationship and provides selective use of an array of interventions. For example, behavioral techniques replace the violent response with exercise, talking it out, and an anger log noting both the stressors and the buildup of physical tension. Cognitive techniques point out the automatic violent response to anger and frustration learned from a parent and offer other interpretations and responses. Thus we challenge attitudes and behaviors carried from the family of origin and seek substitutes for the "faulty" belief. Psychodynamic techniques address underlying issues such as low self-esteem and fear of abandonment, the need to be perfect to be lovable, insecurity, and trust. Preventing further couple violence is a step toward breaking the cycle of violence passed from generation to generation.

Couple violence can be viewed as a cycle of repetitive episodes of abuse, as a straight-line continuum from mild to severe abuse, or as a zigzag series of interactions between partners. These two-dimensional planes become multidimensional forms when family-of-origin influences, generational dynamics, and the couple's external environment are included in the assessment. Each of these areas serves as a tool for assessment of violence in relationships. They are discussed below.

Assessing the Cycle of Violence

Langen and Innes (1986) reported that 32% of abused women had been abused during an average six-month period following the initial abuse. These repeat victims accounted for 57% of detected incidents of domestic violence over a four-year period.

Bern (1982) traces abuse from a single violent incident to a cyclical pattern between partners. Walker (1979, 1989) describes the cycle of violence as a tension-building phase followed by the acute battering incident followed by a calm period afterward. Deschner (1984) describes the cycle of violence as having seven stages: mutual dependence, the noxious event, coercions exchanged, the "last straw" decision, primitive rage, reinforcement for battering when the victim is silenced, and repentance. Mack (1989) emphasizes the systemic nature of the feedback loop, which leads to the "last straw" decision and reinforcement for battering when the victim is silenced. Mack adds two more stages: feelings of rejection and abandonment on the part of the abuser, which fuel the anger, and fear in the abused partner following the violent episode.

What to Look for

The violent episode, which marks the beginning and end of the cycle, is brief, intense, dangerous, and dramatic. Violence is the point in the cycle that has received media and public attention, resulting in laws, shelters, and services for abused women and abusive men. The couple, however, may view the violence as an unhappy aberration, whereas the nonviolent period of the cycle, which may last for months, is considered the norm and the true state of their relationship.

The dynamics of the abusive relationships are different immediately after the violence occurs and later in the cycle. In the crisis stage the clinician sees a female client with physical bruises or worse who is angry, hurt, frightened, and perhaps determined to end the relationship. The abusive partner demonstrates remorse. While initially blaming each other, each partner recognizes that he or she was a participant in the development of violence and that the violence was the culmination of a progressive cycle of events. Often, both parties wish to reconcile their differences, promising each other—and believing—that it will not happen again. A honeymoon period follows, during which calm is restored and denial sets in. However, as tensions begin to rise as a result of stresses from external events and the relationship, the couple become more cautious in their interactions until eventually violence occurs again. Incidents gradually increase in both frequency and severity. The dynamics of the nonviolent period depend upon where the couple are along the violence continuum and the thematic reactive sequences between partners.

In the early stages, the nonviolent period includes good times as well as caring and understanding behavior toward the partner. For example, one woman, following a fight the previous week, reported the following:

> We had a really nice week. We hired a baby-sitter and went out, just the two of us, Saturday night. We're both trying to make this work. We really do love each other. I just have to remember that he gets envious of my family sometimes and thinks I care about them too much and don't care about him.

In the severe stage, in contrast, in which violence is deliberate, premeditated, and dangerous, the period between actual violent incidents offers no respite from punishing behaviors, domination, fear, jealousy, accusations, and criticism.

> I told her I know she's been seeing someone. She's lying to me, but I've been following her and I'm checking up. I warned her I've got a gun, and when I catch her, I'll blow them both away. I'm just waiting for her to slip up.

These two examples illustrate themes of jealousy and fear of loss of the partner, contrasting responses in the mild and the severe ends of the continuum.

How to Find It

After violence has been disclosed, the clinician moves through the cycle of interactions with the couple. Both ongoing assessment and interventions should be matched to the clients' current stage in the cycle, while anticipating the next stage. Generally, cycles are completed once or twice a year initially. Gradually, the cycles become more frequent until they occur within a period of a few weeks. If the worker knows how frequently cycles recur, he or she can anticipate when the couple are nearing the crisis stage.

If violence is not the presenting problem, the interviewer should ask during the initial intake how the couple handle disagreements and whether arguments ever get out of hand, whether things are broken, or anybody gets hurt. If violence exists but the couple are not ready to disclose it, the clinician may discover its potential or probability through the dynamics that are revealed in the course of treatment. In this case, the clinician should ask again about violence.

Assessing the Violence Continuum

McLeer (1981) suggests that abuse between intimates falls on a quantitative spectrum from mild to severe as well as on a qualitative spectrum from emotional to physical. Neidig and Friedman (1984) chart the difference between expressive violence that is part of the emotional life of the couple and instrumental violence that is used to punish or control the partner.

What to Look for

Early stage. On the continuum of violence, physical abuse is seldom the beginning point. Prior to any physical threat, one or both partners may become verbally and emotionally abusive and perhaps have broken objects in their environment. As these behaviors escalate, the first physical blow is generally minor—a slap or a punch. The couple react with shock and attempt to reverse the escalation of violence. At this stage, the couple may have many strengths and a generally healthy emotional bond. The dynamics of their relationship are not yet set in a dysfunctional pattern. The partners can learn and apply basic skills of communication and conflict management and prevent further violence from occurring. Prevention is most easily accomplished at this stage. Thus, it is important that the clinician evaluate the direction toward which the couple are headed and not to dismiss mild forms of abuse as insignificant.

Middle stage. Without intervention, the pattern of conflict becomes set over time. The couple develop a history of recurring themes and unresolved issues. As these themes are replayed the intensity of their interactions increases, resulting in increased verbal and physical abuse. Underlying issues of power and control, intimacy, and autonomy begin to surface when even minor conflict occurs. As their negative exchanges become more frequent, the positive aspects of their relationship begin to fade. However, the emotional and sexual bond between them is usually strong, and a sense of loyalty may motivate them to keep the violence secret from family, friends, and clinician.

How to Find It

Initially, the clinician should see each partner individually at least once in order to gain accurate information about the violence without renewing anger, blame, and defensiveness on the part of the other partner. The clinician can learn about the couple's dynamics by having them provide a detailed account of a violent episode working chronologically backward from the violent incident, including exactly what each partner said and did and felt immediately before the violence occurred. One will discover the recurring themes and their meaning to each partner, the areas of hurt and sensitivity, and how the couple bring forth underlying issues of power and intimacy or autonomy. One can learn the couple's conflict script in order to intervene later. The specific trigger to the violence will be minor and of little importance.

Similarly, an account of events following the violent incident will reveal the couple's emotional strengths, reciprocal needs, and defenses, such as denial, which are used in order to maintain the relationship. The clinician can explore the clients' cognitive interpretations of events and emotional themes such as fear of abandonment. The partners do not react to the event per se, but to the meanings they attribute to it.

The clinician can obtain additional information from psychological tests for violence potential as well as from a medical examination and medical records of both partners to address any physical factors, including depression, that may contribute to the problem.

Severe stage. Neidig and Friedman (1984) refer to the above stages as involving "expressive violence," wherein the violence is part of the overall emotional cycle of the couple: violence arising from anger, followed by remorse, promises that it won't happen again, forgiveness, and making up. Both partners engage in this process with reciprocal actions.

215

By contrast, their description of "instrumental violence" (violence used by one partner to maintain dominance and power by intentionally inflicting fear, humiliation, and injury on the partner) would be found at the far end of the continuum, incorporating relatively fixed perpetrator and victim roles with a high frequency and severity, violence consistent with values, and lack of remorse or motivation for change. Because violence at this end of the continuum is severe and dangerous the clinician should consider the children at risk for abuse. One can assess for the severe stage by questioning the child and the mother and through psychological testing and the child's medical records.

Violence at this stage is unlikely to be a secret. The family will have a history of injuries requiring medical attention, police intervention or court procedures, and shelter visits. The woman may come to an interview with visible bruises or injuries. Their partners are unlikely to come for treatment unless they are court ordered. Even then, they are unlikely to remain in treatment.

Like Bern (1982) and Weitzman and Dreen (1982), the author believes that marriage counseling is not advisable if violence has reached the severe stage. It will not be effective and may endanger the woman. Because the relationship has virtually no positive aspects at this juncture, the clinician needs to assess the woman's overall ego strengths and areas of competent functioning as well as her current level of depression and possible suicidal or homicidal ideation. If sexual abuse is evident, the practitioner should inquire whether she was sexually abused in the past and assess current reinforcement of early sexual trauma that may add to her sense of helplessness and despair. The practitioner should identify concrete services (shelter, financial and housing assistance, legal assistance) and a support group to help her.

Assessing Reciprocal Couple Interactions

Cook and Franz-Cook (1984) found that violent couple systems have low levels of differentiation and an inability to communicate and negotiate as equals, intergenerational triangles and coalitions that leave the partners vulnerable to pressures from parents and in-laws, identifiable sequences in their violent interactions, and themes of complementarity.

What to Look for

When violence is part of the couple system, it is usually confined to that system, occurring only in the home out of public view and only within the context of the ongoing intimate relationship.

Verbal arguments. In verbal arguments each partner reacts to and contributes to the exchange. The partners forget the source of their original conflict as they attack each other in ways that diminish self-esteem, create feelings of vulnerability, and activate fears of rejection and abandonment. During this cyclical progression, the woman may have superior verbal skills, which she uses effectively to gain an edge on her partner, whereas the man has greater physical strength, which he uses. The first physical blow changes the nature of their exchanges and the relationship becomes charged with a new and growing intensity.

Dependency and fear of rejection and abandonment. The couple's primary emotional system includes both partners' unmet emotional needs, unrealistic expectations, and disappointments, which in turn create anger, strong dependency needs, and consequent fear of rejection and abandonment. Virtually every argument begins to touch these themes. After a violent episode, denial sets in and positive behaviors return; hope is reinstated, which leads to renewed expectations and a repeat of the violence cycle.

One couple's first violent episode happened in this way:

> The new baby was one month old, colicky, and seldom stopped crying. The parents were exhausted and ragged. E was resentful that his wife, formerly an eager partner and willing listener, was now unavailable to him because all of her attention was focused on the baby. L felt resentful, in turn, because all the night duty fell on her. E worked and needed his sleep, and she was home all day with the baby. "It was his baby, too; why wouldn't he help more?" E watched her cradle the baby and was ashamed of his jealous feelings. When L said, "We're out of diapers, you'll have to run to the store," E snapped, "I'm not your damn errand boy." L countered, "Well, you're sure as hell not a man and a father, either." He hit her.

One wife explained why she had accepted abuse for so many years:

> It's a typical hooker–pimp relationship. He beats me and then turns to leave. I panic, thinking, that's it, that's all I'll ever get. Nobody else will ever love me. I fall down on my knees and I beg him, please, please don't leave me. And he turns, comes back, and beats me again.

Shifting power balance. In the early and middle stages of the continuum, the couple's conflict forms part of their shifting balance of power. The apparent power lies with the man, who is physically stronger and thus able to impose his will. If he resorts to violence, however, he is perceived by both himself and his partner as being out of control, which is not a position of power (as any parent driven to yelling at a two-year-old is aware). He reaches that point as a result of feelings of frustration, vulnerability, and impotence, which he defends against with anger and physical violence. In doing so, he intimidates and silences his partner and gains the upper hand in the relationship. However, he also runs the risk of public disclosure and condemnation, possible police charges, and personal rejection and abandonment by his partner, on whom he is emotionally dependent.

As he becomes increasingly violent, his spouse counteracts his display of power by increasingly strong actions such as leaving the home temporarily to stay with her mother, with a friend, or in a shelter; by getting a civil protective order, then letting her partner back into the house; by calling the police but not pressing charges; by pressing charges and later dropping them; or by going to court with the hope that the partner will be forced into counseling. Most of her actions are later reversed, and none alone is necessarily indicative of a wish or decision to end the relationship.

Although the woman may perceive herself, and is generally perceived as, helpless, people generally do not accept a position of powerlessness on an ongoing basis without attempting to equalize the balance of power in some way. Verbal skills are one way to counteract the abuser's power. Sexual indifference or rejection diminishes the self-esteem of the abuser.

How to Find It

When the couple are together in sessions, they often will reenact their arguments in front of the clinician. It is useful to observe this process, but the clinician needs to keep the argument under control. By noting what each partner says to the other and the affective reaction, the practitioner can identify the emotional themes as they arise.

As sessions progress, it is possible to see the parallel processes of each partner's efforts to acquire power. The practitioner is able to discern the reciprocity and complementarity between partners that was not apparent initially. Client efforts to increase autonomy and differentiation and decrease enmeshment should be identified and encouraged.

Other Dynamics of Violent Relationships

Violent relationships share several general characteristics. Both partners generally assume rigid roles. Communication does not occur on a personal or feeling level, and the couple neither recognize nor negotiate legitimate differences between them. Therefore, couples in such relationships have no safe or acceptable way to handle disagreements or anger. When the violence remains secret, an enmeshed family system lacking appropriate personal boundaries or limits may develop. Both partners seem unable to place limits on the kind of treatment they will accept or how they will treat each other. Both partners suffer from low self-esteem and a resulting strong emotional dependency. The more firmly these patterns are set, the greater potential for physical abuse in the relationship.

Assessing the Functions of Violence

What to Look for

Violence serves a purpose in the couple's interaction and thus is not easily relinquished. In assessing the functions of violence in the system the practitioner can find specific interventions. The following addresses the primary functions of relationship violence, ordered from the perspective of the clinician, from the simplest to the most complex or difficult. Several functions can operate simultaneously.

1. *Violence releases tensions.* During the gradual and cyclical buildup of tension in the relationship, the woman becomes more cautious, more passive, and more depressed. Tension is generally released in a burst of anger and violence, triggered by an insignificant event, thus offering relief and calm as the cycle begins anew.

2. *Violence is a crude means of conflict resolution.* Violence does "settle things" momentarily in that the specific argument is terminated and perhaps avoided permanently thereafter. For a time, the warning signals of impending violence may serve to stop an argument.

3. *Violence maintains the status quo.* In rigidly structured relationships, change is threatening. The present system is known and understood by both partners, however unsatisfactory it might be. When changes are introduced, a violent episode often serves to reestablish the *status quo.*

In the following two functions, it is important that the therapist distinguish which function is at work or whether both are used alternately as a way of regulating emotional distance. Accurate assessment serves as a guide to therapy; inappropriate interventions will create further problems. For example, in cases in which violence is a distancing mechanism, one should not choose interventions designed to enhance intimacy.

4. *Violence creates emotional distance.* In an enmeshed system in which neither partner has adequate self-focus or clear boundaries, violence serves as a distancing mechanism. If enmeshment with an inability to tolerate intimacy (as, for example, with borderline personality disorder) is evident, the internal anxiety created by intimacy may be resolved by violence. Depersonalizing sex may create distance; if sex is not depersonalized, the intensity and intimacy of the act may create an anxiety so great that an equally intense violent response is used to reestablish distance. Thus, some clients report that violence occurs after apparently satisfying sexual activity.

5. *Violence facilitates intimacy.* Almost everyone is familiar with the process of "making up" after a quarrel to restore the normal emotional connection or to adjust for excessive distancing. The "honeymoon period" following violence not only serves this function, but may in fact stimulate emotional closeness, which would not occur without the violence to facilitate it.

In a couple system characterized by an almost total lack of meaningful personal communication, violence suddenly and dramatically breaks down the emotional barriers between partners, presenting a full range of ambivalent feelings—from rage and hate to love, need, fear of loss, and vulnerability. During this brief period, the emotions are both raw and genuine. Because this period may represent the only true emotionally intimate moments available to the couple, both partners may anticipate the harmony that occurs after a violent episode and understand it as a true expression of their love.

Similarly, sex following violence may be particularly intense and exciting. The sexual bond between partners can be exceptionally strong and loyal. Assessment should recognize the strength of this bond and how it is expressed. For example, the following incident was recounted by a 37-year-old woman who was married for 17 years:

> I knew what I was doing and I just couldn't stop myself. I was at him for about three days. Everything I said was sarcastic; then I'd get scared and self-pitying and accuse him of being interested in B, this woman at the office. I know he's not, really. When he came home Tuesday I pitched a fit and was screaming at him, accusing him. I threw his jacket on the porch and told him he could get out and go to B, because he was so hot for her. He called me a bitch and punched me real hard, and I fell. He didn't come back 'til about two or three in the morning. I was crying. When he came in I just grabbed him and he grabbed me. We made love right there in the living room. We didn't even go up to bed for the rest of the night. It was fantastic sex, and he just kept telling me he didn't care about B—he really loves me. He said he doesn't want anyone else, ever. Anyway, I'm exhausted. I know this is sick, and I've got to stop doing it.

The juxtaposition of sex with violence for arousal and gratification should surprise no one familiar with television or movie "entertainment." However, clinicians may experience personal and/or ideological discomfort with this material when it arises in therapy.

6. *Violence reinforces a domination/submission relationship pattern.* At the severe stage, domination/submission is the primary dynamic process in violent relationships. Each partner may attempt to intimidate, coerce, humiliate, and degrade the other. Such behavior may occur in the sexual act as well, wherein the abuser attempts to humiliate and inflict physical pain. When the dynamics of the relationship have reached this level and if children are in the home, the practitioner should consider them at risk both for physical and sexual abuse.

How to Find It

Tracking specific sequential behaviors and accompanying feelings, perceptions, and meanings as described in earlier sections helps practitioners discern the functions of violence in the couple system. Often clients are able to express accurately and with insight the purpose of violence in their relationships. Knowing the cycle of violence, that is, what happens before and after the particular episode, helps to explain why the violence occurs.

Violence across Generations

What to Look for

Violence is often transmitted from one generation to the next by both men and women. The single characteristic that has been reliably correlated with an adult violent relationship is witnessing domestic violence in one's own family as a child (Herman, 1989). In the author's experience over a nine-year period, approximately two-thirds of both the men and women in violent relationships were raised in violent families, and approximately one-third of the female clients in violent relationships were sexually abused as children.

Commonly, the young child will identify with his or her mother's helplessness, sympathize with her, and be hostile to or afraid of the man's abusive behavior. However, a young adolescent who initially feels protective of the mother may begin to exhibit aggressive and abusive behavior toward her. The following case illustrates the transition:

> By age 13, J had watched his father beat his mother for many years, hating his father for it. This time he grabbed a bat and beat his father so severely that the father was hospitalized. J's initial sense of triumph and power ("He won't try that again with me around") quickly gave way to confusion and shame as he saw his mother crying when she took towels to mop up the blood, as the police questioned him, as he recognized his own potential for violence. Shame gave way to resentment of his mother for her part in the arguments, for not stopping the abuse years ago, for her drinking, and for providing such a miserable home life. "Why didn't you just shut up? Why are you always yelling at him, anyway?" He grew disgusted with her nagging and complaining, with her weakness. Much later, he mumbled to the worker, "You know, sometimes I think she asks for it."

In some cases, transmission of violent behavior has been demonstrated in adolescent-to-parent violence (Gelles & Cornell, 1985). By the time a young male reaches his mid-teenage years, he generally identifies with the adult male's position of strength and aggressive behavior. Thus the child who was his mother's protector at age 13 may at 17 feel contempt for her victimization, abuse her verbally, mimicking his father's language, and even be physically abusive. The father may applaud this new ally and his demonstration of manhood. The young male who demonstrates abusive behavior toward his mother almost always exhibits the same dynamics and some level of verbal or physical abuse in his dating relationships in high school and later. This path, of course, is not predetermined. A substitute positive role model (an aunt, uncle, grandparent, coach, teacher, neighbor, or adult friend), teachings from church and school, and the youth's own inner determination not to live his or her life with violence can all help to break the intergenerational cycle of violence.

A female child or adolescent usually identifies with her mother and exhibits a similar low self-esteem, sense of helplessness, caution, emotional dependency, and chronic depression, which carries into adulthood and influences her choice of a mate.

Thus children of both sexes often learn and repeat in their adult lives that which they feared and hated while growing up. When children are physically or emotionally abused and lack sufficient nurturing, they carry into adulthood unmet emotional needs and dependencies and may repeat the dysfunctional interactions they learned during their developmental years. A chosen mate may mirror familiar internal processes and learned patterns. Often, adult children will enter into successive violent relationships, thus illustrating the power of these internalized patterns.

How to Find It

Family-of-origin material reveals not only the existence of prior violent behavior in the extended family, but also the degree and patterns of family dysfunction, emotional themes, extent of emotional nurturance or deprivation, and strengths and weaknesses within each family system. A couple involved in an intense, violent relationship lack the emotional resources and capacity to attend to their children's needs. Through discussion of the couple's parenting practices, including discipline, the practitioner can elicit information on current strengths or dysfunction.

External Stressors and Influences

Poverty, debts, illness, accidents, and unemployment can create situational stressors that tax a couple's resources and resilience and contribute to violence (Gelles & Cornell, 1985). Women are at a greater risk for abuse during pregnancy (Gelles, 1987), especially if the pregnancy is unplanned or unwanted. In families prone to violence, holidays and family celebrations carry a high risk for an abusive episode. Seasonal surges in violence have been noted, with violent episodes increasing during hot weather or prolonged inclement weather in winter, when people become isolated and closed in. If the therapist can alleviate situational stress through referrals and liaison with other social service agencies, interventions are generally more effective.

Situational stress alone, however, is not sufficient to cause violence. Everyone experiences stress at some point; only some persons react with violence. External stress can trigger violence when other internal factors, which have been discussed in earlier sections, are present. External factors that help perpetuate couple violence include legal and societal acceptance of domestic abuse (Gelles & Cornell, 1985; Straus, Gelles, & Steinmetz 1980), as is evident in the violence and sexual abuse portrayed by the entertainment industry. The practitioner needs to evaluate the degree to which the complementary roles of abuser and abused have been learned and reinforced through family-of-origin influences (Walker, 1979), their current social network, and societal attitudes toward violence.

Assessing Prognosis

Practitioners must be realistic about what they hope to accomplish therapeutically with a violent couple. The following lists factors to consider when considering prognosis. The most promising prognosis will occur when the following is evident:

1. Clients voluntarily seek help.
2. The abusive partner accepts responsibility for the violent behavior and wishes to stop.
3. Clients seek help early in the development of their pattern of violence, while violence occurs relatively less frequently and is less severe.
4. The therapist can work with both partners.
5. The violence is a secret, and clients would have much to lose through disclosure, either in their employment, family, or community position.
6. The couple have outside social resources.

Prognosis is less hopeful when the following is evident:

1. One or both partners comes from a violent family of origin.
2. Violence is tacitly accepted in the couple's social milieu.
3. A strong power imbalance in the relationship is reinforced by fear.
4. The partners exhibit excessive and long-standing dependency needs and little differentiation.

The poorest prognosis occurs among couples who exhibit the following:

1. One or both partners abuse alcohol or drugs.
2. Either or both partners have a history of multiple abusive relationships.
3. A personality disorder is evident.
4. The abusive client is court-ordered and resistant.
5. The client has a previous record for other crimes or the client has learned to evade the criminal justice system and scorns it.
6. Abuse includes physical or sexual brutality, acts are premeditated, and/or aggravated assault occurs.

Barriers to Detection of Violence

Violence often goes undetected by professionals, especially in the early stages. Several factors contribute to this.

Professional bias. If the practitioner assumes that violence occurs only with a certain type of client or certain segment of the population, the interviewer might automatically and unconsciously exempt clients who are articulate, educated, charming, well-dressed, professional, church-going, or "nice," and not inquire about violence out of fear of offending the client. Like alcoholism, however, violence crosses all socioeconomic lines (Schulman, 1979; Walker, 1979; Straus, Gelles, & Steinmetz, 1980).

Subject matter. The details of abuse as well as the emotional intensity of the clients can be draining. More severe violence is horrifying, and the interviewer may begin to erect defenses and ultimately avoid the subject altogether.

Therapist collusion with clients. Clinicians who are uncomfortable with violence can enter into collusion with a couple not to identify the problem or may diminish its importance. This is especially true during the early stages, when violence is mild and not considered an important treatment focus.

Client secrecy. Clients may attempt to resolve some problems while keeping the abuse secret. Clients who are not ready to disclose will evade or deny the problem.

Client fear of professional authority. Clients may fear the power of social workers to investigate the family and perhaps break it up, punish its members, and destroy a highly dependent system. Disclosure means being found out and found wanting.

Conclusion

Accurate assessment of the cycle and stages of violence, reciprocal couple interactions and their meanings, the functions of violence in the system, intergenerational transmission of violence, and external factors contributing to violence in the system is essential for treatment planning, not only to prevent escalation to the crisis state but also to offer partners a real chance to preserve their relationship. Practitioners who initially find violent material emotionally draining and anxiety provoking will become more effective if they conceive the problem as a process and not limit their focus to the act of violence and the crisis that ensues. Agencies can expand their focus and services to include program development and in-service training directed toward work with couples and families to prevent the continuation of violence.

REFERENCES

Bern, E. H. (1982). From violent incident to spouse abuse syndrome. *Social Casework, 63,* 41–45.

Bureau of Justice Statistics. (1983). *Report to the nation on crime and justice.* Washington, DC: U.S. Department of Justice.

Cook, D., & Franz-Cook, A. (1984). A systemic treatment approach to wife battering. *Journal of Marital and Family Therapy, 10,* 83–94.

Deschner, J. P. (1984). *The hitting habit: Anger control for battering couples.* New York: Free Press.

Gelles, R. J. (1987). *Family violence.* Newbury Park, CA: Sage Publications.

Gelles, R. J., & Cornell, C. P. (1985). *Intimate violence in families.* Beverly Hills, CA: Sage Publications.

Herman, J. L. (1989). Wife beating. *Harvard Medical School Mental Health Letter, 5*(10), 4.

Langen, P. A., & Innes, C. A. (1986). Preventing domestic violence against women. *Bureau of justice statistics special report.* Washington, DC: U.S. Department of Justice.

Mack, N. (1989). Spouse abuse: A dyadic approach. In G. Weeks (Ed.), *Treating couples.* New York: Brunner/Mazel.

McLeer, S. (1981). Spouse abuse. In G. P. Sholevar (Ed.), *The handbook of marriage and mari-*

tal therapy. New York: SP Medical and Scientific Books.

Neidig, P. H., & Friedman, D. H. (1984). *Spouse abuse*. Champaign, IL: Research Press.

Schulman, M. A. (1979). *A survey of spousal violence against women in Kentucky*. Washington, DC: U.S. Government Printing Office.

Straus, M., Gelles, R., & Steinmetz, S. (1980). *Behind closed doors*. New York: Anchor Press/Doubleday.

Walker, L. (1979). *The battered woman*. New York: Harper & Row.

Walker, L. (1989). *Terrifying love*. New York: Harper & Row.

Weitzman, J., & Dreen, K. (1982). Wife beating: A view of the marital dyad. *Social Casework, 63*, 259–265.

A Model for Assessment of Incestuous Families

James D. Orten and Linda L. Rich

17

Successful treatment of incestuous families has been described as a difficult clinical task (Taylor, 1986; Sgroi, 1982; Gentry, 1978). Nonetheless, the core ingredients of effective intervention, especially with father–daughter incest, are beginning to emerge. A model for assessment of incestuous families that may aid practitioners in planning and conducting treatment is presented here. Specifically, the instrument is designed to facilitate the organization of vital information, the clarification of risk factors and treatment goals, and the communication of this information among professionals who work with such families.

Components of Effective Treatment

Protection

Perhaps the most fundamental fact to emerge from epidemiological studies and clinical reports is that the incest victim needs two types of protection. The first is from continued sexual and emotional abuse. The second is from what Conte (1984) called "system-induced trauma."

Intrafamilial sexual abuse of children is rarely a one-time event (Spencer, 1978). Incest generally progresses over time, advancing through predictable stages of increasingly intimate and intrusive activity (Summit & Kryso, 1978). The perpetrator's behavior has been described as compulsive, repetitive, and as having the characteristics of an addiction (Stark, 1984). Despite the father's (or father-figure's) expressions of remorse and promises to desist, his abusive behavior often continues. The perpetrator's denial, minimizations of the effects on the child, and lack of empathy for others maintain the pattern of abuse (Sgroi, 1982).

The child, in a dependent position and usually fearful, cannot assure her own protection. Recent studies indicate that the initial molestation of most children occurs between ages five and nine years (Herman & Hirschman, 1977; Stark, 1984; Spencer, 1978). Summit (1983) noted that children in this age group adopt strategies for emotional survival in situations of abuse that often render them less capable of seeking protection and more likely to act out or delay reporting. This may lead professionals to question the truthfulness of their accusations (Rosenfeld et al., 1979).

Some mothers move quickly to protect their daughters once sexual abuse is disclosed. Others react with disbelief or ambivalence. When the mother is economically or emotionally dependent on the perpetrator, her support of her daughter may weaken as the sobering realities of single parenthood become apparent (Myer, 1984). Without the presence of a strong adult ally in the home and effective intervention from the community, the child remains at risk for repeated sexual abuse despite disclosure (Server & Janzen, 1982).

Although early investigators such as Bender and Blau (1937) questioned the harmful effects of incest, evidence indicates that sexual abuse usually has severe and long-lasting consequences. Low self-esteem, depression, drug and alcohol abuse, suicide, prostitution, hysterical seizures, borderline pathology, sexual dysfunction, pelvic pain, and marital problems are all documented sequelae of incest (Gelinas, 1983; Gross, 1979; Herman & Hirschman, 1981). The percentage of incest victims who suffer serious physical injury may be low; however, the psychological damage to the developing personality is real and long-lasting. The distortion of affection, the betrayal of trust, and the abuse of authority in an incestuous parent–child relationship undermine the child's capacity to form close relationships. Premature sexual experiences flood her with feelings she is unable to discharge or to integrate.[1] The coercion used to continue incestuous activities does violence to the child's emotional development. Perceptions of self, sexuality, intimacy, and responsibility are all distorted. Geiser (1978) noted that in his clinical work with adult incest survivors, he observed a subtle yet pervasive damage to self that resulted not only from the sexually abusive behavior, but also from his clients' adaptation to ongoing exploitation, role reversal, and denial of reality.

In addition to the danger of continued sexual exploitation, the child is vulnerable to psychological pressure from the perpetrator, other family members, and from her own feelings that she may have destroyed her family by disclosing the incest. This pressure causes many victims to

1. Sigmund Freud first advanced this principle in his studies of hysteria but, under pressure from colleagues, later retracted it. See Strachey, J. (Ed.). (1955). *The complete works of Sigmund Freud* (Vol. 3, p. 203). London: Hogarth Press.

retract their original charges. Such children need positive emotional support and reliable protection from emotional abuse.

A child who is subjected to severe psychological pressure by remaining in an unsupportive home suffers in specific ways. Trapped in a hostile environment, she may doubt her own senses because important people are saying that what she experienced did not happen. If she remains in touch with reality she will likely become cynical, because either her report was not believed or trusted adults could not be relied on for protection.

For professionals in positions to make protective decisions or who are involved in the therapeutic or legal process, it is essential that the factors contributing to lasting trauma be understood. As in physical abuse, it is not the tissue damage or physical pain itself that is most traumatic, but the fact that the daughter was misused by those to whom she looked for care and protection. The trauma of removal from the home must be weighed against the possibility of continued sexual and emotional abuse within it.

In the authors' judgment, continued protection for the child is the most important factor in successful treatment of incestuous families. By an unequivocal consideration of the child's best interest, professionals send powerful messages to all family members. They also model for parents skills in which the parents are deficient: having empathy for the child, establishing clear behavioral limits and generational boundaries, and facing uncomfortable realities.

System Coordination

The second type of protection needed by the child, protection from system-induced trauma, highlights another necessary ingredient of successful treatment. System-induced trauma results from agencies and professionals working at cross purposes. Laws in almost all states mandate professionals to report suspected sexual abuse. Incestuous families cannot restrict the working out of their problem exclusively within the privacy of the therapist's office. Whenever two or more professionals are involved with the same family, as happens in cases of incest, system coordination is needed. Usually an attorney for the child and one for the offender are involved. A child welfare worker will be assigned, as well as therapists for different family members. It is not uncommon for half a dozen professionals to be in regular contact with these troubled families.

Because each member of this cadre of professionals has a different, sometimes legally mandated focus and because they are seeing different family members, strained relationships and uncooperative attitudes readily develop. For example, the legal system is interested in prosecution of the offender and protection of the child. A prosecuting attorney may want open-court testimony from the child, which the child protection worker sees as too traumatic to be allowed. The father's therapist, believing his client to be cooperative and wishing to help him, may push for a quick reunion of the family, which other members of the treatment team oppose.

An alert offender can use this situation to manipulate himself out of vigorous prosecution; a child victim's interests can easily be neglected within it.

Perhaps the most serious consequence of an uncoordinated system is that it discourages professionals from working within it and encourages them to "go it alone." Despite the legal necessity and, in the authors' view, the therapeutic necessity to report sexual abuse, some clinicians do not do so. Selective reporting and advocacy against legal involvement altogether have appeared in the literature (Schoeman & Reamer, 1983). Two therapists described their treatment of a family before disclosure was mandated, during which they knew the molestation continued and did not report it to the authorities (Eist & Mandel, 1968).

When a child victim does not receive protection from the community, the cynicism that began with parental misuse is intensified. Also, the offender realizes he can outwit a system that he may already hold in contempt. Escaping legal consequences may reinforce a pattern of antisocial behavior.

Assuming the competence and goodwill of the professionals involved with incestuous families, the goals of one group do not have to be accomplished at the expense of those of others. On the contrary, each professional (or agency) needs the services of the others to successfully do his or her job. This conclusion is demonstrated by the fact that the most successful treatment programs are those that have developed means for coordinating legal, protective, and therapeutic services (Giaretto, 1977).

Assessment

The third ingredient in successful treatment of incestuous families is assessment. A careful assessment is needed in all forms of mental health practice, but factors in these families make the role of assessment even more critical. These same factors may compromise workers' abilities to do assessment objectively.

One factor that makes assessment difficult is that therapists tend to react emotionally to incest more often than they do in the case of other psychosocial problems. As Giaretto (1981) has pointed out, "The image of a five-year-old child performing fellatio on her father in submission to his authority does not engender compassion for her parents" (p. 183). Such a vision is apt to produce feelings of revulsion, which may lead to punitive, nontherapeutic action. Emotional involvement can also make a worker deny what he or she sees. For example, in the case of a remorseful, middle-class family, the worker may tend to believe the family's denial of the continuing risk or its minimization of the seriousness of the abuse. An inexperienced worker may fall for the family's diversionary tactics, losing sight of the problem of incest amid concerns about alcohol abuse and adolescent acting out. Even experienced workers without appropriate assessment practices can become overwhelmed by the multiple crises that frequently accompany the disclosure of incest.

Another factor that makes assessment difficult is that the earliest writers on the subject tended to take rigid theoretical positions rather than to classify the behavior of incestuous families. One could speculate that the emotions of these pioneer writers influenced their theories. Sigmund Freud, for example, could not believe that the incestuous acts that his female patients described were all true, so he postulated other explanations such as oedipal fantasies and seductive children (Strachey, 1955). These and other psychoanalytic explanations, for example, psychotic offender and frigid, orally fixed mother, have for the most part been shown to be unfounded (Peters, 1976). Unfortunately, these explanations are still among the loose collections of beliefs that guide many professionals' assessment of incestuous cases.

The leap from observed behavior to its cause is always tricky, and psychoanalytic writers are not the only ones who have been challenged in this regard. Family-systems theorists have documented characteristic interactions in incestuous families seen in a variety of treatment settings (Alexander, 1985). Their explanation of the dynamics of this behavior, however, has been challenged by feminist therapists, who have demonstrated that the systems theorists' "typical incestuous family" does not differ in many respects from other dysfunctional American families: The father is dominant, the mother is passive–dependent, and the child is expected to be obedient to parental authority (McIntyre, 1981).

Researchers are finding various patterns in the behavior of offenders, victims, and mothers of victims. For example, Groth (1979) identifies three classes of offenders. Myer (1984) classifies mothers of victims into three categories; James and Nasjleti (1983) describe four maternal types. Commenting on the diversity among the families in her study, Myer (1984) states, "We have found that a careful assessment of each mother, as well as the father, child and family members, is essential and that no one solution or approach to an incestuous family will work" (p. 136).

The importance of assessment relative to treatment is especially great in cases of incestuous families because one person's safety depends on the other's therapeutic growth. Reunification of the family is a worthwhile goal, but ought not to be allowed until the home can offer a safe environment to the child. In the absence of well internalized controls by the father, a daughter's security depends heavily on the mother's ability to protect her. Thus the growth of all family members must be measured as precisely as possible.

The dynamics of incestuous families and their assessment are more complex than early theorists recognized. Nevertheless, research and clinical experience have begun to delineate the behavioral and attitudinal characteristics related to a positive emotional adjustment by the child victim, her freedom from continued abuse, and successful reunification of the family. The model of assessment presented here focuses on these behavioral factors, rather than on psychodynamics. This approach enables clinicians to formulate realistic protection and treatment plans and to observe more precisely when reunification is feasible for some families and if it is possible for others.

A Multimodal Treatment Approach

The fourth characteristic of effective intervention is a multimodal treatment approach. This includes individual counseling, group therapy, family sessions, and self-help groups. It will likely also include work with family dyads or subsystems, such as marriage counseling and mother –daughter or mother–children sessions. Although some programs may emphasize certain approaches, and may use them more extensively with some family members than with others or at different points in their service to a family, most programs use the gamut of treatment formats (Giaretto, 1981; Taylor, 1986).

Assessment typically begins with individual sessions with father, mother, and child victim. The mix of formats in which each family member will be subsequently involved depends on the treatment team's assessment of that member and the team's theoretical bent.

The use of groups is becoming generally accepted in incest treatment programs. The power of the group to confront or support is well documented in professional literature (Gazda, 1984). This power to break through perpetrators' denial, to support their growth as it occurs, and to support and empower mothers and victims probably accounts for the widespread use of groups. Group counseling is also an important vehicle in the treatment of adult incest survivors (Tsai & Wagner, 1978).

Assessment Scale for Families
With Father–Daughter Incest

The assessment scale presented in this chapter (Figure 1) is intended to assist clinicians objectively to evaluate incestuous families' strengths and degrees of pathology. The behavioral and attitudinal characteristics included are those that, according to the literature and the authors' experience, are most directly related to treatment success. They relate as well to the issue of risk of continued abuse to the victim. The scale can be used in the initial assessment and at various points during the treatment process as a means of estimating progress.

The initial assessment for each family member should be done by the treatment team after individual and family interviews. In that different family members often have different therapists, several practitioners might work together in the evaluation. This will not present a problem in using the scale, because scoring for each family member is done independently. Such a procedure should enhance the cooperation of all practitioners involved in the case. The scale is purposely presented in lay language so that professionals who are not trained therapists may contribute to the process. For example, an attorney or probation officer might participate in the evaluation of an offender, and a child welfare worker in the assessment of a child. Again, this common ground should help to unify the thinking of all professionals working with the family.

Each factor in the assessment format is cast on a five-point, Likert-type continuum from least to most severe indication of pathology. Thus lower scores suggest a better prognosis. Scores that become lower during treatment indicate progress. The authors caution against attaching a great deal of significance to changes in scores on single items or to small changes on overall ratings. The general pattern of scores is important.

Assessment of the Father

"Father" refers to one who occupies the father role. This may be the biological father, stepfather, common-law husband, or live-in boyfriend of the mother. The significant feature is that this is a male who, because of his relationship to the mother and his place in the family, wields power over family members and should be one whom the children can trust.

Experienced clinicians have found that the first three items in the assessment of the father have the highest correlation with good rehabilitation (Kroth, 1979). If early in the disclosure process the father acknowledges the incestuous behavior, is open with therapists and other appropriate persons, and takes personal responsibility for his behavior, he demonstrates a level of maturity that makes prognosis favorable. The more cautious the offender is on these matters, the more guarded the prognosis must be. If the father appears to understand the impact of his behavior on the child and shows remorse, the prognosis is even better. Conversely, statements such as "We just played around" or "She enjoyed it too" are negative indications.

Item four can be seen as a behavioral manifestation of item three. Genuine empathy for the daughter may restrain sexually abusive acts, even in the presence of the father's temptation. Thus the more empathy, the less likely the molestation is to have involved force, injury, or outright terror for the victim. Item five is designed to reveal the degree of empathy in the relationship history of father and daughter. The treatment outlook is better if the sexual abuse is inconsistent with the father's personality rather than a part of an overall pattern of antisocial behavior. Items six through eight are intended to reveal such a pattern.

An offender may score anywhere from a low of 8 points (indicating the lowest level of pathology) to a high of 40 points. Values higher than 8 suggest a risk of repeated abuse. The authors believe that some items on the scale are more significant than others are. Offenders whose scores cluster to the right side of the scale are poor candidates for normal types of therapeutic intervention. They will likely need legal coercion to continue in treatment and often respond only to specialized treatment to increase impulse control.

Figure 1. Family assessment: Father–daughter incest.

		Father or father-figure			Score
1	2	3	4	5	
Admits incestuous behavior		Cautious or vague in acknowledging incestuous behavior		Categorically denies abuse	____
1	2	3	4	5	
Accepts responsibility for incest		Projects blame onto wife, alcohol, etc.		Blames victim	____
1	2	3	4	5	
Seems to understand impact on child and shows remorse		Minimizes seriousness of incident and impact on child		Main concern is about consequences for self	____
1	2	3	4	5	
Abuse limited to touching, fondling, exposure; no use of force		Abuse included manual or oral–genital contact or intercourse, use of threats		Rape through threat or force, injured or terrorized child, involved child in pornography	____
1	2	3	4	5	
Past relationship with child showed general empathy		Role reversal, lack of empathy for child		History of physical abuse or extreme discipline	____
1	2	3	4	5	
No history of alcohol or drug abuse		Sporadic alcohol or drug abuse		Alcoholism or drug addiction	____
1	2	3	4	5	
No history of antisocial behavior or criminal acts		Few and less serious law infractions		Extensive antisocial behavior, criminal record	____
1	2	3	4	5	
No previous history of sexual abuse		History of sexual abuse of current victim and/or other children in family		Past or current sexual abuse of children outside family	____
				Total	____

		Mother			Score
1	2	3	4	5	
Believes child		Vague about incident, doubts child's reports		Does not believe child, denies abuse	____
1	2	3	4	5	
Historically adequate relationship with child		Ambivalent bond to child, role reversal		History of abuse, neglect, inadequate parenting	____
1	2	3	4	5	
Quickly forms bonds with therapist		Forms bond with therapist after resistance		Distrustful, resists help	____

234

1	2	3	4	5	
Takes action to protect child, i.e., reports incident		Minimizes need to protect or takes ineffectual action		Primary concern is protection of partner and self	

1	2	3	4	5	
Demonstrates ability to be independent		Dependent on partner but can act independently with support		Strong dependency on partner	

1	2	3	4	5	
Active social support system		Limited social support system		Socially isolated	

1	2	3	4	5	
Holds adults responsible for limits of sexuality and for protection of children		Partially blames daughter or blames alcohol, etc.		Blames daughter for incestuous behavior	

1	2	3	4	5	
No history of alcohol or drug abuse		Sporadic alcohol or drug abuse		Alcoholism or drug addiction	

1	2	3	4	5	
No physical or mental handicap that limits ability to protect		Intellectual, physical, or psychiatric condition that compromises ability to protect child		Serious physical, intellectual, or psychiatric handicap	

Total _____

Child

Score

1	2	3	4	5	
Adolescent, age 13 years or older		Latency, age 6 through 12 years		Preschool age, age 5 years or younger	

1	2	3	4	5	
Normal intellectual, emotional, and physical functioning		Borderline intelligence, mild physical or emotional handicaps		Vulnerable child—serious mental, physical, or emotional handicap	

1	2	3	4	5	
Expresses confidence in mother's ability to protect		Protective of mother or sees mother as being unable to protect		Fearful of mother or sees her as potential abuser	

1	2	3	4	5	
Can identify available adult resource person outside family		Can identify possible adult resource persons		Socially isolated, distrustful of adults	

1	2	3	4	5	
Easily develops rapport with therapist		Able to develop bond with therapist after being cautious initially		Distrustful, resists therapist and other helpers	

Total _____

Although this scale was not developed in conjunction with Groth's (1979) typology of offenders, the two may overlap. Offenders whose scores are high on this scale may be like Groth's "fixated offender," and those with low scores may be considered "regressed offenders." Treatment considerations for each group would also probably be similar.

Assessment of the Mother

An evaluation of the mother in incestuous families is twofold. It includes an assessment of her personal strengths and her potential for individual growth and an assessment of her ability to protect her daughter. These two areas are not inimical, and growth in both occurs at the same time and by the same means. As the mother relinquishes her dependence on her partner and establishes herself as an autonomous person, she will simultaneously become better able to empathize with and protect her child.

The first three items on the scale are designed to test the mother's ability to empathize with and protect her child. If she can see her daughter as believable and if she has had an adequate relationship with the child, prognosis is better. Presumably, her ability to form a bond with the therapist would tap the same quality.

The next section of the scale (items four through six) is intended to determine the mother's ability to grow into a more autonomous individual. Items four and five measure her ability to act independently of her partner. Item four asks about this characteristic in relationship to the daughter; item five measures this ability on a more general level. Because no one is able to stand completely alone, the mother's ability to stand against her partner and for her daughter's protection will be partly determined by the type of support she has outside the nuclear family. Typically, incestuous families are isolated. Item six looks at this factor.

Items seven through nine test additional features of the mother's intellectual and physical condition that may affect her role performance. Is she, for example, intellectually mature enough to recognize that adults, not children, must be held responsible for limiting sexual behavior? Does she have physical handicaps, mental limitations, or addictions (for example, alcoholism) that make it difficult for her to be an adequate mother?

A mother might score as low as 9 points or as high as 45. In the authors' experience, mothers in incestuous families will rarely be rated at the lowest level by professionals who know them well. They have frequently endured life experiences that have undermined these types of personal qualities.

Assessment of the Victim

The evaluation of a child is intended to elucidate her potential for self-protection and for constructive emotional adjustment to the experience of sexual abuse. "Self-protection" does not refer to physical self-defense but rather to the complex of mental and behavioral skills that children of all ages employ to seek assistance in times of threat. As in the case of the mother, a child's increased self-confidence will serve both healing and preventive functions.

Item one is a straightforward ranking by age. The older a child is at the onset of abuse, the more ability and mobility she generally has to seek help. Many adolescents run away from home for this reason. Intelligence is an asset in undoing the damage of sexual abuse and in protecting oneself from it. Some victims have found ingenious ways of keeping out of an offender's clutches. A bright and strong 13-year-old girl described how she studied every room in her home and planned escape routes after her stepfather's intentions toward her became clear. No child should have to protect herself from a father, and most are not capable of doing so. A more common response is disassociation or acting out.

Items three through five are intended to measure the child's ability to trust, a prerequisite to asking for help, and the ability to name specific individuals on whom she can rely. If the system around the child responds appropriately when she discloses sexual abuse, her trust and, thus, her ability to obtain help will increase. The authors recall an alert 15-year-old who believed she could not tell her mother about her stepfather's molestation because she believed her mother would side with the father. The mother–daughter relationship had been poor for several years. In addition, the mother's marriage to the stepfather had helped the family financially. When the daughter was hospitalized for attempted suicide, however, and the incest was disclosed to an alert and sympathetic staff, the mother responded promptly and effectively. Through discussions with the mother, the daughter also found that an aunt, who lived nearby, was an equally good ally. The rapport a child develops with a competent therapist will also serve a curative and protective function.

Theoretically, a child victim could be scored as low as five, although that is not likely on initial evaluation. Such protective skills can come, with therapeutic growth, in intelligent older victims. A child can never be realistically expected to protect herself from an adult male, even with good skills. But they do add to her self-confidence and serve as added insurance in a troubled family.

Research Suggestions

The authors have employed the assessment scale described here in clinical practice and found it useful. Empirical studies are needed to confirm its value objectively. Three research suggestions are outlined below.

Validity

The scale attempts to predict treatability of incestuous family members and to measure therapeutic progress. Perhaps the most basic research question is whether it does in fact do so. The validity of the instrument could be tested in various types of formats. The ideal one would be its use with a number of families at the beginning and throughout treatment to observe whether it measured progress as seen by clinicians and predicted treatment success. In this case, the integrity of the measurement would require that those doing the treatment and those doing the measurement be different practitioners. Alternatively, one might employ the scale retrospectively in a blind study of closed cases and see whether low and high scores correlated significantly with successful and unsuccessful outcomes.

Reliability

The reliability of the instrument could be checked by asking pairs of professionals, in which the members of each pair knew the same incestuous family members, to rate the members. The ratings could then be compared for interrater reliability. Items that showed poor reliability could be discarded or refined for greater behavioral specificity. This should make it easier for different raters to get similar results.

Sensitivity

Most researchers, including the authors, are fond of instruments that yield precise interval scores. This one does. The authors believe that significant differences in scores are therapeutically meaningful. However, very small differences, such as one or a few points, would not be significant. Thus the magnitude of difference in scores that is required to denote significant differences for clinicians needs to be established. Factor analysis of different items would be helpful in this regard.

Conclusion

The number of incestuous families requiring treatment has increased dramatically in past decades. Greater public awareness and better case-finding procedures have probably accounted for most of the increase. Perhaps, too, societal confusion about sexual mores has instigated an increase in the incidence of incest. In any event, the problem of treating incestuous families is staggering and not apt to decrease. For this reason, the need for objective and clinically effective measures of assessment is very great.

The assessment format described here is designed to help practitioners objectively evaluate the risks in leaving victim and offender in the same home and in deciding whether to reunify the family during treatment. It is also intended to facilitate the communication of professional goals and the coordination of the system that responds to incestuous activities. In addition, it focuses on behavioral rather than psychodynamic factors in order to assist clinicians in formulating realistic plans to protect and treat incest victims and their families.

238

REFERENCES

Alexander, P. C. (1985). A systems theory conceptualization of incest. *Family Process, 24,* 79–88.

Bender, L., & Blau, A. (1937). The reaction of children to sexual relations with adults. *American Journal of Orthopsychiatry, 7,* 500–518.

Conte, J. (1984). The justice system and sexual abuse of children. *Social Service Review, 58,* 556–568.

Eist, H., & Mandel, A. (1968). Family treatment of ongoing incest behavior. *Family Process, 7,* 216–232.

Gazda, G. M. (1984). *Group counseling: A developmental approach* (3rd ed.). Boston: Allyn and Bacon.

Geiser, R. (1978). Incest and psychological violence. *International Journal of Family Psychiatry, 2,* 291–300.

Gelinas, D. J. (1983). Persisting negative effects of incest. *Psychiatry, 46,* 312–332.

Gentry, C. E. (1978). Incestuous abuse of children: The need for an objective overview. *Child Welfare, 57,* 355–364.

Giaretto, H. (1977). Humanistic treatment of father–daughter incest. *Child Abuse and Neglect, 1,* 411–426.

Giaretto, H. (1981). A comprehensive child sexual abuse treatment program. In P. B. Mrazek & C. H. Kempe (Eds.), *Sexually abused children and their families* (p. 183). Oxford: Pergamon Press.

Gross, M. (1979). Incestuous rape: A cause for hysterical seizures in four adolescent girls. *American Journal of Orthopsychiatry, 49,* 704–708.

Groth, N. (1979). *Men who rape: The psychology of the offender.* New York: Plenum Press.

Herman, J., & Hirschman, L. (1977). Father–daughter incest. *Journal of Women in Culture and Society, 2,* 735–756.

Herman, J. L., & Hirschman, L. (1981). *Father–daughter incest.* Cambridge, MA: Harvard University Press.

James, B., & Nasjleti, M. (1983). *Treating sexually abused children and their families.* Palo Alto, CA: Consulting Psychologists Press.

Kroth, J. A. (1979). *Child sexual abuse: Analysis of evaluation report on the child sexual abuse demonstration and treatment project.* Report prepared for the California Office of Child Abuse Prevention, Sacramento, CA.

McIntyre, K. (1981). The role of mothers in father–daughter incest: A feminist analysis. *Social Work, 26,* 462–467.

Myer, M. H. (1984, March). Research dispels incestuous family myth. *NASW News, 19,* 2–4.

Peters, J. (1976). Children who are victims of sexual assault and the psychology of offenders. *American Journal of Psychotherapy, 30,* 398–421.

Rosenfeld, A. A., et al. (1979). Fantasy and reality in patients' reports of incest. *Journal of Clinical Psychiatry, 40,* 159–164.

Schoeman, F., & Reamer, F. (1983, August). Should child abuse always be reported? *The Hastings Center Report, 13,* 19–20.

Server, J., & Janzen, C. (1982). Contraindications to reconstitution of sexually abusive families. *Child Welfare, 61,* 279–288.

Sgroi, S. M. (1982). *Handbook of clinical intervention in child sexual abuse.* Lexington, MA: Lexington Books.

Spencer, J. (1978). Father–daughter incest: A clinical view from the corrections field. *Child Welfare, 57,* 581–590.

Stark, E. (1984, May). The unspeakable family secret. *Psychology Today, 18,* 41–46.

Strachey, J. (Ed.). (1955). *The complete works of Sigmund Freud* (Vol. 3). London: Hogarth Press.

Summit, R. (1983). The child sexual abuse accommodation syndrome. *Child Abuse and Neglect, 7,* 177–193.

Summit, R., & Kryso, J. (1978). Sexual abuse of children: A clinical spectrum. *American Journal of Orthopsychiatry, 48,* 237–251.

Taylor, J. W. (1986). Social casework and the multimodal treatment of incest. *Social Casework, 67,* 451–459.

Tsai, M., & Wagner, N. (1978). Therapy groups for women sexually molested as children. *Archives of Sexual Behavior, 7,* 417–427.

Detecting Childhood Sexual Abuse in Couples Therapy

Ferol E. Mennen and Lynn Pearlmutter

18

T he ability of couples therapists to detect an undisclosed history of childhood sexual abuse is a requisite but underrecognized skill. Many articles and books deal with incidence, outcome, detection, and treatment strategies for individuals who have been sexually abused. An equally extensive array of literature describes couples therapy. However, professional literature on detecting an abuse history in partners in therapy is scarce. This chapter discusses how couples therapists can detect an abuse history in a couple, introduce this issue into the couple's treatment, and begin to integrate sexual-abuse issues into treatment.[1]

Schnarch (1991) makes only fleeting references to childhood sexual abuse in his otherwise encyclopedic book on sex therapy. Dinsmore (1991) devotes a chapter to integrating the issues that arise in treating partners when one or both have been sexually abused, yet these works do not discuss how to detect abuse. Sprei and Courtois (1988) briefly mention detection in their discussion of treating sexual dysfunction following sexual assault. Although the literature on extramarital affairs has increased greatly in the past few years, only cursory references are made to childhood sexual abuse as a dynamic in marital infidelity (Pittman, 1989; Moultrup, 1990; Brown, 1991).

---

1. The information presented is not specific to gender or sexual orientation. Because most sexual-abuse survivors in treatment are females, the feminine pronoun is used. However, the information presented also applies to male clients.

When sexual abuse is addressed in the literature, it is assumed that the abuse will be disclosed as part of the presenting problem or in the psychosocial history (Ingram, 1985; Johnson, 1989) or is related to sexual dysfunction arising from childhood sexual abuse (McCarthy, 1990; McGuire & Wagner, 1978; Rowe & Savage, 1988; Talmadge & Wallace, 1991; Weiner, 1988). Although the literature cited above contains valuable information, clinical experience suggests that self-identified clients represent only a small percentage of sexual-abuse victims among the population seeking couples therapy. Because many victims of sexual abuse fail to disclose their abuse to the therapist, do not remember it, or minimize its impact, couples therapists are advised to consider the possibility of sexual abuse as a factor in couples' problems.

Several factors may account for the dearth of literature on the detection of sexual abuse in couples treatment. Despite increasing professional attention to the prevalence of childhood sexual abuse in adults, many professionals either wittingly or unwittingly perpetuate denial among their clients. Reliance on theoretical frameworks that discount the importance of childhood victimization may lead clinicians to fail to recognize sexual abuse in their clients or to discount it as a factor in the etiology of the presenting dysfunction and problem (Schetky, 1990). Also, some training programs on couples therapy may fail to stress the relationship between sexual abuse and couple dysfunction. The emphasis on "change first" in systems-oriented therapies has resulted in deemphasis on extensive history taking (Fisch, Weakland, & Segal, 1982; Haley, 1981; Stuart, 1980), which may result in failure to learn about childhood sexual abuse in one or both partners.

Researchers currently estimate that between 19% and 42% of all women and a minimum of 16% of all men have been sexually abused in childhood (Finkelhor, 1984; Finkelhor, Hotaling, Lewis, & Smith, 1990; Russell, 1983; Wyatt, 1985). Higher rates are evident in those seeking psychotherapy services (Briere & Runtz, 1987; Swett, Surrey, & Cohen, 1990). As more couples seek treatment, it can be assumed that sexual-abuse survivors will represent a larger percentage of people in treatment.

Detecting Abuse in Couples Therapy

The first step in understanding and diagnosing childhood sexual abuse in couples therapy is to recognize sexual abuse as a contributing factor in psychological and interactional dysfunction. Couples therapists, like all therapists, need education about and to become sensitive to the existence of childhood sexual abuse. The importance of becoming aware of sexual abuse and the ability to use such knowledge in therapy cannot be overstated; without such awareness, therapists will not recognize abuse and therefore will not introduce it into the treatment setting (Mennen, 1990).

Therapists need to be knowledgeable about the constellations of symptoms that may indicate sexual abuse. Abused children develop strategies that allow them to survive the assault on their bodies, emotions, and souls (Summitt, 1983). However, for adults, these strategies may become maladaptive and thus manifested as "symptoms" (Briere, 1989).

Symptoms can be quite provocative and may lead to a diagnosis of "mental illness." The survivor may be labeled with a diagnosis and treated (albeit unsuccessfully) with no attention to the underlying cause of the symptoms. Couples therapists who see these kinds of problems in practice need to be cognizant of their etiology. However, therapists also must be careful not to overreact to isolated symptoms. Symptoms must be understood within their context. Because sexual abuse can create a wide variety of symptoms, therapists must be careful not to assume a history of abuse. Symptoms may be evident in the individual and/or in the couple dyad.

Symptoms in Individuals

Multiple symptoms. One partner may exhibit a constellation of symptoms: anxiety, depression, low self-esteem, past or present history of self-destructive or self-mutilating behavior, substance abuse, and/or eating disorders (Briere, 1989; Courtois, 1988; Herman, 1988; Herman, Russell, & Trocki, 1986; Kluft, 1990). Although a single symptom does not necessarily indicate abuse, when a partner presents with a constellation of symptoms, the possibility of abuse should be considered.

Borderline personality. Borderline personality characteristics can be an important indicator of past sexual abuse. Studies indicate that the majority of patients with borderline personality have a history of childhood sexual abuse (Bryer, Nelson, Miller, & Krol, 1987; Herman, Perry, & van der Kolk, 1989; Ludolph, Westen, Misle, Jackson, Wixom, & Wiss, 1990). The emphasis on early object deprivation as the essential feature in the development of borderline personality (Kernberg, 1975, 1984; Masterson, 1981) conceals the importance of sexual abuse in the evolution of symptoms. As a result, partners may have had their sexual abuse dismissed or minimized in previous therapy (Tarnopolsky, 1992).

> W was referred to a therapist after having seen a number of different therapists, all of whom dismissed her as difficult to treat due to her borderline personality. Treatment revealed an extensive history of abuse by her brother, father, and grandfather that had not been acknowledged in previous therapy.

Physical complaints. A history of numerous, vague physical complaints, frequently with little medical cause, may indicate past abuse. Headaches, stomach pain, pelvic pain, hypoglycemia, spastic colitis, heart palpitations, and asthma have all been found to be common in women with a history of sexual abuse (Cunningham, Pearce, & Pearce, 1988; Walker, Katon, Neraas, Jemelka, & Massoth, 1992). In such cases, the spouse may complain of his partner's frequent medical problems, their impact on the relationship, and question their validity.

243

G entered treatment through referral from a physician after having undergone numerous medical procedures, including a hysterectomy, without relief from chronic pain. Years of therapy had failed to uncover a history of sadistic sexual abuse. The psychiatrist, who was sensitive to issues of sexual abuse, was able to relate her physical symptoms to past abuse.

Repression and dissociation. Repression results not only in the inability to remember the abuse, but it also inhibits memory of other periods of childhood (Herman & Schatzow, 1987). Survivors may have significant memory lapses. Frequently, clients present with only isolated memories of childhood. For example, one woman was unable to remember anything that happened when she was nine and had a vague "suspicion" that she might have been sexually abused. As treatment progressed, she recovered memories of her stepfather's ongoing sexual abuse. The most violent and sadistic abuse had occurred during her ninth year.

Survivors also use dissociation as a defense (Chu & Dill, 1990), ranging from feelings dissociated from the accompanying events to the development of multiple personalities (Norton, Ross, & Novotny, 1990). Dramatic symptoms include perceptual and cognitive distortions such as extreme dissociation, fugue states, depersonalization, derealization, psychic numbing, and hallucinations (Ellenson, 1985, 1986; Gelinas, 1983), all of which are frequently misdiagnosed as psychosis. If such symptoms do occur in couples therapy, the therapist is advised to seek consultation with and/or referral to a professional who is an expert on treating dissociation in survivors of childhood sexual abuse. All multiple-personality cases should be considered possible victims of sexual abuse (Kluft, 1985).

Presentation of Past Abuse

Lack of trust. The capacity for developing intimate adult relationships is compromised by the betrayal that occurs when a trusted adult sexually abuses a child (Wooley & Vigilanti, 1984). When clients exhibit a pervasive lack of trust in their partner without substantial basis, a history of childhood sexual abuse may be indicated.

"Trust is the paramount issue for incest survivors," says Lew (1988, p. 168). This issue may be manifested in the areas of fidelity, love, protection, and so forth. Survivors often distort life events to confirm a perceived lack of trust, including misinterpreting the therapist's intentions. A therapist may be inclined to dismiss this phenomenon as hypersensitivity or paranoid behavior. However, it is important to realize that lack of trust may have been learned as a defense against further victimization. Perpetrators often initiate abuse with kindness or special favors to gain the child's trust. Often, the perpetrator expresses love and affection, which causes the victim to become confused about the safety of future relationships.

When J and P entered therapy, P was convinced, despite lack of objective evidence, that J did not really care about him and that she wanted to have an affair. Therapy revealed that P had been sexually abused by a trusted and much loved neighbor when he was a child.

Sexual problems. Sexual problems are common in abuse survivors; more than half of survivors report some type of sexual dysfunction (Becker, Skinner, Abel, & Treacy, 1982). Such problems may be related to desire, arousal, or response. In such cases, the therapist needs to be sensitive to the possibility of undisclosed or repressed sexual abuse. A careful sexual history or a genogram may reveal patterns indicative of abuse (Hof & Berman, 1986).

Difficulties with desire may include forms of hyposexuality and hypersexuality. In some instances, a woman may lack interest in sex and complain that her partner is "oversexed." These women may have never gained any pleasure in sex, finding it "nasty" or "dirty." In other instances, couples will report having had a fairly normal sexual relationship until the birth of a child, after which the woman may lose interest in sex.

Other survivors may report that they are overly preoccupied with sex. Persons with histories of compulsive sexual behavior often report that sexual activity fails to bring pleasure. Many abuse survivors can engage in or enjoy sex only if they are in control of the situation. Other survivors report that sex is enjoyable only with a partner with whom they are not emotionally intimate. For example, one client reported that she had experienced sexual gratification in casual relationships before her recent marriage, but was now uninterested in sex with her husband, whom she loved deeply.

In other cases, survivors may have an almost phobic response to sex. A particular touch or particular positions may make them withdraw or feel frightened or anxious. A survivor may report periods of dissociation during sex in which she feels "out of her body." Clients who have repressed past abuse are unable to connect their sexual problems with past abuse without assistance.

B, who had no conscious recollection of sexual abuse, could not stand her husband approaching or touching her from behind. As therapy progressed and she recalled her abuse, she remembered that her father had approached her from behind and fondled her.

Infidelity

This issue has not received appropriate attention in the professional literature on sexual abuse. Maltz and Holman (1987) have described many of the sexual complications experienced by survivors but conspicuously omit discussion of infidelity. Moultrup (1990) described infidelity as a complex systemic process involving interlocking triangles caused by lack of differentiation in the family of origin. However, no reference is made to sexual abuse as a factor contributing to infidelity. Pittman

(1989) briefly discusses how the "guilty aftereffects of childhood sexual abuse" can be expressed by survivors' lashing out against their loved ones by "inflicting harm upon themselves" (p. 61). Brown (1991) highlighted childhood sexual abuse as an important causative factor in sexual addiction affairs, ignoring its importance in other kinds of infidelity.

Many sexual addicts have a history of childhood sexual abuse (Carnes, 1989). Naive, inexperienced, inadequately trained therapists or those with therapeutic blind spots may find it difficult to inquire into possible abuse (Brown, 1991). Lew (1988) described how a partner's promiscuity can wear down the other partner's efforts to keep the relationship going. Therapists need to be willing to assess sexual addiction and to confront its possible connection with childhood sexual abuse. In such instances, couples therapy may need to be delayed until after the sexual addiction is under control.

> S requested marital therapy and, in the presence of her partner, openly discussed during the first interview that she did not understand why she had had a series of brief extramarital sexual encounters. With considerable encouragement from her husband, she eventually shared her childhood history of incest. He perceived the connection between his wife's past abuse and present infidelity. She expressed surprise when the therapist saw the connection too.

Recurrent patterns of victimization. Revictimization is common among sexual-abuse survivors, who repeat patterns learned in childhood when they were unable to extricate themselves from an abusive situation. For example, they may report being victims of sexually violent experiences such as rape, abusive romantic relationships, and physical violence (Briere & Runtz, 1987). In the couple dyad, a pattern of victimization may occur. Victimization may occur in areas of physical abuse, emotional abuse, or a sadomasochistic sexual relationship. The female sexual abuse victim may be a sexual addict who repeatedly becomes involved as the "third party" (Brown, 1991).

> D and K entered treatment because D complained that K, his wife, was not interested in sex. Through gentle probing, the therapist learned that D sometimes physically abused K, refused to give her enough money for food despite his more than adequate salary, and sometimes stayed out all night. Upon questioning, K divulged a history of sexual abuse by a grandfather. Her intimate relationships indicated a pattern of physical and emotional abuse, of which her marriage was the most recent example.

Introducing the Topic of Sexual Abuse

After a therapist realizes that a client may have been sexually abused, the therapist must introduce this possibility into therapy. Few clients enter therapy with an understanding of their childhood victimization and how it relates to their current distress. Thus, it is imperative that therapists be willing to ask the right questions in order to gain the necessary information. In a sample of female admissions to a psychiatric emergency room, a chart review revealed a victimization rate of 6%. However, direct questions about an abuse history revealed a 70% history of sexual molestation (Briere & Zaidi, 1989). Even therapists who are quite comfortable asking individual clients about abuse may fail to screen for abuse in couples work. By asking about abuse, the therapist initiates the corrective process of challenging the secrecy and shame that accompany sexual abuse.

Some agencies and practitioners attempt to solicit information about past abuse through written forms completed by couples. However, this approach, albeit valuable, limits the therapist's ability to observe nonverbal communication, perpetuates the message that sexual abuse cannot be talked about, and risks depersonalizing a highly emotional experience. Thus, a more direct approach is needed.

Questions about sexual abuse need to be asked before the end of the first interview. For example, a therapist might say, "We are learning that sexual abuse in children is quite common and that it can have a negative impact on relationships. Does either of you have a history of any kind of sexual contact as a child that made you feel uncomfortable?" If a couple presents with problems of jealousy, affairs, and/or sexual dysfunctions, the therapist might state, "My experience has been that when clients present with these symptoms, sometimes a history of abuse has occurred in one or both partners' families of origin. Could you tell me about any such incidents in your families?"

Questions about sexual abuse may elicit various responses. Clients may deny past sexual abuse or one or both partners may admit to having been abused and have some insight into the role of abuse in their relationship. In the latter case, treatment for past abuse can be integrated · into the couple work. For clients who present with a history of sexual abuse, the marital therapy literature offers a number of resources for treatment (Ingram, 1985; Johnson, 1989; Maltz, 1988).

Other responses to questions about sexual abuse may be more problematic. One or both partners may admit to a history of childhood victimization but discount its current relevance. Survivors frequently deny the impact of childhood victimization on their present functioning, a once-useful strategy that helped them survive as a child. Other people in the client's life (particularly family members who knew about the abuse) may have encouraged denial by minimizing the abuse or advising the survivor to "let bygones be bygones."

Because denial and minimization are often successful in warding off the pain of abuse, the client may be reluctant to admit the emotional impact of abuse. The therapist can educate the couple about the effects of sexual abuse in a nonthreatening way. The therapist might discuss the dynamics of sexual abuse and let the couple know that the kinds of problems they are experiencing are common among sexual-abuse survivors.

Although painful and difficult to resolve, issues associated with victimization are treatable. The therapist needs to instill a realistic hope for change. Using analogies to post-traumatic stress disorder (such as the trauma experienced by Vietnam veterans) can help illustrate the long-lasting effects of trauma as well as the possibility of working through it.

Therapists should avoid becoming involved in power struggles with clients about the impact of sexual abuse on their lives. A survivor might seem to acquiesce to the therapist's suggestions or may adamantly deny that abuse occurred. Both scenarios reflect the client's perception of a powerful adult (therapist) imposing his or her will on a child (client). In such instances, therapy can even revictimize the client. Abuse may be introduced as a possible cause of dysfunction, but the client's perceptions must be respected until a trusting relationship can be established. Readings, casually suggested during the session, may help clients deal with their past experiences (Armstrong, 1978; Bass & Davis, 1988; Jarvis-Kirkendall & Kirkendall, 1989; Petersen 1991). Couples will be more invested in treatment if the therapist respects boundaries.

Partners who have previously undergone treatment for abuse may believe that the problem has been resolved and may not understand its current effects. Past therapy may have dealt with the abuse at an intellectual level but failed to confront its powerful affective component (Cornell & Olio, 1991). If the therapy occurred before the survivor became involved in an intimate adult relationship, the issue of relationships may have been difficult to address. In discussing previous therapy, therapists should be respectful of the previous therapy and therapist, while making new connections between the abuse and the couple's marital or relationship problems. Dealing with sexual abuse issues can be conceptualized as an incremental process with different stages. The previous therapy may be conceived of as an initial step that has led to the next step of working through the abuse in the context of an intimate relationship. If the client feels dissatisfied about the previous therapeutic experience, the clinician may acknowledge the disappointment while suggesting that current therapy may be more effective.

Sometimes clients may deny abuse because they fear their partner's or their therapist's reaction. Sexual abuse has been acknowledged and discussed widely by the professional community and the public only since the late 1970s (Rush, 1980). Many people still blame victims for their abuse or see them as "damaged goods." Thus, the shame and guilt that survivors experience result not only from the abuse experience but from society's reaction to sexual abuse.

Both the survivor's and her partner's reactions need to be monitored. Although most partners of abuse survivors are supportive and understanding, some blame the partner or believe that she was a willing participant, thus reinforcing the survivor's feelings of shame and guilt (Brittain & Merriam, 1988). Or the partner may use the past abuse to reinforce his view that the abused partner is "the problem." Discussion of roles can be useful for eliciting important content and observing the couple's interactions. For example, the therapist might say, "You seem to overfunction in this relationship. I wonder if you learned that as a child." If disclosure of abuse is met with less than an empathic response by the partner, the therapist should proceed slowly and carefully in further joint discussions of the abuse.

Individual sessions, as part of the assessment process, can free a partner and therapist to explore sexual abuse without dealing with the reactions of the other partner (Scharff & Scharff, 1991). If the client discloses past abuse, the therapist and client can develop a plan for sharing the experience with the partner. The therapist should not conspire to keep this information from the nonvictimized spouse. Secrecy is an important dynamic in sexual abuse and is responsible for much of the shame experienced by victims (Finkelhor & Browne, 1985).

When a client continues to deny abuse in the face of clear symptoms of an abuse history, complications ensue. Sometimes, the client may even leave therapy. The subject may threaten the tenuous defenses of the survivor. In fact, the majority of victims have repressed at least a portion of their abuse history (Herman & Schatzow, 1987). In such cases, the therapist should focus on developing a therapeutic relationship that allows for exploration of painful material.

Survivors need a trusting, supportive environment to deal with and work through a past that threatens to overwhelm them. Couples therapists need to create a supportive atmosphere by focusing on empathic communication and building trust with the couple. Therapists must avoid being judgmental and overly confrontive.

In some instances, referral for concurrent individual or group therapy with a therapist who is skilled in dealing with sexual abuse may be necessary. Referral can prevent overfocus on one partner during couples therapy. The couples therapist should explain that problematic pre-relationship issues may be best addressed individually or in a group in order to maximize the benefits of couples therapy. In such cases, couples work can continue with consultation with the individual therapist. Of course, the couple's ability to afford concurrent therapies needs to be taken into consideration.

Conclusion

Childhood sexual abuse is a contributing, but often unrecognized, factor in couple dysfunction. To detect and integrate childhood sexual abuse into therapy, a couples therapist must probe sensitively while maintaining therapeutic distance, balance diagnostic activity with nonreactivity, and respect the client's childhood history while focusing on current problems. These skills will improve therapists' abilities in both assessment and intervention with couples.

REFERENCES

Armstrong, L. (1978). *Kiss daddy goodnight: A speak-out on incest.* New York: Pocket Books.

Bass, E., & Davis, L. (1988). *The courage to heal: A guide for women survivors of child sexual abuse.* New York: Harper and Row.

Becker, J. V., Skinner, L. J., Abel, G. G., & Treacy, E. C. (1982). Incidence and types of sexual dysfunctions in rape and incest victims. *Journal of Sex and Marital Therapy, 8,* 65–74.

Briere, J. (1989). *Therapy for adults molested as children: Beyond survival.* New York: Springer.

Briere, J., & Runtz, M. (1987). Post sexual abuse trauma: Data and implications for clinical practice. *Journal of Interpersonal Violence, 2,* 367–379.

Briere, J., & Zaidi, L. Y. (1989). Sexual abuse histories and sequelae in female psychiatric emergency room patients. *American Journal of Psychiatry, 146,* 1602–1606.

Brittain, D. E., & Merriam, K. (1988). Groups for significant others of survivors of child sexual abuse: A report of methods and findings. *Journal of Interpersonal Violence, 3,* 90–101.

Brown, E. M. (1991). *Patterns of infidelity and their treatment.* New York: Brunner/Mazel.

Bryer, J. B., Nelson, B. A., Miller, J. B., & Krol, P. A. (1987). Childhood sexual and physical abuse as factors in adult psychiatric illness. *American Journal of Psychiatry, 144,* 1426–1430.

Carnes, P. J. (1989, October). *Contrary to love: The sex addict.* Paper presented at the meeting of the American Association for Marriage and Family Therapy Conference, San Francisco.

Chu, J. A., & Dill, D. L. (1990). Dissociative symptoms in relation to childhood physical and sexual abuse. *American Journal of Psychiatry, 147,* 887–892.

Cornell, W. F., & Olio, K. A. (1991). Integrating affect in treatment with adult survivors of physical and sexual abuse. *American Journal of Orthopsychiatry, 61,* 59–69.

Courtois, C. (1988). *Healing the incest wound: Adult survivors in therapy.* New York: W. W. Norton.

Cunningham, J., Pearce, T., & Pearce, P. (1988). Childhood sexual abuse and medical complaints in adult women. *Journal of Interpersonal Violence, 3,* 131–144.

Dinsmore, C. (1991). *From surviving to thriving.* Albany, NY: State University of New York Press.

Ellenson, G. S. (1985). Detecting a history of incest: A predictive syndrome. *Social Casework, 66,* 525–532.

Ellenson, G. S. (1986). Disturbances of perception in adult female incest survivors. *Social Casework, 67,* 149–159.

Finkelhor, D. (1984). *Child sexual abuse: New theory and research.* New York: Free Press.

Finkelhor, D., & Browne, A. (1985). The traumatic impact of child sexual abuse: A conceptualization. *American Journal of Orthopsychiatry, 55,* 530–541.

Finkelhor, D., Hotaling, G., Lewis, I. A., & Smith, C. (1990). Sexual abuse in a national survey of adult men and women: Prevalence, characteristics, and risk factors. *Child Abuse and Neglect, 14*(1), 19–28.

Fisch, R., Weakland, J. H., & Segal, L. (1982). *The tactics of change.* San Francisco: Jossey-Bass.

Gelinas, D. J. (1983). The persisting negative effects of incest. *Psychiatry, 46,* 312–332.

Haley, J. (1981). How to be a marriage therapist without knowing practically anything. In J. Haley (Ed.), *Reflections on therapy and other essays.* Chevy Chase, MD: Family Therapy Institute.

Herman, J. L. (1988). Father–daughter incest. In F. M. Ochberg (Ed.), *Post-traumatic therapy and victims of violence.* New York: Brunner/Mazel.

Herman, J. L., Perry, J. C., & van der Kolk, B. A. (1989). Childhood trauma in borderline personality disorder. *American Journal of Psychiatry, 146,* 490–495.

Herman, J., Russell, D., & Trocki, K. (1986). Long-term effects of incestuous abuse in childhood. *American Journal of Psychiatry, 143,* 1293–1296.

Herman, J. L., & Schatzow, E. (1987). Recovery and verification of memories of childhood sexual trauma. *Psychoanalytic Psychology*, *4*(1), 1–14.

Hof, L., & Berman, L. (1986). The sexual genogram. *Journal of Marital and Family Therapy*, *12*, 39–47.

Ingram, T. L. (1985). Sexual abuse in the family of origin and unresolved issues: A gestalt/systems treatment approach for couples. *Family Therapy*, *12*, 173–183.

Jarvis-Kirkendall, C., & Kirkendall, J. (1989). *Without consent: How to overcome childhood sexual abuse*. Scottsdale, AZ: Swan Press.

Johnson, S. M. (1989). Integrating marital and individual therapy for incest survivors: A case study. *Psychotherapy*, *26*(1), 96–103.

Kernberg, O. F. (1975). *Borderline conditions and pathological narcissism*. New York: Aronson.

Kernberg, O. F. (1984). *Severe personality disorders*. New Haven, CT: Yale University Press.

Kluft, R. P. (1985). *Childhood antecedents of multiple personality*. Washington, DC: American Psychiatric Association.

Kluft, R. P. (1990). *Incest-related syndromes of adult psychopathology*. Washington, DC: American Psychiatric Press.

Lew, M. (1988). *Victims no longer*. New York: Nevraumount.

Ludolph, P. S., Westen, D., Misle, B., Jackson, A., Wixom, J., & Wiss, C. (1990). The borderline diagnosis in adolescents: Symptoms and developmental history. *American Journal of Psychiatry*, *147*, 470–476.

Maltz, W. (1988). Identifying and treating the sexual repercussions of incest: A couples therapy approach. *Journal of Sex and Marital Therapy*, *14*, 142–170.

Maltz, W., & Holman, B. (1987). *Incest and sexuality*. Lexington, MA: Lexington Books.

Masterson, J. L. (1981). *The narcissistic and borderline disorders*. New York: Brunner/Mazel.

McCarthy, B. W. (1990). Treating sexual dysfunction associated with prior sexual trauma. *Journal of Sex and Marital Therapy*, *16*, 142–146.

McGuire, L. S., & Wagner, N. N. (1978). Sexual dysfunction in women who were molested as children: One response pattern and suggestions for treatment. *Journal of Sex and Marital Therapy*, *4*, 11–15.

Mennen, F. E. (1990). Dilemmas and demands: Working with adult survivors of sexual abuse. *Affilia*, *5*(4), 72–86.

Moultrup, D. O. (1990). *Husbands, wives, and lovers: The emotional system of the extramarital affair*. New York: Guilford Press.

Norton, G. R., Ross, C. A., & Novotny, M. F. (1990). Factors that predict scores on the dissociative experiences scale. *Journal of Clinical Psychology*, *46*, 273–277.

Petersen, B. (1991). *Dancing with daddy: A childhood lost and a life regained*. New York: Bantam Books.

Pittman, F. (1989). *Private lives*. New York: W. W. Norton.

Rowe, W., & Savage, S. (1988). Sex therapy with female incest survivors. *Social Casework*, *69*, 265–271.

Rush, F. (1980). *The best-kept secret: Sexual abuse of children*. Englewood Cliffs, NJ: Prentice-Hall.

Russell, D. E. H. (1983). The incidence and prevalence of intrafamilial and extrafamilial sexual abuse of female children. *Child Abuse and Neglect*, *7*, 133–146.

Scharff, D. E., & Scharff, J. S. (1991). *Object relations couples therapy*. New York: W. W. Norton.

Schetky, D. (1990). A review of the literature of the long-term effects of childhood sexual abuse. In R. Kluft (Ed.), *Incest-related syndromes of adult psychopathology*. Washington, DC: American Psychiatric Press.

Schnarch, D. M. (1991). *Constructing the sexual crucible*. New York: W. W. Norton.

Sprei, J. E., & Courtois, C. A. (1988). The treatment of women's sexual dysfunctions arising from sexual assault. In R. A. Brown & J. R. Field (Eds.), *Treatment of sexual problems in individual and couples therapy* (pp. 267–299). College Park, MD: PMA Publishing.

Summitt, R. (1983). The child abuse accommodation syndrome. *Child Abuse and Neglect, 7,* 177–193.

Stuart, R. B. (1980). *Helping couples change.* New York: Guilford Press.

Swett, C., Surrey, J., & Cohen, C. (1990). Sexual and physical abuse histories and psychiatric symptoms among male psychiatric outpatients. *American Journal of Psychiatry, 147,* 632–636.

Talmadge, L. D., & Wallace, S. C. (1991). Reclaiming sexuality in female incest survivors. *Journal of Sex and Marital Therapy, 17,* 163–182.

Tarnopolsky, A. (1992). The validity of the borderline personality disorder. In D. Silver & M. Rosenbluth (Eds.), *Handbook of borderline disorders* (pp. 29–52). Madison, WI: International University Press.

Walker, E. A., Katon, W. J., Neraas, K., Jemelka, R. P., & Massoth, D. (1992). Dissociation in women with chronic pelvic pain. *American Journal of Psychiatry, 149,* 534–537.

Weiner, L. J. (1988). Issues in sex therapy with survivors of intrafamily sexual abuse. *Women in Therapy, 7*(2–3), 253–264.

Wooley, M. J., & Vigilanti, M. A. (1984). Psychological separation and the sexual abuse victim. *Psychotherapy, 3,* 347–352.

Wyatt, G. E. (1985). The sexual abuse of Afro-American and White-American women in childhood. *Child Abuse and Neglect, 9,* 507–519.

Part 4

Assessment Techniques

Self-Observation:
An Empowerment Strategy
In Assessment

Judy Kopp

19

T hrough their commitment to client self-determination and to building on client strengths, social work practitioners use empowerment strategies to counteract the consequences of negative valuations and powerlessness. Solomon (1976) defined empowerment as "a process whereby the social worker engages in a set of activities with the client or client system that aim to reduce the powerlessness that has been created by negative valuations based on membership in a stigmatized group" (p. 19). The consequences of belonging to a stigmatized group include varying degrees of alienation from and mistrust of societal institutions, lowered self-esteem, and fatalism—all potential obstacles to the development of a successful treatment relationship. Solomon points out that it is critical for clients to see the social worker as a helping person.

Solomon's observations about powerlessness in minority groups can be generalized to many clients seen by social workers. Sometimes coerced or required to seek help, perhaps estranged from usual sources of support, clients may experience agencies and social workers as a foreign and powerful system. In such a context, empowerment means providing clients with opportunities to recognize their personal value and to attain their goals through their own efforts.

Although the literature on empowerment emphasizes the importance of incorporating empowering techniques into practice, ideally during the initial contact (Gray, Hartman, & Saalberg, 1985), few techniques have been specified for practitioners, especially during the assessment phase. Rather, empowerment has often been limited to advocacy through social action groups (Hepworth & Larsen, 1986). The technique of self-observation, however, helps obviate a client's sense of powerlessness during the social work assessment process. The information gathered during the problem-definition and formulation stages is controlled by the client. By recording information about themselves, clients are able to select the problem focus, determine what needs to be changed, decide what information to record (using the worker as a consultant), collect information about their experiences, and interpret the data collected. Although workers' positive attitudes and expectations about clients' potential for change help facilitate a sense of power in the client, attitudes also need to be operationalized into "activities [that] make it possible for the client to perceive of self as causal agent in achieving the solution to his problem rather than as hapless victim" (Solomon, 1976, pp. 333–334). By giving the client control over some of the information used in intervention planning, power shifts from the worker to the client. A collaborative relationship develops; the worker is no longer the lone expert who assesses the client's problem.

Although self-monitoring is often linked to cognitive–behavioral practice due to its inclusion in behaviorally oriented self-control programs as a measurement tool, it is not bound by theory. Recording events in a diary is a valuable technique for clients whose social workers are psychodynamically or behaviorally oriented. Self-observation is often used in time-limited treatments regardless of the theoretical approach, especially between the first and second sessions (Fisch, Weakland, & Segal, 1982; Wells, 1982). Self-observation increases self-knowledge in the client and allows both worker and client to measure the severity of the problem.

Empowerment Strategies

For empowerment to occur, practice skills and activities need to be designed to achieve four goals (Solomon, 1976):
1. To help the client perceive him- or herself as a causal agent in achieving a solution to his or her problem or problems
2. To help the client perceive the practitioner as having knowledge and skills that the client can use
3. To help the client perceive the practitioner as peer–collaborator or partner in the problem-solving effort
4. To help the client perceive the "power structure" as being multipolar, as demonstrating varying degrees of commitment to the status quo, and therefore as being open to influence

Thus the overall goal is to help clients who have been subjected to negative valuations to perceive themselves as causal forces capable of bringing about a desired effect. In short, instead of the worker giving the client aid, the client and worker form a collaborative, complementary relationship "to prevent the reinforcement or extension of the client's feelings of powerlessness" (Solomon, 1976, p. 353).

Leigh (1987) developed assessment strategies for operationalizing empowerment in cross-cultural interactions. His ethnographic interviewing approach places the client in the role of teacher and the social worker in the role of learner. Hirayama and Cetingok (1988) discussed the relevance of empowerment tactics in work with Asian immigrants. Solomon (1976) suggests that practitioners develop an "opportunity profile" that weighs the environmental obstacles (e.g., negative expectations from employers) against the client's environmental supports (e.g., a supportive extended family network). Failure to recognize environmental and personal strengths may lead to what Solomon (1976) describes as

> inappropriate pessimism regarding the possibility of change. The pessimism of practitioners often gets transmitted to clients and instead of "hanging-in" to obtain assistance in maximizing available opportunities, they "drop-out" and create another example of a self-fulfilling prophecy (p. 333).

Sometimes workers expect less from clients than clients are capable of achieving. For example, mothers who had received Aid for Dependent Children grants for long periods and who were considered "hopeless" by their workers were invited to attend a group for parents interested in learning new techniques for relating to their children and helping their children change (Kopp, 1972). The group leaders, who were not employees of the state agency, hoped that each parent would work on one issue but suggested they might collect information on up to four concerns. Several mothers collected assessment data on four issues and with the help of group members designed their own intervention plans.

Self-Observation as an Empowerment Strategy

Definition of Self-Observation

Self-observation, self-recording, and self-monitoring are interchangeable terms that describe clients' written descriptions and records of their feelings, behaviors, and thoughts. Self-monitoring has been defined as a two-step process: (1) the individual first recognizes the occurrence of the event, then (2) systematically records the observation (Thorensen & Mahoney, 1974). A third step, charting or graphing the information, increases awareness of the phenomenon and facilitates its observation and assessment over time.

Clients can record observations about themselves in various ways: by frequency counts (counting each time an event occurs), by duration of events, by severity of experiences graded by self-anchored scales,[1] by diaries

1. Self-anchored scales are self-constructed scales, usually with three to seven personal statements describing a continuum of feelings or experiences.

or logs, and by checklists or other validated measures, such as the Assertion Inventory (Gambrill & Richey, 1975). Recording the frequency of thoughts, feelings, or behaviors is the most common self-monitoring technique described in the literature. Frequency counts can easily be converted into rates by dividing the number of times the event occurred by the number of minutes or hours during which the events were observed. A daily rate represents two dimensions, frequency and time, and allows comparisons across days, even if observation periods vary. Furthermore, frequency data are less demanding to record than are durations or written descriptions.

On the other hand, descriptions of events and the surrounding circumstances help operationalize problems and define appropriate places where interventive efforts can be focused. When the presenting problem is complex and additional information about a situation is needed, descriptive records—even if they are kept only for a week or two—are highly productive. A combination of measures may be used. For example, a client might record the situation at the time he or she felt depressed, accompanying thoughts, and, using a self-anchored scale, rate the severity of his or her feelings. Focusing their attention leads clients naturally to insights about their situations. As they discuss their self-records, clients spontaneously operationalize goals and suggest ideas for change. Thus the worker becomes a consultant/collaborator who suggests ways clients can implement their ideas. Assuming an active role in the intervention planning process helps clients develop confidence in their ability to affect their own situations.

Self-Observation in the Context of Assessment

Commonly (and appropriately), social workers act as experts whose professional knowledge and judgment are the central resource for assessing client situations. During the assessment process, practitioners usually rely primarily on clients' oral accounts of their situations and concerns. Other assessment resources include past records, forms completed by clients, direct observations, collateral observations, and standardized questionnaires. Clients' oral reports are considered indirect information sources because they are based on recall; that is, information is provided retrospectively, sometimes long after the event has been experienced. "Though it is the primary source of information, verbal report is vulnerable to error because of possibly faulty recall, distorted perceptions, biases, and limited self-awareness on the part of the client" (Hepworth & Larsen, 1986, p. 168). Self-observation or self-recording, on the other hand, is a direct information source. It can increase the accuracy of assessment information; information monitored concurrently is more accurate than are retrospective estimates (Frederiksen, Epstein, & Kosevsky, 1975).

Clearly, information recorded while an event is experienced complements self-exploration during counseling sessions. Knowledge is a source of power; the new knowledge and heightened insight that clients experience through focusing their attention on a particular dimension of their lives is unquestionably empowering. Through close observation of specific events, clients acquire new information about themselves, their relationships with others, and the relationship between their behavior and their environment (or environmental context). For example, two weeks of self-monitoring with Wolpe's Subjective Anxiety Scale increased clients' self-knowledge about their anxiety (Hiebert & Fox, 1981). Some clients said that the focused attention required to self-monitor increased their awareness of early feelings of anxiety and of coping mechanisms they could use to control their anxiety; others reported post-monitoring changes in their internal dialogue.

It may be necessary to acquire client-monitored data for problem clarification before a contract is negotiated, or it may be part of the first contract between the client and the practitioner. Client-monitored data are also useful for providing information to other professionals. For example, in an interdisciplinary case staffing situation, self-monitored records convinced other professionals that a nonverbal child was more able than psychological tests showed. These records were the basis for accepting the social worker's recommendation that the client be admitted to a particular classroom (Kopp, 1972). Evidence shows that self-monitoring can be used by a wide range of clients in diverse practice settings and in relation to various problems (Green & Morrow, 1972). The literature describes self-monitoring by children, adolescents, and adults, with and without mental and physical handicaps.

In summary, self-observation during the assessment phase may be used by clients (1) as a source of information about a problem or situation, (2) to gain knowledge about the environmental context of a problem, (3) to increase self-awareness and stimulate insights, and (4) to increase involvement and control. The following sections describe applications of self-observation in assessment through case examples and practice tips and summarize data on the reliability and accuracy of self-records (for additional information on self-monitoring in clinical settings, see Ciminero, Nelson, & Lipinski, 1977; Nelson, 1977).

Case Examples

When a client mentions a problem, workers usually try to understand its severity, frequency, context, history, and importance to the client. The following three case examples show how self-observation contributes to understanding in these areas. In addition, the cases exemplify how self-observation empowers clients to modify initial evaluations and distorted perceptions of their problems.

Clarifying the Problem

Clients do not always reveal their most troubling problems during initial interviews. In the first case, the presenting concern changed after a week of focused observation (Kopp, 1972). A seven-year-old boy was brought by his family to a multidisciplinary child center for evaluation. The presenting problem was tantrums. During the initial assessment interview, the parents said the tantrums occurred "all the time." When asked how severe the tantrums were, they expressed concern that their son might hurt himself. The parents were asked to record each tantrum during the following week and to write what was happening at the time the tantrum began as well as their responses to their son. A format for the record was outlined; the worker emphasized that the information was needed in order to complete the assessment for the interdisciplinary case staffing. When they returned the following week, the parents reported only two tantrums. During this second session, the mother revealed that tantrums were not the central issue. In reviewing their diary of responses to their son, the clients began to discuss their real concerns and feelings. In short, self-observation empowered these parents to give their worker important information.

Locating the Problem

In the second case, monitoring was used to focus on a client's immediate perceptions of the problem in order to help her change this conceptualization (Kopp, 1972). Both parents brought their 10-year-old adopted son for evaluation, certain that something was wrong with him. He was not doing as well in school as was their natural-born, younger daughter, and his mother said she had to nag him constantly to complete his chores and homework. They expected him to earn all A's and to complete his homework and chores every day. He appeared to be a normal but very anxious boy. Psychological testing confirmed he had no developmental delays and average intelligence. He worried about not meeting his parents' above-average expectations. He agreed to record completed homework and chores each day on a large chart; his mother agreed to record her nagging and reminders. A week's data showed he was doing about half his assigned tasks. However, the mother's records indicated that she nagged and reminded him at a high rate—sometimes every two minutes. The son agreed to continue his record and to work toward completing all his tasks if his mother would stop reminding him.

After several months, the son was doing well with his tasks, and his mother had begun to recognize that her expectations of her son were too high. She began to record and increase her compliments and positive comments to him. Also, as she realized that her personal needs were identified with his achievements, she enrolled in college courses and began to do volunteer community work. These outside activities diverted some attention and pressure away from her son. Even though during the initial interview the worker had recognized that the problem was related more to the mother's attitudes and behaviors than to the son's, the worker did not share this perception because of concern that the mother would not return. Giving the mother time, focusing on her definition of the central concern, empowering the son without directly threatening the mother's control, and providing the mother with a tool for self-discovery was successful: the mother identified the areas within herself that needed to be changed. In short, self-monitoring served as a relatively nonthreatening route to recognizing her role in problems that were initially attributed to another family member as well as increasing the son's power and control.

Controlling the Problem

A client's increased attention to the presenting problem can result in better understanding of the issue, a refined definition of the problem, and heightened awareness of its relationship to the environmental context, thus stimulating the client's ideas for handling the problem. A 25-year-old woman referred herself to a family service agency, stating that she "needed to find out about her feelings and wanted to improve her communication" (Kopp, 1972). She had experienced a series of disappointments and failures while living on her own in another city: the loss of her job and male partner and the accumulation of debts. She had not developed close friends during four years away from home, only a series of acquaintances to whom she had difficulty saying no. She decided to escape personal and economic pressures by returning to her parents' home. She saw her return home as another failure. She hoped to become economically independent again, but in the meantime was experiencing difficulties adjusting to living with her parents and reestablishing relationships with old friends. She said that she felt depressed.

During the initial interview, the worker provided information about agency services and procedures and helped the client explore her reasons for seeking help, her past experiences with counseling, her personal strengths and resources, and her goals. Emphasizing the client's primary role in determining the focus of future sessions, the concept and advantages of self-monitoring were introduced.

In addition to exploring the client's feelings of helplessness about her situation, during the second interview the worker introduced the idea of keeping a log or diary. Careful not to suggest problem areas, the worker encouraged the client to select the focus for their work together. The client said that she wished to express her thoughts and feelings more effectively and more comfortably. The client believed that improving her communication skills would enhance her job search and her relationships with parents and friends. Emphasizing that the client knew herself better than anyone else knew her, the worker suggested that a diary would increase self-understanding and further define the problem(s). The client decided to record situations in which she felt she had not expressed her feelings effectively. The client and worker collaborated on developing a recording format, and the worker expressed her confidence in the client's ability to keep a log. The client said she felt hopeless, helpless, and out of control. The log was perceived as a tool to help change these perceptions.

The client reviewed her log with the worker at the beginning of their third session. She saw that she rarely expressed her feelings and thoughts assertively, especially in response to daily requests from her mother to take her on errands. The client's log described the anger and low moods she experienced when she acquiesced to her mother's demands rather than asserting her own plans. On one occasion she had responded with an angry outburst; an impassioned argument ensued, which ended when her mother said she wished herself dead. The client felt intense guilt and helpless to change her situation; she worried that she would become like her mother, who spent long periods in her room rarely communicating with others. In addition to the log, the client completed two assertiveness questionnaires to measure her assertiveness.

During the fourth session, the client and worker reviewed the log. The client expressed interest in assessing her skill and comfort levels in situations in which she had opportunities to be assertive. With the worker's help, she designed two self-anchored scales. Her self-assessments on these scales were used to identify situations in which she felt least competent and most uncomfortable. In the next session the client used her log to specify the skills she wanted to improve and situations she wanted to role-play to practice assertive behaviors. She increased her sense of control and her positive expectations that she could become more assertive.

Practice Tips: The Application of Self-Observation

Parameters of recording, such as how long the record is kept each day, how many days to record, what specific information to record, and how to record the information, depend upon each client's particular situation and how much information is needed to understand the presenting problem(s) and to develop an effective intervention plan. Thus these decisions are functional and individualized. Clients should not collect information that is not used in the assessment process. Clients should be the primary determiners of what and how to record.

Some clients respond enthusiastically to the idea of recording information about themselves, whereas others do not follow through with a monitoring plan. Both the worker's attitude about the importance of the self-monitored record and expressed expectations regarding the client's ability to self-record affect whether the client follows through with the recording plan. Explaining that the information is necessary in order to develop an individualized intervention plan communicates to clients the importance of their data. Expressing optimistic expectations that they can self-monitor also increases the probability that clients will implement recording plans. Again, these expectations, plus the offer of a collaborative relationship, are important empowerment strategies.

The task of recording the frequency of behaviors can be simplified by the use of convenient counters, such as the inexpensive, cumulative counters some shoppers carry, wrist golf-score counters (Lindsley, 1968), bead-wrist counters (Mahoney, 1974), knitting stitch counters, or a piece of masking tape or paper placed in a strategic location. Generally, the closer the recording device is to the behavior, the more accurate the record will be (Nelson, Lipinski, & Boykin, 1978). Durations of events can be monitored with pocket parking-meter timers, a stopwatch function on a wrist watch, or kitchen timers.

How demanding the recording plan is may predict whether a client will follow through with the plan. Although continuous recording (noting each event throughout the period in which the event could occur) is more reliable and provides more information, it is more demanding than is intermittent recording (Frederiksen et al., 1975; Mahoney et al., 1973; Rehm et al., 1981. Continuous recording throughout the client's waking hours may be initially preferable to provide maximum information. If an event occurs frequently throughout the day, time samples (an hour or two a day) may provide adequate information. If the behavior occurs infrequently, an all-day record may not be too demanding. Monitoring can be conceptualized on continuums from a lot of information to a little information, from precise information to general estimates, and from a demanding recording and reporting schedule to a simple plan. Both degree of precision and amount of information collected depend on the client's concerns, goals, and pre-monitoring knowledge. At times, it is important to record several behaviors. However, it is wise to keep the recording plan simple by devising simplified forms and checklists for the client to use. Checking with clients by telephone several days after the monitoring plan is initiated serves as a reminder and gives clients an opportunity to ask questions and obtain help with problems during their initial efforts to self-observe.

Because social support may encourage clients to continue observing themselves, it is important to decide who will see their records. Sharing the information by displaying charts or graphs on walls at home, in a classroom, or in an office may encourage clients to continue recording. Public display of information generally elicits responses and support from significant others, which in turn encourage ongoing monitoring. Worker attention to client records and praise for recording encourages clients to self-monitor. More important, as clients experience the value and importance of their self-monitored records in the assessment phase, they tend to continue monitoring their behaviors and responses. Group meetings for clients involved in self-help efforts offer mutual support and ideas for maintenance of records as well as for change efforts. In order for the data to be used functionally, it is helpful to chart or graph the data to facilitate observation of weekly or daily patterns. The opportunity to observe oneself over time is itself rewarding, especially because most people change in the desired direction from the process of self-observation (Kopp, 1987). If the behavior changes during the initial self-monitoring phase and the client is satisfied with the rate of change, self-monitoring alone offers an inexpensive, efficient intervention procedure.

As contradictory as it may seem, self-observation often results in change of the issue being monitored while serving as a reliable source of information for assessment purposes. The following section clarifies this apparent contradiction.

Reliability and Accuracy of Self-Monitored Records

Studies of reliability have compared self-monitored frequency records with an observer's frequency record, using objective observers' records as the criterion against which to measure the consistency and the accuracy of the self-record. In general, clients provide reasonably accurate records of their progress. Accuracy may vary somewhat, depending on what is being monitored. For example, a significant, positive correlation was found between diabetics' reported visits to a diabetes center and clinic-recorded data (Turkat, 1982), whereas adults suffering from anxiety tended to overestimate their relaxation practice (Hoelscher, Lichstein, & Rosenthal, 1984). Although one might assume that clients would record desirable behaviors more accurately than they would undesirable behaviors, as Willis and Nelson (1982) point out,

> negatively valenced behaviors, especially verbal behavior, tended to be self-recorded with greater accuracy than positively valenced behaviors, especially positive verbal behavior. In terms of the assessment functions of self-monitoring, the finding of high levels of accuracy for negatively valenced responses is of particular interest since the target behavior to be assessed in clinical settings is frequently one evaluated negatively by the client (pp. 409–410).

In general, self-monitored records are likely to show lower than actual levels of occurrence for both desirable and undesirable behaviors (Willis & Nelson, 1982).

If reliability and accuracy of client records are of concern, steps can be taken to enhance both. For example, rewards for accurate and reliable records (distinct from rewards for behavior change) increased the accuracy and reliability of self-monitored data (Bolstad & Johnson, 1972; Fixsen, Phillips, & Wolf, 1972; Layne, 1976; Thomas, 1976; McLaughlin & Truhlicka, 1983). Actually, 75% of a group of young children accurately monitored themselves without rewards (Bolstad & Johnson, 1972). In addition, obtrusive reliability checks have increased reliability and accuracy (Layne, 1976; Lipinski & Nelson, 1974; Thomas, 1976). Reliability tends to be higher when persons who self-monitor believe that they are being periodically monitored by independent observers (Lipinski et al., 1975). In other words, if greater than 90% accuracy is critical, random accuracy checks by independent observers might be planned, if this is agreeable to the client. In home settings, the observer might be a family member; in work or school settings, a colleague, peer, supervisor, or teacher may serve as observer. Given the goal of empowerment, the fact that self-monitored records are more than 70% accurate without special efforts to increase reliability, and that service, not research, is the primary objective, reliability checks are not recommended.

Training persons to self-monitor their behavior the same way observers in research projects are trained can increase the accuracy of records (Bornstein et al., 1978; Fixsen et al., 1972). Thus, including opportunities for clients to practice monitoring their behavior in the practitioner's office may increase the accuracy of their records (Nelson et al., 1978). Also, maximizing the accessibility and obtrusiveness of monitoring devices can increase accuracy (Nelson et al., 1978). In addition, continuous, concurrent self-monitoring was more reliable than were frequency estimates at the end of each day or each week, although reliabilities for each of the three recording methods were high (greater than 85%) (Frederiksen et al., 1975). One study found low day-to-day reliability between self-monitors and observers, yet the median frequencies across a week were highly reliable (Broden, Hall, & Mitts, 1971). If behavior rates are variable from day to day, the median rate and the rate of change on a chart may be the important measures (Pennypacker, Koenig, & Lindsley, 1972).

In summary, if accuracy is important, it can be increased. However, data support the relative accuracy of self-monitoring. Reported levels of accuracy and reliability without special efforts are likely to be acceptable to practitioners, including those committed to practice research and evaluation. If a feeling, thought, or behavior changes in the desired direction within the first three weeks of recording, as research indicates (Kopp, 1987), self-monitoring serves as an information source as well as a helpful intervention. Most practitioners would applaud such effects. If change occurs as the client is monitoring, the client still has a more reliable record than is usually produced through retrospective accounts and benefits from opportunities outside sessions to acquire increased self-understanding.

Howe (1976) recommended a neutral stance on the part of the social work practitioner regarding the potential change effects of self-monitoring in order to decrease the possibility of clients distorting data to conform to practitioners' expectations. It is possible to be neutral about the potential change effect of self-monitoring, yet enthusiastic about the value of the record. Or self-monitoring can be introduced as an information source without suggesting to clients that it might in fact result in change. On the other hand, workers sometimes may want to discuss the potential change from self-monitoring, hoping to enhance its effect.

Conclusions

Considering the range of clients and their problems, social work practitioners have an opportunity to increase knowledge about the applicability of self-monitoring in assessment and its reliability and validity. Textbooks on practice ask questions related to presenting problems that need to be answered before an adequate assessment can be made. Usually, however, these books do not explain how to collect the needed information other than through oral interviewing skills aimed at concreteness and specificity. Concrete exploration, while important, remains an indirect source of information, whereas self-monitoring is a direct measure. Asking clients to record information about themselves increases their activity and sense of control in the assessment process while decreasing the aura of professional authority. As the client and practitioner discuss the information collected by the client, they act as collaborators in assessment and intervention planning, with the social worker often assuming a consulting role. This transfer of responsibility to the client is an important step toward empowerment. Relatively powerless clients, who are initially suspicious of the worker's commitment to help them, are not dependent on the "expert's" assessment of their situation. Instead, they become experts about themselves—the sources of the data on which the intervention plan is based.

In clinical settings, self-monitoring is valuable for understanding interactions among family members and for determining skill deficits and unproductive cognitions. New areas where it is helpful await exploration. Social workers are concerned about events that can only be observed and recorded by the client. Social workers want to provide self-help tools to clients, empower them through the assessment process, and at the same time, obtain relevant, thorough information on which to base an assessment and develop an intervention plan. These goals justify increased use of self-observation in social work practice.

REFERENCES

Bolstad, O. D., & Johnson, S. M. (1972). Self-regulation in the modification of disruptive classroom behavior. *Journal of Applied Behavior Analysis, 5,* 443–454.
Bornstein, P. H., et al. (1978). Self-monitoring training: Effects on reactivity and accuracy of self-observation. *Behavior Therapy, 9,* 545–552.
Broden, M., Hall, R. V., & Mitts, B. (1971). The effect of self-recording on the classroom behavior of two eighth grade students. *Journal of Applied Behavior Analysis, 4,* 191–199.
Ciminero, A. R., Nelson, R. O., & Lipinski, D. P. (1977). Self-monitoring procedures. In A. R. Ciminero, K. S. Calhoun, and H. E. Adams (Eds.), *Handbook of behavioral assessment* (pp. 195–232). New York: John Wiley.
Fisch, R., Weakland, J. H., & Segal, L. (1982). *The tactics of change: Doing therapy briefly.* San Francisco: Jossey-Bass.
Fixsen, D. L., Phillips, E. L., & Wolf, M. M. (1972). Achievement place: The reliability of self-reporting and peer-reporting and their effects on behavior. *Journal of Applied*

Behavior Analysis, 5, 19–30.

Frederiksen, L. W., Epstein, L. H., & Kosevsky, B. P. (1975). Reliability and controlling effects of three procedures for self-monitoring smoking. *The Psychological Record, 25,* 255–264.

Gambrill, E., & Richey, C. (1975). An assertion inventory for use in assessment and research. *Behavior Therapy, 6,* 547–549.

Gray, S. S., Hartman, A., & Saalberg, E. S. (Eds.). (1985). *Empowering the black family: A roundtable discussion with Ann Hartman, James Leigh, Jacquelynn Moffett, Elaine Pinder-hughes, Barbara Solomon and Carol Stack.* Ann Arbor, MI: National Child Welfare Training Center, School of Social Work, University of Michigan.

Green, J. K., & Morrow, W. (1972). Precision social work: General model and illustrative student projects with clients. *Journal of Education for Social Work, 8,* 19–29.

Hepworth, D. H., & Larsen, J. A. (1986). *Direct social work practice: Theory and skills* (2nd ed.). Chicago, IL: Dorsey Press.

Hiebert, B., & Fox, E. E. (1981). Reactive effects of self-monitoring anxiety. *Journal of Counseling Psychology, 28,* 187–193.

Hirayama, H., & Cetingok, M. (1988). Empowerment: A social work approach for Asian immigrants. *Social Casework, 69,* 41–47.

Howe, M. (1976). Using clients' observations in research. *Social Work, 21,* 28–31.

Hoelscher, T. J., Lichstein, K. L., & Rosenthal, T. L. (1984). Objective versus subjective assessment of relaxation compliance among anxious individuals. *Behavior Research and Therapy, 22,* 187–193.

Kopp, J. (1972). Unpublished case material from a Midwestern child evaluation clinic and from a public child welfare agency. Seattle, WA: University of Washington.

Kopp, J. (1987). *Self-monitoring: An evaluation of reactivity, reliability, and validity.* Seattle, WA: University of Washington.

Layne, C. C. (1976). Accuracy of self-monitoring on a variable ratio schedule of observer verification. *Behavior Therapy, 7,* 481–489.

Leigh, J. (1987, June). *Ethnographic interviewing.* Workshop presented at the National Association of Social Workers Conference on Minority Issues, Washington, DC.

Lindsley, O. R. (1968). A reliable wrist counter for recording behavior rates. *Journal of Applied Behavior Analysis, 1,* 77–78.

Lipinski, D. P., & Nelson, R. O. (1974). The reactivity and unreliability of self-recording. *Journal of Consulting and Clinical Psychology, 42,* 118–123.

Lipinski, D. P., et al. (1975). Influence of motivational variables on the reactivity and reliability of self-recording. *Journal of Consulting and Clinical Psychology, 43,* 637–646.

Mahoney, K. (1974). Count on it: A simple self-monitoring device. *Behavior Therapy, 5,* 701–703.

Mahoney, M. J., et al. (1973). Effects of continuous and intermittent self-monitoring on academic behavior. *Journal of Consulting and Clinical Psychology, 41,* 65–69.

McLaughlin, T. F., & Truhlicka, M. (1983). Effects on academic performance of self-recording and self-recording and matching with behaviorally disordered students: A replication. *Behavioral Engineering, 42,* 69–74.

Nelson, R. O. (1977). Assessment and therapeutic functions of self-monitoring. In M. Hersen, R. M. Eisler, & P. Miller (Eds.), *Progress in behavior modification* (pp. 264–309). New York: Academic Press.

Nelson, R. O., Lipinski, D. P., & Boykin, R. A. (1978). The effects of self-recorders' training and the obtrusiveness of the self-recording device on the accuracy and reactivity of self-monitoring. *Behavior Therapy, 9,* 200–208.

Pennypacker, H. S., Koenig, C. H., & Lindsley, O. R. (1972). *Handbook of the standard behavior chart.* Kansas City, KS: Precision Media.

Rehm, L. P., et al. (1981). An evaluation of major components of a self-control therapy program for depression. *Behavior Modification, 5,* 459–489.

Thorensen, C. E., & Mahoney, M. J. (1974). *Behavioral self-control.* New York: Holt, Rinehart, and Winston.

Solomon, B. B. (1976). *Black empowerment: Social work in oppressed communities.* New York: Columbia University Press.

Thomas, J. D. (1976). Accuracy of self-assessment of on-task behavior by elementary school children. *Journal of Applied Behavior Analysis, 9,* 209–210.

Turkat, I. D. (1982) Diabetics' self report of medical utilization: A test of validity. *Psychological Reports, 50,* 1160–1162.

Wells, R. A. (1982). *Planned short-term treatment.* New York: Free Press.

Willis, S. E., & Nelson, R. O. (1982). The effects of valence and nature of target behavior on the accuracy and reactivity of self-monitoring. *Behavioral Assessment, 4,* 401–412.

Self-Perception in Family Systems: A Diagrammatic Technique

Ronald R. Van Treuren

20

A mong the advances in the practice of family therapy, diagrammatic assessment has played an important role. Such graphic representations as the genogram, eco-map, and Minuchin's family mapping techniques assist workers in their struggle to understand family dynamics. Despite such representations, the adaptation of diagramming techniques to understand how the family perceives itself has been largely overlooked. This chapter proposes a paradigm of diagrammatic assessment that can be used easily and creatively to learn how a family has organized itself to deal with a presenting problem. The proposal is rooted in the existing literature on family diagrams. It differs, however, because it attempts to elicit the family's own perception of their internal functioning.

The genogram as a method of family assessment has been described by Guerin and Pendagast (1976) and by Hartman (1978). This tool was born out of a multigenerational approach and has the distinct advantage of identifying intrafamilial patterns over time. A cross-generational analysis can yield essential data about the extended family network that may not be obtained in a conventional intake interview. Another advantage is that the family members are actively involved in the process of creating the genogram. When it is completed, each member can see that he or she is part of a collective whole. This facilitates the worker's task of relating the symptom to family dynamics. The genogram, however, does not give a clear picture of internal functioning and organization within the nuclear family. Questions pertaining to the quality of relationships, hierarchical structures, and subgroup boundaries all remain unanswered.

Hartman (1978) has also presented the eco-map as another technique to demonstrate to the worker and the family that many social influences affect the functioning of family members. Grounded in eco-systemic epistemology, the eco-map places the family system in the context of the larger social matrix. The relationships of such societal structures as schools, religious institutions, and welfare agencies to the family are evaluated as strong, tenuous, or stressful. Although the eco-map is syntonic with systems theory, in general, its main limitation is that the relational structures analyzed exist largely outside the nuclear family unit. Again, the family's internal functioning has not been addressed.

Minuchin's (1974) diagrams of family structure delineate most clearly the dynamics that contribute to family functioning and symptom organization. Minuchin presented a paradigm for mapping the intricacies that make each family unique. He used cleverly designed symbols to represent boundaries (clear, diffuse, rigid), affiliations, overinvolvements, conflicts, coalitions, and detouring among family members. Such mapping is a valuable tool in helping the worker formulate his or her perception of what is operating within the system. All future hypothesizing, planning, and intervening must be congruent with the worker's understanding of family dynamics. Although Minuchin has devised an adequate method of mapping family structure, clearly the map is only a representation of the actual territory. At best, the worker's perceptions are still the observations of a spectator. The worker's perception of reality belongs to that class of second-order realities that Watzlawick (1976) has so aptly described. Concurrently, family members perceive family reality from a unique perspective, forming a class of meta-realities of their own.

The contention of this chapter is that an assessment instrument is needed to account fully for each family member's perception of reality regarding family organization around the presenting symptom. Three qualities are essential to such an instrument.

Simplicity. An assessment instrument for use with families must be as easy to explain as it is to understand. Considering the potentially wide range of ages within families, it must be adaptable for use both with small children and adults. A simple tool should not be overly time consuming. Ideally, the worker should be able to administer the instrument in one session.

Applicability. The data obtained from such an instrument must directly apply to the problem at hand. The family should be able to correlate the presenting symptomatology to the total functioning of the family system. The instrument itself should be flexible enough to be adaptable to the variety of family types in today's society.

Creativity. Creative endeavors are most likely to hold the attention of the participants. This is particularly important in work with children, because they can be easily distracted during discussions of the problem within the family session. One basic assumption here is that all people have a creative potential, whether latent or manifest. Another such assumption is that successful therapy allows each participant to tap his or her own creativity to find effective alternative solutions to the problems being faced.

A Paradigm

A paradigm to meet the requirements of simplicity, applicability, and creativity is suggested. This model combines essential features from the genogram, eco-map, and Minuchin's (1974) family diagrams to create an instrument that can be utilized by each family member to portray his or her own perception of family functioning.

Step 1

Each family member is asked to work individually and to represent symbolically his or her observations of how the family has organized itself to deal with the presenting problem. Family members place themselves on a sheet of paper relative to one another. Circles may be used to depict females and squares to depict males; however, members are encouraged to choose any other object or shape that fits their understanding of the person to be represented. Utilization of all the space is stressed to show relative closeness and distance between members.

Once this task has been completed, family members are instructed to draw connecting lines to indicate their perceptions about the quality of the relationships. The basic symbols used are adopted from the eco-map. A solid line is used to indicate a strong connection, "railroad tracks" show stress or tension, and a broken line represents a tenuous midway state (see Figure 1).

Step 2

Once the drawings are completed, family members present them in the family session. Instructions are given beforehand to examine each drawing carefully for similarities and differences. Members are told not to ask questions until the presenter has finished. The therapist offers no interpretation or comment so family members can form their own impressions. This provides members with immediate feedback regarding how they have organized themselves to deal with the presenting problem. Using this feedback, the worker is then able to formulate a hypothesis, the testing of which can provide the foundation for future therapeutic work.

Variations

Variations have occurred during use of this instrument with families. Because the emphasis of this technique is on creativity, family members are given the freedom to adapt this tool to meet their need for expression. Some families have used symbols creatively in representing them-selves. For example, in one family, a 15-year-old boy used a baseball hat to represent himself, a bow and arrow to represent his brother, and an attaché case to represent his father. All the items chosen had particular meaning for him. In another family, the father drew a door next to him-self to signify his movement in and out of the family. In still another fam-ily, a seven-year-old boy was caught between his parents, who had separat-ed and were in the middle of a hostile divorce. He was living with his mother and clearly seemed trapped in a double bind: To visit his father meant he must face his mother's feelings of rejection for having taken his father's side. If he did not visit his father, then his father would feel rejected. The boy was the only member of the family to put his father in a diagram of the family, drawing him as a giant clam. In the discussion afterward, he explained that he felt closed off from his father. The metaphoric expression of a clam seemed to move beyond the family's left-hemispheric analysis of his position to a right-hemispheric under-standing of his dilemma.

Colored crayons can be used in making the diagrams. Each family member selects the colors that accurately portray his or her perceptions of the family. Colors may reflect moods or feeling tone or correspond to various traits of members.

Some families chose to delineate structures or boundaries, such as walls, doors, and windows that separate individuals or subgroups within the system. One particular family, in describing a wall between the par-ents, took great care to label the construction material (wood, brick, or stone), which had a particular meaning.

Families can tap into the creative energy they possess with a little encouragement. When this is accomplished, the diagrams are rich in metaphoric content. The literature in family therapy has expanded our understanding of the use of metaphor in treatment. A generation of therapists, such as Haley (1973, 1976); Madanes (1976); Minuchin and Fishman (1981); and Watzlawick, Weakland, and Fisch (1974), have stud-ied the therapeutic utilization of metaphor with families. All seem to agree that the most useful metaphors come from the family itself.

An Example

The following illustration is taken from the author's clinical practice. This particular family was chosen because its diagrams were simple and could be reproduced accurately. The use of color, although interesting, will not be discussed here because of printing limitations. The diagram-ming took place during the second session, with all family members pre-sent. As the emphasis is on the use of this tool in the assessment phase, the discussion will be confined to the generation and testing of a hypoth-esis, not the implementation of a treatment plan.

Session One

During the first session with the D family, a brief history was taken. The Ds are a middle-class Irish American family. Mr. D, a blue-collar worker, put in long hours to help meet the financial needs of the family. Mrs. D worked part-time as a playground monitor at the children's elementary school but spent the bulk of her time raising the children and managing the household. She mentioned that she had seen a psychiatrist approximately three times for treatment of depression several years ago. The identified patient was their oldest daughter, 12-year-old J, who was experiencing problems in school with peers and declining grades. The school child-study team felt that J had a "poor self-image." In addition, five months earlier, the family had learned that J had scoliosis. The process of diagnosis and treatment of this disorder involved a series of visits to specialists and the prescription of a back brace. This brace not only restricted J's movement, but was also unsightly, as she had to wear loose-fitting clothing rather than designer jeans. Her 10-year-old sister, K, was bright, attractive, and did well in school. R, a seven-year-old boy, seemed verbal and engaging. No problems were reported for either K or R.

It was clear that Mr. and Mrs. D felt that the school blamed J's apparent difficulties on their being bad parents. Mrs. D, in particular, felt that the referral for family therapy somehow implied that they were the problem. Although the mother and father appeared united, differences arose in how they wanted to handle the school. Mr. D had become peripheral to the child-study team evaluation process, immersing himself in his work. Mrs. D, on the other hand, became overinvolved by going to meetings, talking with team members and teachers privately, and even taking the job as playground monitor at the school, where she had ready access to her daughter and school personnel.

Session Two

By session two, hypotheses about the D family were already being generated. Diagramming was used with this family to test them. The diagrams done in this session are reproduced in Figure 1. All members chose similar facial representations to depict family members, with the exception of Mrs. D, who chose the conventional circles for females and squares for males. Spatial orientation and relationship lines are drawn to scale.

After the family completed the diagrams, a discussion of similarities and differences was initiated. The most striking observation was the degree of intensity with which Mrs. D and J perceived stress within the family, in contrast with Mr. D's diagram in which tension was perceived as at a minimum. From this, it could be hypothesized that Mrs. D and J, through possible enmeshed status, shared similar perceptions of the family. The peripheral father seemed to take a metaposition to this overinvolved dyad.

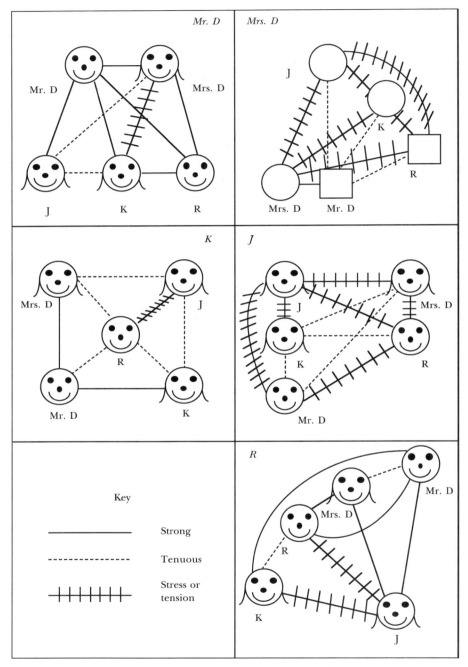

Figure 1. Diagrams drawn by the D family during the second session.

All the family members perceived a strong connection between Mr. and Mrs. D except J and R. It seemed reasonable that J sensed marital conflict, as she was the identified patient. It was possible that R might become the next symptom bearer once the present cycle was broken.

J's diagram also showed her mother and father on opposite ends of her family structure. This would seem to support the notion that she perceived her father as a peripheral figure, existing largely outside the subsystem of mother and children.

The initial hypothesis was that J's scoliosis and subsequent problems in school served a protective function in the family. As Madanes (1976) has pointed out, a child's problematic behavior can provide parents a focus for their concern and respite from their own troubles and difficulties. Perhaps they avoided marital conflicts by detouring their energies through J. The plan to test this hypothesis was to move the peripheral father into a more active role with the school and J's doctors in an effort to deintensify J's relationship with her mother and to increase marital interaction.

The clinical approach taken was that of structural family therapy. Within three months of initial contact with the family, the therapy was progressing as planned. Mr. D had become more involved with his wife in dealing with the child-study team. He had even taken time off from work to accompany his daughter to visit the doctor. J's grades improved as she began doing her own homework without her mother's help. J continued wearing her back brace diligently, and with the favorable reports on her progress, she was able to reduce her time in the brace to 17 hours a day. This allowed her enough time to leave the brace home during school hours.

As the parents began to function more as a team, marital tension seemed to increase. Mr. and Mrs. D planned to begin marital therapy together. At this point, something unexpected happened. While Mr. D was away on a weekend hunting trip, K experienced what was later diagnosed as a grand mal seizure. The seizure occurred one-half hour after her father left the house. She was taken to the hospital for treatment, which marked the beginning of another series of visits to specialists for the family. She was ultimately diagnosed as having a hysterical neurosis, conversion type, after an independent complete psychiatric workup.[1]

1. A grand mal seizure will generally rule out a diagnosis of conversion disorder, because, although a seizure can be precipitated by an environmental stressor, its etiology may still be organic. The diagnosis of hysterical neurosis here reflected the findings of a team of independent medical specialists. Nearly one year later, another specialist found some organic basis for K's rare grand mal seizures. Most of K's subsequent seizures were petit mal and persisted in spite of chemotherapy. A finding of organicity, however, does not preclude our understanding of the dynamics of this family, which had previously been organized around J's scoliosis.

Two years after termination, the Ds came in for one consultation around J's relationship with a particularly troublesome peer. They reported that K was no longer experiencing seizures. They were dealing with J's problem together, rather than letting it become an occasion to split them apart.

Retrospective

With the onset of K's seizures, the initial hypothesis was reexamined. Having access to the family's early diagrams helped here by providing early data that might offer additional clues. The development of K's problem could be seen as a classic move to reestablish the equilibrium within the family system. As the parents began functioning together, J was able to disengage from her intense relationship with her mother. As a result, marital tensions became more evident, but then K's seizures launched the family into a strikingly similar pattern of visits to doctors for special treatment.

A retrospective analysis of the initial diagrams from the family was then performed. The initial focus was on K's drawing. The most obvious feature was that K had no perceived connection with her mother except through R. This was corroborated by R's diagram, which exhibited a similar interactional pattern. K's diagram showed that J experienced a similar indirect connection with her father. This supported the notion that Mr. D was a peripheral figure for J. In contrast, the relationship K had with her father was the only strong connection she experienced in the family.

It could be hypothesized that when Mr. D shifted to a more active role within the parental unit, major systemic changes occurred. For this to happen, the mother had to disengage somewhat from J, and the father had to disengage somewhat from K. When marital tensions increased, the mother's and K's intense connection with each other was a natural phenomenon to reestablish order. In this way, the system appeared to correct itself.

Guidelines for General Use

This form of diagrammatic assessment has been used with a variety of family types from intact nuclear to single parent to reconstituted families. It has been equally effective in all situations. The clearest indication for use would be with families in which the representational system is primarily visual. Such families are more apt to see things clearly when they are graphically portrayed. Family diagramming is not necessarily contraindicated for persons whose dominant representational system is auditory or kinesthetic. Switching sensory modalities can be an effective lever for change. Extra care must be taken in the presentation with such family members to facilitate its acceptance. For a complete description of visual, auditory, and kinesthetic modalities in client work, the reader is referred to Bandler and Grinder (1975, 1979) and Grinder and Bandler (1976).

As with any therapeutic intervention, the framing is essential for its introduction into the family session. Two particular guidelines may be useful. First, a minimum of direction will ensure maximum creative expression. When questions arise regarding particular details on how to complete the drawing, simply encouraging the family member to search for his or her own answers is usually sufficient. Second, if the therapist wishes to stimulate the right brain and encourage metaphoric thinking, the task of diagramming can be introduced with a metaphor. One example is that each diagram will be like a set of fingerprints: No two will be alike and each will be highly characteristic of the individual member. This metaphor has been particularly effective with children who are fascinated by the uniqueness of their own fingerprints. This fascination can then be transferred to making their diagram. The worker can also use this task to establish rapport with small children, as they can draw together while the rest of the family members complete their own diagrams.

In keeping with the general thesis of this chapter, the practitioner is encouraged to tap into his or her own creative energies and adapt this instrument to fit the needs of families seeking help.

REFERENCES

Bandler, R., & Grinder, J. (1975). *The structure of magic.* Palo Alto, CA: Science and Behavior Books.

Bandler, R., & Grinder, J. (1979). *Frogs into princes.* Moab, UT: Real People Press.

Grinder, G., & Bandler, R. (1976). *The structure of magic II.* Palo Alto, CA: Science and Behavior Books.

Guerin, P. J., & Pendagast, E. G. (1976). Evaluation of family system and genogram. In P. J. Guerin (Ed.), *Family therapy: Theory and practice.* New York: Gardner Press.

Haley, J. (1976). *Problem solving therapy.* San Francisco: Jossey-Bass.

Haley, J. (1973). *Uncommon therapy: The psychiatric techniques of Milton H. Erickson M.D.* New York: W. W. Norton.

Hartman, A. (1978). Diagrammatic assessment of family relationships. *Social Casework, 59,* 465–476.

Madanes, C. (1976). *Strategic family therapy.* San Francisco: Jossey-Bass.

Minuchin, S. (1974). *Families and family therapy.* Cambridge, MA: Harvard University Press.

Watzlawick, P. (1976). *How real is real?* New York: Random House.

Watzlawick, P., Weakland, J., & Fisch, R. (1974). *Change: Principles of problem formulation and problem resolution.* New York: W. W. Norton.

Genetic Family Histories: An Aid to Social Work Assessment

21

*Barbara Bernhardt
and Julia B. Rauch*

S eventy-six years ago, Mary Richmond (1917) recommended that social workers obtain genetic family histories:

> In cases, for instance, where the social worker has reason to suspect the presence of mental disease, he must aim to get at facts of heredity which would assist a physician in forming an opinion of the patient's condition. The pertinent data would cover the condition of health and cause of death of parents, grandparents, brothers and sisters, uncles and aunts. The items should be especially clear and detailed whenever, in any of these relatives, there seems to be a question of consanguineous marriage, miscarriage, tuberculosis, alcoholism, mental disorder, nervousness, epilepsy, cancer, deformities or abnormalities, or of any exceptional ability (p. 187).

Richmond's advice is still pertinent. Advances in the science of human genetics make genetic family histories (GFH) more necessary and relevant than before. New diagnostic techniques and therapies are also available because of the rapidly expanding capabilities of genetic technology. Increasingly, social workers will need to obtain GFHs and use the information in assessment and intervention (Rauch, 1988).

The purpose of this chapter is to inform social workers about GFHs. It reviews the rationale for obtaining histories, describes types of genetic disorders and genetic services, presents referral criteria, and discusses approaches to GFHs.

Why Obtain Genetic Family Histories?

Health Promotion/Disease Prevention

Genetic factors underlie all aspects of health and disease. The information contained in GFHs contributes to disease prevention and health promotion. For example, many common diseases of adulthood, such as coronary artery disease, diabetes, and cancer are known to have a genetic basis. Knowing this, relatives of affected people can improve their chances of staying healthy by avoiding risk factors such as high-fat diets or smoking. Physicians can screen and monitor family members for symptoms of disease and promptly begin treatment if such signs appear. Because allergies and responsiveness to certain medications tend to run in families, a GFH can also help physicians select safe, effective medications.

Clients whose ability to function is impaired may need assistance with health maintenance. In such cases, practitioners can use GFHs to determine whether clients are at risk for familial health problems. The practitioner can then obtain information about the problem, educate the client about the risk, encourage wellness behaviors, help monitor clients for symptoms of the disorder, and facilitate access to and utilization of health services.

Genetic Disorders Are Common

Frequency. In the aggregate, genetic disorders constitute a major health problem. Three to four percent of newborns have birth defects; 80% of these have a major genetic cause. Approximately 40% of infant mortality and 30% of pediatric-hospital admissions can be attributed to genetic diseases (Robinson, 1988). Many diseases of adulthood, for example, diabetes, cardiovascular disorders, Alzheimer's disease, and some cancers, have genetic determinants (Pyeritz, 1989). Evidence suggests that schizophrenia and mood disorders are inherited, biological disorders (McGuffin & Murray, 1991). Thus, millions of Americans are affected, or are likely to be affected, by genetic disorders.

Genes and chromosomes. Genes, which control the body's appearance and functioning, are extremely small components of every cell in the human body. Genes normally come in pairs, and groups of genes are packed together and stored in larger structures called chromosomes. Genes and chromosomes alone and together transmit traits from one generation to the next.

Humans normally have 23 pairs of chromosomes, for a total of 46, in every body cell. The exceptions to this rule are sperm and ova, which have 23 chromosomes each, or one of each chromosomal pair. Each person's life begins when a sperm penetrates an ova, creating a single cell with a full complement of genes and chromosomes.

Types of genetic disorders and birth defects. There are four types of genetic disorders and birth defects: (1) single gene, (2) chromosomal, (3) multifactorial, and (4) environmentally induced.

Single-gene disorders occur when the genetic blueprint is changed by an abnormality in a single or in a matched pair of genes. The disorders are transmitted from parents to children in different patterns. Autosomal dominant disorders are passed from an affected parent to an affected child (e.g., neurofibromatosis). Autosomal recessive disorders are passed from both unaffected parents to an affected child (e.g., cystic fibrosis). In the third pattern, X-linked recessive, the disorder is passed from an unaffected or mildly affected mother to an affected son (e.g., hemophilia).

Chromosomal disorders occur as a result of a change in the number or structure of chromosomes. For example, Down syndrome, a common cause of mental retardation, is caused by an extra chromosome number 21. Many chromosomal disorders are incompatible with fetal development and are an important cause of miscarriage, stillbirth, and infertility.

Multifactorial disorders are caused by the interaction of multiple genes with environmental factors. Spina bifida, cleft lip and palate, and club-foot are examples of birth defects with multifactorial causation. Schizophrenia and mood disorders may also be multifactorial conditions. Some of the so-called life-style disorders, such as cardiovascular disease, alcoholism, and lung cancer, are also multifactorial, in that a genetic predisposition interacts with environmental factors to produce manifestations of the disease.

Environmental agents may interfere with normal developmental processes without directly damaging genes or chromosomes. Prenatal exposure to alcohol, for example, may lead to fetal alcohol syndrome, an increasingly important cause of mental retardation in the United States.

Our understanding of gene–environment interactions is expanding the knowledge of disease processes. Conditions once thought to be primarily environmental in origin are now known or suspected to have a genetic component. For example, evidence suggests a genetic component to alcoholism in some families (Anthelli & Schucket, 1990; Russell, Henderson, & Blume, 1985). Also, bacterial and viral diseases may be caused by the interaction of bacteria and viruses with genetic resistances and vulnerabilities (Childs, Moxon, & Winkelstein, 1990).

Clients Have Genetic Concerns

The number of social work clients with genetic concerns is increasing. Media attention stimulates public awareness of genetics. People who have relatives with a serious health problem may wonder if the problem is genetically related and, if it is, what its ramifications may be for themselves and their children. Anxiety may be exacerbated by misinformation and misconceptions. Genetic concepts are complex and difficult to understand. For example, people may confuse carrying a gene for a particular disorder with having the disorder. If the information is not understood, client confusion may have serious consequences, even if the person has had genetic counseling (Black, 1981).

Deinstitutionalization is another factor that increases the number of clients with genetic concerns. Individuals who are returned to the community with handicapping conditions and their families may have questions about inheritance and reproductive risks, especially if the handicapped person is sexually active and fertile. In addition, improved diagnosis and treatment are increasing the life expectancy of children with genetic conditions such as hemophilia, cystic fibrosis, sickle-cell disease, and other inherited diseases. Survivors of such diseases now deal with questions regarding having children of their own, knowing that the condition may limit their ability to parent and that the illness may be passed on to their offspring.

Members of families in which a genetic disorder is known are likely to have many concerns. In general, genetic disorders are "permanent, chronic, familial, complex, labeling and threatening" (Schild, 1977, pp. 34–35). A known or possible genetic disorder touches intimate, private aspects of an individual and family's life: sexuality, decisions to conceive, or decisions to terminate pregnancy for genetic reasons. A parent who has transmitted genes for a genetic disorder to his or her child may feel tremendous guilt. Parents may blame each other, and the affected child may be angry at his or her parents for transmitting the disorder (Weiss, 1976; Weiss, 1981). Feelings are likely to be particularly intense when a child has a birth defect due to maternal behavior, such as alcohol abuse during pregnancy (Anderson & Grant, 1984; Wright, 1981).

Because genetic disorders are stigmatizing, family members may feel defective and ashamed of their "bad" genes. They may also keep family secrets such as incest, adultery, or suicide. Because clients may initially hide genetic concerns, practitioners must be tactful and sensitive when taking a GFH.

Asking about GFHs indicates to clients that a worker is aware of genetic issues, and the history-taking process may stimulate disclosure of clients' concerns. If it does not do so, the history and the client's behavior while giving the history can alert the worker to the possibility of disguised genetic anxieties.

Assessment and Service Planning

Practitioners have always used family and developmental histories in psychosocial assessment. Adding GFHs to this process is helpful, even essential, in assessing some problems, for example, sadness and depression (Rauch, Sarno, & Simpson, 1991). A history of affective disorders in the family of a depressed person strongly suggests an inherited, biological condition that may respond to medication. In some instances, an affective disorder may be masked by alcohol or drug abuse, both of which can be forms of self-medication for depressed people. A relationship also appears to exist between depression and anorexia nervosa (Pope & Hudson, 1989). When the presenting problem is depressed feelings, alcohol or drug abuse, or an eating disorder, social workers should obtain a GFH and, if it is appropriate to do so, refer the individual to a biologically oriented psychiatrist for evaluation and possible antidepressant therapy.

The GFH is vital in assessment of schizophrenia. For example, lacking family-history information, Huntington disease, an autosomal dominant disorder, may be labeled as schizophrenia and the movement symptoms as tardive dyskinesia, a side effect of medication. Wilson disease, an autosomal recessive disorder of copper metabolism, may also be misdiagnosed as schizophrenia; however, it is readily treated if recognized early. A history showing the presence of a single-gene disorder or an inheritance pattern that is compatible with single-gene inheritance may facilitate timely, accurate diagnosis and treatment of conditions that masquerade as schizophrenia.

Family histories also contribute to assessment of psychosocial dysfunction in children. Many learning disabilities, such as dyslexia or attention-deficit disorder, are known to run in families (Ludlow & Cooper, 1983). The family history can contribute to early, accurate diagnosis and intervention, averting the devastating emotional and behavioral effects of school failure.

Genetic family histories are essential in evaluating children with attention-deficit hyperactivity disorder (ADHD). In some children, ADHD is an early symptom of manic depression (Biederman, Faraone, Keenan, & Tsuang, 1991). If a practitioner knows that a relative of a child with ADHD has manic depression or another affective disorder, she or he can refer the child for psychiatric evaluation and a possible trial of lithium. If the lithium is effective, the child and family may be spared years of misdiagnosis, ineffective treatment, and unnecessary suffering.

Diagnosis of developmental disabilities and handicapping conditions in children also depend on GFHs. The same symptom or condition can have different causes, both genetic and environmental. For example, mental retardation may be caused by many different single-gene and chromosomal disorders, maternal alcohol abuse during pregnancy, birth trauma, high fever, and so forth. The etiology of learning disabilities, developmental disabilities, and handicapping conditions has ramifications for prognosis, treatment, and reproductive risks for the parents, the affected individual, and other relatives. Identification of specific areas of dysfunction may be sufficient for education and physical, speech, and other therapies for the child but do not necessarily indicate the etiology of the condition and the chances for recurrence in other family members.

Unfortunately, practitioners cannot rely consistently on other professionals to obtain GFHs. Depending upon when and where they were trained, many professionals, including physicians, are unaware of or not up to date on genetic factors in handicapping conditions. Even though GFHs are increasingly recognized as essential to good medical care, many physicians do not obtain them. Thus, practitioners may need to obtain the GFH, bring important family data to the attention of other professionals involved with the client, and advocate for a genetic-service referral.

Genetic Family Histories in Adoptions

Genetic family histories are vital in the adoption process (Burns, 1984). They can help potentially adoptive parents to make informed decisions, anticipate a child's special needs, negotiate adoption subsidies, arrange for postadoption services, and contribute to improved health care for the adopted individual. In addition, many adult adoptees seek access to closed records in order to learn about inherited conditions in their biological families (Sachdev, 1989).

State adoption laws are likely to change to require inclusion of genetic histories in adoptees' records (President's Commission for the Study of Ethical Problems, 1983). In some states, adoption regulations require GFHs (Plumridge, Burns, & Fisher, 1990). In 1989, the Institute of Medicine, National Academy of Science, convened an interdisciplinary panel that identified issues of health and genetic information in adoptions (Health and Medical Information in Adoption, 1989). Three national organizations (Alliance of Genetic Support Groups, Council of Regional Networks in Genetic Services, and American Society of Human Genetics) endorsed a policy statement in 1990 declaring that every person should have the right to gain access to his or her medical record, including genetic data (American Society of Human Genetics Social Issues Committee, 1991). These and other events suggest that adoption agencies and professionals will increasingly be expected to provide a sound genetic family history; obtain a genetic evaluation of the child, if it is indicated; and provide full information to the adopting parents, informing them that genetic counseling is available. Failure to provide such information could provide grounds for wrongful-adoption suits. Similar expectations are likely to hold for children in long-term out-of-home care; for example, if an agency fails to arrange for carrier testing and genetic counseling for an adolescent in foster care who has a family history of a single-gene disorder, the agency may be guilty of malpractice.

Genetic Services

The 1976 National Genetic Diseases Act authorized federal support of a national genetic-diseases testing, counseling, and education program, mandating that such services be made available to all individuals on a voluntary basis (National Genetic Diseases Act, 1976). Public, voluntary, and proprietary genetic services are available in every state. Networks of genetic service providers coordinate services, research, and education within each region of the United States. Genetic services have developed so rapidly that many people are unaware of their existence and their capabilities.

Genetic services available nationally include screening, diagnosis, treatment, and counseling. Four types of genetic screening are available. *Neonatal screening*, which is now routine in most hospitals, identifies the possible presence of a serious, and often treatable, genetic disease shortly after birth, even if the baby has no symptoms. *Carrier screening* detects the presence of genes that might be harmful to potential offspring. *Presymptomatic screening* ascertains whether a person has inherited the gene for a late-onset condition, such as Huntington disease. *Prenatal screening*, now a routine part of obstetric care, detects the possible presence of a genetic disorder in a fetus.

Prenatal diagnosis involves testing to ascertain whether a fetus has certain specific conditions, such as spina bifida or Down syndrome.

Diagnostic evaluation involves review of medical and family-history information and performing a physical examination and appropriate laboratory tests to diagnose a suspected genetic disorder. These evaluations are provided by physicians trained as clinical geneticists who may treat individuals with genetic disorders, although people with more common inherited disorders, such as cystic fibrosis and sickle-cell diseases, are often followed by physicians who specialize in those conditions. Anticipated breakthroughs in gene therapy and genetic engineering offer hope that eventually it will be possible to prevent, provide improved treatment, and/or cure genetic disorders, most of which are currently incurable.

Genetic counseling is a core modality that is usually provided with other genetic services as well as independently. Genetic counselors provide clients with information about the disorder—the way in which heredity contributes to its causation, risks of recurrence, and reproductive or treatment options. These professionals also support clients in choosing an appropriate course of action.

Persons with relatives who have a genetic disorder may seek genetic counseling for various reasons: learning about the possibility of being affected by a familial disorder and the probability of offspring being affected; deciding whether to have biological children, to obtain prenatal diagnosis once conception has occurred, or to terminate a pregnancy for genetic reasons; and deciding whether to obtain carrier or presymptomatic screening. Genetic counseling is also recommended for adoptive parents who have questions about the implications of their child's medical or family history, including evidence of maternal drug and alcohol abuse during pregnancy.

Specialized counseling for psychiatric disorders is available in some clinical genetic centers and psychiatric facilities (Targum & Schulz, 1982; Stancer & Wegener, 1984). Except for some known single-gene disorders, such as Huntington and Alzheimer diseases, the etiology of most psychiatric disorders remains uncertain. Psychiatric genetic counselors provide empirical risk estimates that are derived from large epidemiological studies. In addition, the counselor reviews the family history to discern whether a pattern suggests a particular mode of inheritance. Empirical risks, the client's history, the closeness of the biological tie between the clients and affected family member(s), the severity of the condition, and the client's age are assessed jointly to develop an individualized risk estimate (Kay, 1980).

Criteria for Referral to Genetic Services

Referrals for genetic services can be initiated by health care professionals, teachers, social workers, or the individual. Social workers who are not sure whether a referral is warranted can obtain telephone consultation by calling a local genetic service provider. Most major university hospitals provide genetic services. Information about the location of genetic services can be obtained from state departments of health, local chapters of the March of Dimes Birth Defects Foundation, and the National Center for Education in Maternal and Child Health (703-824-8955).

Individuals and families should be informed of the availability of genetic services if they express genetic concerns. On the whole, social workers should avoid giving an opinion about the disorder of concern, its treatment, recurrence risks, and so forth, unless they have had genetics training and keep up to date with the field. Incorrect or incomplete information may have serious consequences for clients, such as unnecessarily avoiding having children or failure to obtain indicated medical treatment or testing.

Criteria for social work referral for genetic services for individuals who are pregnant or who are contemplating a pregnancy include the following:
- A genetic disorder or birth defect in one partner
- Previous child with or a positive family history of a known or suspected genetic disorder
- Maternal age 35 years or older
- Maternal exposure to drugs, alcohol, infections, or chemical or radiological agents known to cause or suspected of causing birth defects
- Multiple miscarriages or stillbirths
- Membership in an ethnic group with incidence of specific genetic disorders higher than that of the general population

Criteria for referral for genetic evaluation of infants, children, and adolescents include the following:
- Developmental delay or mental retardation
- Major physical anomalies, such as cleft lip or palate, clubfoot, severe curvature of the spine, extra or missing fingers, short stature, or unusual body proportions
- Major organ malformation, such as congenital heart defect or missing kidney
- Complete or partial blindness or hearing loss
- Abnormal sexual development, including precocious or markedly delayed puberty

- Loss or deterioration of motor, speech, or other capacities in a child with no previous indications of such problems
- Evidence of maternal drug or alcohol abuse during pregnancy; of infection with a sexually transmitted virus; or of exposure to other viral, chemical, or radiological agents known to cause or suspected of causing birth defects
- Known hereditary disorder in the family

Health insurance coverage can be a major problem in referring clients for genetic services. Depending on the state, carrier or neonatal screening may be provided through the state health department at minimal or no cost. Medicaid usually pays for prenatal diagnosis and genetic evaluation of children. Services covered by other third-party insurers vary greatly, but for the most part, prenatal diagnosis and diagnostic evaluations are covered. Carrier and presymptomatic screening may not be covered. Genetic counselors are able to advise clients about services that are covered within a specific state and how to advocate for coverage.

Content of the Genetic Family History

Optimally, GFHs cover three generations, that is, the health and medical history of the client's living and deceased biological relatives, including full and half siblings, parents, aunts, uncles, cousins, and grandparents. To begin, the country of origin (ethnicity) of each grandparent or the grandparents' families should be documented. Other important content includes:
- Whether the client's parents are blood relatives and, if they are, the nature of their relationship
- The cause and age of death of all deceased relatives
- Any health problems or pertinent medical information of all relatives
- Any unusual health problems, birth defects, genetic disorders, psychiatric disorders, or mental retardation in more distant relatives, including the gender and relationship of the affected persons

Approaches to Obtaining Genetic Family Histories

Asking about GFHs requires tact and sensitivity on the part of practitioners. The practitioner should explain to the client that such information is routinely obtained, the reason it is important, and how it will be used. The worker should also (1) note the confidentiality of the information and state whether and to whom it will be divulged, for example, adoptive parents, and (2) state the client's right to refuse to provide the information. The practitioner should also comment that GFHs sometimes touch on issues that may be difficult to discuss.

Practitioners can use several approaches to obtain and record genetic family histories. One approach is to ask a few broad questions derived from the referral criteria listed above, for example, "Is anyone in your family mentally retarded?" "Has anyone in your family had a psychiatric hospitalization?" The practitioner should ask specifically about the cause and

Name of child _____

Disorder	Check if yes	Relationship to child	Age at onset	Comments, name of disorder (if known)
Spina bifida (open spine) defect				
Misshapen skull				
Kidney/ bladder				
Heart				
Fingers/toes (e.g., webbing, extra, missing)				
Cleft palate				
Cleft lip				
Ears: tags (pieces of skin) or pits next to ear				
Other (specify)				
Down syndrome				
Other (features dissimilar from those of other family members)				

Note: Adapted from a form developed by Karen Hofman, Johns Hopkins University Hospital, Baltimore, Maryland.

Figure 1. Sample from a genetic family history form.

age at death of deceased family members. The information obtained can be recorded in narrative form. It is helpful to have the information located in one place in the chart rather than buried in the ongoing record. Although taking this broad approach is easiest, important information about the client's history may be overlooked.

Another approach is to use a standardized form on which the worker checks or circles the appropriate response. Figure 1 provides the contents of one page from a longer form developed by Karen Hofman of Johns Hopkins University Hospital for use by child welfare workers in Maryland. As can be seen, the form inquires about a specific condition, the relationship between the client and the affected individual, and the age of onset of the condition. Interested agencies could use similar forms or create their own form in consultation with a genetic professional.

Genetic professionals usually record GFHs in a diagram called a pedigree. This format presents a visual picture indicating the family composition and health status of living and deceased relatives. Pedigrees are efficient and save space; new information can be easily added to them. They are similar to genograms, with which many social workers are familiar (see Figure 2). Figure 3 presents symbols used in drawing a pedigree and their meaning.

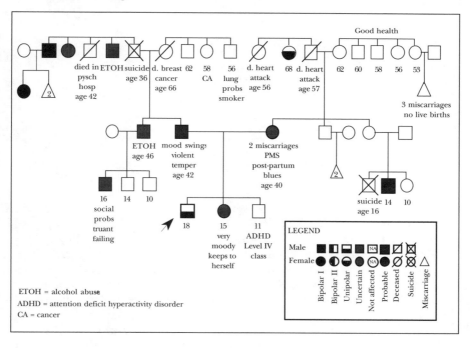

Figure 2. Example of pedigree.

289

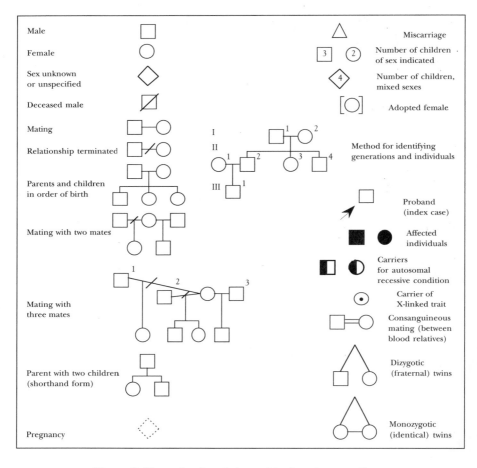

Figure 3. Example of symbols used in drawing a pedigree.

An easy way to start a pedigree is by using a form divided into three sections that shows the client's parents and grandparents. The client is placed beneath the parents and grandparents and is designated by an arrow.

Figure 4 presents step-by-step directions for drawing a pedigree. The history taker asks about the health of each family member. It is also beneficial to ask for a mood and behavioral description of each individual.

In selecting an approach, agency administrators and practitioners should take into account the way in which the genetic family history will be used. For example, if the practitioner is assessing depression in a generally competent person, relatively focused questioning can ascertain whether a family history of mood disorders exists. However, for adoptees, obtaining the most complete information is recommended.

Problems in Obtaining Genetic Information

Clients are often unfamiliar with their genetic family histories. In some instances, they may be able to obtain the information from a relative and in some circumstances it may be appropriate for the practitioner to ask permission to interview a relative. Another problem is that relevant information may not be accessible, for example, if the father of a child is unknown or the informant is cognitively impaired.

Often the informant is unclear about details or does not know the medical terms for a condition. In such instances, practitioners should record the informant's statement. For example, age of onset might be given as "when she was a teenager" or "when he was old." The informant may only know that "something was wrong with his heart" or "she died in a mental hospital" or describe a parent as "like Dr. Jekyll and Mr. Hyde." The informant may also use colloquial terms such as "low sugar" (diabetes). People from other cultures may use disease categories different from those of Western medicine, such as the Latin American concepts of susto or hot and cold diseases. Again, the worker should record the informant's words exactly. They can be valuable clues to a physician or genetic professional.

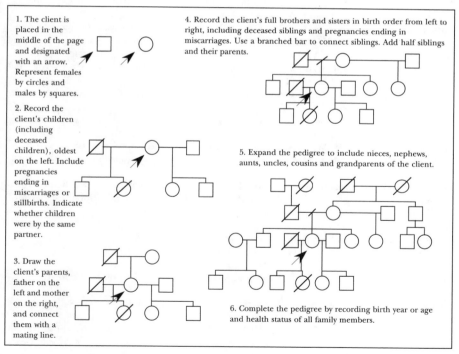

1. The client is placed in the middle of the page and designated with an arrow. Represent females by circles and males by squares.

2. Record the client's children (including deceased children), oldest on the left. Include pregnancies ending in miscarriages or stillbirths. Indicate whether children were by the same partner.

3. Draw the client's parents, father on the left and mother on the right, and connect them with a mating line.

4. Record the client's full brothers and sisters in birth order from left to right, including deceased siblings and pregnancies ending in miscarriages. Use a branched bar to connect siblings. Add half siblings and their parents.

5. Expand the pedigree to include nieces, nephews, aunts, uncles, cousins and grandparents of the client.

6. Complete the pedigree by recording birth year or age and health status of all family members.

Figure 4. Step-by-step directions for drawing a pedigree.

Conclusion

Genetic family histories can be very helpful to practitioners. The purpose of the history, its focus, depth, and utilization vary according to the agency function and the client's presenting problem. Failure to obtain GFHs can result in inaccurate assessment and incomplete or misdirected services. In the worst-case scenario, failure to obtain the information and to advise of available genetic services are potential grounds for malpractice and wrongful-adoption suits.

This chapter discussed approaches to obtaining and recording genetic family histories and presented criteria for referral to genetic services. However, the authors recommend that agency administrators consider consulting with a genetic professional to determine the appropriate focus of GFHs within the agency, design a protocol, and arrange in-service training in using the protocol.

REFERENCES

American Society of Human Genetics Social Issues Committee. (1991). Report on genetics and adoption: Points to consider. *American Journal of Human Genetics, 48,* 1009–1010.

Anderson, S. C., & Grant, J. F. (1984). Pregnant women and alcohol: Implications for social work. *Social Casework, 65,* 3–10.

Anthelli, R. M., & Schucket, M. A. (1990). Genetic studies of alcoholism. *International Journal of the Addictions, 25*(1A), 81–93.

Biederman, J., Faraone, S. V., Keenan, K., & Tsuang, M. T. (1991). Evidence of familial association between attention deficit disorder and major affective disorders. *Archives of General Psychiatry, 48,* 633–642.

Black, R. B. (1981). Risk-taking behavior: Decision making in the face of uncertainty. *Social Work in Health Care, 6*(1), 11–25.

Burns, J. (1984). *Genetic family history: An aid to better health in adoptive children.* Washington, DC: National Center for Education in Maternal and Child Health.

Childs, B., Moxon, R., & Winkelstein, J. (1990). Genetics and infectious diseases. In R. A. King, J. I. Rotter, & A. Motulsky (Eds.), *The genetic basis of common disease.* New York: McGraw-Hill.

Health and Medical Information in Adoption: Report of an Institute of Medicine Workshop. (1989, August 15). Washington, DC: Institute of Medicine, National Academy of Science.

Kay, D. W. (1980). Assessment of familial risks with functional psychoses and their application in genetic counseling. *Advances in Family Psychiatry, 2,* 335–365.

Ludlow, C. L., & Cooper, J. A. (1983). (Eds.). *Genetic aspects of speech and learning disorders.* New York: Academic Press.

McGuffin, P., & Murray, R. (1991). *The new genetics of mental illness.* Boston: Oxford, Butterworth-Heinemann.

National Genetic Diseases Act. (1976, April 22). P.L. 94-278. Title IV, sec. 403(b)(c), 90 Stat. 409, 42 U.S.C.

Plumridge, D., Burns, J., & Fisher, N. (1990). ASHG activities relevant to education. Heredity and adoption: A survey of state adoption agencies. *American Journal of Human Genetics, 46,* 208–214.

Pope, H. G., & Hudson, J. I. (1989). Eating disorders. In H. I. Kaplan & B. I. Sadock (Eds.),

Comprehensive textbook of psychiatry (5th ed., vol. 2) (pp. 1854–1864). Baltimore, MD: Williams & Wilkins.

President's Commission for the Study of Ethical Problems in Medicine and Biomedical Behavioral Research. (1983). *Screening and counseling for genetic conditions: The ethical, social and legal implications of genetic screening, counseling and education programs.* Washington, DC: U.S. Government Printing Office.

Pyeritz, R. E. (1989). Assessing the role of genes in diseases of adulthood. *Maryland Medical Journal, 38,* 949–952.

Rauch, J. (1988). Social work and the genetics revolution: Genetic services. *Social Work, 33,* 389–395.

Rauch, J., Sarno, C., & Simpson, S. (1991). Screening for affective disorders. *Families in Society, 72,* 602–609.

Richmond, M. (1917). *Social diagnosis.* New York: Russell Sage Foundation.

Robinson, A. (1988). Genetics and the health professional. In *Genetic applications: A health perspective* (pp. 1–3). Lawrence, KS: Learner Managed Designs.

Russell, M., Henderson, M. A., & Blume, S. (1985). *Children of alcoholics: A review of the literature.* New York: Children of Alcoholics Foundation, Inc.

Sachdev, R. (1989). *Unlocking the adoption files.* Lexington, MA: D. C. Heath.

Schild, S. (1977). Social work with genetic problems. *Health and Social Work, 2*(1), 58–77.

Stancer, H. C., & Wegener, D. K. (1984). Genetic counseling: Its need in psychiatry and the directions it gives for future research. *Canadian Journal of Psychiatry, 29,* 289–294.

Targum, S., & Schulz, C. S. (1982). Clinical applications of psychiatric genetics. *American Journal of Orthopsychiatry, 52,* 45–57.

Weiss, J. O. (1976). Social work and genetic counseling. *Social Work in Health Care, 2*(1), 5–12.

Weiss, J. O. (1981). Psychosocial stress in genetic disorders. *Social Work in Health Care, 6*(4), 17–31.

Wright, J. M. (1981). Fetal alcohol syndrome. The social work connection. *Health and Social Work, 6*(1), 5–10.

The Social Network Map: Assessing Social Support in Clinical Practice

*Elizabeth M. Tracy
and James K. Whittaker*

22

C linical practitioners increasingly recognize the importance of their clients' sources of informal social support and make these resources a focal point in case planning and design of service delivery systems (Whittaker & Garbarino, 1983; Gottlieb, 1983). In many ways, the current interest in social support reflects the rediscovery of a concept closely linked to the origins of social work practice (Richmond, 1918). Almost by definition, social work has long recognized the importance of social networks in clients' lives, but in the past decade or so, interest in the significance of informal helpers and their role in the provision of formal services has been renewed (Collins & Pancoast, 1976; Owne, 1986).

Unfortunately, even though a person-in-environment focus has long been a part of social work tradition, practice technologies for assessment, intervention, and evaluation of supportive environmental helping approaches have, until relatively recently, been less well-developed than have those for person-centered approaches (Grinnel & Kyte, 1975). More often, the "person" has received greater emphasis than the "situation" (Gitterman & Germain, 1981). The development of explicit practice principles and techniques for assessing and intervening with clients' informal social and environmental resources is critically needed (Tracy & Whittaker, 1987). Clients are rarely isolated; rather, they are surrounded by social networks that may support, weaken, substitute for, or supplement the helping efforts of professionals. Being embedded in a social network and the availability of social resources responsive to stressful events have been shown to have direct and stress-buffering effects on the well-being of clients (Cohen & Wills, 1985). Thus, given the importance of social support, valid and reliable measures of social support resources are needed that can be used in routine assessments and that are clinically useful.

The assessment tool described in this chapter—the social network map—was developed as part of a larger research and development effort called the Family Support Project (Whittaker, Tracy, & Marckworth, 1989). The goal of this project was to develop practical strategies for assessing and enhancing social support resources for families at risk of disruption as a result of out-of-home placement. The project was undertaken in conjunction with Homebuilders, an intensive family-preservation program designed to prevent unnecessary out-of-home placement (Kinney, Haapala, Booth, & Leavitt, 1990).

This chapter describes the development and pilot use of the social network map with 45 families served by Homebuilders, along with qualitative findings regarding its clinical utility. A process for social support assessment that focuses both on the structure and function of the personal social network is proposed. The assessment information generated from this approach allows both clinicians and clients to evaluate several aspects of informal support: (1) existing informal resources, (2) potential informal resources not currently utilized by the client, (3) barriers to involving social network resources, and (4) factors to be considered and weighed in the decision to incorporate informal resources in the formal service plan. A final section deals with pertinent questions for assessing social support as well as with strengths and limits of the previously described instrument.

Conceptualizing and Assessing
Social Networks and Social Support

Social support has been conceptualized in various ways, and it is important at the outset to establish a common definitional and conceptual language. *Social support* here refers to the many different ways in which people render assistance to one another: emotional encouragement, advice, information, guidance, tangible aid, or concrete assistance (Barrera & Ainley, 1983; Gottlieb, 1983; House & Kahn, 1985; Wood, 1984). Social support can be provided spontaneously through the natural helping networks of family and friends or can be mobilized through professional intervention. Social support that is provided through an informal helping network is typically characterized by a mutuality, reciprocity, and informality not often evident in professional helping relationships.

The term *social network* refers to the structure and quantity of a set of interconnected relationships (Mitchell & Trickett, 1980). Barnes's (1954) analyses of relationships in a Norwegian fishing village and Bott's (1957) study of marital patterns among London families are generally thought to be the beginning of what is now referred to as *social network analysis*. A *social support network* refers to a set of relationships that provide nurturance and reinforcement for coping with life on a daily basis (Whittaker & Garbarino, 1983), though not all networks are socially supportive, nor do they always reinforce positive social behaviors.

It is important, then, to distinguish the structural links of the social network from the resources or "supports" exchanged within that network. More social network resources do not necessarily imply more social support, nor is it the case that all exchanges are supportive. For this reason, some authors have viewed social support within social exchange theory (Wellman, 1981; Specht, 1986). In addition, the perception that others would be available to render help may be a key factor in mediating stress (Cohen & McKay, 1984; Wethington & Kessler, 1986). Because of these complexities, social support is increasingly viewed as a multidimensional construct, consisting of social network resources, types of supportive exchanges, perceptions of support availability, and skills in accessing and maintaining supportive relationships (Heller & Swindle, 1983).

In recent years, researchers have developed several measures for assessing social support (Tardy, 1985). *Structural measures* describe the existence or quality of social relationships, for example, marital status, contacts with friends, church affiliation. *Functional measures* assess various types of supportive exchanges. The supportive functions of social networks are also assessed in various ways. The frequency of specific supportive events can be determined; in addition, the perceived availability or adequacy of support can be evaluated. The difficulty with many social support measurement tools is their length, complexity, and tenuous relationship to direct-practice needs. Many instruments were designed for purposes other than treatment planning, for example, to identify the components of support or the mediating role of social support in stress and coping. Not only were they developed for different purposes, but they were often difficult and time consuming to administer. The dilemma for practitioners is how to assess social support in a clinically meaningful manner.

The eco-map is an extremely useful method for portraying client–environment relationships (Hartman, 1978; Hartman & Laird, 1983). Although the eco-map was designed to help public child welfare workers examine family needs, this tool is now used in a wide variety of practice settings. Although it can be used to illustrate an individual's connections, it is most often used to portray the total family system's relationship with the outside world. The advantages of the eco-map are its visual simulation of connections between a family and the environment, its ability to demonstrate the flow of energy into and from the family, and its depiction of nurturant as well as conflicted relationships. One disadvantage of the eco-map is its imprecise terms, which make it difficult to determine the exact nature of the relationships portrayed. For example, strong versus tenuous relationships can be defined in many different ways. In fact, the eco-map provides a much more complete portrayal of structure than it does of function.

In a manner analogous to the eco-map, social network mapping techniques begin by identifying and visually displaying network composition and membership. However, social network mapping attends to both structure and function in a more detailed fashion than does the eco-map. In general, social networks are constructed for a single individual— an egocentric network—and list each person known to that individual. Social network data collected in this manner have been used to determine a number of variables, including size, composition, and density. Social network mapping techniques are fully compatible with eco-map procedures but provide more detailed, anchored responses regarding the quality and functioning of social connections.

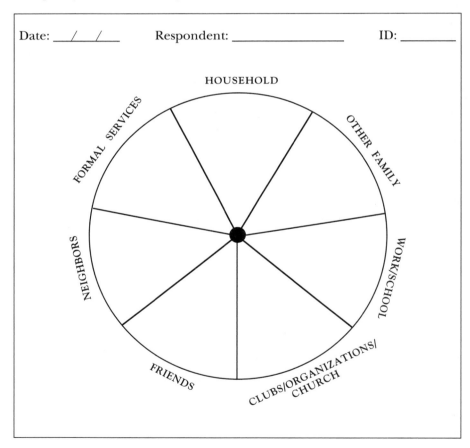

Figure 1. Family Support Project social network map.

The Social Network Map

The social network map described here uses a circle mapping technique reported as useful by a number of social network researchers, including Biegel, Shore, and Gordon (1984) in their work with frail elderly, Kahn and Antonucci (1981) in their national study of support networks of older adults, Fraser and Hawkins (1984) and Hawkins and Fraser (1985) in their work with drug abusers, and Lovell and Hawkins (1988) in their study of abusive mothers. The map displays network membership visually but reveals little information in itself about the functioning of network relationships. Therefore, an accompanying grid was included to record responses about the supportive and nonsupportive functions of network relationships, for example, who provided what types of supports, what relationships were reciprocal, what relationships were conflicted, and so forth (R. Catalano, personal communication, June 1987). The advantage of the network grid lies in the added specificity of network functions and the fact that information directly relevant to the target population can be collected. For example, Fraser and Hawkins (1984) used this approach to gather information on a number of drug-related behaviors among network members.

Administration of the Social Network Map

The social network map collects information on the total size and composition of the network, the extent to which network members provide various types of support, and the nature of relationships within the network as perceived by the person completing the map. Administering the map involves listing network members in each of seven domains: (1) household (people with whom you live); (2) family/relatives; (3) friends; (4) people from work or school; (5) people from clubs, organizations, or religious groups; (6) neighbors; and (7) agencies or other formal service providers. Names or initials of network members are visually displayed on the circle "map" (see Figure 1). After the composition of the network has been identified, a series of questions are asked regarding the nature of network relationships (see Figure 2). These questions cover the types of supports available (emotional, informational, and concrete), the extent to which network members are critical of the individual, the direction of help, the closeness of relationships, frequency of contact, and length of relationships. Responses to these questions are recorded on a network grid (see Figure 3).

Specifically, the social network map provides information on the following aspects of social network functioning. For each aspect, both absolute numbers as well as proportions can be calculated; the use of proportions allows practitioners to make comparisons across social networks of different sizes.

1. *Network size*: total number of people identified in the network
2. *Domain size*: total number/proportions of people in each of the seven domains
3. *Perceived availability of emotional, concrete, and informational support*: proportion of network rated as "almost always" available to provide these types of support
4. *Criticalness*: proportion of network perceived to be "almost always" critical of the individual
5. *Closeness*: proportion of network perceived to be "very close"
6. *Reciprocity*: proportion of network relationships in which "help goes both ways"
7. *Directionality*: proportion of network relationships in which help goes primarily from client to network and proportion of network relationships in which help goes primarily from network to client
8. *Stability*: length of relationships (how long known)
9. *Frequency*: frequency of contact (how often seen)

Social network data collected from 45 families revealed some interesting and clinically useful relationships among these variables. For example, although network size was a poor indicator of perceived social support, network composition appeared to be a relevant factor. Both number and proportion of friends within the network were associated with higher levels of support in this sample. In addition, reciprocity was positively related to concrete support. The proportion of critical network members was negatively related to emotional support. Overall, findings indicated that the families perceived a number of supportive resources within their networks. A network's composition and functioning, however, could create additional stress and strain (Tracy, 1990).

In order to ease administration and make the network map more engaging to complete, respondents can be supplied sorting cards and slips of paper onto which the names of their network members have been recorded (M. Lovell, personal communication, June 1987). When asked, for example, how close they feel to members of their network, respondents can easily sort the slips of paper into three piles—people with whom they feel very close, somewhat close, and not very close. This method is more visual and tactile than typical paper and pencil tools. Respondents view the process as "fun," more like a game than a test.

Despite the amount of detail the social network map provides, completion of the measures may take surprisingly little time. For the practitioners interviewed, the length of time to complete the social network map with individual family members ranged from 15 minutes to an hour, with an average completion time of approximately 20 minutes. Completion time appears to depend on the size of the network and the extent to which the respondent wants to talk about network members. It should be pointed out that the family members, generally mothers, were in crisis at the point of referral to the agency, and this factor may have

Step One: Developing a Social Network Map

Let's take a look at who is in your social network by putting together a network map. (Show network map.) We can use first names or initials because I'm not that interested in knowing the particular people and I wouldn't necessarily be contacting any of the people we talk about.

Think back to this past month, say since [date]. What people have been important to you? They may have been people you saw, talked with, or wrote letters to. This includes people who made you feel good, people who made you feel bad, and others who just played a part in your life. They may be people who had an influence on the way you made decisions during this time.

There is no right or wrong number of people to identify on your map. Right now, just list as many people as you come up with. Do you want me to write, or do you want to do the writing?

First, think of people in your *household*—whom does that include?

Now, going around the map, what *other family members* would you include in your network?

How about people from *work or school?*

People from *clubs, organizations, or religious groups*—whom should we include here?

What *other friends* haven't been listed in the other categories?

Neighbors—local shopkeepers may be included here.

Finally, list *professional people* or people from *formal agencies* whom you have contact with.

Look over your network. Are these the people you would consider part of your social network this past month? (Add or delete names as needed.)

Step Two: Completing the Social Network Grid

(If more than 15 people are in the network, ask the client to select the "top fifteen" and then ask the questions about only those network members. For each of the questions use the appropriate sorting guide card. Once the client has divided up the cards, put the appropriate code number for each person listed on the network grid.)

Now, I'd like to learn more about the people in your network. I'm going to write their names on this network grid, put a code number for the area of life, and then ask a few questions about the ways in which they help you. Let's also write their names on these slips of paper too; this will make answering the questions a lot easier. These are the questions I'll be asking (show list of social network questions), and we'll check off the names on this grid as we go through each question.

The first three questions have to do with the *types of support* people give you.

Who would be available to help you out in *concrete* ways—for example, would give you a ride if you needed one or would pitch in to help you with a big chore or would look after your belongings for a while if you were away? Divide your cards into three piles—those people you can hardly ever rely on for concrete help, those you can rely on sometimes, and those you'd almost always rely on for this type of help.

Now, who would be available to give you *emotional support*—for example, to comfort you if you were upset, to be right there with you in a stressful situation, to listen to you talk about your feelings? Again, divide your cards into three piles—those people you can hardly ever rely on for emotional support, those you can rely on sometimes, and those you almost always can rely on for this type of help.

Finally, whom do you rely on for *advice*—for example, who would give you information on how to do something, help you make a big decision, or teach you how to do something? Divide your cards into the three piles—hardly ever, sometimes, and almost always—for this type of support.

Look through your cards and this time select those people, if any, in your network who feel are *critical* of you (either critical of you or your life-style or of you as a parent). When I say "critical," I mean critical of you in a way that makes you feel bad or inadequate. Divide the cards into three piles—those people who are hardly ever critical of you, sometimes critical of you, and almost always critical of you. Again we'll put the code numbers next to their names.

Now look over your cards and think about the *direction of help*. Divide your cards into three piles—those people with whom help goes both ways (you help them just as much as they help you), those whom you help more, and those who help you more. OK, let's get their code numbers on the grid.

Now think about how *close* you are to the people in your network. Divide the cards into three piles—those people you are not very close to, those you are sort of close to, and those you are very close to—and then we'll put a code number for them.

Finally, just a few questions about *how often* you see people and *how long* you've known the people in your network. Divide the cards into four piles—people you see just a few times a year, people you see monthly, people you see weekly, and people you see daily (if you see someone twice or more than twice a week, count that as "daily"). OK, we'll put their numbers on the grid.

This is the last question. Divide the cards into three piles—those people you have known less than a year, from 1 to 5 years, and more than 5 years.

Now we have a pretty complete picture of who is in your social network.

Figure 2. Instructions/script for social network map.

influenced administration time to some extent. Most practitioners found administration of the map to be an interactive exercise. Several mentioned the potential of this form of assessment as an ice-breaker or relationship-building activity.

Clinical Usefulness

As part of the project, practitioners administered the social network map with clients at two points in time, within the first two weeks of intervention and again at termination. A structured qualitative interview was conducted with each of the 23 participating practitioners regarding the use of the map, including administration of the instrument, interpretation of the information gathered, use of this information in service delivery, and barriers to use of social support assessment information. All practitioners indicated that they intended to continue using the map even after the project's completion. Use of the social network map was cited as helpful in identifying and assessing stressors, strains, and resources within the client's social environment.

The map also enabled therapists to gather information about social and environmental resources in a more systematic manner. Rather than describing social support in global terms (e.g., "relatives live in the area"), practitioners were better able to describe specific aspects of the client's social environment (e.g., types of support, presence or absence of close relationships, the direction of help). Through the use of the social network map, information was often obtained about other potentially useful resources as well as the client's perception of these resources.

In addition to its value as an assessment tool, therapists also cited the social network map as a clinically useful activity. The instrument helped people review their resources and identify potential resources. Often this process revealed unexpected information, indicating more supportive resources than the client or worker had initially realized were present. For example, one client who had initially "bad-mouthed" neighbors realized after completing the social network map how often those same neighbors provided support in various ways.

Another example of the clinical utility of social support assessment is the case of a young single mother who often left her child alone and unattended. When asked about child-care resources, the mother reported none was available. In the process of completing the social network map, two people were identified who could help with babysitting. With therapist coaching, the mother asked these individuals for help and a child-care schedule was established. In this situation, the information gathered about social support was directly relevant to averting the need for placement of the child outside the home.

Similarly, the social network map often provided a vehicle for discussing other issues with the client. These discussions were helpful in

Name	#	Area of life 1. Household 2. Other family 3. Work/school 4. Organizations 5. Other friends 6. Neighbors 7. Professionals 8. Other	Concrete support 1. Hardly ever 2. Sometimes 3. Almost always	Emotional support 1. Hardly ever 2. Sometimes 3. Almost always	Information/ advice 1. Hardly ever 2. Sometimes 3. Almost always	Critical 1. Hardly ever 2. Sometimes 3. Almost always	Direction of help 1. Goes both ways 2. You to them 3. They to you	Closeness 1. Not very close 2. Sort of close 3. Very close	How often seen 0. Does not see 1. Few times/yr. 2. Monthly 3. Weekly 4. Daily	How long known 1. Less than 1 yr. 2. 1–5 yrs. 3. More than 5 yrs.
	01									
	02									
	03									
	04									
	05									
	06									
	07									
	08									
	09									
	10									
	11									
	12									
	13									
	14									
	15									
1–6		7	8	9	10	11	12	13	14	15

ID _____
Respondent _____

Figure 3. Family Support Project social network grid.

understanding current stressors experienced by families. For example, one woman commented that "support from the men in my life is exactly the same as from my children; it's mostly my helping them and they're mostly critical of me." In another example, each member of an entire family placed a deceased relative's name on the social network map, providing an opportunity for the worker to discuss issues of grief and loss. Several workers reported that the map worked well with women in abusive relationships, helping these women to identify what they were actually getting from the relationship. For example, one female client recognized that social support was reciprocal with the majority of her relationships, yet she continued to rely primarily on a particularly abusive one-way relationship with her boyfriend.

Some project practitioners viewed completing the social network map as an empowering activity. Clients began to understand their networks better as well as the steps they could take to get more of their needs met by the network. The visual display of the information gathered made insights readily available to clients. They could be actively engaged in assessing their network and generating options for change. For example, one client realized in working on her map that because she had recently moved, she felt isolated from usual sources of support. A specific intervention was developed to initiate contacts with neighbors.

Guidelines for Assessing Social Support

Based on the experience of the practitioners who participated in this project, a number of assessment guidelines and practice principles can be tentatively proposed. It is essential to evaluate social network data in relation to the presenting problems and needs of the client. Practitioners need detailed ways of conceptualizing their clients' social resources in order to develop individualized social support goals and accompanying interventions.

The following questions, based primarily on information generated from the social network grid, were helpful in translating social network and social support data into appropriate service goals:

1. Who is in the network, how are they related to the client, and who could be potential members?
2. What are the strengths and capabilities of the social network? In particular, which members of the network provide emotional support, concrete assistance, and information or advice?
3. What are the gaps in social support needs? Is there a lack of fit between the types of support the network is willing to provide or capable of providing and the types of support the client needs or desires?
4. What relationships in the network are based on mutual exchange? Does reciprocity seem to be an issue for the client? Is the client

always giving to others and thereby experiencing stress? Or does the client appear to be a drain on the network, with the result that network members are stressed and overburdened?

5. What network members are identified as responsive to requests for help, effective in their helping, accessible, and dependable? Do sufficient numbers of network members meet these conditions?

6. What network members are critical of the client in a negative or demanding way? Is the client surrounded by a network that is perceived as negative, nonsupportive, and/or stress-producing?

7. What obstacles to utilizing social network resources exist? Does the client lack supportive resources or skills in utilizing available resources? For example, the client may lack skills in accessing social network resources or otherwise be reluctant to accept or ask for help. On the other hand, network members may be unable to provide more assistance due to lack of skills or knowledge.

8. How are social support needs prioritized in relation to other presenting problems and needs?

Implications for Future Clinical Applications

With the assessment guidelines presented above, Homebuilder therapists were able to design and develop a variety of social support interventions as part of their clinical work with families. For example, some families were extremely isolated and needed new, additional sources of support. Other families were involved in large social networks, but those networks were not necessarily supportive of the family's efforts to work toward change. For these families, interventions to modify the quality of network relationships were viewed as more appropriate to implement. Through the Family Support Project, a series of case consultations were held in order to assist in clinical decision making. In addition, a social support training module was developed that is now available for use by other family preservation programs. The training module covers both social support assessment and intervention techniques.

Information gathered via the social network map, however, is limited in that the data generated are self-reported and therefore may be affected by recall problems, recent history, and social desirability. For these reasons, social network data are difficult to subject to usual tests of reliability. Little is known about the stability of social networks—whether changes in networks represent true changes or unreliable instruments (Tracy, Catalano, Whittaker, & Fine, 1990).

Objective verification of the validity of social network data is a related measurement issue. It is very difficult to determine "true" network size because so much depends on the method of data collection. For example, the time or the manner in which questions are asked could influence the numbers and types of people included in an individual's social network. From a clinical point of view, it is helpful to know the extent to which the network described by the client does, in fact, exist. Perceiving a large supportive network may cushion the experience of stress. Unrealistic expectations of others, however, can also lead to disappointment and feelings of rejection.

Another limitation in the information gathered from the social network map involves the unit of attention, that is, the individual rather than total family focus. The map provides information about an individual's personal social network but does not yield information about the collective impact of personal social networks within a family or group. The family's relation to the social environment would seem to require more than simply summing individual network maps. For example, the overlap—or lack of overlap—in network maps among different family members might be helpful to understand.

Finally, self-reported information about social networks may be influenced by the problem or need precipitating referral for services. It is difficult to know whether social network characteristics are a contributing factor to the presenting problem or a result of the presenting problem, which suggests the need for monitoring changes in social networks over time.

Obviously, more work is needed on the measurement properties of social network assessment information. For example, do the dimensions of support—concrete, emotional, and informational—correlate with other social support measures? In determining the reliability of network data, shorter test–retest intervals are needed in addition to methods of verifying self-reported network membership. It would be helpful to obtain measures of support received in relation to support perceived. The relationship between levels and types of social support and service outcomes needs further examination. Measures of *change* in social support from intake to termination may be correlated with treatment outcomes (Fraser, Pecora, & Haapala, 1988).

Conclusions

The experiences of family practitioners utilizing the social network map in a very brief intervention highlight the importance of assessing both structural and functional features of clients' social networks. This type of social support assessment information enables practitioners to gain a better sense of the types of support available to clients, the gaps that exist in support availability, and the resources available or potentially available to fill these gaps. It is important to avoid making assumptions about social networks and social support resources; even seemingly isolated clients are often able to identify supportive resources. The need for individualized assessments and corresponding individualized social support interventions is apparent; it is unlikely that one form of intervention will be suitable for all clients.

If social workers are to assess and intervene with clients' informal sources of support, then expanded practice models that combine the best of person-centered and environment-centered strategies will be needed (Whittaker, 1986). Social support as a construct can enable practitioners to understand better their client's social environment, the impact of that environment on the client, and how best to create more supportive and nurturant environments. The social network map is one tool that workers can use in gathering specific, clearly defined, and individualized social support assessment information relevant to the planning of social support interventions.

Although the social network map was developed as an assessment tool and practice technique, we believe that it contributes to a new model of practice that links formal and informal helping resources. Consistent with current ecological perspectives, such a practice model helps clients become more competent in dealing with the environment while helping to make the environment more supportive and nurturant of the client (Whittaker, Schinke, & Gilchrist, 1986).

REFERENCES

Barnes, J. A. (1954). Class and communities in a Norwegian island parish. *Human Relations, 7*(1), 39–58.

Barrera, M., & Ainley, S. L., (1983). The structure of social support: A conceptual and empirical analysis. *Journal of Community Psychology, 11*, 133–144.

Biegel, D. E., Shore, B. K., & Gordon, E. (1984). *Building support networks for the elderly: Theory and application.* Beverly Hills, CA: Sage Publications.

Bott, E. (1957). *Family and social network.* London: Tavistock.

Cohen, S., & McKay, G. (1984). Social support, stress and the buffering hypothesis: A theoretical analysis. In A. Baum, J. E. Singer, & S. E. Taylor (Eds.), *Handbook of psychology and health* (Vol. 4, pp. 78–89). Hillsdale, NJ: Erlbaum.

Cohen, S., & Wills, T. A. (1985). Stress, social support and the buffering hypothesis. *Psychological Bulletin, 98*, 310–357.

Collins, A. H., & Pancoast, D. L. (1976). *Natural helping networks: A strategy for prevention.* Washington, DC: National Association of Social Workers.

Fraser, M. W., & Hawkins, J. D. (1984). The social networks of opioid abusers. *International Journal of the Addictions, 19*, 903–917.

Fraser, M. W., Pecora, P. J., & Haapala, D. A. (1988). *Families in crisis: Final report on the family-based intensive treatment project.* Salt Lake City, UT: Social Research Institute, University of Utah.

Gitterman, A., & Germain, C. B. (1981). Education for practice: Teaching about the environment. *Journal of Education for Social Work, 17*(3), 44–51.

Gottlieb, B. H. (1983). *Social support strategies.* Beverly Hills, CA: Sage Publications.

Grinnel, R. M., & Kyte, N. S. (1975). Environmental modification: A study. *Social Work, 20*, 313–318.

Hartman, A. (1978). Diagrammatic assessment of family relations. *Social Casework, 59*, 465–476.

Hartman, A., & Laird, J. (1983). *Family-centered social work practice.* New York: Free Press, 1983.

Hawkins, J. D., & Fraser, M. W. (1985). The social networks of street drug users: A comparison of descriptive propositions from control and differential association theories. *Social Work Research and Abstracts, 21*(1), 3–12.

Heller, K., & Swindle, R. W. (1983). Social networks, perceived social support and coping with stress. In R. D. Felner, L. A. Jason, J. Morisugu, & S. S. Farber (Eds.), *Preventive psychology: Theory, research and practice* (pp. 87–103). New York: Pergamon.

House, J. S., & Kahn, R. L. (1985). Measures and concepts of social support. In S. Cohen & S. L. Syme (Eds.), *Social support and health* (pp. 83–108). Orlando, FL: Academic Press.

Kahn, R. L., & Antonucci, T. C. (1981). Convoys of social support: A life course approach. In S. B. Kiesler, J. N. Morgan, & V. C. Oppenheimer (Eds.), *Aging: Social change*. New York: Academic Press.

Kinney, J., Haapala, D., Booth, C., & Leavitt, S. (1990). The Homebuilders model. In J. K. Whittaker, J. Kinney, E. M. Tracy, & C. Booth (Eds.), *Reaching high-risk families: Intensive family preservation in the human services* (pp. 31–64). New York: Aldine de Gruyter.

Lovell, M. L., & Hawkins, J. D. (1988). An evaluation of a group intervention to increase the personal social networks of abusive mothers. *Children and Youth Services Review, 10*, 175–188.

Mitchell, R. E., & Trickett, E. J. (1980). Social networks as mediators of social support. *Community Mental Health Journal, 16*(1), 27–43.

Owne, D. (1986). Formal and informal patterns of social care. *British Journal of Social Work, 16* (Suppl.), 5–14.

Richmond, M. (1918). *Friendly visiting among the poor*. New York: Macmillan.

Specht, H. (1986). Social support, social networks, social exchange, and social work practice. *Social Service Review, 60*, 218–240.

Tardy, C. H. (1985). Social support measurement. *American Journal of Community Psychology, 13*, 187–202.

Tracy, E. M. (1990). Identifying social support resources of at-risk families. *Social Work, 35*, 252–258.

Tracy, E. M., Catalano, R. F., Whittaker, J. K., & Fine, D. (1990). Research note: Reliability of social network data. *Social Work Research and Abstracts, 26*(2), 33–35.

Tracy, E. M., & Whittaker, J. K. (1987). The evidence base for social support interventions in child and family practice: Emerging issues for research and practice. *Children and Youth Services Review, 9*, 249–270.

Wellman, B. (1981). Applying network analysis to the study of support. In B. H. Gottlieb (Ed.), *Social networks and social support* (pp. 171–200). Beverly Hills, CA: Sage Publications.

Wethington, E., & Kessler, K. C. (1986). Perceived support, received support, and adjustment to stressful life events. *Journal of Health and Social Behavior, 27*, 78–89.

Whittaker, J. K. (1986). Formal and informal helping in child welfare services: Implications for management and practice. *Child Welfare, 65*, 17–25.

Whittaker, J. K., & Garbarino, J. (1983). *Social support networks: Informal helping in the human services*. New York: Aldine Publishing.

Whittaker, J. K., Schinke, S. P., & Gilchrist, L. D. (1986). The ecological paradigm in child, youth, and family services: Implications for policy and practice. *Social Service Review, 60*, 483–503.

Whittaker, J. K., Tracy, E. M., & Marckworth, M. (1989). *The family support project: Identifying informal support resources for high risk families*. Seattle, WA: University of Washington, School of Social Work.

Wood, Y. R. (1984). Social support and social networks: Nature and measurement. In P. McReynolds & G. J. Chelvne (Eds.), *Advances in psychological assessment* (Vol. 6, pp. 312–353). San Francisco: Jossey-Bass.

The Family Intervention Scale: Assessing Treatment Outcome

Janet Taynor, Robert W. Nelson, and W. Keith Daugherty

23

Professionals who conduct family therapy in applied community settings and funders of their service need methods and tools to evaluate the outcome of family therapy. Service providers wish to monitor the effectiveness of treatment in order to provide the best services to their target populations. Funders, quite understandably, want to know if scarce dollars are producing beneficial changes in the lives of service recipients and over the past decade have begun to ask that providers demonstrate that treatment produces such changes.

Even though professionals need to demonstrate the effectiveness of family intervention in their own settings, not enough has been done to address the problem. Although exemplary outcome studies of family treatment have been conducted periodically (e.g., Beck, 1988; Beck & Jones, 1973; Sacks, Bradley, & Beck, 1970; Geismar, 1980), evaluating the outcome of family therapy in applied community settings has been considered beyond the reach of most service agencies.

The reasons for this belief are rooted in the fact that resources and technology for conducting such evaluations are scarce. Technological limitations stem from the fact that even in settings staffed and funded to perform basic research, assessing the outcome of therapy is a very complex issue (Bergin & Lambert, 1978; Cromwell, Olson, & Fournier, 1976; Gurman, 1977; Gurman & Kniskern, 1981; Gurman, Kniskern, & Pinsof, 1986; Hazelrigg, Cooper, & Borduin, 1987; Lambert, Shapiro, & Bergin, 1986). When the everyday demands of service delivery and administration are added to the purely methodological ones encountered in more academic situations, the difficulties can seem insurmountable. Consequently, although professionals who deliver services in busy agencies contend that family intervention is very effective, they must rest their contentions on belief rather than on outcome data. This situation does not satisfy professional and management needs, nor does it meet the accountability demands of funders of services. Thus efficient and methodologically sound procedures to assess the outcome of family treatment must be found.

This chapter describes a method and a scale that can be used to assess the outcome of family intervention in a family service agency where resources that can be allocated to outcome evaluation are scarce. Our intention is to share how an evaluation process can be shaped to fit a particular agency's evaluation needs while reflecting that agency's intended outcomes of treatment.

Early Decisions

The first issue that confronted us when determining how we would evaluate the outcome of family intervention was *what to measure*. Various approaches have been used to measure the outcome of psychosocial intervention. General outcome measures intended to be used across a variety of treatment settings and modalities have been used (Ciarlo & Reihman, 1977; Derogatis, 1977; Ellsworth, 1975; Kane, Kane, & Arnold, 1985). Assessment of the attainment of individualized client goals has also been the focus of evaluation (Kiresuk & Sherman, 1968). Tailor-made outcome measures that assess what a particular program is trying to accomplish have been employed (Ball, 1981; Schacht & Strupp, 1984) and used successfully in low-budget projects in public service agencies (Taynor, 1978, 1979). In this project we decided to focus upon the areas of clients' lives at which the service providers most often aimed their intervention and to measure whether change occurred in these life areas.

The second issue to be resolved centered on the *source of measurement*. In social service agencies with few resources, usually either the client or the service provider serves as the source of data. Clients as the source of measurement both strengthen and weaken evaluation efforts (Gurman, 1977; Kane et al., 1985; Lebow, 1981; Taynor, 1978; Wynne, 1984). Likewise, using service providers as the source of information has advantages and disadvantages (Bergin & Lambert, 1978; Gurman & Kniskern, 1981; Mintz, 1977).

Given the practical consideration of our own project, we chose the service workers as the source of information about families' functioning to be used for outcome evaluation. We made this choice for several reasons: the incidence of missing data is usually lower when service providers are the source of data,[1] language on the questionnaire can be more abstract,[2] and the response format can be made more complex.[3]

We knew, however, that we would have to take precautions to control potential rater bias. Service providers must be able to "buy in" to the evaluation process, perceive its value, and feel some ownership of it. Also, they would have to be assured that the outcome results would *not* be used to monitor the quality of their individual performance.

For methodological reasons, we decided that providers would *not* be asked to make retrospective comparisons of family functioning before and after treatment in order to determine whether the families got better, worse, or stayed the same. Instead, we asked them to make an *absolute* judgment of families' functioning *in specific life areas* at the beginning of intervention and to make another assessment at the end of treatment.[4] Our experience in evaluating treatment outcome in other settings (Taynor, 1978, 1979; Taynor & Schwartz, 1986) led us to believe that these procedures would yield meaningful data from treatment providers.

Finally, we determined how *change would be assessed*. Because assessments of family functioning would be made at the beginning of intervention and again when the family left the agency, change during intervention was determined statistically by comparing group prescores and postscores.

Our aim was to implement a cost-efficient and meaningful assessment technique to be used in the agency's monitoring and planning processes. First, we decided to tailor an outcome measure to focus upon the areas of clients' lives at which intervention was aimed. We chose service providers as the source of data. An absolute measure was taken of family functioning at the beginning and the end of intervention and a statistical comparison was made between aggregate pre- and postscores. Our choices were guided by what was considered feasible but still methodologically sound.

Building the Scale

Intention Analysis

In order to measure change, it was necessary to know what providers anticipated would change. To do this, an "intention analysis" was con-

---

1. In a setting such as ours, clients usually leave when they feel ready, regardless of whether they have tidily completed a postmeasure.
2. Questions posed to providers can be cast in the language in which they conceptualize and describe cases. When using a client measure, questions must be aimed at the lowest literacy level in the target population.
3. The metric of the response format can contain more response options than that used for clients of various literacy levels or for clients in crisis who should not be asked to respond to complex language on questionnaires.
4. In so doing, the providers would not have access to the premeasures when they rated the postmeasures, so they could not compare the postscores with the prescores and thereby bias their postratings. In addition to this "blind" postrating, our workers carry heavy case loads, so it is very difficult for them to remember a family's prescore when completing the postmeasure.

Figure 1. Family intervention scale.

Family name _____   Number _____
Today's date _____   Rater _____   Pre _____
Last contact date _____ Number of contacts _____   Post _____
Program _____   Case terminated after one session _____

The satisfaction and distress family members experience in their family very often are due to the way the family operates as a unit. In some families, members experience a great deal of satisfaction in the family because all the members of the family perform their roles appropriately. In other families, the members feel very distressed because of the breakdown of roles in the family.

Family role	High satisfaction Satisfaction *much* greater than distress due to role performance	Moderate satisfaction Satisfaction greater than distress due to role performance	Balance between satisfaction and distress due to role performance	Moderate distress Distress greater than satisfaction due to role performance	High distress Distress *much* greater than satisfaction due to role performance
	11 10	9 8	7 6 5	4	3 2 1

Families have varying degrees of interaction with and support from friends, acquaintances, and extended family. One family may be just about right in terms of the amount and kind of interaction with its social environment. On the other hand, another family may be too isolated, and still another family may be involved in outside interests to the exclusion of family concerns.

What is the nature of this family's interaction with and support from friends, acquaintances, and extended family?

Social support	Very satisfactory Interaction and support *much* more satisfactory than problematic	Moderately satisfactory Interaction and support more satisfactory than problematic	Balance between satisfactory and problematic interaction and support	Moderately problematic Interaction and support more problematic than satisfactory	Very problematic Interaction and support *much* more problematic than satisfactory
	11 10	9 8	7 6 5	4	3 2 1

How adequately does the family support itself with respect to money, food, shelter, clothing, and safety of its members?

Physical maintenance

11	Very adequately Support *much more* adequate than inadequate	10	9	Moderately adequately Support more adequate than inadequate	8	7	Balance between adequate and inadequate support	6	5	Moderately inadequately Support more *inadequate* than adequate	4	3	Very inadequately Support *much more inadequate* than adequate	2	1

When the family has a need to be met, how adequately does it use community resources to address this need? (Examples of community resources are welfare, health care, legal aid, public transportation, clinics, banking, library, and cultural.) Consider the *frequency* of use, the *match* between the need and the resource, and the *skill* the family uses to get what it needs.

Community resources

11	Very adequately Uses community resources *much more* adequately than inadequately	10	9	Moderately adequately Uses community resources more adequately than inadequately	8	7	Balance between adequate and inadequate use of community resources	6	5	Moderately inadequately Uses community resources more *inadequately* than adequately	4	3	Very inadequately Uses community resources *much more inadequately* than adequately	2	1

How adequate are the family's skills for maintaining emotional well-being (managing feelings, solving emotion-laden problems)?

Emotional well-being

11	Very adequate Skills are *much more* adequate than inadequate for maintaining emotional well-being	10	9	Moderately adequate Skills are more adequate than inadequate for maintaining emotional well-being	8	7	Balance between adequate and inadequate skills for maintaining emotional well-being	6	5	Moderately inadequate Skills are more *inadequate* than adequate for maintaining emotional well-being	4	3	Very inadequate Skills are *much more inadequate* than adequate for maintaining emotional well-being	2	1

313

ducted. The intention analysis method has been used successfully in field situations similar to this one (Taynor, 1979; Taynor, Perry, & Frederick, 1976; Taynor & Schwartz, 1979). This method to elicit the intended outcomes of intervention entails in-depth discussions with service providers and the asking of a series of related questions: "What do you intend to have happen in the families' lives? What areas of the families' lives do you want to see changed? What do families look like when they begin treatment? What do they look like when they leave treatment?"

Instead of using a single evaluator to gather this information from service providers, advanced graduate students pursuing a doctoral degree in psychology were used. Students participated in this effort as a partial requirement in a regularly scheduled course in the evaluation of treatment outcome. They interviewed service providers to identify life areas upon which treatment was focused, asking them the types of problems families were experiencing in the life areas, what they expected to occur in these life areas if treatment were successful, and what was anticipated if it were not successful.

After this interview was completed, a short list of life areas that were most often mentioned as target areas of intervention by the agency's providers was obtained. We returned to the agency's professional staff with this list and shared the findings with them. The staff had cogent comments and suggestions, which were heeded. The life areas, in what was to become the Family Intervention Scale, were then operationalized and again put before the professional staff for review and comment.

Scale Items

The Family Intervention Scale (Figure 1) consists of five items, each of which is scored on an 11-point Likert scale. These items correspond to the five life areas identified by the intention analysis as the major foci of intervention. The items measure the following:

- Quality of *role performance* in the family
- Family's *connectedness* to the outside community and friends
- How adequately the family provides for its own *physical maintenance* (money, food, shelter, clothing, and safety)
- How adequately the family uses *community resources* to meet its needs
- Family's skills for *maintaining emotional well-being*

Data Collection

As stated earlier, service providers were the source of the data. Each counselor rated families on each of the five dimensions stated above when the family entered counseling. After this was done, the scale was taken from the family's record and sent to a secretary who coded the data. When the family terminated services, the counselor rated the family again. (Note that the counselor did not have access to the prescore when rating the postscore.) A counselor typically completed the scale in two to three minutes. Post-ratings were made within 30 days of the last contact with the family.

Early Pilot Testing

Our first effort at testing the adequacy of the instrument was to conduct a validity test. Our rationale for this was that if the scale could differentiate *between* high- and low-functioning families, it was reasonable to anticipate that it would show change *within* families. At any rate, we knew that if it did not distinguish between families, it never would do the job of detecting change within families.

Consequently, we asked a senior supervisory counselor to designate a group of families, currently in counseling, as either high or low functioning. These families' own counselors, not knowing to which group their family had been ascribed, then rated them on the scale. A *t*-test was conducted on each of the five items of the scale to determine whether the items distinguished between the high- and low-functioning families.

Each of the five items, when compared statistically, showed that the high-functioning group was rated significantly higher than was the low-functioning group (Table 1). We interpreted these findings as an indication that agency resources would not be squandered if we began collecting pre- and postmeasures, coding data, and analyzing them.

It is important to note the order of events here. In basic research settings, it is customary to conduct an interrater reliability study to learn something about the internal reliability of the scale before undertaking the research. In an applied setting, where one cannot turn the agency upside down to ascertain interrater reliability and assess internal consistency, this procedure is not always the wisest, or even a possible, course of action. Consequently, we did the validating study before doing anything else, assuming that if a scale were valid, it would necessarily be reliable.

Table 1. Differences between high- and low-functioning families on the pilot test of the Family Intervention Scale.

	High functioning		Low functioning				
	m	*sd*	*m*	*sd*	*t*	*df*	*p*
Role performance	5.31	2.024	3.00	1.000	3.82	23	<.01
Connectedness	6.50	2.221	3.44	1.130	4.56	23	<.01
Physical resources	8.50	1.033	4.78	2.108	4.97	23	<.01
Community resources	8.00	1.862	5.00	1.936	3.77	23	<.01
Emotional well-being	6.56	1.931	2.56	1.014	6.80	23	<.01

Note: Number of high-functioning families = 16; number of low-functioning families = 9

Table 2. Item-total correlations on the Family Intervention Scale (n = 39).

	Pretest
Role performance	.770
Connectedness	.847
Physical resources	.748
Community resources	.772
Emotional well-being	.901

Note: All p's < .001

Table 3. Interrater reliability on the Family Intervention Scale (n = 11).

	r	p
Role performance	.765	.006
Connectedness	.036	.917
Physical resources	.875	.004
Community resources	.502	.115
Emotional well-being	.791	.004
Total score	.782	.004

Reliability—Item Analyses

Six months later, sufficient data were available to conduct an item analysis. In this analysis, the relationship between each item and the total score was determined.[5] All correlations (Pearson r) were greater than .77, indicating that the items in the Family Intervention Scale measured the general area of family functioning that the agency sought to improve during treatment (Table 2).

The results of this analysis allowed us to incorporate the total scale score into subsequent analyses, with the *total scale score* now serving as the main measure of accountability when talking with funders about treatment outcome. We use the individual items as well, although they are of interest to us more for our monitoring of service delivery.

Interrater Reliability

Obtaining interrater reliability data for this instrument presented a logistical challenge because the agency did not have readily available a sufficiently large group of families seen regularly by two counselors whose ratings could be compared to obtain a reliability index. However, a small sample of families were seen by more than one service provider. These families participated in an incest-treatment program with multiple counselors, several of whom could assess the families' functioning on the Family Intervention Scale. Eleven families were available for this purpose.[6]

The analyses showed the interrater reliability (Pearson r) of the total scale score to be .78 (p = .004). Interrater reliability for the family role item was .76 (p = .006); for family connectedness, it was .04 (p = .92); for physical maintenance, .88 (p = .004); for the appropriate use of commu-

5. The total score was obtained by adding the items and dividing by 5.
6. With some trepidation, we undertook a preliminary reliability study. We knew we would be limited by the small amount of data (n = 11). We also knew this particular group of families were at the low end of the functioning continuum, thereby restricting the range of scores, which, in turn, would make it difficult to obtain high correlations.

nity resources, .50 (p = .115); and for maintaining emotional well-being, .79 (p = .004) (Table 3).

All correlations were quite respectable, with the exception of the item measuring family connectedness. We did not drop this item, however, because it represented an important area of intervention, obtained a good correlation with the total score, and, as will be described later, showed statistically significant differences between pre- and postscores. The low interrater reliability index obtained in this analysis may be due to the small sample size.

Differences among Items

When analyzing the individual items of the scale, differences among the items emerged. As can be seen in Table 4, the individual items did reflect different levels of functioning among the five life areas at the beginning of treatment and also showed different magnitudes of change.

When entering treatment, families scored lowest on emotional well-being and family role performance. If it is true that families seek counseling when they are experiencing emotional pain, it would be expected that their mechanisms for handling painful feelings would be at a very low point when they begin treatment. The functioning of the family as a unit (family role performance) would also be expected to be very low. Thus, the lower entry scores on these items make sense.

These life areas also showed the greatest change between beginning and end of treatment. Due to counselors' training and the fact that inappropriate ways of interacting and handling discomfort can be observed and corrected in counseling sessions, we suspect that counselors worked hardest on these problems.[7]

On the other hand, the least change was seen in basic physical maintenance and the appropriate use of community resources (Table 4). Families seeking agency services generally were not as dysfunctional in these life areas as they were in others, so their entry scores were higher. In addition, due to their own training and inclinations, some of the counselors were not as ready to work on these problems. Thus the finding of less change is not surprising.[8]

Although these results are interesting from a clinical point of view, even more important is what they suggest regarding the utility of the scale. The items behave as one would expect. In addition, they yield evidence about the appropriateness of using service providers as the source of data. The service providers rated families differently on various life areas of the scale, suggesting that they were making an accurate assessment of their

7. The connectedness item showed nearly as much change as did the family role measure. However, the entry level is higher, as is the score at the end of treatment.
8. Higher entry scores accompanied by smaller amounts of change might make one suspect that a "ceiling effect" explains these findings. However, Table 4 shows that termination scores were also highest on these two items.

Table 4. Results on the Family Intervention Scale.

| | Year 1[a] | | | | | | Year 2 | | | | | |
| | Pretest[b] | | Posttest[c] | | | | Pretest[d] | | Posttest[e] | | | |
	m	sd	m	sd	t	p	m	sd	m	sd	t	p
Role performance	4.16	1.977	5.59	2.432	3.46	.001	4.74	2.195	5.69	1.928	2.75	.007
Connectedness	4.96	2.198	6.37	2.270	3.45	.001	5.34	2.156	6.25	1.786	2.71	.007
Physical resources	6.62	2.414	7.51	1.894	2.32	.022	6.41	1.961	6.93	1.870	1.66	.100
Community resources	6.59	2.066	7.43	1.814	2.39	.018	6.51	1.864	6.72	1.872	.70	.486
Emotional well-being	4.28	2.025	5.73	2.262	3.68	.004	3.59	1.238	5.33	1.886	6.33	.001
Total Score	5.32	1.734	6.53	1.827	3.69	.004	5.32	1.556	6.18	1.605	3.32	.001

[a]Year one consisted of five months of data.
[b]n pretest = 79; [c]n posttest = 49; [d]n pretest = 91; [e]n posttest = 61
Note: If a family is seen only once, their scores are omitted from the analyses.

clients both at the beginning and the end of services. Said another way, it appears that providers were not marking scales just to show improvement and did evaluate the families differently in the various life areas.

Scale Use

This scale was introduced at Family Service Association, Dayton, Ohio. The agency offers a variety of programs to inner-city, suburban, and rural populations. The typical client family lives in the inner city and has an income of less than $15,000 per year. Families usually identify children as "the problem." Referrals from the child protection agency, the court system, and schools are common. The direct service staff are all master's-level clinicians with an average of nine years' experience working with families. Social work is their predominant orientation.

The scale is used for families in family counseling. The outcomes of counseling for individual clients and couples are assessed by instruments similar to the Family Intervention Scale. Only data obtained on the Family Intervention Scale are included in the analyses that follow.

Family Improvement

Two sets of analyses of the outcome of family counseling have been conducted, one at the end of the first year in which the scale was in use and another at the end of the second year of use.

First year. At the end of the first year, the Family Intervention Scale worked as anticipated. In year one (Table 4), total scale scores were significantly higher on the postmeasures than they were on the premeasures ($t = 3.69$; $df = 126$; $p = .001$). These differences in total scale scores, reflecting the general measure of families' functioning, indicate that families did improve between the beginning and end of intervention. (The median number of times a family was seen was five.) Thus the main index of treatment outcome demonstrated that change had occurred in families' lives.

With respect to the specific life areas, statistically significant differences were found between pre- and postscores on each of the subscales. Family role performance, family connectedness, physical maintenance, community resources, and emotional well-being were significantly higher at the end of treatment than they were at the beginning.

The most change was seen in emotional well-being, although family role performance and family connectedness followed closely. Less change was seen in physical maintenance and community resources, even though the differences between pre- and postscores were statistically significant.

Second year. In year two, the main measure of family functioning, the total score on the Family Intervention Scale, again showed that families functioned at a significantly higher level at the end of treatment than they did at the beginning ($t = 3.32$; $df = 150$; $p = .001$).

Family role performance, family connectedness, and emotional maintenance showed significantly higher postscores than prescores. A trend was found for physical maintenance scores to be higher at the end of treatment than they were at the beginning. No significant differences were found in the use of community resources. (Again, the median number of counseling sessions was five.)

The trend and no-difference findings on the physical maintenance and use of community resources items followed the same pattern of least movement as was found in the first year. Our reactions to these findings are mixed. On the one hand, significant change on all the items on the scale would be desirable. On the other hand, it is reassuring that treatment providers are not just making general ratings of improvement; that is, although the total scale scores showed improvement, the individual items showed differing amounts of change.

Implications. The Family Intervention Scale has demonstrated differences between pre- and postscores for two years. We are now able to say to our funders that what we are doing in the community does make a difference: families show improved functioning between the beginning and end of treatment.

Discussion

Several points need to be stressed about evaluation efforts such as the one described here. First, close attention to making appropriate choices regarding what to measure is fundamental to the success of this, or any, outcome evaluation project. Initial contact with service providers must be made to learn the manner in which they conceptualize and talk among themselves about cases, to learn about the target population, and, most important, to learn what they intend to have happen in their clients' lives. We showed drafts of the instrument to service providers on several occasions to incorporate their comments and suggestions. Ex-

319

pending time and effort at the beginning of the evaluation project to learn what an intervention program intends to accomplish is the most important step in evaluating the treatment outcome.

Also, spending time at the beginning to talk with service providers assured them of our benign intentions and allowed them to develop a sense of ownership of the evaluation project. Such ownership is crucial to success if providers are to be the source of measurement and if one wishes to have the evaluation results integrated into the decision-making and planning processes of the service delivery system administrators.

In this project, we found service providers to be an excellent source for outcome data. Philosophically, we believe that professional caregivers who are entrusted to deliver services can be relied upon to provide thoughtful and reliable assessments of family functioning. Empirically, our results support this contention. Service providers differentially assessed their clients in the several life areas of the Family Intervention Scale, giving credence to the notion that they were trying their best to make accurate assessments of their clients.

Taking an absolute assessment at the beginning and again at the end of treatment helps to set the stage for raters being able to give sound, reliable assessments of family functioning. Making statistical comparison to assess change relieved raters from the burden of comparing clients' functioning at the beginning and end of treatment. Absolute measures at pre- and posttreatment also yielded insight into the severity of problems in the various life areas and the amount of change observed by the end of treatment.

The sequence of events during the early validity testing of the scale hastened implementation of the instrument, thus cutting expense for construction of the scale while controlling for the risk of implementing a faulty instrument.

It is too early to say unequivocally that families served by our agency improved as a result of treatment. The aforementioned analyses were obtained in a simple pre–post design; we did not have a randomly assigned control group that would allow us to make incontrovertible causal inferences. The intention of this chapter is to present the scale and the method of its construction so that others may benefit from our experience.

In summary, the Family Intervention Scale is a tool that may be used to efficiently evaluate the outcome of intervention in a family service agency. It certainly could be augmented by other measures, and it does not measure every aspect of family functioning. However, we have made a reasonable start at evaluating the outcome of services in our agency and encourage others to do the same.

REFERENCES

Ball, S. (1981). Outcomes, the size of impact, and program evaluation. *New Directions for Program Evaluation, 9*, 71–86.

Beck, D. F. (1988). *Counselor characteristics: How they affect outcomes.* Milwaukee, WI: Family Service America.

Beck, D. F., & Jones, M. A. (1973). *Progress on family problems: A nationwide study of clients' and counselors' views on family agency services.* New York: Family Service Association of America.

Bergin, A. E., & Lambert, M. J. (1978). The evaluation of therapeutic outcomes. In S. L. Garfield & A. E. Bergin (Eds.), *Handbook of psychotherapy and behavior change: An empirical analysis* (2nd ed.) (pp. 139–190). New York: John Wiley.

Ciarlo, J. A., & Reihman, J. (1977). The Denver Community Mental Health Questionnaire: Development of a multidimensional program evaluation instrument. In R. Coursey, G. Spector, S. Murrel, & B. Hunt (Eds.), *Program evaluation for mental health: Methods, strategies, and participants.* New York: Grune & Stratton.

Cromwell, R., Olson, D., & Fournier, D. (1976). Diagnosis and evaluation in marital and family counseling. In D. H. L. Olson (Ed.), *Treating relationships.* Lake Mills, IA: Graphic.

Derogatis, L. R. (1977). *Administration, scoring and procedures manual-1 for the revised version.* Baltimore, MD: Clinical Psychometrics Research.

Ellsworth, R. B. (1975). Consumer feedback in measuring the effectiveness of mental health programs. In M. Guttentag & E. S. Struening (Eds.), *Handbook of evaluation research: Vol. 2.* Beverly Hills, CA: Sage Publications.

Geismar, L. L. (1980). *Family and community functioning.* Metuchen, NJ: Scarecrow Press.

Gurman, A. S. (1977). The patient's perception of the therapeutic relationship. In A. S. Gurman & A. Razin (Eds.), *Effective psychotherapy: A handbook of research* (pp. 503–543). New York: Pergamon.

Gurman, A. S., & Kniskern, D. P. (1981). Family therapy outcome research. In A. Gurman & D. Kniskern (Eds.), *Handbook of family therapy.* New York: Brunner/Mazel.

Gurman, A. S., Kniskern, D. P., & Pinsof, W. M. (1986). Research on the process and outcome of marital and family therapy. In S. L. Garfield & A. E. Bergin (Eds.), *Handbook of psychotherapy and behavior change.* New York: John Wiley.

Hazelrigg, M. D., Cooper, H. M., & Borduin, C. M. (1987). Evaluating the effectiveness of family therapies: An integrative review and analysis. *Psychological Bulletin, 101*, 428–443.

Kane, R. S., Kane, R. L., & Arnold, S. (1985). *Measuring social functioning in mental health studies: Concepts and instruments* (DHHS Publ. No. (ADM) 85-1384). Washington, DC: U.S. Government Printing Office.

Kiresuk, T. J., & Sherman, R. E. (1968). Goal attainment scaling: A general method for evaluating comprehensive community mental health programs. *Community Mental Health Journal, 4*, 443–453.

Lambert, M. J., Shapiro, D. A., & Bergin, A. E. (1986). Evaluation of therapeutic outcomes. In S. L. Garfield & A. E. Bergin (Eds.), *Handbook of psychotherapy and behavior change* (3rd ed.). New York: John Wiley.

Lebow, J. (1981). Issues in the assessment of outcome in family therapy. *Family Process, 20*, 167–188.

Mintz, J. (1977). The role of the therapist in assessing psychotherapy outcome. In A. S. Gurman & A. Razin (Eds.), *Effective psychotherapy: A handbook of research.* New York: Pergamon.

Sacks, J. G., Bradley, P. M., & Beck, D. F. (1970). *Clients' progress within five interviews.* New York: Family Service Association of America.

Schacht, T. E., & Strupp, H. H. (1984, June). *Psychotherapy outcome: Individualized is nice, but intelligible is beautiful.* Paper presented at the Annual Meeting of the Society for Psychotherapy Research, Lake Louise, Alberta, Canada.

Taynor, J. (1978). The Personal Feelings Booklet: A measure of treatment outcome. *JSAS Catalog of Selected Documents in Psychology, 8*(14), Ms. 1647.

Taynor, J. (1979). The Community Integration Scale: A measure of treatment outcome in the community. *JSAS Catalog of Selected Documents in Psychology, 9,* Ms. 1971.

Taynor, J., Perry, J., & Frederick, P. (1976). A brief program to upgrade the skills of community caregivers. *Community Mental Health Journal, 12,* 13–19.

Taynor, J., & Schwartz, J. (1979). *Assessing treatment outcome in community mental health centers.* Workshop IV. Paper presented at the Evaluation Research Society, Third Annual Meeting, Minneapolis.

Taynor, J., & Schwartz, J. (1986). *Evaluation overview: A seven-year study.* Report to the Medical Director of Greene Memorial Hospital Mental Health Unit, Xenia, Ohio.

Wynne, L. C. (1984, October). *Definable problems in family therapy efficacy research.* Paper presented at the NIMH Conference on the State of the Art in Family Therapy Research, Rockville, MD.

A Computerized Assessment System for Brief, Crisis-Oriented Youth Services

Cynthia Franklin, Jack Nowicki,
John Trapp, A. James Schwab,
and Jerene Petersen

24

I ncreasingly, social service agencies are basing services on models that require social workers to provide rapid assessments and brief crisis interventions to their clients (Franklin & Jordan, 1992; Mattaini & Kirk, 1991; O'Hare, 1991; Tolson, 1990). Brief interventions have complicated the utilization of comprehensive assessment protocols, single-system methodology, and other traditional approaches to assessment and practice evaluation in social work practice. However, recent innovations in collecting data on brief interventions have suggested ways to collect data with assessment tools as a major source of information.

O'Hare (1991) described a clinical–administrative framework for developing and implementing an eclectic, empirically based model for assessment, monitoring, and evaluating brief clinical practice activities. The framework encompasses empirical clinical assessments, including checklists, scales, and other measures to be administered pre- and postintervention; participation of the clinical staff in designing or selecting practice-relevant assessment measures; collaboration between clinician and clients in defining specific, measurable, and achievable intervention goals; and the collection of assessment and outcome information for the purpose of developing a database for program evaluation.

Computerized assessment models have also been suggested as a method for collecting outcome information in the context of brief assessments (Nurius & Hudson, 1993). In addition, computers provide the technology necessary to implement, in a practice agency, empirical assessments such as those mentioned in the aforementioned clinical–administrative framework. Computers simplify and enhance assessment in social work (Gingerich, 1990; Krueger & Ruckdeschel, 1985) and have been widely demonstrated to be effective tools for assessment in clinical psychology and marriage and family therapy (Ben-Porath & Butcher, 1986; Butcher, Keller, & Bacon, 1985; Erdman & Foster, 1986; Kratochwill, Doll, & Dickson, 1985; Moreland, 1985; Murphy & Pardeck, 1986; Roid, 1985; Snyder, Lachar, & Wills, 1988).

For agencies to benefit fully from computerized assessment technologies, professionals involved in the computerized assessment field as well as those involved in information-systems management have recommended integrating the goals of administrative information needs and clinically relevant assessment and practice-evaluation activities (Grasso & Epstein, 1988; Hudson, 1990; Mutschler & Hasenfeld, 1986; Nurius & Hudson, 1988; Nurius & Hudson, 1989a, 1989b; Nurius, Hooyman, & Nicoll, 1988; Skinner & Pakula, 1986). For example, Skinner and Pakula (1986) suggested that computers can be used to develop multifunctional systems that integrate the administrative and clinical interpretation of tests with related functions of information office management.

Nurius and Hudson (1989a) outlined tasks for building linkages between computer technology and service effectiveness. Tasks include

> 1. defining the organization (and service) purpose, 2. defining the organizational (and service) outcomes or productivity, 3. creating measures of outcomes and productivity, 4. setting standards and formatting reports that enhance interpretation and thus utility of the information (p. 73).

According to these authors, the steps needed to develop an integrative computerized assessment and database system are consistent with and mirror the tasks that a clinical practitioner would use to develop a thorough assessment.

Computerized assessment systems that integrate clinical assessment and administrative needs appear to have been delayed by the lack of practice-relevant information systems. Some authorities in the field have suggested that this delay in the development of integrative computerized assessment systems may be explained by the fact that most developers of agency information-management systems have been computer specialists, not clinicians. The developers of computerized systems therefore have not been sensitive to the needs of clinical assessment and practice (Blythe & Briar, 1985; Grasso & Epstein, 1988; Mutschler & Cnaan, 1985; Nurius, 1990a). A few exceptions exist, such as the Computer Assisted Social Services (CASS) developed by Hudson (Hudson, 1989; Nurius & Hudson, 1989b) and the Boysville Management Information System (BOMIS) developed by Boysville, a child and family service agency in Michigan (Grasso & Epstein, 1988). However, only a few models effectively integrate computerized information systems with clinical assessment.

In order for agencies to develop integrative computerized assessment systems that can be used in brief interventions, clinicians, administrators, and computer specialists must work together. Clients also need to offer their input. The research data, however, indicate that clients adjust well to and even prefer computerized assessment systems but that practitioners resist using them (Nurius, 1990b). Clinician resistance has been attributed to the failure of existing data-management systems to provide clinicians with immediate feedback or help with their clinical work as well as to the reluctance of administrators and computer specialists to reckon with the expertise and needs of clinicians in designing computerized data-management systems (Nurius, 1990b).

Few models exist for development or implementation of integrative computerized assessment systems. Agencies, therefore, are left without specific examples to follow in their desire to develop combined computerized assessment and database systems. Bronson and Blythe (1987) suggested that persons knowledgeable about social work practice are ideal specialists for developing computerized database systems. Some experts have suggested schools of social work as important "players" that may fulfill a significant function in the development of practice-relevant technologies (Bronson & Blythe, 1987; Franklin & McNeil, 1992).

This article reports on an integrative computerized assessment system developed for a youth-services agency. The Middle Earth Computerized Assessment System (MECAS) was developed to be compatible with the brief, crisis-oriented interventions delivered by the agency. The MECAS was designed to provide empirical clinical assessments and to collect data on client characteristics and outcomes; it is similar to and consistent with the clinical–administrative framework described by O'Hare (1991). In the following sections, this system is described and illustrated with a case example from the agency. In addition, the development of MECAS is discussed to highlight a process that can be used in establishing similar integrative computerized assessment systems. Development of the system incorporated the tasks for developing integrative computer assessment systems as summarized by Nurius and Hudson (1989a).

Background and Setting

Middle Earth Unlimited, Inc., is a nonprofit youth agency serving multiproblem youth and families. The agency operates several programs, including a shelter program, family counseling center, alternative school, and school-based services program. The agency budget for 1992 was $1.6 million. An outpatient counseling center component of Middle Earth, known as the Counseling Center (CC), was used to pilot MECAS. Funding for this project was provided by a grant from the Travis County Counseling Center and the Department of Health and Human Services Drug and Alcohol Prevention Program.

The CC was established as a support service of the emergency shelter in order to divert youth from shelter care. Clinical practitioners work to resolve family conflicts and disruptions that could lead to an adolescent's separation from his or her family. The work with adolescents and parents is brief, solution-focused, and based on a crisis-intervention model. Youth and families are seen an average of four times in the CC. The CC provides crisis counseling for a range of problems that, if untreated, may lead to adolescents running away from home or being separated from their family. Problems include family conflict, truancy, drug or alcohol abuse, physical or sexual abuse, emotional problems, and gang activity. Referrals are made to other agencies for longer-term interventions when such interventions are needed.

Clinical practitioners and administrators at the CC wanted to design an assessment system that could provide empirical data on the characteristics of youth and families and could be used to monitor the effectiveness of the brief-intervention services provided by the agency. Both clinicians and administrators were interested in feedback regarding client characteristics and practice evaluation, but from different perspectives. Administrators were compelled to document the need for and evaluation of their services because of demands for accountability and the increasingly competitive environment of nonprofit funding. Clinicians, on the other hand, were more interested in finding a better way to conduct assessments and to receive feedback on their clinical work with clients.

Administrators believed that total restructuring and computerization of data-collection efforts were necessary to establish more effective and efficient means for collecting and reporting assessment and practice-evaluation data. Administrators contracted with faculty of the University of Texas at Austin School of Social Work to help accomplish this restructuring and computerization effort.

Procedures

The agency formulated a work group consisting of one administrative staff member, a clinical administrative supervisor, a clinical practitioner, one clinical faculty member trained in clinical assessment and practice-evaluation methods, and one computer technologist who had experience in automating social service agencies. Peer leaders who had been former agency clients were also asked to provide continual feedback on the developing system, as were support staff who would be using the system.

Members of the work group clarified agency needs and sought to design a system to meet those needs. An important goal was to design a system that practitioners could easily utilize to assist with assessment and practice-evaluation activities. The group operated from the assumptions that a computerized assessment system would (1) simplify agency record keeping and reporting, (2) give clinical staff tools in order to perform assessments, (3) enhance staff motivation for collecting data by giving them a method for immediate clinical feedback, (4) provide a mechanism that could produce data for funding sources, and (5) generate hypotheses about effective interventions for particular presenting problems.

Initially, the work group met twice a month for three months to define agency goals and needs. The computer technologist did not attend these early meetings. However, the clinical faculty member kept the technologist abreast of the issues. In addition, the clinical faculty member worked with the agency to develop an integrative method for collecting assessment information and guided it through the process of selecting outcome measures and developing structured forms for data collection. After three months, the work group began to meet once a month for approximately eight months in order to complete the computerized assessment system. In the final several months of the development of the system, the computer technologist participated in the meetings together with a second computer technologist.

As the work group met to discuss and plan how the proposed system could be implemented, the clinical supervisor met with clinicians to analyze the existing assessment system. Clinical staff recommendations served as the basis for proposing changes that would be incorporated in the new assessment system. Clinical staff coined watchwords for the system they wanted: a system that would specify, simplify, and quantify. The work group and clinical staff agreed on three outcomes that were relevant to agency clients and, therefore, were important to measure: (1) improvement in family functioning, (2) decreases in substance use and abuse, and (3) specific behavioral outcomes that could be individualized from client to client. In addition, the work group and clinical staff agreed that an operational, outcome-oriented treatment plan was desirable for each client and that three other structured forms were necessary to meet the requirements of funding sources and agency operational procedures. These forms and the assessment system will be illustrated in the case example.

Assessment Measures

Three standardized rapid-assessment measures and a self-anchored-scale approach were chosen by the work group. The group understood that not all three measures would be used in every case but posited that at least one measure should be used in each case and a self-anchored scale should also be developed for each case. The clinical practitioner who was responsible for individualizing the assessment would decide which measure(s) to use.

FACES III

The Family Adaptability and Cohesion Scale III (FACES III) is a standardized 20-item self-report instrument that attempts to operationalize the Circumplex Model of Marital and Family Systems. Originally, the Circumplex Model was developed as a curvilinear model to classify family functioning along three major dimensions—family cohesion (bonding), family adaptability (flexibility), and communication (Olson, Portner, & Lavee, 1985). However, it was recently rescored and interpreted as a linear model (Olson, 1991; Olson & Tiesel, 1991). The new linear FACES III or Three-Dimensional (3-D) Circumplex Model was developed to address previous issues concerning the validity of the measure's constructs.

The FACES III 3-D Circumplex Model measures the cohesion and flexibility dimensions of family systems. Each dimension is measured on an eight-point continuum ranging from low cohesion (disengaged) to high cohesion (very connected) and from low flexibility (rigid) to high flexibility (very flexible). With the linear interpretation of FACES III, high scores on cohesion and adaptability are conceptualized as measuring balanced family types, and low scores on these two dimensions indicate extreme family types.

Family Satisfaction Inventory

The Family Satisfaction Inventory (FSI) is a 14-item standardized measure that was developed to measure satisfaction across the Circumplex Model. The main hypothesis of the Circumplex Model is that balanced families function more adequately. However, this model fails to take into account cultural life-cycle dimensions and normative expectations of different families. The FSI takes into account such variables and assesses satisfaction with one's family regardless of its level of functioning. Satisfaction is believed to be a more incremental measure than structure or functions in families and, therefore, may be more sensitive to brief, crisis-oriented interventions. Construct validity for the FSI has been established by means of factor analysis. Internal consistency reliability has also been demonstrated with alphas of .86 for subscales and .90 for the total scale (Olson & Wilson, 1982).

Personal Experience Screening Questionnaire

Drug use was measured by means of the Personal Experience Screening Questionnaire (PESQ). The PESQ is a 38-item self-report screening questionnaire for use with adolescents suspected of using drugs. Content covered includes (1) drug-use problem severity (18 items), (2) drug-use frequency (4 items), (3) other mental health and behavior problems (8 items), (4) defensiveness/faking good (5 items), and (5) infrequency/faking bad inattention (3 items). Internal consistency reliability is .90–.94. Construct and criteria validity have also been established with studies of substance abusers, juvenile offenders, and school samples (Winters, 1988).

Self-Anchored Scales

Self-anchored scales were selected as a method for measuring individualized behavior problems. Self-anchored scales are "do-it-yourself" scales constructed by the client and practitioner. The scales exist on a seven-point continuum and are developed with anchors that are concrete and operationalized dimensions of the client's presenting problems as identified in their service plan (Bloom & Fischer, 1982; Jordan & Franklin, in press). Practitioners develop these scales together with the client in the first session. A reconstructed baseline is encouraged for gaining a more consistent picture of the client's functioning historically and across time.

Training

After the work group finalized measurement instruments and structured forms, which were reworked by clinical staff, and selected a structure and format for conducting assessments, the clinical staff were trained in all facets of the new assessment structure. Clinical staff began using the new assessment structure and provided feedback on needed changes during staff meetings. After staff agreed they were comfortable with the assessment structure, the clinical faculty member was brought in to do more specific training in practice assessments and evaluation. Specific training was provided for the clinical use of the four new measurement instruments selected by the work group. Practitioners were encouraged to begin gradually to use the instruments to enhance their assessment skills. In the beginning, the measurement instruments were administered to clients at intake by clerical staff and results were included in the practitioner's case records. The practitioners were asked to score the forms manually and to use the information to understand family functioning and to guide subsequent interventions. Simultaneously, discussion of how to use self-anchored scales to quantify and measure service objectives became a part of every clinical staff meeting. Training was provided by the clinical supervisor on how to develop the self-anchored scales. Clinical staff members were given the option of using the new system concurrently with the old, specifically with regard to the self-anchored scales. During the next few months, staff were slowly encouraged to score and use the information from their measurement instruments and also to create self-anchored scales for all their cases.

During this period, management and the clinical administrator offered only positive feedback about using the measures and new assessment structure. As practitioners used the new structure and discovered many ways in which they could use the information it generated, the work group reviewed and finalized the computer version of the assessment structure. When the first version of the computer system was installed, data-entry and clinical staff were trained to use the computer to build a database and to produce graphics illustrating the results of the measurement instruments. Staff were encouraged to use the computer because computer scoring of measures was much easier and the graphics clearly showed clinical patterns and progress in practice efforts with clients.

Computer System Development

The MECAS was designed to run on a 68030 CPU series Macintosh computer with a hard disk drive. The program was developed with a relational database management system called FoxBase+/Mac. FoxBase was chosen for several reasons: (1) it is a fast relational database system; (2) the dBASE III® clone language is well known, allowing program modifications and support independent of the original programmers; (3) FoxBase provides programming routines consistent with Macintosh user interface guidelines; and (4) FoxBase has a Runtime module allowing the program to run without the agency having to purchase the FoxBase+/Mac application.

Computer technologists were also social work practitioners, which offered an important advantage in MECAS development. The integration of computer technology into social work practice involves a process not unlike the introduction of an alternative clinical assessment or therapy strategy. Technologists must provide not only technical support and knowledge, but they must be sensitive to the issues and impact of the new technology on the agency. The following sections provide summaries of some of the issues and discussions that arose during the collaborative project and subsequent program testing sessions. Discussion illustrates the types of issues that need to be addressed in the development and implementation of a computerized system. For convenience, issues are grouped into client, clinical, and administrative concerns; however, the same issues can and should be examined from each participant's perspective.

Client Concerns

For the agency's clients, the introduction of the new technology raised issues of confidentiality, accessibility, and dehumanization. Confidentiality was addressed in decisions about the physical location of the computer system, who would have access to the computer, and what types of information would be password protected within MECAS. Client accessibility to their own information was less of an issue because the system was designed to hold client information supplied voluntarily, such as demographics, and assessment data accessible through the practitioners. The argument that computerization of client records can be dehumanizing was addressed in the work group and among the clinical practitioners by carefully considering the wording on data-collection instruments and category coding. Decisions about the types of information that would be collected were made with client concerns in mind. Also, staff recognized that the ultimate purpose of the system is to enhance client services.

Staff Concerns

The concerns of the clinical staff for the most part echoed the results of research focusing on clinician resistance to computerized data collection (Nurius, 1990b). The driving questions for these users were how much extra work the system involved and how MECAS was relevant to practice. Active participation of the clinical staff in the design of MECAS assured their support and understanding of empirical assessment as a means of enhancing service effectiveness. The technologists and administrators tried to alleviate work-load concerns by engaging clinicians in discussions about computer anxiety, by having them identify data-collection needs and data-entry strategies, and by designing a user-friendly system with on-screen directions, immediate feedback mechanisms, and a consistent user interface.

Administrative Concerns

Administrative concerns focused on the mechanics of the actual program: the ease of transition from the existing information system, data integrity, system maintenance, and future expansion. To simplify the transition to the new system and to aid in user training, the flow of the program, data coding, entry screens, and reports were designed to match the existing information system. Data integrity was ensured by error checking, maintenance, and backup schemes built into the program. Also, an expert module was included to accommodate speedy direct entry for a trained entry person. Future expansion is an important

---

ID number: 000906A01   Date: 03/04/91

Client name: Last name: First name: N   Initial:

Services:

03/04/91	Crisis Counseling	Hours: 2.00	Staff: JN	Kept: Y
03/12/91	Family Counseling	Hours: 1.50	Staff: JN	Kept: Y
03/19/91	Family Counseling	Hours: 1.25	Staff: JN	Kept: Y
03/26/91	Family Counseling	Hours: 1.00	Staff: JN	Kept Y
04/02/91	Family Counseling	Hours: 0.00	Staff: JN	Kept: C
04/09/91	Family Counseling	Hours: 1.00	Staff: JN	Kept: Y

Service entry:

05/17/92   Hours: 0 ..00   Staff:

Appointment kept: Y=Yes / C=Cancel

Accept entry   Cancel

Figure 1. Counseling log.

Important: Please fill out for shelter residents:

Full name: N

Case #:

Types: INT = Intake, IC = Individual, SO = Significant other, CC = Crisis, FC = Family, GC = Group, CM = Case management, OB = Observe

Date	Hours	Type	Fund	Description
03/04/91	2.0	CC	Rat/Fee	Mom & N in for crisis session. According to mom, N scratches and bites mom when they argue with each other. Last incident was when N wanted to go to subway and mom said no. They fought and mom finally walked away from situation. Mom very concerned about where and with whom N goes whenever she is out. These fights occur every other month or so. N wants to learn to control temper—she loses it when she is told no by mom. Plan: 1. Work w/ mom and N on N showing mom she is more responsible. 2. Share information w/ mom about teen development. 3. Help mom/N negotiate agreement. 4. Help N control temper and become more assertive.
03/12/91	1.5	FC	Rat/Fee	Mom and N in for session. They maintained their agreement not to fight physically last week, but their yelling arguments increased dramatically. Developed self-anchored scale for fighting. Explained to mom/daughter about power struggles and how it is impossible for parents to win them. According to N, she argued with mom this week because mom won't let her stay with a friend overnight during spring break. Also, this week is her birthday and N believes that mom should let her stay overnight on her B-day. During the session, mom decided that she would allow N to spend night with L in exchange for mom getting to take N out to dinner for her birthday *and* N's promise that she would work on controlling her temper. At end of session, mom brought up that she was angry that N had had a boy visit at the house today. N replied that it was really D and that she'd lied to mom earlier. Now she tells the truth because mom called her a slut. *Homework:* 1. N to call D and tell him she doesn't want him to come to her house when mom's not there. 2. N should write down what happens when she loses her temper.

Date	Hours	Code		Notes
03/19/91	1.25	FC	Rat/Fee	Session w/ mom and N. Last week better. N made it through the rest of spring break w/ no problems. Spent time working on N's temper. Talked about the process of N losing her temper and how she does it, specifically. It appears there is an auditory cue, "Gripe, gripe, gripe." *Homework:* 1. N must lose temper 5x in next week and each time change auditory submodality to examine its effect on temper. 2. If she and mom have a *real* fight, N to discuss her responses and program for losing her temper.
03/26/91	1.0	FC	Rat/Fee	N and mom in for a session. N reports losing temper 3x last week. Changed response to auditory stimuli and didn't yell. Talked about what she can do to expel energy, since she isn't yelling anymore. N said walking helps—she is walking w/ mom and their roommate. N said she thinks that not a lot of negative energy has built up. Also talked to N about boyfriend—cooling it now. Talked to mom about learning to let go a little so that N can learn by experience. Both have reservations about discontinuing counseling. *Next:* 1. I-statement to describe feelings. 2. Reflective listening. 3. Natural/logical consequences. 4. Check last homework.
04/02/91		CNX		
04/09/91	1.0	FC	Rat/Fee	Last session. Reviewed progress. Covered today's topic areas and talked about what N and mom can do in future to deal w/ problems themselves.
05/15/91		CM	Rat/Fee	Close case.

Figure 2. Counseling log with case notes.

issue for agencies, especially given questions concerning ownership of the data. For example, can the agency retrieve its information from the program without the original programmers? One reason FoxBase was chosen is that the database structure has an open storage format, allowing access to the data from a variety of applications independent of the program code. In addition, the reporting structure of the program was designed with a generic approach that exports all data items into text files for easy incorporation into specific agency documents.

Case Example

The following case example illustrates the use of MECAS. Case information is reported in the abbreviated form that exists in the agency records and also the format of MECAS.

Client history: Referral: Single Hispanic mom called for help with her 14-year-old daughter, N, who is physically attacking mom when she doesn't get her way. Mom also reported that daughter has run away from home two times and skips school. Daughter is a good student and has a boyfriend. Mom employed and

FACES III for N			
Adapt-ability	Cohesion		
	Pretest Disen Separ Conne VConn	Posttest Disen Separ Conne VConn	Follow-up Disen Separ Conne VConn
Rigid Struc Flex VFlex	C M	M C	

Codes: C = Client   F = Father   M = Mother   S = Sibling   O = Other
Disen = Disengaged   Sep = Separated   Conne = Connected   VConn = Very connected
Rigid = Rigid   Struc = Structured   Flex = Flexible   VFlex = Very flexible

Family type		
Pretest Extre MidRa ModBa Balan CM	Posttest Extre MidRa ModBa Balan CM	Follow-up Extre MidRa ModBa Balan

Extre = Extreme   MidRa = Mid-range   ModBa = Moderately balanced   Balan = Balanced

FACES III for N					
Relation	Time period	Cohesion		Adaptability	
		Score	Type	Score	Type	Family Type
Client	Pretest	36	3	21	3	3
Client	Posttest	41	5	32	7	6
Mother	Pretest	22	1	26	5	3
Mother	Posttest	38	4	29	6	5

Figure 3. Computerized and graphic scoring of the FACES III.

Family cohesion				
	Client	Mother	Father	Sibling	Other
%tile	Pre Pos Fol	Pre Pos Fol	Pre Pos Fol	Pre Pos Fol	Pre Pos Fol
76–100	•				
51–75	•	•			
26–50					
1–25		•			

Family adaptability				
	Client	Mother	Father	Sibling	Other
%tile	Pre Pos Fol	Pre Pos Fol	Pre Pos Fol	Pre Pos Fol	Pre Pos Fol
76–100	•				
51–75		•			
26–50	•				
1–25		•			

Total family satisfaction				
	Client	Mother	Father	Sibling	Other
%tile	Pre Pos Fol	Pre Pos Fol	Pre Pos Fol	Pre Pos Fol	Pre Pos Fol
76–100	•				
51–75	•	•			
26–50					
1–25		•			

Family Satisfaction Scale scores for N						
Relation	Time period	Family cohesion		Family adaptability		Total satisfaction	
		Score	%tile	Score	%tile	Score	%tile
Client	Pretest	29	67	18	34	47	52
Client	Posttest	33	91	25	91	58	91
Mother	Pretest	20	4	15	7	35	1
Mother	Posttest	29	67	21	64	50	64

Key: %tile = Percentile, Pre = Pretest, Pos = Posttest, Fol = Follow-up

Figure 4. Family Satisfaction Scale for N.

successfully running household consisting of herself, daughter, and an unrelated female friend needing a temporary place to stay.

The computerized assessment and database system stores all information that is relevant to the clinical management of the case. Figures 1

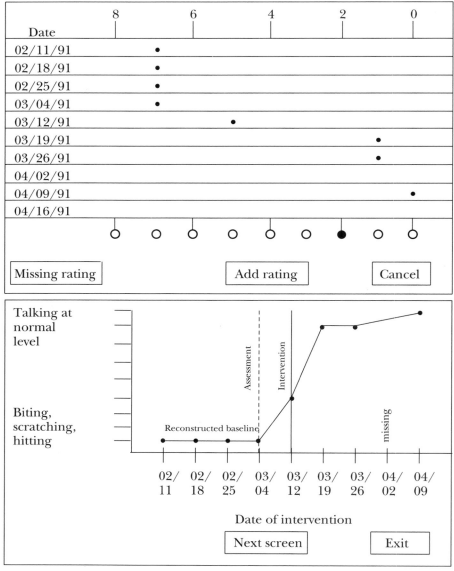

Figure 5. Self-anchored scale: N/mom level of disagreements.

and 2 provide examples of the contact information, known as a counselor log, completed on the teenage client in this family. Figure 1 illustrates the contact information kept in the database and Figure 2 the clinical case notes on the case.

Figure 3 illustrates the computerized and graphic scoring of the FACES III, and Figure 4 the computerized scoring of the Family Satisfaction Inventory at assessment and at end of treatment. The PESQ was not

2-21-91	Initial call for counseling
3-4-91	1st session FACES III Family Satisfaction Inventory Self-anchored scale Plan: 1. Mom and N learn to discuss disagreements without yelling or hitting. 2. Teach N more effective ways to get what she wants. 3. Teach N to control temper. *Homework:* No physical fighting.
3-12-91	2nd session Discussed arguments over week. Negotiated exchange. N spend night for Mom taking her out to dinner on B-day. *Homework:* 1. N to write down what happens when she loses temper. 2. N to tell boyfriend she doesn't want him coming over when mom isn't home.
3-19-91	Discussed last week. Doing better. Worked on N's temper—process she goes through. (The program she knows.) Determined there are auditory cues. Changed submodality. *Homework:* 1. N must lose temper 5x and do it differently. 2. Document fights w/ Mom.
3-26-91	Report. N. Lost temper 3x w/o yelling, walking off anger instead.
4-9-91	Worked on I-statements, reflective listening, natural/logical consequences. No further temper losses. Mom satisfied and better able to communicate/negotiate w/ N.

Figure 6. Treatment summary.

administered in this case. The graphic presentation of the assessment information makes the scoring user friendly to practitioners. Positive changes in the client are visible in the improvements in scores between the assessment and postintervention, indicating the system's clinical monitoring capacities.

A self-anchored scale (Fig. 5) was constructed to assess the level of disagreements between client and mother across time. The scale is also presented in graphic form, tracking the occurrences of the client's problem from week to week. More than one scale may be constructed, if desired.

Finally, Figure 6 illustrates a closing treatment summary on the client. All measures and data-collection forms are related to the assessment and clinical monitoring of the case.

Summary and Conclusion

An integrative computerized assessment system was developed for a crisis-oriented youth agency with the help of a school of social work. This agency's experience may serve as an example for other agencies to create integrative systems that meet the needs of practitioners, administrators, and clients. As of January 1993, the computerized system has been operational for approximately one year and is currently serving the agency's needs. It continues to be updated and revised as needed, although the basic structure remains the same. The agency's goals are to transform their computerized assessment system into a database that can provide data for funding sources and to help guide decisions concerning practice activities. In addition, future plans, contingent upon funding, call for expanding the computerized assessment system to the shelter services and other programs of the agency.

The development of MECAS provides valuable experience in designing integrative computerized database systems for social service agencies. Consistent with the literature on this subject, MECAS (1) demonstrates the important roles that schools of social work may have in the development of practice-relevant technology (Bronson & Blythe, 1987); (2) demonstrates that computerized systems can serve multiple functions and meet the needs of clinicians and administrators (Skinner & Pakula, 1986); and (3) affirms that Nurius and Hudson (1989a) may be correct that computerized clinical assessment aids service effectiveness. This is evident in that MECAS is nothing more than an empirically based, computerized clinical-assessment system with the capacity to serve multiple data functions within the agency environment. Acceptance of MECAS by clinical practitioners provides further evidence that the key to developing effective and efficient database systems may be found in computerized clinical-assessment systems.

Finally, MECAS demonstrates that computerized assessment technologies can turn the clinical–administrative framework discussed by

O'Hare (1991) into a workable solution for data collecting and providing a database on brief interventions. Developing mutual goals on the part of both administrators and clinicians and maintaining a consensus in the agency concerning the components of the computerized assessment system were important tasks in the successful development of this system. Essentially, this type of information-management system was created through a combination of "bottom up" and "top down" management approaches. Those on the bottom were allowed to make decisions about MECAS and to become involved in the development of the system. The group processes used to establish the system are consistent with the tenets of quality management and the participatory strategy that was used helped establish staff "ownership" of the database system (Franklin, in press). At the same time, agency administrators set the direction and provided a guiding philosophy of service effectiveness to anchor the restructuring effort. This process is consistent with the tasks suggested by Nurius and Hudson (1989a) for the development of integrative computer-based assessment systems.

Thus, MECAS was developed through a participatory decision-making and group planning process that resulted in both clinicians and administrators having a personal investment in the system. This sense of personal ownership was extremely helpful during the implementation phase of the system, in that motivation and commitment were maintained through the difficult transition to using a new system. Clinicians liked the system because they helped develop it and because MECAS provided useful clinical assessment and outcome-monitoring information.

Steps for Developing a Computerized Assessment System

Based on our experience, the following steps may serve as guidelines for agencies wishing to develop a computerized assessment system.

1. Obtain a commitment from the top administrators and board for developing a database system that will restructure agency intake procedures, assessment, and data-collection methods.

2. Set aside or secure funds and personnel release time to accomplish this task. Planning and preparation may take at least one year of committed effort. Each agency should calculate its own cost in both time and funds.

3. Obtain the commitment of clinical administrators and staff for building a new intake, assessment, and clinical evaluation system that uses computer technology.

4. Construct an agency team that represents the multiple constituencies of administrators, clinicians, support staff, and clients.

5. Contract with an outside facilitation team that can guide the process and has the clinical and technical expertise to help develop the computerized assessment system.

6. Establish a process for consensus building, participatory input, and decision making. Ask for feedback on each step of the system's development from clinical staff and other users, such as clients. Modify the proposed system accordingly.

7. Define major service-delivery outcomes for client populations and identify or develop assessment measures, data-collection forms, and outcome indicators.

8. Develop a structure and process for assessment and data collection in conjunction with the uses of assessment measures and data collection-forms. This structure should become a routine part of the clinical process in the agency.

9. Automate the system and obtain feedback on its user friendliness. Improve the system on the basis of user feedback.

10. Provide ongoing and systematic training in use of the new assessment system. Accept ongoing feedback about improvements.

11. Develop a plan for incremental implementation of the assessment system, with rewards and positive feedback for usage. Build in feedback loops after each step of implementation.

12. Be flexible with and supportive of staff during implementation. Constantly reevaluate and modify the computerized assessment system in relationship to the needs of clinicians and clients.

These 12 steps provided guidelines for the successful development of MECAS and illustrate the links by which clinical assessment and practice and agency administrative processes are integrated. Computerized clinical-assessment systems may provide the practice technologies whereby the integration of these functions can be operationalized.

REFERENCES

Ben-Porath, Y. S., & Butcher, J. N. (1986). Computers in personality assessment: A brief past, an ebullient present, and an expanding future. *Computers in Human Behavior, 2,* 167–182.

Bloom, M., & Fischer, J. (1982). *Evaluating practice: Guidelines for the accountable professional.* Englewood Cliffs, NJ: Prentice-Hall.

Blythe, B. J., & Briar, S. (1985). Developing empirically based models of practice. *Social Work, 30,* 483–488.

Bronson, D. E., & Blythe, B. J. (1987). Computer support for single-case evaluation of practice. *Social Work Research and Abstracts, 23*(3), 10–13.

Butcher, J. N., Keller, L. S., & Bacon, S. F. (1985). Current developments and future directions in computerized personality assessment. *Journal of Consulting and Clinical Psychology, 53,* 573–580.

Erdman, H. P., & Foster, S. W. (1986). Computer-assisted assessment with couples and families. *Family Therapy, 13*(1), 23–40.

Franklin, C. (in press). Assessment centers for children: A promise worth considering. In Eileen Gambrill (Ed.), *Controversies in child welfare.* Boston: Allyn and Bacon.

Franklin, C., & Jordan, C. (1992). Teaching students to perform assessment. *Journal of Social Work Education, 28,* 222–241.

Franklin, C., & McNeil, J. S. (1992). The Cassata project: A school–agency partnership for practice research integration. *Arete, 17*(1), 47–52.

Gingerich, W. J. (1990). Expert systems and their potential uses in social work. *Families in Society, 71,* 220–228.

Grasso, A. J., & Epstein, I. (1988). The Boysville experience: Integrating practice decision-making, program evaluation, and management information. *Computers in Human Services 4,* 85–94.

Hudson, W. W. (1989). *Computer assisted social services.* Tempe, AZ: Walmyr.

Hudson, W. W. (1990). Computer-based clinical practice: Present statistics and future possibilities. In L. Videka-Sherman & W. J. Reid (Ed.), *Advances in clinical social work research* (pp. 105–117). Silver Spring, MD: National Association of Social Workers.

Jordan, C., & Franklin, C. (in press). *Clinical assessment.* Chicago: Lyceum Books.

Kratochwill, T. R., Doll, E. J., & Dickson, W. P. (1985). Microcomputers in behavioral assessment: Recent advances and remaining issues. *Computers in Human Behavior, 1,* 277–291.

Krueger, L. W., & Ruckdeschel, R. (1985). Microcomputers in social service settings: Research applications. *Social Work, 30,* 219–224.

Mattaini, M., & Kirk, S. (1991). Assessing assessment in social work. *Social Work, 36,* 260–266.

Moreland, K. L. (1985). Computer-assisted psychological assessment in 1986: A practical guide. *Computers in Human Behavior, 1,* 221–233.

Murphy, J. W., & Pardeck, J. T. (1986). Computerized clinical practice: Promises and short-comings. *Psychological Reports, 59,* 1099–1113.

Mutschler, E., & Cnaan, R. A. (1985). Success and failure of computerized information systems: Two case studies and human service agencies. *Administration in Social Work, 9,* 67–79.

Mutschler, E., & Hasenfeld, Y. (1986). Integrated information systems for social work practice. *Social Work, 37,* 345–349.

Nurius, P. S. (1990a). A review of automated assessment. *Computers in Human Services, 6,* 265–281.

Nurius, P. S. (1990b). Computer literacy in automated assessment: Challenges and future directions. *Computers in Human Services, 6,* 283–297.

Nurius, P., Hooyman, N., & Nicoll, A. E. (1988). The changing face of computer utilization in social work settings. *Journal of Social Work Education, 2,* 186–197.

Nurius, P. S., & Hudson, W. W. (1988). Computer-based practice: Future dream or current technology? *Social Work, 33,* 357–362.

Nurius, P. S., & Hudson, W. W. (1989a). Workers, clients, and computers. *Computers in Human Services, 4,* 71–83.

Nurius, P. S., & Hudson, W. W. (1989b). Computers and social diagnosis: The client's perspective. *Computers in Human Services, 5,* 21–35.

Nurius, P. S., & Hudson, W. W. (1993). *Human services: Practice evaluation and computers.* Pacific Grove, CA: Brooks Cole.

O'Hare, T. M. (1991). Integrating research and practice: A framework for implementation. *Social Work, 36,* 220–223.

Olson, D. H. (1991). Commentary: Three-dimensional (3-D) Circumplex Model and revised scoring of FACES III. *Family Process, 30,* 74–79.

Olson, D. H., Portner, J., & Lavee, Y. (1985). *FACES III manual.* St. Paul, MN: Department of Family Social Science, University of Minnesota.

Olson, D. H., & Tiesel, J. (1991). *FACES III-Linear scoring and interpretation.* St. Paul, MN: Department of Family Social Science, University of Minnesota.

Olson, D. H., & Wilson, M. (1982). *Family satisfaction.* St. Paul, MN: Department of Family Social Science, University of Minnesota.

341

Roid, G. H. (1985). Computer-based test interpretation: The potential of quantitative methods of test interpretation. *Computers in Human Behavior, 1,* 207–219.

Skinner, H. A., & Pakula, A. (1986). Challenge of computers in psychological assessment. *Professional Psychology: Research and Practice, 17,* 44–50.

Snyder, D. K., Lachar, D., & Wills, R. M. (1988). Computer-based interpretation of the marital satisfaction inventory: Use in treatment planning. *Journal of Marital and Family Therapy, 14,* 397–409.

Tolson, E. R. (1990). Why don't practitioners use single-subject designs. In L. Videka-Sherman & W. J. Reid (Eds.), *Advances in clinical social work research* (pp. 58–66). Silver Spring, MD: National Association of Social Workers.

Winters, K. (1988). *Personal experience screen questionnaire (PESQ) manual.* Los Angeles, CA: Western Psychological Services.

Part 5

Assessment and Ethnic Diversity

Clinical Diagnosis among Diverse Populations: A Multicultural Perspective

Alison Solomon

25

$\mathbb{C}$linicians often assume that issues of discrimination and the improvement of services to minority clients will be addressed by professionals whose work is policy oriented. It is imperative, however, that clinicians who provide direct service to people of all racial and ethnic backgrounds examine their own practice with minority clients.

Much has been written about the treatment of minorities in the psychotherapeutic relationship (Hines & Boyd-Franklin, 1982; Boyd-Franklin, 1989; Bryant, 1980; Canino & Canino, 1982; de Anda, 1984; Jue, 1987; Pinderhughes, 1982). Before clients enter into such a relationship, however, they are evaluated and diagnosed. This diagnosis is key to the type of treatment they will subsequently receive. Moreover, once a psychiatric label is attached to a client, it often sticks. Thus, a diagnosis of schizophrenia is not usually changed, even if the person no longer shows symptoms of the illness. The schizophrenia is considered in remission, but the person is not considered cured of the illness. It is crucial, therefore, that clinicians become aware not only of racial and cultural bias in the *treatment* of minority members but also of racial and ethnic biases inherent in present forms of psychiatric *diagnosis.*

This chapter highlights and discusses differences in psychiatric diagnoses applied to various racial and ethnic groups. The focus is primarily on instances in which the differences are caused by misdiagnosis. Ways to minimize misdiagnosis are suggested.

Cultural Differences in the Literature

Researchers have described various diagnoses that appear to be connected to the race, class, cultural background, or gender of the client:

- African Americans and Hispanics are more likely to be diagnosed with affective or personality disorders, whereas whites are more likely to be diagnosed with organic disorders (Hines & Boyd-Franklin, 1982; Jones, Gray, & Parson, 1983).
- African Americans and Hispanics are more likely to be misdiagnosed as schizophrenic when they are, in fact, suffering from bipolar affective disorder (Mukherjee, Shukla, & Woodle, 1983).
- African American children are diagnosed as hyperactive more often than are white children, who are, in turn, diagnosed as hyperactive more often than are Asian American children (Sata, 1990).
- Lower-class children are more frequently described in terms of psychosis and character disorder, whereas middle-class children are described as neurotic and normal (Harrison et al., 1965).
- When diagnosed with psychotic or affective disorders, minority clients are more likely to be labeled as having a chronic syndrome than an acute episode (Sata, 1990).
- Adult white males of all ages have a much lower rate of admission to outpatient psychiatric facilities than do white women and nonwhite men and women (Chesler, 1972).
- Research in the 1960s found a higher rate of schizophrenia among Puerto Ricans than among the general population (Padilla & Padilla, 1977).
- Puerto Ricans on the mainland are more likely to be diagnosed with mental illness than are Puerto Ricans in Puerto Rico. Depression is diagnosed more frequently in Puerto Ricans than among other Hispanic groups, including Cuban Americans and Mexican Americans (Canino, 1990).
- Alcohol abuse is at least four times more prevalent among Puerto Ricans in Puerto Rico than it is among the non-Puerto Rican population in the United States (Canino, 1990).
- Studies often show that Puerto Ricans use mental health resources at a higher rate than do non-Puerto Rican populations (Canino, 1990).

Findings such as these require explanations, which in some cases are readily available. For example, Padilla and Padilla (1977) explain the high rate of schizophrenia among Hispanics by the fact that the Hispanic population is poor and psychotic disorders are more prevalent among the poor. Social conditions, migration, prejudice, and language barriers make Hispanics more vulnerable to psychotic disorders. In a similar vein, Sedgewick (1982) notes that although the factor of racism should not be ignored, labels of psychopathology are social indicators of the stress experienced by populations that lack power; thus, we should expect the oppressed and underprivileged to show more psychopathology.

In addition, behavior that is considered "normal" in one country or ethnic group may be considered pathological or dysfunctional in another country or locale. For example, the consumption of large quantities of alcohol is considered more acceptable in Puerto Rico than it is in the United States. Thus, although alcoholism is a significant problem in Puerto Rico, fewer people are considered "dysfunctional alcoholics" there because Puerto Rican society makes allowances for heavy alcohol use (Canino, 1990).

Although explanations for diagnostic differences are sometimes reasonable, misdiagnosis often occurs. Four basic reasons for misdiagnosis are (1) cultural expression of symptomatology, (2) unreliable research instruments and evaluation inventories, (3) clinician bias and prejudice, and (4) institutional racism.

Cultural Expression of Symptomatology

People from different cultures express the same feelings in different ways. Conversely, they also express feelings in ways that may suggest different symptoms in different cultures. For example, in depression one feels unable to cope with daily life; individuals show depression by manifesting symptoms that contradict normal expressivity in a given culture or society. In a culture in which extroversion is valued, depression will be expressed as quiet, introverted behavior. In a culture in which subdued, less expressive behavior is valued, depression is indicated through acting-out behaviors. Moreover, if someone from an "introverted" culture acts out in American culture, he or she is likely to be misdiagnosed with mania or antisocial personality.

In some cultures, the division between psychological and somatic problems is less clearly delineated than it is in American culture. Canino (1988) cites research indicating that Mexicans do not dichotomize or separate emotional illness from somatic diseases. Thus various psychological or emotional disorders that are indicative of grief in Western societies—agitated depression, feelings of helplessness—may be manifested as somatic symptoms among Mexicans (Canino, 1988). Kleinman and Good (1985) note that Asian Indians and Iraqis often present to physicians with somatic complaints rather than affective ones (i.e., "my stomach hurts" rather than "I'm depressed").

Various religions and cultures have quite different ways of expressing grief, including what Westerners might term "hallucinations," "grandiosity," and "hearing voices." Such differences can lead to misdiagnosis. For example,

S, a Ghanian woman, presented to an outpatient psychiatry service with feelings of apathy, confusion, and depression. S and her husband were in America while he worked on his postdoctoral studies. S had little social life and found caring for her children, which she had previously enjoyed, burdensome. During the mental-status portion of her interview with a psychiatric resident, she was asked if she ever heard voices other people didn't hear or saw things that other people didn't see. She replied that she had vivid visions of her recently deceased mother, who came to S's room and talked to S. She was asked whether she simply envisioned her mother or literally saw her mother standing before her. S replied that the latter was the case. She was then asked if she ever felt as if someone else controlled her thoughts. S replied that her mother's voice was constantly inside her head, telling her what to do. S mentioned that her mother had died four months earlier but that she and her husband could not afford to go home for the funeral. The attending physician deemed that the sudden and dramatic changes in S's life had triggered a psychotic episode, a form of schizophrenia, and she was started on a course of psychotropic medication.

During this interview, no questions were asked regarding S's spiritual/religious beliefs, nor were cultural aspects of her grieving process examined. Normal grieving in some cultures includes elements that Western culture might view as psychotic (e.g., seeing the dead and communicating with them as they were in life or as transformed into birds, animals, or spirits). Had this aspect of S's reactions been examined, a more appropriate diagnosis of depression or bereavement might have been made.

In discussing cultural variants of depression, Kleinman and Good (1985) provide an excellent argument for the essential importance of considering cultural background in psychiatric diagnosis:

> Because the analytic categories of professional psychiatry so fundamentally share assumptions with popular Western cultures . . . the complaints of patients are viewed as reflecting an underlying pathological phenomenon. From this perspective, culture appears epiphenomenal; cultural differences may exist, but they are not considered essential to the phenomenon itself. However, when culture is treated as a significant variable, for example, when the researcher seriously confronts the world of meaning and experience of members of non-Western societies, many of our assumptions about the nature of emotions and illness are cast in sharp relief (p. 492).

Unreliable Research Instruments and Evaluation Inventories

To recognize symptoms of mental disorder, a normative measure is required. However, whose norm should be employed? As with educational testing, psychiatric testing in America is clearly biased toward the dominant white, male, Western cultural experience and thus is not culturally syntonic for people outside this population. When I was a student doing field practice in an outpatient psychiatric clinic, clients were asked during the mental-status exam if they ever heard things other people didn't hear. In one instance, an educated, middle-class, white male replied, "If you're asking me if I'm schizophrenic, then the answer's no!" In another instance, a 60-year-old working-class African American woman replied, "Well, yes, sometimes when I'm alone in the house, I think I hear voices." Her response led to the question, "And are other people really there?" She said, "No, when I go to look, I never find anyone." Thus, people who are unaware of psychiatric procedures and jargon tend to answer such questions honestly, unaware that they may be setting themselves up for misdiagnosis. People who live in a dangerous neighborhood may indeed hear things other people do not hear. And clients whose grief expression is non-Western may see things other people do not see.

Canino (1990) pointed out that women are more often diagnosed as mentally ill than are men, yet the research instruments measuring mental disorders often do not include items concerning alcohol abuse and antisocial personality ("male" disorders) though they do include anxiety and depression scales ("female" disorders). Canino also pointed out the importance of geography in research on ethnic minorities, noting that studies comparing Hispanics in New York with Cuban Americans in Miami may yield different results because life in New York, especially in the areas where Hispanics typically live, is more difficult than life in Miami. He also pointed out that seeking mental health care is less stigmatizing for Puerto Ricans on the mainland than it is in Puerto Rico, which may explain the higher rate of mental illness among Puerto Ricans here. Moreover, whereas Puerto Ricans may use mental health facilities more, they may use other health facilities less (Canino, 1990). In other words, one must look at their total use of all medical and mental health services offered. Also, the difficulties of intergroup comparisons among persons of the same (or different) ethnic background should not be underestimated. Are immigrant populations compared with nonimmigrant populations? Are people who have come to the United States voluntarily compared with those who were forced to flee their home country?

Clinician Bias and Prejudice

Misdiagnosis can also be caused by clinician bias. Spurlock (1985) and Gardner (1990) note that many psychiatrists do not perceive African Americans' psyche as being as complex as that of whites. Therefore, the same symptoms that would be labeled emotional or affective disorders among whites are labeled schizophrenic among African Americans. Sata (1990) notes that psychiatry's focus is exclusively on individual pathology and not on social, cultural, and political realities. This focus is inherently racist due to its detrimental effects on clients from the nondominant culture. Gardner (1990) points out that even African American doctors are not immune to such bias—when they don the physician's white coat, they often don its values, too. Language barriers, both obvious and the not so obvious, also exist, complicating the problem of making cross-cultural psychiatric diagnoses. Clearly, immigrants whose English is poor have difficulty making themselves understood. However, even if minority clients speak English well, communication may still be impeded by cultural barriers. For example, Teichner (1981) found that because Puerto Ricans are underrepresented in the mental health professions, professionals' lack of knowledge of Puerto Rican culture is likely to lead to misdiagnosis.

Gardner (1990) takes the problem one step farther, asking whether psychiatrists really want to understand their clients or whether it is easier for most psychiatrists to "blame" clients by labeling them noncompliant or resistant. To examine the meaning behind such labels, one must examine psychiatrists' own values, attitudes, and countertransference issues. Psychiatric training does little to raise awareness of professionals' bias and prejudices. Psychiatric social workers should be aware of this during team diagnosis, and social workers in general should consider the possibility of bias in reports from psychiatric professionals. Most psychiatrists are not aware of their own bias and therefore do not do adequate assessments and history taking.

Institutional Racism

Institutional racism can also cause misdiagnosis. For example, the *Diagnostic and Statistical Manual of Mental Disorders* (American Psychiatric Association, 1987) claims to be objective and nonpolitical but in fact contains inherent assumptions regarding pathology and mental disease that demonstrate a Western bias. Some of its earlier assumptions have been challenged and changed in later editions—for example, it no longer classifies homosexuality as a mental disorder. However, many diagnostic assumptions that affect women and minorities are less overt and have not been adequately questioned. For example, wife-battering is considered a crime but not a psychiatric disorder. If it were labeled a psychiatric disorder, perpetrators could be hospitalized involuntarily. As another example, schizophrenia is characterized by hostility, suspicion, and paranoia. An African American in today's society may manifest all of these emotions in the course of daily survival.

At the other extreme, Spurlock (1985) notes that in their efforts to avoid cultural bias, mental health care providers often miss pathology when they preidentify it as a cultural trait. Thus, a therapist facing an Asian American who is withdrawn may consider such behavior typical of Asian American peoples instead of recognizing it as a sign of possible depression. Alternatively, if a symptom is dystonic within a particular culture, but not dystonic within the dominant culture, it may not be recognized as pathology. Thus, as noted earlier, Asian American children are often underdiagnosed with hyperactivity because they are measured against the white American cultural norm instead of against their own cultural norm (Sata, 1990).

In a mental-status examination, affect is measured. White Americans may be more open to sharing their feelings than are African Americans, who, although they are very expressive in their mode of communication, may have learned not to share their inner feelings, especially with someone whom they do not know well. Asian Americans learn not to be overtly expressive; thus what appears as blunting of affect to non-Asians may actually represent self-control to Asians. Also, many Asian Americans believe that what is spoken is not as important as that which is left unsaid. Hispanic men verbalize their anger but rarely express fear or anxiety (Jue, 1987). Direct eye contact is viewed as disrespectful in some cultures; thus these clients should not be considered shy or hostile unless these diagnoses are supported by other factors in the interview. Other nonverbal cues, such as the way the client sits, may have less to do with pathology than with cultural dictates. The clinician needs to be familiar with such behaviors if he or she is to interpret them correctly.

Treatment Issues

Diagnosis may be reached after a single evaluation session or may occur during treatment. Thus, treatment must be evaluated when the possibility of misdiagnosis is considered.

Many authors have discussed the importance of clinician awareness of minority cultures and issues during therapy (Jue, 1987; Hines & Boyd-Franklin, 1982; Boyd-Franklin, 1989; Pinderhughes, 1982; de Anda, 1984). Therapists need to be aware of their own biases and of clients' self-perception and understanding of therapy so that client behaviors can be placed in their proper context. For example, behaviors that help African Americans to survive in the larger society affect their behavior and consequent diagnosis in the therapeutic environment. African Americans may be especially wary of the motives of authority figures and thus may test relationships before allowing themselves to develop a trusting and intimate bond with a therapist. Asian Americans, in contrast, are taught to be cooperative in social relationships and respectful toward authority figures. They may thus maintain a low profile as a survival technique. Hence, in therapy, they may smile and nod in agreement even when they do not agree or understand.

Stereotypes concerning minority clients once permeated the mental health professions and may still influence therapists' behavior in some instances. For example, Hines and Boyd-Franklin (1982) cited various studies indicating that African American clients were less likely than were white clients to be in psychotherapy. African American clients were also discharged sooner than were whites. Fewer than one-third of African American clients were referred to group or individual therapy, whereas one-half of the white patients were referred to such treatment (Yamamoto, James, & Palley, 1968).

351

An accusation often leveled against minority clients by clinicians in public health institutions is that they have no respect for time constraints and often are late for or miss appointments (Kupers, 1981). However, therapy appointments are often scheduled to meet the needs of the therapist, not the client. Problems with transportation and baby-sitting may cause clients to miss appointments. Moreover, poor minority clients' experiences with institutions and services in other areas of their life do not serve as models for responsible behavior. For example, why should a client who typically waits four hours in a welfare line believe that his or her 9:00 A.M. appointment for outpatient psychiatry will be any different?

Depending on cultural background, clients may use Western medicine or psychiatry in conjunction with other forms of healing techniques. Most cultures have spiritual healers—priests, rabbis, shamans, spiritualists—whose advice is sought on mental health issues. In a random sample of Puerto Ricans in New York City, Canino (1990) found that 31% had seen a spiritualist at least once. Canino also found that 73% of a group of outpatients at a New York City mental health clinic reported visiting a spiritualist prior to seeking psychiatric consultation. Clinicians need to be aware that their advice or opinion may conflict with that of the spiritual healer and to respect and integrate differing approaches in the best interests of clients.

Recommendations

How can clinicians ensure that misdiagnosis does not occur when dealing with clients from different cultural backgrounds?

First, clinicians need to examine critically the means used to categorize pathologies and illnesses. Kleinman and Good (1985) recommend that more clinical/descriptive research should be conducted to serve as a basis for evaluating the cross-cultural validity of our current diagnostic categories of mental illness. They also hold that new standards for cross-cultural epidemiological studies should be developed and emphasize that cross-cultural research can help us better understand the relationships among emotions, social influences, causes of illness, cognitions, and somatization. In addition, they believe that serious consideration should be given to adding a cultural axis to the *Diagnostic and Statistical Manual of Mental Disorders* (American Psychiatric Association, 1987).

Perhaps most important, clinicians should focus on the specific personal, familial, and cultural history of the client. Accurate assessment of a client's history includes:

- Immigrant-generation status of the client
- Level of cultural assimilation—that is, is the client monocultural (e.g., a new immigrant), bicultural (balancing and integrating nondominant culture into the dominant culture), or unicultural (assimilated to the point of no longer identifying with ethnic background)?

- Level of integration within cultural assimilation—that is, the client isolated, marginal, acculturated?
- Religious beliefs
- Social class
- Child-rearing practices
- School influence

Jones (1985) recommends that clinicians consider the following when assessing the psychological adaptation of African Americans: (1) reactions to racial oppression, (2) influence of the majority culture, (3) influence of African American culture, and (4) individual and family experiences and strengths. The model is interactive; that is, each set of factors has an influence on psychological functioning and an influence on the operation of the other factors. Thus factors such as political activism within the family, personal experience with discrimination, and attendance at a predominantly white or black school and how these factors influence one another would be considered in the assessment.

Some authors have suggested that, depending on the cultural background of the client, one form of therapy may be more culturally syntonic than another. Canino and Canino (1982) recommend goal-oriented, directive, structural family therapy for low-income Hispanic clients. They describe this approach as being appropriate for cultures in which men are expected to assume a dominant role and women and children a passive role. However, clinicians from the dominant culture should not impose their values on those from other cultures, this does not mean that issues of abuse, such as wife-battering or degradation of women, should be overlooked because of different cultural attitudes toward women.

In familiarizing themselves with different cultures, clinicians must note that diversity exists within a population as well as between different populations. The term "Middle Eastern" covers peoples from Syria to Algeria to Lebanon. African Americans include Americans whose origins are spread across the whole continent of Africa. Stereotypes of economic class for different populations must also be avoided. Clinicians need to understand the cultural nuances of their clients and remain curious and open to the information that the client presents.

Conclusion

Clinical treatment usually follows and is dependent on a given diagnosis. Research has shown that particular racial or ethnic groups are frequently diagnosed as having particular disorders. Although these diagnostic differences are sometimes valid, they can also reflect misunderstandings based on ethnocentric and racist assumptions of the profession.

Cultural background can affect clients' presentation of symptoms. Behaviors that are considered dysfunctional or abnormal in the dominant culture may be considered functional and normal in another cul-

353

ture. Because research instruments and treatment modalities are often based on experiences and needs of the white, male, Western client, they may not reflect the cultural realities of minority clients. Moreover, studies that examine the cultural differences among particular communities often do not take into account factors such as immigrant status, geographical location, and economic status.

Clinician prejudice, bias, and lack of familiarity with different racial and ethnic groups can also result in misdiagnosis. Clinicians need to examine their own potential bias, in that diagnoses are based on deviations from normative measures. If the normative experience of clients from a given cultural background is not considered, diagnosis is likely to reflect the majority culture's bias.

To minimize misdiagnosis, more cross-cultural research is needed. Clinicians must examine their own prejudices and biases so that assessment procedures can better reflect the reality of clients' experience.

REFERENCES

American Psychiatric Association. (1987). *Diagnostic and statistical manual of mental disorders* (3rd ed., rev.). Washington, DC: Author.

Boyd-Franklin, N. (1989). *Black families in therapy*. New York: Guilford.

Bryant, C. (1980). Introducing students to the treatment of inner-city families. *Social Casework, 61*, 629–636.

Canino, G., & Canino, I. (1982). Family therapy: A culturally syntonic approach for migrant Puerto Ricans. *Hospital and Community Psychiatry, 33*, 299–303.

Canino, I. (1988). The clinical assessment of the transcultural child. In C. Kestenbaum & D. Williams (Eds.), *Clinical assessment of children and adolescents*. New York: New York University Press.

Canino, I., (1990, April). *Working with persons from Hispanic backgrounds*. Paper presented at the Cross-Cultural Psychotherapy Conference, Hahnemann University, Philadelphia.

Chesler, P. (1972). *Women and madness*. New York: Doubleday.

de Anda, D. (1984). Bicultural socialization: Factors affecting the minority experience. *Social Work, 29*, 101–107.

Gardner, G. (1990, April). *Working with persons from African American backgrounds*. Paper presented at the Cross-Cultural Psychotherapy Conference, Hahnemann University, Philadelphia.

Harrison, S. I., et al. (1965). Social class and mental illness in children: Choice of treatment. *Archives of General Psychiatry, 13*, 411–417.

Hines, P. M., & Boyd-Franklin, N. (1982). Black families. In M. McGoldrick, J. Pearce, & J. Giordano (Eds.), *Ethnicity and family therapy*. New York: Guilford.

Jones, A. (1985). Psychological functioning in black Americans: A conceptual guide for use in psychotherapy. *Psychotherapy, 22*, 363–369.

Jones, B., Gray, B., & Parson, E. (1983). Manic-depressive illness among poor urban Hispanics. *American Journal of Psychiatry, 140*, 1208–1210.

Jue, S. (1987). Identifying and meeting the needs of minority clients with AIDS. In C. Leukenfeld & M. Fimbres (Eds.), *Responding to AIDS*. Washington, DC: National Association of Social Workers.

Kleinman, A., & Good, B. (Eds.). (1985). *Culture and depression*. Los Angeles: University of California Press.

Kupers, T. A. (1981). *Public therapy.* New York: Free Press.

Mukherjee, S., Shukla, S., & Woodle, J. (1983). Misdiagnosis of schizophrenia in bipolar patients: A multiethnic comparison. *American Journal of Psychiatry, 140,* 1571–1574.

Padilla, E., & Padilla, A. (Eds). (1977). *Transcultural psychiatry: An Hispanic perspective.* Los Angeles: Spanish Speaking Mental Health Research Center (UCLA).

Pinderhughes, E. (1982). Afro-American families and the victim system. In M. McGoldrick, J. Pearce, & J. Giordano (Eds.), *Ethnicity and family therapy.* New York: Guilford.

Sata, L. (1990, April). *Working with persons from Asian backgrounds.* Paper presented at the Cross-Cultural Psychotherapy Conference, Hahnemann University, Philadelphia.

Sedgewick, P. (1982). *Psycho politics.* New York: Harper and Row.

Spurlock, J. (1985). Assessment and therapeutic intervention of black children. *Journal of American Academy of Child Psychiatry, 24,* 168–174.

Teichner, V. (1981). The Puerto Rican patient. *Journal of the American Academy of Psychoanalysis, 9,* 277.

Yamamoto, J., James, E., & Palley, N. (1968). Cultural problems in psychiatric therapy. *Archives of General Psychiatry, 19,* 45–49.

The Emergent Nature of Ethnicity: Dilemmas in Assessment

Donald E. Gelfand
and Donald V. Fandetti

26

The literature on ethnicity has been expanding in a number of important directions. Devore and Schlesinger (1981) and Jenkins (1981) concentrate on the role of the worker in interactions with individuals from various ethnic groups as well as the development of agencies oriented to particular ethnic groups. Collections have also focused on the importance of ethnic background in delivering health care as well as family therapy (Harwood, 1981; McGoldrick, Pearce, & Giordano, 1982). In all of these volumes, the traditional culture of the ethnic group is the starting point in the intervention. In the case of Asians, Caribbeans, and "white ethnics," the traditional culture is assumed to be the culture brought to the United States by the original immigrant generation.

The wider acceptance of the potential importance of ethnicity is welcomed. We believe, however, that the wide use of an approach based on traditional immigrant cultures is not always warranted and may hamper advancement of our understanding of pluralism in American society as well as the effectiveness of many interventions.

In this chapter, we argue that although calling attention to ethnicity is valuable for clinical practice, the use of traditional models or paradigms of ethnic cultures is fraught with serious problems. The most fundamental problem is that ethnic culture is now being proposed as a variable that is *ipso facto* vital in an individual or family situation, rather than as a concept whose importance must be assessed along with other potentially significant factors. Even when this problem is recognized, the tendency is to slip into reification of ethnic culture, that is, to attribute an independent or real existence to a mental creation.

Analyses of Ethnicity

Contributors to recent literature have admitted that the picture of ethnic groups they present may be based on a simplification of the values, norms, and beliefs of individual groups. It is also possible, they acknowledge, that characteristics of ethnic cultures may be based on attitudes and behaviors that have changed under the influence of many variables, including modernization, urbanization, and industrialization. McGoldrick et al. (1982), however, do not see a danger in using stereotypes. They argue that extensive generalizations about cultural differences should be used in clinical intervention.

Accepting traditional ethnic culture as a given leads to a number of possible analytical errors, including reductionism and unwarranted generalizations. Reductionism occurs when the effects of factors such as class and religion are mistakenly assumed to be the effects of ethnicity. Unwarranted generalizations take many forms, but among the most common are characterizations about ethnic groups that ignore important intra-ethnic group differences. Even a quick sampling of the recent literature on ethnicity reveals a large number of attributions that may be questionable in relation to contemporary ethnic populations in modernized, industrialized societies such as the United States. For example,

> Norwegians have always attributed great importance to the body—its health and diseases—and have neglected the psychological side of life (Midelfort & Midelfort, 1982, p. 45).

> However, since everyone outside the family is mistrusted until proved otherwise, gaining acceptance as an outsider is the first hurdle in dealing with Italians (Rotunno & McGoldrick, 1982, p. 352).

> Feeling inadequate is a core British-American symptom (McGill & Pearce, 1982, p. 470).

Although these generalizations may be accurate in describing the immigrant, their applicability to second-, third-, or fourth-generation descendants of the original immigrant generation is questionable.

Moreover, many generalizations about ethnic groups are based on traditional ethnic cultures that were formed in agrarian societies. With industrialization, the value systems in the native country may also change dramatically. Indeed, many Japanese Americans find modern Japan baffling and discordant with their impressions of traditional Japanese culture. A recent Japanese immigrant to the United States may therefore have different value orientations than did the Japanese immigrant who arrived in the United States at the end of the 1800s.

Ethnicity and Societal Change

The economic and social changes in European, Asian, and Latin American countries may also alter the reliance on the informal network that is often assumed to be intrinsic to many ethnic groups. This change may be most evident among immigrants from countries with extensive public social services, such as the socialist and former communist countries. An example can be found in the attitudes of elderly Russian Jews who emigrated to the United States in the 1970s (Gelfand, 1986). In a sample of 259 older individuals (mean age 67 years) living in New York, respondents indicated a preference for using social agencies rather than informal support networks for assistance. This preference may arise from the feeling that relatives, primarily children, are unable to provide the assistance needed even if they are willing when called upon. More important, however, is that the use of social agencies appears to be a societal pattern. Soviet citizens were constantly required to deal with governmental agencies in order to meet a wide gamut of social and economic needs. This pattern of Soviet life has been transplanted to the United States by immigrants who have great difficulty understanding that voluntary agencies are not arms of the government.

Thus ethnic culture is not only emergent to conditions in the new country but may change in response to political and social changes in the country of origin. Assuming that culture brought to the United States by recent immigrants is the same as the culture brought by immigrants in the late 1800s is a mistake for clinicians in contact with ethnic families.

Whatever the culture of the ethnic group, a high degree of intermarriage may be important in altering these values. Indeed, all ethnic groups have viewed intermarriage as a major threat to their continued cultural existence. Alba and Kessler (1979) reported on the continued growth of intermarriage among all white and nonwhite ethnic groups with the basic exception of Hispanics. As this trend continues, some groups, such as Jews, have begun to fear for their survival, whereas other groups fear that the rate of intermarriage will hinder their continued cultural development. Thus the idea of a "pure" ethnic family or individual becomes more tenuous for the practitioner who attempts to understand the factors that have an impact on individual and family needs and problems.

In order to emphasize the complexity of assessing ethnic culture among contemporary ethnic groups, we must first turn our attention to the social factors that affect the maintenance, or attenuation, of traditional immigrant culture in the United States. Then we must focus on the need to be cognizant of "intra-ethnic" as opposed to ethnic differences. Finally, rather than adopting a position advocating for or against the utilization of ethnicity as a factor in clinical practice, we attempt to provide the practitioner with some assistance in determining the basis of ethnic family interaction and participation in social institutions.

Several factors have been cited as having an effect on the degree of cultural allegiance and ethnic affiliation of the family. These factors include immigration experience, the language spoken at home, race and country of origin, place of residence, socioeconomic status, education, social mobility, emotional processes in the family, and political and religious ties of the ethnic group (Gelfand, 1982; Harwood, 1981; McGoldrick et al., 1982). Because these factors are detailed in a number of publications, we briefly examine those that are most directly related to maintenance of the culture or change with the ethnic group.

Socioeconomic Status

Individuals of low socioeconomic status may maintain strong ethnic values after they arrive in a new country. Their scarce economic resources and low educational levels may retard their social mobility by limiting the jobs they can obtain. These lower-class family members may also not feel comfortable with individuals from other ethnic groups because of their limited educational background.

Facing what may seem to be a threatening environment, the new lower-class immigrant may seek jobs that were considered traditional in the old country. Besides not requiring new skills, these jobs may act as a bulwark against the pressures of adjusting to the new society, even if the jobs offer only little opportunity for social mobility.

Language Fluency

A lack of fluency in the language of the new country affects the new immigrant in much the same way as does low economic status, including an inability to obtain many jobs. Lack of language fluency also makes it difficult to obtain more advanced education to assist in enhancing socioeconomic resources. Individuals who only speak the language of the home country are also retarded in their ability to develop primary, personal interaction with members of other ethnic groups. Primary interaction is viewed as the most important step in acclimatization, leading eventually to intermarriage among ethnic groups (Gordon, 1964). In a positive sense, as McGoldrick (1982) noted, "The language of the country of origin will serve to preserve its culture." This function of language is clearly evident among recent Spanish-speaking and Asian immigrants to the United States. However, Stevens (1985) recently showed that if only one parent is foreign born, a child is significantly less likely to speak the so-called mother tongue.

Religion

For many ethnic groups, especially Catholics and Jews, religion may also be a bulwark against the pressures of adjusting to a new society. This may be significantly more true in religious groups that are organized around the specific nationality of the immigrant, a unique feature of American Catholics. As in the case of language, education, and traditional jobs, affiliation and participation in a nationality-based parish has allowed immigrants from Italian, Polish, French, or other backgrounds to continue to associate with individuals from the same background and thus avoid drastic shifts in their values or life-style.

Residential Patterns

One important element in the intergenerational transmission of ethnic values has been the socialization of children into ethnic traditions and values. This socialization process is obviously more easily undertaken when the family is living within a homogeneous ethnic community. In a homogeneous area, the values of the community correspond to those of the nuclear or extended family unit. Living within the ethnic community may thus help to reinforce the traditional cultural values and norms of behavior. At the same time, remaining within the ethnic community as a geographic unit may retard the immigrant's adjustment to a larger society with values discrepant with the ethnic culture. Residence in an ethnic community may limit interaction with members of other groups. If the extended family is also clustered within the same ethnic community, traditional family values, including traditional ways of dealing with problems, may also be reinforced. The family network may continue to be more important than professional practitioners as a source of assistance.

Generational Succession

Inability to obtain or lack of interest in more advanced education, failing to gain fluency in the language of the new country, remaining in jobs comparable to those of the old country, and living within a homogeneous ethnic community may enable a first-generation immigrant to retain his or her ethnic identity at a level comparable to that of the "old country." For the immigrant's children, however, historical evidence does not indicate that this low level of "acculturation" should be regarded as satisfactory. Whether as slaves, refugees from political turmoil, or as legal and illegal immigrants seeking better economic opportunities, second-generation ethnic-group members usually manifest a great desire for better life conditions than were available to their parents.

This betterment means greater adjustment to the new society. As this adjustment takes place, the ethnic culture subtly and inevitably changes. Yancey, Ericksen, and Juliani (1976) note that the dialectical nature of contact between the traditional ethnic culture and the new society produces an ethnic culture that is "emergent" and thus a unique blending of the ethnic subgroup culture and the culture of the larger society. In this emergent ethnic culture, standard descriptions that are based on traditional cultures are suspect and should be considered questions rather than givens. Second-, third-, and even fourth-generation American ethnic persons may also have achieved higher education, be employed in professional occupations, and live away from the homogeneous ethnic community of their forebears. In his classic study of an Italian American working-class community in Boston, Gans (1958) concluded that acculturation had almost completely eroded ethnic cultural patterns among the second generation. Gans went so far as to predict that remaining traces of ethnic cultural heritage would be erased in the third generation. Moreover, he saw the features of group life among Italian Americans as associated with working-class life-styles common to many ethnic groups in American society.

The importance of ethnicity as an emotional bond and source of distinctive norms and values may thus be greatly lessened among second-, third- or fourth-generation individuals of ethnic origins who are professionals and living in heterogeneous neighborhoods. Indeed, appeals to the ethnic background may be resented by these individuals. In a study of professional Italian men living in a heterogeneous suburb of Baltimore, a strong negative reaction was registered to any suggestion that these men might cast a vote for a candidate because he was Italian (Fandetti & Gelfand, 1976). For this group, the role of the church, often stressed as a basis for interaction and community networks, may also be lessened.

Ethnic Complexity

It is not difficult to describe how change produces complexity with respect to ethnicity. However, the relevance of change and complexity for the clinician can be best observed by examining specific examples. The following vignettes of four families residing in a northeastern urban area illustrate intra-ethnic group variation and the subsequent difficulties in generalizing about ethnic cultural traits. These vignettes depict families from similar ethnic groups with differing attitudes toward attributes such as educational achievement, kin and other social relationships, residential patterns, participation in religious and community associations, and language.

Vignette 1

Mr. V is a 40-year-old Italian-American who is employed in oil furnace repair. He is also active in a housing rehabilitation program in the ethnic neighborhood where he resides. Despite his obvious intelligence, he left high school without graduating. His parents are second-generation Italian Americans, and his father operated a small heating-oil delivery business in the ethnic neighborhood. Mr. V decided to leave high school in the 10th grade, feeling that he was more suited for employment in the heating-oil and furnace-repair business. His parents accepted his decision to quit school and raised no concerns about his failure to graduate or pursue a college education. Indeed, his parents made it clear that they shared his attitudes about higher education, perceiving it as inadequate preparation for dealing with life in the "real world" of the urban ethnic neighborhood.

Despite being involved in business activities in the neighborhood, Mr. V and his parents avoid participation in community associations. They do, however, enjoy speaking Italian with friends and neighbors. The Vs are not active in the local parish and attend church only sporadically. The Vs' life revolves around the city, as all Mr. V's siblings live in the same city in which the ethnic neighborhood is located. Mr. V is very conscious of his ethnic heritage and is very comfortable when relating to fellow Italians. His discussions of political issues and especially of other ethnic groups provide ample evidence that his background as an Italian American is very important to how he views the world.

Vignette 2

Mrs. D is in her forties and of Irish American heritage. She dropped out of high school before graduating, married, and is now a homemaker with two children. Mrs. D's only sibling is a high school graduate and a homemaker. Mrs. D's parents were born in the United States. For most of his working career, her father was employed in the costume-jewelry manufacturing industry where he worked as a solderer. He was indifferent to the value of higher education, an attitude that was shared by the entire family.

Although Mrs. D's mother attends church occasionally, other members of the family rarely attend. Mrs. D and her sister are very attached to their parents and live close by in the same neighborhood. They have daily contact with one another. The family members also confine their leisure time primarily to socializing with one another and indicate little interest in news, politics, community-association issues, civic events, or international problems.

Vignette 3

Mr. G is a 35-year-old Italian American who is employed as a chemist by a large oil corporation. Raised in an ethnic neighborhood, he remained there until graduating from an Ivy League university. Mr. G's parents are both high school graduates, and his father owned a small tobacco wholesale business that supplied markets and corner stores in and around the ethnic neighborhood. Mrs. G has three siblings, all of whom attended college. After obtaining a doctoral degree in chemistry and marrying, Mr. G moved with his wife and child to another state.

Mr. G's father is an articulate and engaging individual in his social and business relationships. He attends church occasionally, but his wife attends more regularly. She is also considered to be a person of charm and grace. Mr. G's father and mother are the only family members still living in the ethnic neighborhood. Mr. G's siblings reside out-of-state with their families. Neither Mr. G nor his siblings are able to speak Italian.

Vignette 4

Mr. B and his wife are third-generation Irish Americans. They are both in their mid-forties and are college graduates. Mr. B has completed graduate studies. The Bs have five children. Mr. and Mrs. B and their old-est child are devout Catholics. Their oldest child is very bright and received a merit scholarship to a major northeastern university. Mr. B's parents are also college graduates.

Mr. B is a very attractive and outgoing individual. He has raced in a marathon. His wife is also a runner. The Bs are very active in church and participate in the social ministry sponsored by the archdiocese. They regard themselves as liberal in social and political outlook. Mr. B's par-ents and siblings do not live in the same state and personal contact among family members is infrequent, usually on an annual basis. The Bs live in an upper-middle-class suburban neighborhood. They do not belong to any ethnic association or mention their ethnic background, and do not seem intent on passing their heritage on to their children.

Discussion

The Italian family in vignette one resembles the Irish family in vi-gnette two. Neither family is strongly oriented toward high educational achievement. Both are enmeshed with the extended family and tend to avoid participation in community associations. These two families are similar, despite the continuing use of Italian and the sense of ethnic identification in the Italian family.

Similar observations can be made about the two families in vignettes three and four. Again, the Irish and Italian families in these vignettes are more similar to one another than they are to the families sharing their respective ethnic backgrounds. Orientation to high educational achieve-ment is evident in both families, and both families live at a considerable distance from their extended-family kin. Rather than confining them-selves to members of the family circle, these two families have frequent interaction with nonfamily members. Social relationships are not orient-ed to members of the extended family. A positive attitude toward partici-pation in community activities and the church is shared by these families, yet neither exhibits a strong sense of ethnic identity.

The four vignettes highlight the danger in making generalizations based on ethnic groups and the pitfalls involved in assuming that common cultural traits and patterns exist in families by virtue of their membership in a given ethnic group. Indeed, the four families described in these vignettes demonstrate that variation within ethnic groups is often as significant as variation among different ethnic groups. Although the vignettes focus on Euro-Americans, similar processes are at work among nonwhite groups.

Assessing the Ethnic Family

As the vignettes illustrate, the relative importance of ethnicity for an individual or family should be assessed. To assist in this endeavor, a two-step process is suggested.

Step 1

The questions listed below can be used as the first step. These questions are similar to those developed by Harwood (1981) but focus upon general clinical practice rather than the more limited issue of health care. The questions help determine whether cultural differences are a factor in individual and family functioning.

1. What is the generation of immigration of the client (first, second, third, fourth)?
2. Does the client and his or her family live in an ethnically homogeneous neighborhood?
3. Does the client only speak English or is the individual bilingual, and to what extent is the "old" language used (at work, at home regularly, at home occasionally)?
4. To what extent is the client active in the traditional religious group?
5. What is the socioeconomic status of the client (income, educational background, profession)?
6. Is the client self-referred?

Question six is included because self-referral rather than referral by another person tends to occur more among assimilated middle-class families than it does among individuals who strongly adhere to the ethnic culture. Working-class ethnic families often utilize intermediaries such as older brothers and relatives when requesting services from social agencies; the intermediaries may assist their relatives in overcoming feelings of strangeness and possible lack of confidence in negotiating organizations outside the family and the ethnic neighborhood (Levine & Herman, 1972).

Evaluating the responses to these questions is not merely an additive process in which a certain number of "yes" responses indicates that strong cultural differences exist. In the same manner, a lack of positive responses to all of these questions does not indicate that ethnic background is unimportant for an individual. In general, however, responses that show the client and his or her family to be third- or fourth-generation immigrants who do not use the old language extensively, who have higher socioeconomic status, and who live outside a homogeneous ethnic community should alert the practitioner to the possibility of an attenuation of cultural differences.

This attenuation may not only be evident in formal patterns of membership in ethnic organizations, but in beliefs and behaviors as well. In a study of mental-health attitudes, second-generation residents in a working-class area of Baltimore indicated a preference for professional helpers rather than local helpers (Fandetti & Gelfand, 1978). A greater emphasis on local helpers was found among their first-generation counterparts. In another study that compared inner-city Italian Americans with more affluent suburban Italian Americans who were living in a heterogeneous community, the individuals in the suburbanized sample were more willing to use nursing homes for their bedridden elderly relatives (Fandetti & Gelfand, 1980). A significantly smaller proportion of the suburban Italian Americans wanted to have ambulatory older relatives living in their home.

These differences represent important indications of movement away from very prized traditional values of assistance and care among this ethnic group. Indeed, the concept of emergent ethnicity means that a number of the traditional generalizations commonly made about ethnic groups may not be applicable to present-day individuals and families.

Step 2

The dilemmas of ethnic assessment become clear in this step. We have already argued that the immigrant paradigm among white and nonwhite groups is an increasingly inappropriate baseline for use in ethnic assessment. In addition, the clinician is confronted with the fact that little empirical information is available with respect to the emergent properties associated with many ethnic groups in our society. However, as Montalvo and Gutierrez (1984) suggest, it is important that practitioners move beyond their limitations in assessing ethnicity toward a full assessment of other social factors that form the basis for interaction within the ethnic family and for ethnic family participation in social institutions of the society.

Figure 1 provides a family–institution interaction approach based on the six questions of the first step. The social institutions include workplace, school, social services, health and mental-health services, and the community. The social characteristics related to ethnicity have already been discussed. Generation of immigration has been omitted from Figure 1 because characteristics attributable to a specific generation of immigration are reflected in the other items, for example, place of residence.

Ascertaining the interaction between the individual or family and the institutions in Figure 1 will help the practitioner shift from a static view of ethnicity to an interactional view of social factors that affect ethnic family interaction and participation in social institutions. For example, finding that the primary language of the individual or family is not English, the practitioner would probe how the use of a foreign language affects the interaction of the individual with the social institutions listed in the figure; that is, does the primary use of foreign language make the individual hesitant to join nonethnically related community organizations? This hesitation may limit his or her contacts with individuals from other ethnic groups.

Socioeconomic status can also have an impact across many of these institutions. For example, low educational levels may limit the ability of parents to assist and support their children in school. Educational background may also be a factor in the family's knowledge about a variety of social and medical services or its willingness to use these services. Low

Social characteristic	Institution				
	Work	School	Social services	Medical services	Community
Language	————	————	————	————	————
Socioeconomic status	————	————	————	————	————
Residence	————	————	————	————	————
Religion	————	————	————	————	————

Figure 1. Ethnic family–institution interactions.

income may make it difficult for the family to pay for advanced education or for needed social and medical programs.

Residential location can have numerous implications for assessment of ethnic families. In close-knit, homogeneous neighborhoods where neighborhood attachment and local orientations are strong, support for local parochial schools may be evident, and the school may be viewed as an extension of the family. Orientation toward the local network of individuals and institutions may predispose residents to use local physicians, priests, and other helping persons. Unfortunately, strong local attachments may also favor the development of "we–they" attitudes toward individuals residing in other neighborhoods.

Among the effects of adherence to traditional religious values may be the development of strong attitudes toward health- and human-services access and utilization (Kahn, 1969). Traditional religious values may thus promote an emphasis on divine intervention as a cause for recovery from illness, and individuals professing these beliefs may use formal health providers only when strongly urged by a family member (Biegel & Sherman, 1979).

The six questions and the framework exemplified in Figure 1 will not provide a complete picture of possible differences among ethnic families. However, using these two steps will provide the practitioner with a beginning point for more dynamic clinical assessment of family social functioning.

Conclusion

All too frequently, ethnicity is accepted as a given. However, clinical assessment must also consider the "emergent" nature of ethnicity and the dilemmas this emergent nature introduces. As members of ethnic groups and their descendants come into contact with new and changing social environments, change or attenuation of ethnicity inevitably occurs. In a dialectical process, ethnicity is transformed as emergent properties surface. Unfortunately, the tendency has been to underestimate the complexity of ethnicity in contemporary society and to fall back on immigrant culture for an understanding of ethnicity. When ethnicity is simplified in this way, however, families are viewed in terms of cultural models that may be increasingly inaccurate with the passage of time. The need to view ethnicity as an emergent phenomenon is important for blacks, Hispanics, and Asians as well as whites.

In the current situation it is extremely difficult, perhaps impossible, to generalize accurately about ethnicity in clinical practice and to separate the effects of ethnicity from other social factors such as religion and socioeconomic status. The process of ethnic assessment has given rise to a problem that is exceedingly difficult to resolve; that is, as interest in ethnicity increased among professionals, the ability to document core cultural characteristics of many ethnic groups in our society became less and less possible. The rediscovery of ethnicity in clinical practice has been accompanied by much enthusiasm and many expectations. It is possible, however, that this enthusiasm has resulted in a process of denial and lack of realism about the limits of our knowledge on this topic. Although these limitations are especially evident in regard to many ethnic groups in American society, they are especially evident with white ethnics. We must deal with these limitations and move toward a less static and less stereotypical approach to ethnic assessment.

REFERENCES

Alba, R., & Kessler, R. (1979). Patterns of interethnic marriage among American Catholics. *Social Forces, 57,* 1124–1140.

Biegel, D., & Sherman, W. (1979). Neighborhood capacity building and ethnic aged. In D. E. Gelfand & A. J. Kutzik (Eds.). *Ethnicity and aging: Theory, research and policy.* New York: Springer Publishing.

Devore, W., & Schlesinger, E. (1981). *Ethnic sensitive social work practice.* St. Louis: C. V. Mosby.

Fandetti, D. V., & Gelfand, D. E. (1976). Care of the aged: Attitudes of white ethnic families. *Gerontologist, 16,* 544–549.

Fandetti, D. V., & Gelfand, D. E. (1978). Attitudes toward symptoms and services in the ethnic family and neighborhood. *American Journal of Orthopsychiatry, 48,* 477–485.

Fandetti, D. V., & Gelfand, D. E. (1980). Suburban and urban white ethnics: Attitudes toward care of the aged. *Gerontologist, 20,* 588–594.

Gans, H. (1958). *The urban villagers.* New York: Free Press.

Gelfand, D. E. (1986). Assistance to the new Russian elderly. *Gerontologist, 26,* 444–448.

Gelfand, D. E. (1982). *Aging: The ethnic factor.* Boston: Little, Brown.

Gordon, M. (1964). *Assimilation in American life.* New York: Oxford University Press.

Harwood, A. (Ed.). (1981). *Ethnicity and medical care.* Cambridge, MA: Harvard University Press.

Jenkins, S. (1981). *The ethnic dilemma in social services.* New York: Free Press.

Kahn, A. J. (1969). *Theory and practice of social planning.* New York: Russell Sage Foundation.

Levine, I., & Herman, J. (1972). The life of white ethnics. *Dissent,* 286–294.

McGill, D., & Pearce, J. (1982). British families. In M. McGoldrick, J. Pearce, & J. Giordano (Eds.), *Ethnicity and family therapy.* New York: Guilford Press.

McGoldrick, M. (1982). Ethnicity and family therapy: An overview. In M. McGoldrick, J. Pearce, & J. Giordano (Eds.), *Ethnicity and family therapy*. New York: Guilford Press.

McGoldrick, M., Pearce, J., & Giordano, J. (Eds.). (1982). *Ethnicity and family therapy*. New York: Guilford Press.

Midelfort, C. F., & Midelfort, H. P. (1982). Norwegian families. In M. McGoldrick, J. Pearce, & J. Giordano (Eds.), *Ethnicity and family therapy*. New York: Guilford Press.

Montalvo, B., & Gutierrez, M. (1984, July–August). The mask of culture. *Family Therapy Networker*, 42–46.

Rotunno, M., & McGoldrick, M. (1982). Italian families. In M. McGoldrick, J. Pearce, & J. Giordano (Eds.), *Ethnicity and family therapy*. New York: Guilford Press.

Stevens, G. (1985). Nativity, intermarriage and mother-tongue shift. *American Sociological Review, 50,* 74–83.

Yancey, W., Ericksen, E., & Juliani, R. (1976). Emergent ethnicity: A review and reformulation. *American Sociological Review, 41,* 391–403.

Intergenerational Relationships Across Cultures

Paulette Moore Hines,
Nydia Garcia-Preto,
Monica McGoldrick, Rhea Almeida,
and Susan Weltman

27

T he powerful influence of ethnicity on how individuals think, feel, and behave has only recently begun to be considered in family therapy training and practice as well as in the larger human services delivery system.

In our efforts to promote the melting-pot myth and the notion that all individuals are equal, we tend to perpetuate the notion that to be different is to be deficient or bad. Although similarities exist across individuals and groups in this country and the push for acculturation is strong, differences among groups need to be recognized, valued, and integrated into our thinking and practice of family therapy. Human behavior cannot be understood properly in isolation from the context in which an individual is embedded.

Ethnicity is a critical, but not sufficient, consideration for understanding personal development and family life throughout the life cycle. McGoldrick (1982) defined ethnicity as a sense of commonality transmitted over generations by the family and reinforced by the surrounding community. Our cultural values and assumptions, often unconscious, influence every aspect of our being, including what we label as a problem, how we communicate, beliefs about the cause of a problem, whom we prefer as a helper, and what kind of solutions we prefer.

The rules governing intergenerational relationships in families throughout the life cycle vary across cultures. For instance, considerable differences exist among ethnic groups as to the degree of intergenerational dependence and sharing expected between adult children and their aging parents. Whereas Italians or Greeks are likely to grow up with the expectation that eventually they will take care of their parents, white Anglo-Saxon Protestant (WASP) parents' worst nightmare might be that eventually they will have to depend on their child for support. Minimal interdependence is expected or fostered so that adult children feel relatively guilt free when they have to put their parents in a nursing home. Conversely, adult children avoid asking their parents for support beyond paying for their education.

Another significant difference among groups is the way in which cultures define responsibilities and obligations according to gender roles. Groups differ profoundly in their expectations of motherhood and fatherhood as well as in their treatment of sons and daughters. Families evolve through the life cycle and encounter conflicts at different developmental phases. Marriage, child rearing, leaving home, and caring for the elderly demand changes in relationships that are inherently stressful, especially when ascribed cultural rules for dealing with these stages are challenged or cease to be functional. When conflict erupts, families usually attempt resolution by drawing on the strengths and legacies passed from one generation to the next.

Needless to say, it is difficult to share personal and clinical observations about our respective ethnic groups without generalizing. Thus, readers should understand that, among other variables, the following portraits of ethnic groups are affected by gender, generation, residence, education, socioeconomic status, and migration as well as by the life experience of the authors. We acknowledge that significant variations exist within groups and that ethnic values and practices are constantly evolving.

Clinicians need to remain open to what families tell us about themselves and take care to enter the therapeutic process without predetermined conclusions about families based merely on ethnic generalizations. Equally important is the fact that clinicians neither formulate theories nor conduct interventions in a vacuum. Our cultural lenses dictate our world view and what we consider "normal." It is also useful to have a point of departure in one's work that is larger than one's own limited experiences; hypotheses are simply starting points from which one proceeds to look for data that support or contradict one's initial notions. In the interests of offering that starting point for practitioners, this chapter addresses rules for relationships, common conflicts, resources, and/or legacies that promote or hinder conflict resolution, and implications for assessment and intervention with African American, Hispanic, Irish, Asian Indian, and Jewish families.

African American Families

African traditions, the experience of slavery, assimilation into the American mainstream, the psychological scars of past and current discrimination, age, education, religion, and geographic origins allow for great heterogeneity within African American culture. However, survival issues based on interdependence and oppression due to racism are commonalities that transcend individual and group differences.

Despite conscious and consistent efforts by members of the dominant culture to erase all remnants of African culture from the memories and practices of African slaves and their descendants, a sense of "oneness," as exemplified in the practice of greeting one another as "sister" or "brother," is critical to understanding the dynamics of relationships among African Americans. A general assumption exists among African Americans that regardless of the educational or economic advantages of individuals, the legacy of slavery, racism, and oppression is a common bond.

Family relationships, moreso than bank accounts, represent "wealth" and guarantee emotional and concrete support in the face of negative feedback from the larger society. The emotional significance of relationships is not determined solely by the immediacy of blood ties. In fact, "family" is an extended system of blood-related kin and persons informally adopted into this system (Hines & Boyd-Franklin, 1982; Boyd-Franklin, 1989). Extended-family systems tend to be large and constantly expanding as new individuals and their families are incorporated through marriage. Commonly, three or four generations live in proximity, sometimes residing in the same household.

Strong value is placed on loyalty and responsibility to others. This value is reinforced through the belief that everything one does in the public domain reflects on one's family and other African Americans. Similarly, African Americans often believe that one does not succeed just for oneself but for one's family and race as well. In essence, African Americans believe that "you are your brother's keeper."

Among African Americans, respect is shown to others because of their intrinsic worth and character, not for their status or what they have accumulated in material wealth. Personal accomplishments are considered the dual consequence of individual effort and, importantly, also due to the sacrifice of others. Success is to be acknowledged and celebrated but not overemphasized, as positive outcomes cannot be guaranteed despite one's efforts in a racist environment. Furthermore, even when success is achieved, it may be short lived. Intelligence and education without character and "common sense" have little value. Good character involves respect for those who helped one succeed and survive difficult circumstances. Family members are expected to stay connected and to reach out and assist others who are in need (McGoldrick, Garcia-Preto, Hines, & Lee, 1989).

The elderly are held in reverence. Older women, more than men, are called upon to impart wisdom as well as to provide functional support to younger family members. Older adults are testimony to the fact that one not only can survive but can transcend difficult circumstances as well.

They serve as models for self-sacrifice, personal strength, and integrity. By example, they show that although suffering is inevitable, one can grow from hardship and adversity. Children and adults are expected to show verbal and nonverbal "respect" to the elderly. Titles such as Mr., Mrs., Aunt, and Uncle are used to convey respect, deriving from the slavery and post-slavery eras during which African American men and women, irrespective of their age, were treated and referred to as objects or children.

Children and adolescents may express their feelings and opinions but are not allowed to argue with adults after a final decision has been made. Although adults have the liberty to voice dissenting opinions to those who are older, younger adults are expected to acknowledge respectfully the older adult's opinion and perspective. To fail to do so shows disrespect for the life experience of the older person. Use of profanity in an intergenerational context is generally not acceptable.

Young adulthood for African Americans is a critical period during which poor decisions and impulsive behavior can have life-long consequences (Hines, 1989). The usual stressors on intergenerational relationships during this phase of the family life cycle can be both eased and complicated by the numerous adults who may be intensely concerned about a young adult's well-being. Young adults with few employment possibilities and who find it difficult to achieve adult status while living at home may move in with relatives until they become economically self-sufficient. They remain subject, however, to older family members' collective efforts to protect them from life hardships that might be avoided.

Some young African American adults fear failure and disappointing significant others. Others fear success as a result of internalizing the older generation's concerns about losing one's cultural connectedness. Some young adults are ambivalent about personal success because they are materially comfortable while significant others, especially parental figures, are struggling for basic survival. Conflicts may arise when younger adults believe that the advice of older adults is not appropriate to the context in which the young adult operates. Sometimes older adults may minimize the concerns and distress of younger people because they feel that such concerns are trivial compared with their difficult life experiences. Consequently, some young adults find it difficult to seek help within their families for fear of being perceived as weak; others are afraid that they will overwhelm family members who are already burdened by other life stresses. Young adults may be reluctant to pursue help from appropriate professionals in the work setting for fear of being negatively labeled as well as adversely affecting opportunities for other African Americans. The consequence of these scenarios is over- or underfunctioning, which may result in or exacerbate internal and intergenerational conflicts.

Similar intergenerational issues may surface in families with young children and adolescents. The role flexibility (exchange of responsibilities) characteristic of African American families allows adults to help children thrive in environments with many "mine fields" (Hines, 1990). The proverb "It takes a village to raise a child" works well as long as roles are clearly defined, rules are consistent, and ultimate authority is clearly established. However, boundaries may not be clearly delineated, which creates confusion. Intergenerational conflicts are most likely to arise as a result of a child's "disrespectful" behavior at home or school, poor academic functioning, and behaviors that may put the youth at risk of compromising his or her personal freedom. The primary concerns are that male adolescents will get into trouble with legal authorities and that female adolescents will act out sexually or, worse, become pregnant. Parents may resort to overfunctioning (i.e., become inflexible) and turn to relatives for help. Male adolescents from female-headed households are particularly inclined to rebel against the power and influence of their mothers and other females in positions of authority (Hines, 1990).

Although African Americans have the capacity to be openly expressive of their feelings, such expression may be held in check in an effort to minimize intergenerational conflicts. Such conflicts threaten unity and diminish energy needed to deal with everyday life. Conflict often occurs when individuals are perceived to have lost hope, self-respect, and/or self-responsibility; when they are perceived to be wallowing in sorrow, engaging in self-destructive behaviors, or pursuing individual interests without concern for significant others, particularly children and older adults.

Intergenerational conflicts may revolve around whether children are being taught traditional values basic to the survival of African American people. Parents who invest in providing material things and opportunities to their children that were not available to them while growing up may be perceived by other family members as "spoiling" their children. Conflicts are likely to focus on how to teach children survival skills without depriving them of the fruits of the previous generation's labor.

The therapist's ability to communicate genuineness; familiarity and respect for the cultural, historical, and current sociopolitical context; and an openness to learning the idiosyncracies of a particular client/family are critical to effective joining and intervention with African American clients (McGoldrick, Garcia-Preto, Hines, & Lee, 1991). It is important to keep in mind that African American families typically share one another's joy, pain, frustration, and shame. Therapists are likely to encounter difficulty if they label any family member as a "villain" or "bad," regardless of how angry, disappointed, or rejecting family members may be of that individual's behavior. To attack one family member is to attack the entire family, causing members to resist help. This phenomenon does not mean that family members absolve one another of responsibility for problematic behaviors; however, families often express anger, sometimes rage, about the tendency of individuals in mainstream society to ignore the pernicious effects of racism and poverty. Families more than likely will be concerned about their therapist's attitude toward such issues if they are to share personal information and be open to the therapist's influence. African Americans attend to nonverbal as well as verbal communication; therapists must attend to both levels as well. Giving family members permission to express freely their concerns and feelings facilitates trust so that the family can devote its attention to problem solving.

Family members should be given the opportunity to share family stories and rules with regard to roles and relationships. In so doing, family members are able to explore the ways in which, consciously and unconsciously, they have continued family legacies to their advantage and disadvantage. Because they are so invested in maintaining family unity, family members sometimes need to be encouraged to address "forbidden" or difficult topics. One way to accomplish this is to offer concrete examples to highlight how suppression of important emotional issues can damage relationships.

Therapists should avoid suggesting that clients focus on their own needs over those of significant others (Hines, 1990). Behavioral changes can be encouraged more effectively by emphasizing the short- and long-term negative effects on significant others if the client does not modify his or her behavior.

When several persons share caretaking responsibility for a child, the therapist should attempt to involve family members in clarifying who makes which decisions and how other family members can be supportive. Single female parents, especially those raising male adolescents, may benefit greatly when others within their social support systems are recruited to serve as a mentor or role model rather than another disciplinarian for their child.

When making referrals to self-help groups, therapists should be aware that some African American clients are uncomfortable in groups in which, as the sole African American participant, their problems might seem to be "exceptional" or different from everyone else's. Clients should be offered the opportunity to discuss such concerns, and alternatives should be made available. Young adults should also be encouraged to develop and use natural support groups within their work and social environments if they are struggling under the weight of unrealistic family- or self-imposed expectations as well as challenged by the inherent stress of working in a bicultural setting.

Hispanic Families

The web of relationships that extends across generations in Hispanic families provides a support network sustained by rules of mutual obligation. These rules are perpetuated by patterns of caretaking that fulfill expectations of emotional, physical, and economic support for those who need it from those capable of providing it. Rules of respect also play an important role in preserving this intergenerational network of close personal relationships. Children, for example, learn to relate to others according to their age, sex, and social class. When the system works, that is, if sacrifices do not border on martyrdom, the support and emotional acceptance provided can be very healthy and nurturing as well as reassuring and validating.

The sense of responsibility and mutual obligation can be so ingrained among Hispanics that individuals with few resources run the risk of self-sacrifice. Women, in particular, are expected to assume caretaking roles in the family and tend to experience more pressure than do men to devote their lives to the welfare of others. Becoming martyrs gives them special status, in that family members often see their sacrifice as exemplary. However, the price they pay for "carrying this cross" is often too high (Garcia-Preto, 1990). This behavior is reinforced by the cultural concepts of *marianismo* and *hembrismo,* which contribute to the complexity of Hispanic gender roles.

Marianismo stems from the cult of the Virgin Mary, whereby women are considered morally superior to men and, therefore, capable of enduring the suffering inflicted by men (Stevens, 1973). *Hembrismo,* which literally means femaleness, has been described as a cultural revenge to *machismo* (Habach, 1972) and as a frustrated attempt to imitate a male. *Hembrismo,* within a historical context, shares common elements with the women's movement in the areas of social and political goals (Gomez, 1982). *Hembrismo,* according to Comas-Diaz (1989), connotes strength, perseverance, flexibility, and the ability to survive. However, she adds that it can also translate into a woman's attempt to fulfill her multiple-role expectations as a mother, wife, worker, daughter, and community member—in other words, the "superwoman" working a double shift at home and on the job. In therapy, many Hispanic women present symptoms related to *marianista* behavior at home and *hembrista* behavior at work (Comas-Diaz, 1989).

Men, on the other hand, are more likely to assume financial responsibility for elderly parents, younger siblings, and nephews and nieces. This behavior, too, is admired and respected. Grandparents and other elderly relatives, although not expected to contribute financially to the family, often do so indirectly by caring for grandchildren and thus enabling parents to work or go to school. In return for this assistance and by virtue of their being in need, it is expected that the elderly will be cared for by their adult children. If such expectations are not met, intergenerational conflicts are likely to occur throughout the family system.

A common source of intergenerational conflict in Hispanic families who enter therapy is the struggle between parents and children who have grown apart while trying to adapt to American culture. Traditionally, Hispanic children tend to have closer relationships with their mothers than with their fathers. Perhaps because women are responsible for holding the family together, they tend to develop very strong relationships with their children and other family members. This central position in the family system gives them a measure of power, which is reflected in their alliances with children against authoritarian fathers, who are perceived as lacking understanding with regard to emotional issues. Relationships between sons and mothers are close and dependent; it is not uncommon for a son to protect his mother against an abusive husband.

Mothers and daughters also have close relationships, but these are more reciprocal in nature. Mothers teach their daughters how to be good women who deserve the respect of others, especially males, and who will make good wives and mothers. Daughters usually care for their elderly parents, often taking them into their homes when they are widowed. Relationships between Hispanic women and their fathers vary according to family structure. In families in which fathers assume an authoritarian position, the father–daughter relationship may be marked by distance and conflict. While attempting to be protective, fathers may become unreasonable, unapproachable, and highly critical of their daughters' behavior and friends. On the other hand, in families in which men are more submissive and dependent on their wife to make decisions, fathers may develop special alliances with their daughters, who in turn may assume a nurturing role toward them.

When Hispanic families arrive in the United States, the children usually find it easier to learn English and adapt to the new culture than do parents. The parents, on the other hand, may find English too difficult to learn and the new culture unwelcoming and dangerous. They may react by taking refuge in the old culture, expecting their children to do the same. When this occurs, children typically rebel against their parents' rigidity by rejecting parental customs, which are viewed as inferior to the American way of life.

Children may become emotionally distanced from their parents, who often feel they have lost control. Parents usually react by imposing stricter rules; corporal punishment may be used. Commonly, parents will demand respect and obedience, cultural values that are traditionally seen as a solution to misbehavior. Parents may become very strict and overprotective of adolescents, especially if the family lives in a high-crime community where drugs are prevalent. Daughters, especially, may be overprotected because they are viewed as being more vulnerable than males in a society with loose sexual mores. Such patterns of overprotection are more characteristic of families who are isolated or alienated from support systems in the community and when extended-family members are not available (Garcia-Preto, 1982).

Children who are caught in the conflict of cultures and loyalties may develop a negative self-image, which can inhibit their chances for growth and accomplishment. Parents, then, may feel thwarted at every turn and consequently give up on their children. In therapy, it may be useful to see adolescents alone if they are unable to speak freely in front of their parents. Issues of respect and fear about their parents' reactions may inhibit adolescents from speaking about sex, drugs, incest, problems at school, or cultural conflicts at home and in the community. In such instances, obvious goals include helping adolescents define and share with their parents personal issues that affect their relationship in an effort to find compromises. Discussing a family's migratory history and acculturation process may help clarify conflicts over cultural values. The therapist can also encourage parents to redefine privileges and responsibilities and to discuss their genuine concern for the child. By encouraging parents to express their love, concern, and fear to their children, therapists help parents and children relate in a more positive manner (Garcia-Preto, 1982).

Disagreements that parents have with their own parents regarding child discipline can become another source of intergenerational conflict. This is especially true when grandparents live in the household with adolescents who show disrespect toward them and reject Hispanic values. Parents often find themselves caught between two generations, each of which pulls them in opposite directions. Adolescents may feel that their grandparents are too old-fashioned and resent the elders' attempts at discipline. Both adolescents and grandparents may complain to parents, who may try to mediate by explaining cultural differences but end up feeling powerless and confused about their own values.

Asking grandparents to attend therapy sessions, then discussing adolescence in terms of cultural values, is sometimes helpful. The therapist might ask the family to identify the values that cause the most conflict at home. Ensuing discussions might lead to intergenerational compromise. For female adolescents, dating usually presents the greatest source of conflict. In traditional Hispanic culture, dating begins much later than it does in the United States. When dating is allowed, it generally is chaperoned by family or friends. Dating a number of boys is frowned upon, and girls gain bad reputations if they violate this rule of behavior. Parents and grandparents need to understand these cultural differences as well as peer pressures to which adolescents are exposed so that family members can begin to make compromises that benefit the family system.

As stated earlier, intergenerational conflict is often caused by the inability of one generation to provide care for another. Adult children who are unable to care for their elderly parents, especially if the parents are ill, may experience stress and guilt. Conflicts with siblings and other family members may result. Practitioners need to encourage communication among family members in order to help them find ways to contribute to the care of elderly parents. Women who devote themselves to caring for elderly parents may express their stress and resentment through somatic complaints and/or depression. Therapists can help these women express their resentments openly as well as assist them in finding support from other family members or community resources.

Leaving the family system (e.g., through divorce or separation) is extremely risky for both men and women because it implies loss of control, support, and protection. For couples who are still adjusting to American culture, the loss of the family system can be devastating. For example, women usually depend on other women in the extended family for help with child-rearing and domestic tasks, because men are not expected to share these responsibilities. Without the help of their mother, mother-in-law, grandmothers, aunts, or sisters, Hispanic women may become overburdened and begin demanding assistance from their husband. The husband may, in turn, resent these demands and become argumentative and distant, perhaps turning to alcohol, gambling, or extramarital affairs. The extended family can provide a measure of control for aggression and violence by intervening in arguments and providing advice to couples. Helping couples make connections with relatives, friends, or community supports may be the therapist's most crucial task.

Irish Families

Intergenerational relationships among the Irish are not generally characterized by intimacy. Unlike many other groups, such as African Americans, Italians, or Hispanics, who tend to view the extended family as a resource in times of trouble, the Irish tend to take the attitude that having a problem is bad enough, but if your family finds out, you have two problems: the problem and your embarrassment in front of your family. It is said of the Irish that they suffer alone. They do not like others to see them when they are in pain. It is not so much a fear of dependence, as with WASPs, but a sense of embarrassment and humiliation at not being able to keep up appearances. Intergenerational secrets are common. The Irish would often rather tell almost anything to a stranger than to a family member, but if they do share it with a family member it is usually told to someone of the same sex and generation as the teller. Intergenerational boundaries are strongly maintained, even though this approach may be very hurtful for everyone involved.

Within the family, intergenerational relationships throughout the life cycle are handled primarily by the mother. She cares for both the old and the young. She views caretaking as her responsibility, as does everyone else in the family. Her main supporters are her daughters, though she might also call on her sisters.

The Irish sense of duty is a wonderful resource. Parents want to "do the right thing" for their children; it is not a lack of care, but a lack of attention to detail that most often interferes with appropriate nurturing of their children. The Irish tend to focus more on their children's conformity to rules than on other aspects of their child's development, such as emotional expression, self-assertiveness, or creativity. Should a child be brought to the school principal for misbehavior, a traditional Irish mother's reaction to the child might be: "I don't want to hear your explanations or excuses. Just never let it happen that the principal has to contact me again." Traditionally, the Irish have believed that children should be seen and not heard. They should not bring outside notoriety to the family, especially for bad behavior. Less emphasis is placed on being a star student than on not standing out from the group for misbehavior. Irish parents tend to have a superficial sense of child psychology, hoping that keeping their children clean, out of trouble, and teaching them right from wrong will get them through. When children develop psychological symptoms, Irish parents are often mystified. When children act out, parents tend to blame outside influences, although privately they blame themselves.

During the child-rearing phase, the biggest problem in Irish families occurs if a child gets in trouble with outside authorities such as the school system. When the adults have problems at home during this phase, for example, if the father is an alcoholic, Irish children can be remarkably inventive in developing strategies to obey family rules of denial while appearing to function well. However, they may later pay a high price emotionally for having learned at an early age to suppress unacceptable feelings.

During the adolescent phase and the launching years, heavy drinking may become a major, often unidentified, problem that the parents—primarily the mother—do not know how to handle. It therefore may be ignored, often with disastrous consequences.

Irish fathers play a peripheral role in intergenerational family relationships, whereas Irish mothers are at the center. They are indomitable. But the stereotype of the "sainted Irish mother" is not totally positive (McGoldrick, 1991; Rudd, 1984; McGoldrick, 1982; Diner, 1983; McKenna, 1979; Scheper-Hughes, 1979); she can also be critical, distant, and lacking in affection, less concerned about nurturing her children than about control and discipline. She may worry about their dirty underwear lest they be in an accident and she be called in to claim the body. She can be sanctimonious, preoccupied with categories of right and wrong and about what the neighbors think, consciously withholding praise of her children for fear it will give them "a swelled head." Such attitudes and behaviors make sense in a culture with such a long history of foreign domination, in which Irish mothers sought control over "something" through whatever means were available to them and felt a need to keep their family in line to minimize the risk of members being singled out for further oppression.

Sons and daughters rarely voice resentment toward their mothers. To do so is to risk guilt and to undermine their admiration for her stoic self-sacrifice. For generations, Irish women have held rule in their families, including control of the family money. Children tend to speak of "my mother's house," dismissing the role of the father (Diner, 1983). Irish mothers often fail to recognize their own strength or ability to intimidate their children, whether through teasing, ridicule, a disapproving glance, or a quick hand. One Irish mother in therapy described her son's arrest for a drunken escapade as follows:

> Joey's afraid of me. I know he is, because when he got arrested and I went down there to pick him up, the policeman expected when I walked in there that he'd see a big witch of a woman coming through the door, because Joey had said to him, "Just promise me one thing, just protect me from my mother." But I didn't do anything. When I went in there, I just gave him a smack across the face, because I didn't need that nonsense.

Implicit in her comment are ridicule for her son's fear of her and a bold assertion of her own righteousness.

Perhaps because of their history of oppression, the Irish tend to communicate indirectly, often believing that putting feelings into words only makes things worse. They can also be uncomfortable with physical affection (Rudd, 1984; McGoldrick, 1982; Barrabe & von Mering, 1953) and tend to relate to their children through fixed labels: "Bold Kathleen," "Poor Paddy," and "That Joey." Children are loved, but not intimately known (Rudd, 1984).

As a result of her need for ambiguous communication and ambivalence with regard to self-assertion, a mother may indirectly belittle her child for "putting himself ahead" while in the same breath chide him for not being more aggressive and achievement oriented. Irish mothers tend to dote on their sons, overprotecting them and drawing them into powerful bonds more intense than their marital tie. Conversely, Irish parents tend to underprotect their daughters, treating them like sisters and often not allowing them much of a childhood by raising them to be overresponsible and self-sufficient, just like the mothers (Byrne & McCarthy, 1986). This failure to protect daughters teaches them to repress personal needs and contributes to an ongoing fatalism, emotional repression, and stoicism in the next generation of women.

Irish women have little expectation of or interest in being taken care of by a man. Their hopes are articulated less often in romantic terms than in aspirations for self-sufficiency. They are often reluctant to give up their freedom and economic independence for marriage and family responsibilities.

What about Irish fathers and daughters? One pattern involves the "dutiful daughter," especially if the mother is absent, who becomes the caretaker for her father without much real intimacy in the relationship. In other families, the daughter may become "Daddy's girl," even his companion, who is sent to bring him home from the bar or chosen to work with him, especially if there is no son in the family. Generally, however, father–daughter relationships are distant, possibly because the father fears that closeness will be confused with trespass of sexual boundaries. Moreover, Irish families are not very good at differentiating among anger, sexuality, and intimacy. A father may maintain distance from his daughter, or perhaps be sarcastic and teasing, not because such behavior reflects his true feelings but because he is unsure how to approach her.

With sons a father may share sports, work, and jokes, although the teasing and ridicule that are so common in Irish parent–child relationships may be very painful to a son. Some Irish fathers remain silent, almost invisible, in the family. Another common pattern is the father who is jovial or silent, except when drinking, at which time he becomes a fearsome, intimidating, larger-than-life antagonist, who returns to his gentler self when sober with no acknowledgment of this transformation. Children are kept off guard in such relationships. They may be drawn to the humor and fun, yet terrified of the unpredictable and violent moods. In cultures with less dissociation of self from negative behaviors (such as among Italians or Puerto Ricans), children may fear a parent who drinks, but they will not be as mystified by parents' denial of an out-of-control situation.

Resentment over class differences may surface when Irish children marry. The Irish tend to measure others hierarchically as being "better than" or "inferior to" themselves. Thus, parents may criticize children for "marrying up" and putting on airs (which usually means marrying a WASP) or may criticize them for "marrying down." Both of these parental reactions are deeply rooted in tensions stemming from the Irish history of oppression by the British, which left the Irish with a deep sense of inferiority.

When Irish children reach their mid-20s or older, they may begin to resent the denial and emotional suppression of their childhood. Such resentments may be evident in their young-adult relationships with others. Irish communication patterns are generally characterized by a high degree of ambiguity and confusion. Because Irish parents often control their children via indirect communication, such as humor, teasing, sarcasm, and ridicule, outsiders may not understand why children become so frustrated dealing with their parents and feel a need to distance themselves from the family in order to feel "sane." The resentments that Irish children have buried since childhood often continue into adulthood without realization that resolution is possible.

Resentments and distancing may become more intense throughout the adults' life, especially if parents' subtle disapproval continues or if adult children assume caretaking responsibilities for their parents. Unlike other children—such as African American, Greek, Italian, or Jewish—who are freer to express their resentments, Irish children may be extremely sensitive to perceived slights, such as favors shown to siblings, or other imagined wrongs. They may never confront the parent or the sibling with their feelings, dutifully continuing their caretaking responsibilities while maintaining tense silence with regard to their emotional wounds.

As parents age, intimacy typically does not increase. The mother may maintain her matriarchal role within the family. She may be seen as intimidating and indomitable. She may be unaware of the hold she has on her family because inwardly she feels that hold slipping.

Although unmarried children may continue to be emotionally dependent on their parents (and outwardly deny this dependence), they have no strong sense of filial responsibility. For example, placing a parent in a nursing home when the time comes may be acceptable to both children and parents, who prefer to "suffer alone" and never become a burden to their children.

The typical Irish solution to a problem is distancing—pretend it isn't there, dissociate, use denial, humor, or drink to escape pain. Therapeutic interventions designed to help them to address their relationships and problems without resorting to those mechanisms are very helpful. Suggestions usually need to be quite specific because vagueness scares them, as do references to multilayered underlying feelings of anger or sexuality. Therapy sessions that are not too frequent; letters, journals, or other forms of expression that allow a degree of control over expression; clear directions; and a gentle humor free of negative connotations that would feed their already guilty conscience help Irish clients achieve a measure of control and containment over their emotions while moving them toward expression of their feelings.

The most important considerations in the assessment of an Irish family are its members' sense of self-blame for whatever goes wrong and their tendency to avoid or deny problems, even while inwardly tormented by them. Thus, a therapist ought to take seriously any acknowledgment of a problem. If a parent says, "I think my child occasionally drinks a bit too much," one could assume a serious problem with alcohol. The Irish are unlikely to exaggerate. It is important during an assessment to explore thoroughly what they are troubled by, even though it may embarrass them to acknowledge every nuance of the problem. However, if the therapist fails to ask the "right" question, Irish clients will not give the "right" answer. They are also uncomfortable in describing emotional relationships, so it is better to ask them for details of behavior in making an assessment. It is also extremely important to frame observations, especially regarding their intentions, as positively as possible, while gently helping them move beyond denial. A little assistance will go a long way with Irish parents in terms of strategies for helping their children develop. Parents are generally cooperative, especially if therapy gives them a concrete sense of what they can do. It is often preferable to interview the generations, and even sometimes the parents, separately to help them avoid embarrassment in telling their story.

Asian Indian Families

In the past 10 years, Asian Indian immigration to the United States has been opened to nonprofessional classes. Twenty years ago, families immigrating here were primarily of the professional class. Today, however, the influx of uneducated families settling into menial jobs has created many problems similar to those experienced by earlier groups of immigrants from other countries.

Despite the intersecting influences of caste, region, and religion, predictable intergenerational conflicts emerge among family members. Relationships within and across generations are influenced by beliefs in caste and karma. These beliefs are pervasive despite the diversity among Asian Indians in the "old country" and in the United States (Malyala, Kamaraju, & Ramana, 1984). However, the degree to which these beliefs affect adaptation to life in Western society is influenced by level of education and acculturation (Segal, 1991; Matsuoka, 1990). For example, an educated family living in this country for 10 to 20 years will adapt to Western values around education and socialization for their children. However, they frequently revert back to Indian values as the marriage of a child approaches.

The caste system is a stratified social system into which one is born as a result of one's fate or karma. Karma can be changed only through death and subsequent rebirth. It is believed that with each rebirth a person moves from a lower caste (pollution) to a higher caste (purity) until "nirvana" (eternal afterlife) is achieved. These beliefs perpetuate values of passivity and tolerance, suffering and sacrifice. The more accepting one is of one's karma (passivity), the greater assurance one has of achieving spiritual afterlife (tolerance).

Hindu culture portrays women in paradoxical positions. Women are sacred (pure) in the afterlife yet they are devalued (polluted) in present life (Bumiller, 1990; Almeida, 1990; Wadley, 1977). Although men share power with women in the scriptures, in present life the male-centered family system exerts enormous social and economic power over women and children. With its concepts of "purity" and "pollution," the caste system shapes both intragenerational and intergenerational relationships. Prejudices related to lighter vs. darker shades of skin color are deeply embedded within the culture, with light skin symbolizing "purity" and dark skin symbolizing "pollution." These "ideals" are carried into the acculturation process in that Asian Indian immigrants find it easier to connect with white Americans than with non-whites, including other Asians. Asian Indian experiences of racism are generally not talked about, as though acknowledgment of racism might connect them with others who are similarly discriminated against. Although work and educational opportunities are available to all, women and lower-caste men have fewer choices regarding marriage partners. Such contradictions are pervasive and are explained in terms of karma.

Karma focuses on past and future life space. Current life dilemmas are explained in terms of karma. For example, a wife who is mistreated by her in-laws might say, "I must deserve this for something bad I did in a past life. If I endure my current life, I know I will be taken care of by God in a future life." Making choices to alter current life struggles is possible within this belief system. Sacrificial actions may alter one's current life and thus are meaningful. Fasting, praying, somatic complaints, head shaving, and suicide alter "karma" and move one toward a better life. In working with Asian Indian clients, therapists might suggest culturally appropriate constructions of less destructive "solutions" such as limited fasting, praying, meditating, or even haircutting.

Intergenerational patterns are embedded and negotiated within a collective consciousness. Relationships are other-directed rather than self-centered. Spirituality and simplicity are applauded, and family-centered decisions take priority over individual preferences. Within the family of origin, older men assume decision-making authority over all members of the family. Fathers are responsible for the education of their male children and for the care of their elderly parents. Emotional connectedness between sons and fathers, as well as among other extended family members, is not expected. However, intimacy between the son and mother is emphasized. Fathers are responsible for the dowry and marriage of their daughters; uncles or older male siblings take on this responsibility in the event of a father's death. Mothers expect their sons to control their wives with regard to money, work, and social activities. Older women gain status and power through the mother-in-law role. Younger women are socialized by their mothers and sisters to idealize the role of "mother-in-law." The cultural system (i.e., caste and karma, with their values of tolerance and passivity) supported by the male-family lineage (endorsing tolerance and passivity) enables this process. In this system, women realize power by exerting control over women of lesser status. Caretaking of grandchildren and food preparation are used as "covert" means of gaining power in family relations. A mother-in-law, in charge of preparing food while the daughter-in-law works, might cook only according to her son's desires. Young children are generally overprotected by grandparents, while being taught to respect their elders. Children are taught to avoid direct eye contact with their elders and to avoid disagreeing with them. Older sisters-in-law assume a degree of power over younger women entering into the male-centered family system.

Education of male children is considered necessary for the economic needs of the entire family, whereas education for female children increases their marketability as brides. Aging parents are cared for within the family by adult married male children and, in rare instances, by female children who have families of their own.

Child rearing is a shared responsibility of the women in the male-extended-family system. These women can be aunts or friends of the family from India who visit for extended periods during the family's initial years of child rearing. When young mothers are forced to parent without this extended-kinship system, children are more at risk, because family conflicts tend to be expressed in the mother–child dyad rather than in the marital dyad.

Power in Western marriages is directly connected to the economic resources of each partner. This notion of power and relationships is less applicable to Asian Indian families, because a couple's economic resources are distributed across the extended male-oriented family system (Conklin, 1988). Unlike the white, American, middle-class nuclear family, in which marriage stands at the center of the family system, men and their mothers are at the center of the Asian Indian family system. The mother–son tie is prominent in both Hindu and Christian Asian Indian families (Almeida, 1990; de Souza, 1975). Sons provide their mothers and grandmothers with the ultimate pride and status afforded women in "this" life (Issmer, 1989). Young wives do not participate in this system of power, even when they contribute economically to the family unit (Chakrabortty, 1978). Marriage is complicated by overarching problems of caste, dowry, and expensive weddings.

Arranged marriages are the norm in the adopted country as well as in India. When the family chooses to emphasize college education over marriage, or if the child asserts his or her personal rights over the parents' choice of mates or chooses career and money over marriage, major conflicts within the family system arise. Parents expect daughters to be married between 18 and 22 years of age and sons between the ages of 22 and 26. When this does not occur, parents lack a clear role in their adult child's life. The process of differentiation of self from family, which has various implications for Asian Indians as a result of their cultural norms, is particularly problematic at this stage. Despite their efforts to create choices for their sons and daughters, cultural expectations for "arranged" marriages take precedence.

An Asian Indian family entered therapy because of the 21-year-old daughter's difficulty completing her last semester of college. They expressed their helplessness in dealing with her launching. The mother said, "Shiva is very immature and irresponsible; it worries me that she does not know the meaning of money or getting a job, and yet she is about to graduate. I think of her as a selfish brat sometimes. She says she is not ready to think about marriage, and I believe it sometimes, but all of our friends and relatives think I am being neglectful in my responsibility to find her a nice man. If she waits until she is 30, then by the time she is 40, when she should be taking care of us, she and her husband will still have the responsibility of young children. I might be too old to be the kind of grandparent I have to be. Of course, I know that if Shiva gets married, then I will be pushing her to give me grandchildren, so I suppose I have to trust that my husband's and my choice to allow her to be independent will turn out OK.

An Asian Indian woman's status within the family is determined by the gender order of her children. First-born males are preferred. First-born females are vulnerable to conflict between the mother and her in-laws and are perceived as diminishing the father's status with the deities. However, a second-born male child helps normalize the situation. A second-born female child following a first-born female child is at risk for premature death through malnutrition and abuse, even in the United States, if the family does not have sufficient social and economic support. Male children offer the family greater economic support and thereby afford better marital opportunities for the female children in the family. A woman's relationship with her mother-in-law may become strained and the marriage may suffer if she is infertile and thus does not meet the family's role expectations. Sons who are unable to support the elderly family members, widowed mothers, or unmarried sisters extort large dowries from their brides as solutions to this intergenerational legacy (Ramu, 1987).

These intergenerational patterns often conflict with Asian Indian acculturation (Sluzki, 1979). Although most Asian Indians accommodate the work ethic and value of education, they maintain strong cultural ties to Asian Indian concepts of marriage, child rearing, parenting, and the sharing and allocation of economic resources.

Western values of privacy and individualism conflict with Indian values of collectivity and family-centeredness. In the context of separation, less acculturated families view adolescents' and young adults' struggles with independence as disrespect. When Asian Indians speak of *respect*, they mean *obedience* to the family and culture. Similarly, it is difficult for these family members to understand that the Western ideal of love includes separation and independence from the family of origin. Consequently, the Asian Indian concept of love includes control (Mukherjee, 1991).

Families are most likely to enter treatment through referral by outside organizations, such as schools and physicians, although in recent years couples have entered therapy due to troubled marriages. Practitioners need to determine how the presenting problem fits with the belief system of the dominant culture by considering the following factors:

- Life-style in India prior to coming to the United States in order to assess similarity to and difference from current life-style as well as status and story of immigration
- Household composition, social organization, and domestic functioning and activities (concept of household may include relatives in India)
- Religious affiliation
- Details and status of arranged marriage as it relates to current intergenerational anxieties (marital satisfaction, dowry status, women working out of the home presented as "liberal" idea without any negotiation of "second shift" responsibilities)
- Young men's and women's, as well as children's, sense of physical beauty in a culture that values and often eroticizes white-skinned beauty

Clinical observations reveal that Asian Indians do not remain in therapy for long periods (six to nine months is typical). Therapists can help families work through intergenerational conflicts by (1) helping them examine the underlying assumptions of individualism and self-determination as they relate to "success and achievement" and (2) eliciting examples of individualism that demonstrate "disregard for others" (i.e., talking back, visiting friends whose parents are unknown to the family, not accounting for small amounts of money spent, talking on the telephone, and so forth). Such work allows parents to promote their children's success while simultaneously addressing concerns regarding "family disloyalty."

Asian Indians address their problems within the hierarchy of "father knows best" and "mothers and daughters should obey." The emotional difficulties of sons are ignored even when they are severe. Because emotions are neither identified nor acknowledged, families should be encouraged to speak about their problems within the context of their immigrant story and cultural heritage. Therapists must address family members' sense of loss over leaving "home" while struggling to be "successful" in their new country. Engaging the women in stories and myths about strong Asian Indian women can help women achieve balance in their new culture. Therapists should encourage families to discuss these experiences and identify their feelings so that families do not "split" their emotions from real life. Splitting has allowed men and women to uphold values of tolerance and passivity, even when such values are not in their best interests. Therapists must inquire into the family's belief in tolerance (caste) and fate (karma). Asian Indians will not freely discuss these cultural beliefs unless they are specifically asked about them. Their responses might be couched in laughter, denial, or awkwardness. Gentle and respectful persistence will facilitate engagement of the family.

Jewish Families

Judaism has the unusual distinction of being both a religion and an ethnic identity (Farber, Mindel, & Lazerwitz, 1988). Jews, who have a long tradition of intellectual debate and dialogue, carry on a never-ending discussion about who is a Jew and what it means to be a Jew. This debate has been engendered in part by the Jewish history of exclusion, discrimination, and wandering, culminating in the Holocaust and the founding of Israel. As waves of Jewish immigrants entered the United States, including early settlers from Germany who were relatively wealthy, the poor and less assimilated Eastern Europeans before and after World War I, Holocaust survivors, and most recently, Russian and Israeli Jews, the question of essential Jewishness has continued to be debated—a legacy that has led to sensitivity over issues of discrimination and a sense of being "other." Although "Jewishness" may not be apparent to the outsider, most Jews are sensitive to interactions that might be perceived as anti-Semitic and thus may adopt a defensive posture that seems inexplicable to non-Jews.

Jews in the United States have been both fearful of and fascinated by assimilation into the mainstream culture (Herz & Rosen, 1982). Many families are overwhelmingly concerned that family members marry within the faith, or, if members marry outside the faith, that they maintain their Jewish traditions. A primary concern for many parents who move to a new community is whether their children will have other Jewish children with whom to play and date. The issue is further complicated by the diversity of Jewish religious practice; acceptable "Jewishness" in one family may be considered "too assimilated" in another.

Families often enter treatment to deal with conflicting feelings with regard to intermarriage, which may be perceived as destroying the integrity of the family and the faith. Generally, the families' most immediate concerns revolve around who, if anyone, will be expected to convert, who will perform the wedding, and how the grandchildren will be raised. Intermarriage is often felt to be a failure on the part of the parents, who, somehow, should have prevented this from happening. Such feelings exist even in families that are "culturally" rather than religiously observant Jews and are not affiliated with a synagogue.

When intermarriage is an issue, it is important that therapists attempt to gather concerned family members together. The parent or grandparent who is most upset may be difficult to engage. Because Jews traditionally have had a high regard for discourse and the transmission of cultural tradition and history, it can be helpful to review family history and to engage the family in searching for other families for whom intermarriage did not result in leaving the faith. Jewish families respond well to information and the sharing of stories; thus, referrals to a support group and/or interfaith classes run by Reform synagogues can be effective.

Regardless of geographic distance among family members, maintaining close family ties is important to Jewish families. It is important that the therapist identify family members who are critical to the treatment process but who are not immediately available. Soliciting these persons' involvement as consultants (through inclusion in family sessions, a joint phone call, or a letter) can help promote change.

Jewish families' focus on children, particularly their education and nurturing, can be a mixed blessing. Children are expected to be a source of pride and pleasure for parents and grandparents. However, children may find it difficult to be the focus of so much attention, with so many people having an expressed point of view. Young people may find it difficult to operate independently in their own interests (Farber et al., 1988). Separation and individuation are difficult to achieve if the family has rigid definitions of acceptable and successful behaviors. Young Jewish men and women often enter treatment because they are having difficulty dealing with enmeshment issues. Parents may perceive themselves as being generous and supportive and feel hurt by their children's efforts to become more independent. Reframing and relabeling their adult children's need to separate as "successful" and productive behavior can be an effective treatment approach.

The changing mores of late 20th-century American life have been stressful for Jewish families. Traditionally, Jewish women stayed home, complying with the dictum to "be fruitful and multiply." Jewish law has rigidly defined rules for men's and women's behavior, with women having a minor function in religious ritual. Such traditions are less rigidly observed in Reform and Conservative congregations, where women now can be ordained as rabbis and participate in religious ritual. Despite the fact that many Jewish laws concerning gender roles are neglected in all but Orthodox families, these laws still have a subtle influence on role definition and expectations.

In Jewish families, women have traditionally held power at home while the husband faced the work world. Jewish mothers have been responsible for maintaining traditions and culture. However, because many Jewish women were employed outside the home during the Great Depression in the 1930s, many families remember grandmothers or other female relatives who worked out of necessity. Their daughters were primarily homemakers, and their granddaughters now expect themselves to be "supermoms" (Hyman, 1991). The dilemma faced by all three generations has been how to reconcile social expectations with cultural expectations. Women who saw their mothers helping support the family during the Depression came to value their homemaker role. The granddaughters have aspired to raise their family while participating in the educational and professional world. Issues faced by American women in the 1980s and 1990s have been especially complicated for Jewish women due to the emphasis Jewish culture places on education, social consciousness, and tradition. In such situations, the grandmother may serve as a role model for both working and maintaining a family.

Significant shifts in the role of the Jewish husband/father have also occurred. Jewish men have experienced discrimination and violence in the community. Traditionally, their home has been the place where they achieve respect and authority. Because both spouses may work, the father may be called upon or may wish to be a more active parent. But when he does take an active role, he risks the scorn of his own parents, who see him in an unconventional role. The extended family may not be supportive of these changes.

Religion is another source of intergenerational conflict. The majority of Jews in the United States are affiliated with Reform congregations, which do not follow many of the commandments that Orthodox and Conservative Jews follow. Intergenerational conflict may arise over the perceived religious laxity or conservatism of family members. Parents may be disappointed if their child chooses not to be affiliated with a synagogue and not to have a bar mitzvah for their grandson or a bas mitzvah for their granddaughter.

Conversely, some young people have become more observant of the Jewish faith than their families, perhaps joining an Orthodox congregation and living a life-style that is foreign to their families (keeping a kosher home, not traveling on the Sabbath, not practicing birth control). Conflicts in some families may occur if younger family members emigrate to Israel, thus separating parents from their children and grandchildren. Families may enter treatment to deal with feelings of loss and may need help in understanding that their needs are acceptable even if they differ from those of their parents.

Jewish families tend to seek expert opinions and may ask a therapist many questions about professional degrees and competence. Although such inquiries may make practitioners feel uncomfortable and challenged, they may help clients feel more comfortable in therapy. Directing Jewish families to appropriate reading materials about their problems can be helpful, because many Jewish persons place value on being well-informed. Referrals to self-help groups can also be helpful.

Jews are avid consumers of psychotherapy, in part as a result of their comfort with discourse, their search for solutions, and expectation that family life should follow predefined rules (Herz & Rosen, 1982). However, extensive analysis does not always lead to resolution of problems. The therapist may find structural interventions and assigned tasks helpful in challenging verbal interactions that have not led to change. Families may need to be reminded that the goal of therapy is not to tell a good story or to be "right" in the eyes of the therapist, but to resolve the conflict or assuage the pain that brought the family to therapy.

Conclusion

The profiles presented in this paper represent generalizations about the ethnic groups discussed. But, it is important to note that, holding all other variables constant, ethnic groups differ in important ways with regard to relationships, the rules of those relationships, predictable family and personal dilemmas, characteristic strategies for resolving conflict, and considerations essential to effective joining, assessment, and intervention on the part of the therapist.

We do not challenge therapists to become experts on all ethnic groups. We do believe, however, that as therapists we have a responsibility to develop our knowledge about groups with whom we most often work. Without awareness of the ethnic context of clients, therapists are likely to make faulty decisions and initiate ineffective interventions. Culturally sensitive family therapy involves far more than techniques. The comfort, knowledge, and skill required for effective cross-cultural work involve continuous efforts to familiarize oneself with the population, respect for intragroup variation, openness to the idiosyncrasies of every family, and a clear perspective on how one's own ethnic identity influences one's way of seeing and being in the world.

REFERENCES

Almeida, R. V. (1990). Asian Indian mothers. *Journal of Feminist Family Therapy, 2*(2), 33–39.

Barrabe, P., & von Mering, O. (1953). Ethnic variations in mental stress in families with psychotic children. *Social Problems, 1,* 48–53.

Boyd-Franklin, N. (1989). *Black families in therapy.* New York: Guilford.

Bumiller, E. (1990). *May you be the mother of a hundred sons: A journey among the women of India.* New York: Random House.

Byrne, N., & McCarthy, I. (1986, September 15). *Irish women.* Family Therapy Training Program Conference, Robert Wood Johnson Medical School, Piscataway, NJ.

Chakrabortty, K. (1978). *The conflicting worlds of working mothers.* Calcutta, India: Progressive Publishers.

Comas-Diaz, L. (1989). Culturally relevant issues for Hispanics. In V. R. Koslow & E. Salett (Eds.), *Crossing cultures in mental health.* Washington, DC: Society for International Education, Training and Research.

Conklin, G. H. (1988). The influence of economic development and patterns of conjugal power and extended family residence in India. *Journal of Comparative Family Studies, 19,* 187–205.

de Souza, A. (1975). *Women in contemporary India.* New Delhi, India: Manohar.

Diner, H. R. (1983). *Erin's daughters in America.* Baltimore, MD: Johns Hopkins University Press.

Farber, B., Mindel, C. H., & Lazerwitz, B. (1988). In C. H. Mindel & R. W. Habenstein (Eds.), *Ethnic families in America: Patterns and variations.* New York: Elsevier.

Garcia-Preto, N. (1982). Puerto Rican families. In M. McGoldrick, J. K. Pearce, & J. Giordano (Eds.), *Ethnicity and family therapy.* New York: Guilford.

Garcia-Preto, N. (1990). Hispanic mothers. *Journal of Feminist Family Therapy, 2*(2), 15–21.

Gomez, A. G. (1982). Puerto Rican Americans. In A. Gaw (Ed.), *Cross cultural psychiatry* (pp. 109–136). Boston: John Wright.

Habach, E. (1972). Ni machismo, ni hembriso. In *Coleccion: Protesta.* Caracas, Venezuela: Publicaciones EPLA.

Herz, F. M., & Rosen, E. J. (1982). Jewish families. In M. McGoldrick, J. K. Pearce, & J. Giordano (Eds.), *Ethnicity and family therapy.* New York: Guilford.

Hines, P. (1989). The family life cycle of poor black families. In B. Carter & M. McGoldrick (Eds.), *The changing family life cycle: A framework for family therapy* (2nd ed.). New York: Gardner Press.

Hines, P. (1990). African American mothers. *Journal of Feminist Family Therapy, 2*(2), 23–32.

Hines, P., & Boyd-Franklin, N. (1982). Black families. In M. McGoldrick, J. K. Pearce, & J. Giordano (Eds.), *Ethnicity and family therapy.* New York: Guilford.

Hyman, P. (1991). Gender and the immigrant Jewish experience. J. R. Baskin (Ed.), *Jewish women in historical perspective.* Detroit, MI: Wayne State University Press.

Issmer, S. D. (1989). The special function of out-of-home care in India. *Child Welfare, 68,* 228–232.

Malyala, S., Kamaraju, S., & Ramana, K. V. (1984). Untouchability—need for a new approach. *Indian Journal of Social Work, 45,* 361–369.

Matsuoka, J. K. (1990). Differential acculturation among Vietnamese refugees. *Social Work, 35,* 341–345.

McGoldrick, M. (1982). Irish Americans. In M. McGoldrick, J. K. Pearce, & J. Giordano (Eds.), *Ethnicity and family therapy.* New York: Guilford.

McGoldrick, M. (1991). Irish mothers. *Journal of Feminist Family Therapy, 2*(2), 3–8.

McGoldrick, M., Garcia-Preto, N., Hines, P., & Lee, E. (1989). Ethnicity and women. In M. McGoldrick, C. Anderson, & F. Walsh (Eds.), *Women in families.* New York: W. W. Norton.

McGoldrick, M., Garcia-Preto, N., Hines, P., & Lee, E. (1991). Ethnicity and family therapy. In A. Gurman & D. Kniskern (Eds.), *The handbook of family therapy* (2nd ed.) (pp. 546–582). New York: Guilford.

McKenna, A. (1979). Attitudes of Irish mothers to child rearing. *Journal of Comparative Family Studies, 10,* 227–251.

Mukherjee, B. (1991). *Jasmine.* New York: Fawcett Crest.

Ramu, G. N. (1987). Indian husbands: Their role perceptions and performance in single- and dual-earner families. *Journal of Marriage and the Family, 49,* 903–915.

Rudd, J. M. (1984). *Irish American families: The mother–child dyad.* Thesis, Smith College School of Social Work.

Scheper-Hughes, N. (1979). *Saints, scholars, and schizophrenics.* Berkeley, CA: University of California Press.

Segal, U. A. (1991). Cultural variables in Asian Indian families. *Families in Society, 72,* 233–241.

Sluzki, C. (1979). Migration and family conflict. *Family Process, 18,* 379–390.

Stevens, E. (1973). Machismo and marianismo. *Transaction Society, 10*(6), 57–63.

Wadley, S. (1977). Women and the Hindu tradition. *Journal of Women in Culture and Society, 3*(1), 113–128.